Evaluation of
Policy Simulation Models

A Conceptual Approach and Case Study

ROBERT E. PUGH

Information Resources Press I**R**P®
Washington, D.C. 1977

Available from
Information Resources Press
2100 M Street, N.W.
Washington, D.C. 20037

Library of Congress Catalog Card Number 77–82320

ISBN 0–87815–018–8

To **EVELYN**

Foreword

Decision- or policymaking models that enable us to compare alternative solutions or policies to resolve specific problems are being developed and used with increasing frequency at all levels of government and industry. Model developers always have stressed the need for verifying and validating a model prior to accepting its outcomes. Until recently, however, only very basic and limited methodologies for doing so were available, and research in what is now called model evaluation has been rare. In a general sense, evaluation is a process by which interested parties, who were not involved in a model's origins, development, and implementation, can assess the model's results in terms of its structure and data inputs to determine, with some level of confidence, whether or not the results can be used in decision making.

We can attribute the current interest in, and need for, model evaluation procedures to three related events that occurred in the early 1970s: the publishing of *The Limits to Growth* and the attendant voluminous pro and con criticisms of the model's assumptions, structure, and data; the conflicting predictions by the standard econometric forecasting models and the deficiencies in their structures (e.g., not recognizing that unemployment can increase during an inflationary period); and the use of the Project Independence Energy System (PIES) model in preparing the 1974 Project Independence Report, and the extensive critiques of the PIES model.

The Limits to Growth discussions highlighted the fact that there are many different modeling approaches which can be applied to the same policy problem, and there is no agreement on which approach is more appropriate. The breakdown in the old, faithful, economic models revealed the complacency of analysts and users in not continually questioning the assumptions of a model. Finally, the PIES model was so complex that few policymakers, if any, really understood the structure or agreed with the assumptions, and its use was a prime demonstration of the faith in modeling held by policymakers. (This is not to say that

v

the PIES outcomes and recommendations were incorrect; they have not been demonstrated to be correct—an impossible task!)

These three examples (which can be multiplied many times over) illustrate the need for developing and imposing formal evaluation procedures on important and complex policy models. Our concerns in advocating evaluation for complex models are threefold: for many models, the ultimate decision maker is far removed from the modeling process (this is especially true in governmental areas), and a basis for accepting the model's results by such a decision maker needs to be established; users of a complex model that was developed for others must be able to obtain a clear statement of the model's applicability to the new user problem area; and for complex models, even if the decision makers and analysts maintain close working arrangements, it is difficult to assess and to comprehend fully the interactions and impact of a model's assumptions, data availability, and other elements on the model structure and results without some formal, independent evaluation.

The book, *Evaluation of Policy Simulation Models: A Conceptual Approach and Case Study* by Robert E. Pugh, is an important addition to the small but growing body of literature that faces up to the problem of how to evaluate a policy model. The author proposes and uses an evaluation paradigm in the context of a detailed case study of a particular model structure—the urban dynamics model—and its use to resolve specific policy situations. The author's careful analysis and basic approach will be of great value to those readers who want to understand better not only the urban dynamics model but the process and future directions of the emerging field of model evaluation.

SAUL I. GASS
*Professor and Chairman of
the Faculty in Management
Science and Statistics,
University of Maryland*

Preface

In principle, the use of computer simulation models is one of the most promising approaches for dealing with complex policy problems. Computer simulation is defined here as a method for conducting experiments on a computer by using models which are specified by mathematical and logical relationships and which describe the dynamic behavior of a social system over a period of time. The strong appeal of using computer simulation models to cope with policy complexities is their integrative capacity. They can synthesize bits and pieces of theory and information from various perspectives and sources into a comprehensive whole. Such comprehensive representations of policy problems are very attractive to policymakers, who often are forced to rely on fragmentary, partial analyses. The incorporation of this methodology into our policymaking process, however, and realization of its full promise are in an early phase of development.

This book deals with one of the critical problems encountered in incorporating computer simulation into policymaking processes: evaluating policy simulation models. The emphasis is on models that are intended to support analyses of broad-aim, complex policy problems such as urban development, income maintenance, and energy policy. Computer simulation models can assist in policy deliberations related to such problems, but it should be recognized that complex policy questions in these areas are characterized by multiple, difficult-to-measure criteria that must be considered.

It has become evident in recent years that more formal procedures are needed for evaluating complex policy simulation models. In the broadest sense, model evaluation is part of the communication process involved in research and development activities related to policy models. Here, evaluation is considered from the policymaker's point of view—examining a model's utility in providing information relevant to formulating and implementing policy—and encompasses assessments of the problems a model can and cannot deal with, the validity of the model's supporting theory and assumptions, and the performance of the model in actually dealing with policy problems.

As evidenced by recent surveys of policy models referred to in Chapter 1, model evaluation has been neglected in the development and implementation of models, and this neglect has contributed directly to the failure of a large proportion of models in meeting the policy needs for which they were intended. The premise in this book is that improvements in the administration and conduct of modeling research will develop through improved understanding of models and improved approaches to and techniques for evaluating them.

There is no simple formula for evaluating policy simulation models; therefore, this book adopts a case study approach. Chapter 1 sets forth an evaluative paradigm, or a conceptual approach, that is appropriate for evaluating complex policy models. Subsequent chapters discuss various aspects of the evaluative paradigm and illustrate its application by presenting a detailed evaluation of an urban development simulation model.

The evaluative paradigm and case study evaluation are presented in the context of the policymaking process, as well as the role of simulation modeling in that process. This context is developed in Chapter 2 by delineating the intellectual tasks of policymaking and the methodological tools (including simulation modeling) available for assisting with the tasks, and by identifying the role of simulation modeling and examining some of the difficulties encountered in applying the methodology to policy problems.

The model selected for the case study is Professor Jay Forrester's urban dynamics model, described in his book, *Urban Dynamics*. The model is a comprehensive simulation representing many of the demographic and economic developmental processes of an urban area. It has attracted not only widespread favorable attention but strong criticism as well, and continues to be the subject of research. Because the urban dynamics model has not been subject to a full, systematic evaluation, it is an interesting case study candidate. In addition, the model is well documented and manageable in size, which facilitates the evaluation, and it has aroused considerable controversy, which heightens interest in evaluation findings.

The case study evaluation assesses the range of problems the urban dynamics model addresses, the quality of the model's supporting theory and assumptions, and its capability to deal with real-world problems. In the process of assessing the model's capability to deal with real-world problems, an urban dynamics representation of the District of Columbia is developed by empirically estimating model parameters and initial values. Its performance is evaluated by comparing model-computed values for the 1960–1970 period with historical data for the District. Then the model is applied in the analysis of a housing problem for the city by considering several policy alternatives. This application includes an examination of the model projections of policy outcomes for the 1980–1985 period.

An attempt is made throughout the book to serve the interest of two groups of practitioners and students. The first group consists of discipline-oriented researchers: operations researchers, economists, urban planners, sociologists, statisticians, political scientists, and others engaged in the development of models for assisting in policymaking. The second group consists of policymakers: administrators and managers responsible for identifying research needs and for planning to ensure that modeling efforts contribute as much as possible to policy deliberations.

It is impossible to cite all of my intellectual benefactors; however, I must mention a few. The stimulation of Marshall K. Wood, with his insistence on meeting complexity in policy modeling head-on, was a long-term pervasive influence. My sincerest appreciation also is extended to David J. Peterson, Director of the Colgate University Public Policy Study Group in Washington, D.C., and to Laura L. Irwin, of The American University School of Government and Public Administration, for their many helpful insights and suggestions when this undertaking was in a formative stage. Finally, I would like to express my gratitude to the members of the merry modelers—an informal group or invisible college of about 20 colleagues involved in policy simulation modeling—for sharing experiences, perceptions, and judgments that have influenced my thinking in many obvious and subtle ways.

Contents

Contents

Contents

LIST OF FIGURES

FIGURE

LIST OF TABLES

TABLE

CHAPTER 1

Introduction

Models are being used with increasing frequency to cope with policy analysis and planning in a society that is growing in complexity. Policy-oriented models are logical, mathematical representations of the relevant aspects of a particular policy problem and, invariably, make use of the manipulative and computational powers of computers. Designed as analogs to that portion of the real world which is relevant to the policy problem under study, the models are intended to simulate a real-world situation in such a way that inferences useful for policymaking may be drawn from them. In principle, computer-based models—or computer simulation models—can assist in dealing with the complexities of policy analysis in many areas of the social and administrative sciences by developing a general understanding of a real-world situation, by forecasting the future of a real-world system, and by simulating the impacts of alternative policies on the real-world system.

Policy-oriented models vary considerably in complexity, depending on the problems that are being dealt with. Interest here centers on models that address the broad, complex policy questions that frequently arise in social areas and often are characterized by multiple, difficult-to-measure criteria that must be considered in policy deliberations. Examples of such areas include studies of proposed national health insurance programs, policies for improving urban housing, and policies for improving the criminal justice system. Therefore, it is necessary to design and evaluate programs capable of dealing with these many-faceted social problems—for which only imperfect measurement criteria exist.

The broad policy problems are in direct contrast to the more narrowly oriented problems, for which policy-assessment criteria are relatively clear and easily measured. Such problems often are related to specific aspects of organizational efficiency and effectiveness—for example, the design and selection of an inventory policy for which the assessment criterion is to minimize dollar costs to the organization. Although models can assist policymakers in both complex and narrowly oriented policy areas, many difficulties may arise in developing and applying the models to the complex questions, some of which are dealt with in this book.

An approach to model evaluation is proposed in this chapter, and a plan is outlined for treatment of that approach. Four topics are examined: First, there is a discussion of why and how the need arises for an evaluation of policy models; then the approach advanced in this book is described. Second, the evaluative structure—or evaluative paradigm, as it is called—is set forth and examined for appropriateness of use in the evaluation of models that address broad, complex policy questions. Third, the plan adopted illustrates the application of the evaluative paradigm by conducting a case study evaluation of a specific policy model; background information is provided on Professor Jay Forrester's urban dynamics model, which is the one selected for the case study. Finally, an overview is given of the model evaluation presented.

NEED FOR MODEL EVALUATION

The strong appeal of using computer simulation models to cope with policy complexities, as compared with other methodologies, is their integrative capacity. This means that bits and pieces of theory and information of varying quality can be tied together into a comprehensive whole. Such comprehensive representations of policy problems have considerable appeal to policymakers, who often are forced to rely on fragmentary, partial analyses. Harold Lasswell has noted the potential of computer simulation in policy analysis, but he expresses some caution: "Computer simulation provides a spectacular addition to the available means of improving our mastery of complex situations. As yet, however, the technique of incorporating computer simulation is in an early phase of development." [1] This notion is supported by a survey of computer models which examined detailed information on some 250 models and revealed ". . . that at least one-third and perhaps as many as two-thirds of the models failed to achieve their avowed purposes in the form of direct application to policy problems." [2] The gap between models ostensibly developed in support of policymaking and the requirements of policymakers forcefully calls attention to the need for evaluating the usefulness of policy models.

One of the primary factors contributing to this gap is the difference in viewpoints between model builders and policymakers. Model builders are basically researchers—political scientists, operations researchers, economists, sociologists, statisticians, and other discipline-oriented professionals—who often are inclined to maximize the theoretical content of models in order to integrate and develop theory. On the other hand, the policymaker needs information to support decisions and, hence, models that maximize the accuracy of estimates of specific information relevant to policy. These two points of view, or emphases, which may be referred to as the theoretical and the pragmatic, respectively, are not necessarily conflicting. On the contrary, they are complementary, because the development of pragmatic models must rely on theory as much as possible.

Recent research has examined various aspects of the gap between policy models and policymakers. Garry Brewer dealt with the differing viewpoints between model builders and model users in his account of the difficulties encountered by Pittsburgh and San Francisco in their attempts to apply large-scale computer simulation models to policy problems. Although Brewer was dealing with urban models, his analysis was relevant to the general problem of developing models that would have greater policy utility.[3]

Two surveys of policy-related models, sponsored by the National Science Foundation's Research Applied to National Needs program, provide additional insights into this gap. The first survey identified more than 650 nondefense modeling efforts (and this count is far from complete) dealing with some aspect of social policymaking and pro-

[1] Harold D. Lasswell. *A Pre-View of Policy Sciences.* New York, American Elsevier Publ., 1971, p. 72.

[2] Gary Fromm, William L. Hamilton, and Diane E. Hamilton. *Federally Supported Mathematical Models: Survey and Analysis. Volume I: Analysis and Conclusions.* Boston, Data Resources, Inc. and Abt Associates, Inc., 1974, p. 3.

[3] Garry D. Brewer. *Politicians, Bureaucrats and the Consultants: A Critique of Urban Problem Solving.* New York, Basic Books, 1973.

vided detailed information on some 250 modeling efforts. Survey results revealed that a primary reason for not using models was the "distance" between model builders and model users, which created a barrier to communication. One conclusion was that "Under current modes of operation, a number of procedural and institutional factors limit the interaction of policymakers and modelers, and thus increase the likelihood of imperfect communication." [4]

The second survey focused on urban models and included literature reviews, field investigations, a mail survey of 1,500 urban planning agencies, and a conference of model builders and model users. Although the primary contribution of this study was a research design to guide subsequent investigations, the study's conference of model builders and users identified a number of factors that are significant determinants of model utility. These factors include complexity of system being modeled, saliency of policy area addressed, organizational relationship of modeling effort to policymakers, and quality of modeling staff; all suggest practical measures that can reduce the gap between models and policymakers.[5] A number of other research efforts also deal with aspects of the use of models in policymaking.[6]

One way to reduce the gap between models and policymaking is to improve the approaches to and techniques for model evaluation. Evaluation implies a point of view and a purpose; and the point of view taken here is that of the policymaker, whose purpose is to obtain information relevant to formulating and implementing policy. Before accepting a computer simulation model as being useful for his needs, the policymaker should fully understand the capabilities and limitations of the model. Questions such as the following must be asked.

Does the model represent significant aspects of the policy problems? Does the model formulation include variables that can be affected

---

[4] Fromm, Hamilton, and Hamilton. *Federally Supported Mathematical Models*, p. 4.

[5] Janet Rothenberg Pack et al. *The Use of Urban Models in Urban Policy Making: Report on Research to Refine the Relevant Questions and to Provide an Appropriate Research Design*. Philadelphia, The Fels Center of Government, University of Pennsylvania, 1974, pp. 4–11.

[6] Brewer. *Politicians, Bureaucrats and the Consultants;* Saul I. Gass and Roger L. Sisson, eds. *A Guide to Models in Governmental Planning and Operations*. Washington, D. C., Office of Research and Development, Environmental Protection Agency, 1974; Keith E. Marvin. "Getting Involved in Analysis Needed by the Congress of the United States." Paper read at the ORSA/TIMS (Operations Research Society of America/The Institute of Management Sciences) Joint National Meeting, October 16, 1974, San Juan, Puerto Rico.

or controlled by policy actions, as well as quantities that will help to measure the impacts of alternative policy actions?

Are there sufficient data available at acceptable costs to support the use of the model in policy deliberations?

Does the model make use of existing theory related to the policy area represented?

Does adequate theory exist to support the model formulation?

Are the supporting assumptions in the model reasonable for the policy problems to be analyzed?

Specific questions must be devised to fit the particular policy problem and the model under consideration. A set of questions, however, usually will not constitute a definitive evaluation; but unless a reasonable set of such questions can be resolved satisfactorily for a model, its use for policy purposes may be a waste of resources.

The need for improved evaluation of models to increase the probability that modeling research will be useful in policy analysis is not new; in fact, it is an aspect of the general necessity to improve the administration of research so as to increase the payoff from policy-related research. The practice of administering research for policy modeling lags behind research administration practices in other areas, because the use of computer simulation models for policy purposes is a rather recent development. For instance, survey techniques in support of policymaking, as opposed to models, have been used for some time, and, as a result, the administrative practices for the former are more highly developed. Of course, the administration of research for modeling presents some difficulties that are not encountered in research based on other methodologies, because simulation models tend to be broad, comprehensive representations. The premise here is that improvements in administration of research for modeling which is undertaken in support of policy analysis will develop through improved understanding of the evaluation of models and improved approaches to and techniques for evaluation.

PARADIGM FOR MODEL EVALUATION

There is no simple formula that can be applied mechanically to resolve the problems of evaluating the utility of policy models which address complex issues. The approach proposed here is to adopt a broad evaluative structure, or evaluative paradigm, which will provide guidelines by indicating the broad questions or areas that must be addressed. Specific evaluative questions will be prompted by the policy problems and characteristics of the model being considered. Use of the evaluative paradigm ensures that model evaluations will be conducted systematically and completely. An evaluative paradigm follows; then the relationship of the evaluative approach to modeling methodology is analyzed. The evaluative paradigm calls for structuring evaluations in three fundamental facets of the policymaker's purview.

The first facet is the *perspective* the model provides, which raises such questions as:

With what subjects does the model deal?
In how much detail and with what techniques does the model treat its subjects?
In brief, what kinds of policy problems and questions does the model attempt to deal with?

Examination of the model's perspective sets aside the fundamental question of whether the model deals with policy problems well enough to really be useful.

The second facet is concerned with the adequacy of the model representation in *principle*; that is, how acceptable is the model's framework of supporting theory and assumptions, considering the policy questions that must be addressed? The evaluation in-principle may raise such questions as:

How adequate is the underlying research of the model?
Does the research supporting the model formulation satisfy the usual criteria applied to policy-oriented, computer simulation models?

The third facet is concerned with the adequacy of the model in *practice*; that is, how adequately does the model, as a whole, address real-world policy problems? Does the model tie together theory, assumptions, and data so they are useful in practice?

Together, these three facets—in-perspective, in-principle, and in-practice—provide a paradigm for conducting policy-oriented evaluations that will determine the usefulness of existing or proposed models.

The basic question that arises when examining the perspective of a policy model is whether the model addresses the appropriate policy questions. Examination of a model's perspective may take several forms. For example, it could be directed toward determining whether or not the model can be used to develop estimates that will support the analysis of a specific policy question. A more comprehensive examination of perspective could involve the comparison of several models to determine which addresses one or more of a set of questions in a particular policy area. When conducting the in-principle and in-practice phases of model evaluation, the basic question is whether or not the model is a sufficiently valid representation of the real-world policy situation to be useful in analyzing those policy questions encompassed by the model. Model validity in this broad sense cannot, of course, be established with an absolute degree of certainty; at best, only a reasonable assurance can be determined.

The in-principle and in-practice examinations of a model complement each other, and both are essential to an evaluation effort. The in-principle examination can lead only to a tentative conclusion that the model's assumptions appear to be sufficiently realistic to make it useful or that they are unrealistic and, therefore, render the model useless. This follows from the fact that the supporting assumptions inherent in the theory and relationships incorporated into the model are simplifications and abstractions and, by their nature, are unrealistic and untrue representations of the real world. The realism of assumptions is a matter of degree: models with seemingly unrealistic assumptions often prove to be useful, while models with seemingly realistic assumptions do not. The proposed use of the model also must be considered. For example, in the law of falling bodies, the assumptions of a perfect vacuum and no air resistance are never satisfied; yet, this model is a useful representation of some situations, say, dropping a steel ball, but not of others, say, dropping a feather. Because the in-principle examination, in which the reasonableness of the model's assumptions is assessed, cannot be conclusive regarding the model's utility, the in-practice examination is needed.

When conducting an in-practice examination, the model is viewed as an entity, and an assessment is made of its capability to deal with policy questions. This is the heart of the model's utility issue. From this point of view, the examination assesses the model's performance by applying the model to a representative policy problem or by testing its predictive capabilities. As previously mentioned, in-practice examination is made on the premise that models should be judged on their performance and not solely on the reality of their assumptions.[7] It always must be kept in mind, however, that conclusions from the whole evaluation process will provide reasonable assurance that a

---

[7] Otto A. Davis. "Notes on Strategy and Methodology for a Scientific Political Science." *In: Mathematical Applications in Political Science*. Vol. 4. Edited by Joseph L. Bernd. Charlottesville, Va., University Press of Virginia, 1969, pp. 26–29.

model is or is not useful for a particular purpose but not for absolute statements.

Conducting evaluations of the utility of policy models is costly, which partly explains why many models are developed or adopted and used without an adequate evaluation. When models are developed for policy purposes, evaluative steps should be integrated into the development plans—the least costly way to ensure that, when a model is produced, it will be accompanied by a reasonably complete assessment of its policy utility and limitations. By incorporating appropriate evaluative steps into the model development process, evaluation results can be used as feedback for improving the final model. Furthermore, as model evaluation becomes a standard part of model development, the exchange of policy models among organizations will be facilitated.[8]

Further explanation of the evaluative paradigm and its use is made through analogy—the application of the paradigm to a computer simulation model that addresses a broad, complex policy problem. The selection of the urban dynamics model developed by Professor Jay Forrester avoids the necessity of undertaking a model development effort. It illustrates the application of the paradigm and indicates some of the considerations involved in amplifying the paradigm to evaluate a particular model. The case study evaluation is intentionally structured as broad and general, rather than concentrating on the model's capability to deal with specific policy questions. Some background information follows on the urban dynamics model, which serves as the case study model.

THE URBAN DYNAMICS MODEL

In 1969, Professor Jay Forrester, of the Sloan School of Management at the Massachusetts Institute of Technology (MIT), set forth in *Urban Dynamics*[9] a distinctive, computer-based simulation model representing many of the developmental processes of an urban area. The urban dynamics model is built on the basic assumption that three subsystems—industry, housing, and population—and their interactions represent the essence of urban developmental processes. The changes

---

[8] William Lindsay. "Saul Gass Addresses WORC Banquet on Model Evaluation." *Washington Operations Research Council, WORC Newsletter, 13:4,* July 1974; Marvin. "Getting Involved in Analysis Needed by the Congress of the United States," pp. 17–19.

[9] Jay W. Forrester. *Urban Dynamics.* Cambridge, Mass., MIT Press, 1969.

in, and interactions among, these subsystems are assumed to represent the dynamics of the urban socioeconomic structure; and the urban dynamics model representation, based on these assumptions, is intended to address policy problems related to the processes of urban growth and decay.

The model is comprised of 11 sectors. Each of the industry, housing, and population subsystems consists of three sectors. The industry subsystem is stratified according to the age and condition of the enterprise; the sectors are referred to as new enterprise, mature business, and declining industry. Housing also is stratified, according to age and condition, into the sectors of premium housing, worker housing, and underemployed housing. Population is divided into three groups based on occupation: the manager-professional sector consists of entrepreneurs and professionals; the labor sector includes the skilled occupations; and the underemployed sector includes the unskilled and unemployed. In addition to these nine principal sectors, there is a tax sector and a job sector, which primarily tie together the principal sectors.[10]

The urban dynamics model resulted from Forrester's interest in extending his simulation-modeling approach to broader policy problems and from exposure to urban problems through his association with John F. Collins, a former mayor of Boston. Collins had come to MIT as a visiting professor after having been mayor of Boston from 1960 to 1967. Forrester found that Collins' ". . . enthusiasm and his desire to continue to analyze and improve urban processes led to a joint endeavor to structure and model the dynamics of urban decay and revival."[11] Collins organized a series of informal discussions between Forrester and people who had practical experience in urban affairs, which was in accord with Forrester's long-held view that the most valuable sources of information for developing models were people with practical management experience, rather than documents and research reports.[12] This approach to developing the model explains why *Urban Dynamics* carries no references to the urban literature.[13]

Forrester began developing his approach to simulation modeling during the 1950s. His background includes training as an electrical engineer, as well as experience in research and management. He was a

[10] *Ibid.*

[11] *Ibid.*, p. ix.

[12] *Ibid.*

[13] *Ibid.*, p. x.

pioneer in developing servomechanisms and was responsible for designing one of the early high-speed digital computers. He also guided the design of computer technology in the continental air defense system. His modeling approach, which became known as industrial dynamics, drew heavily from this background. In Forrester's view, the approach evolved from four major advances: development of the theory of information-feedback systems, the study of decision making, the experimental-model approach to the design of large systems, and the availability of digital computers.[14] The early applications of industrial dynamics were primarily in developing policy models of corporate and industrial management problems.

Industrial dynamics became an accepted part of the operations research and management science disciplines. The urban dynamics model represents an extension of the modeling approach to a broader and more difficult class of problems. Subsequently, the application of the approach was extended in Forrester's *World Dynamics*[15] and in *The Limits to Growth*[16] by Dennis Meadows and his associates to a still broader, and perhaps more difficult, class of problems. With this trend, the modeling approach became known as system dynamics rather than industrial dynamics. At the Sloan School of Management, Forrester has developed a graduate program devoted to system dynamics research, and the program annually awards several graduate degrees in system dynamics. The System Dynamics Group at MIT is a center for the methodological development and application of Forrester's modeling approach. The group promotes communications through an annual newsletter (*System Dynamics Newsletter*) which is distributed worldwide to teachers and researchers active in system dynamics research.

Although system dynamics has enjoyed a considerable degree of acceptance, it should be noted that the approach has always had strong critics. Some of the criticisms result from claims by Forrester and his followers that system dynamics constitutes not only an approach to developing policy models, but that it is a systems theory of the behavior of organizations, much the same as cybernetics is a theory of social behavior. A recent examination of these claims found little evidence to substantiate this assertion. There is, however, a distinctive character (evident in the urban dynamics model) to Forrester's ap-

[14] Jay W. Forrester. *Industrial Dynamics.* Cambridge, Mass., MIT Press, 1961, p. vii.
[15] Jay W. Forrester. *World Dynamics.* Cambridge, Mass., Wright-Allen Press, 1971.
[16] Donella H. Meadows et al. *The Limits to Growth.* New York, Universe Books, 1972.

plication of the modeling approach, in that he boldly represents the behavior of organizations in a comprehensive fashion, and he makes management decision processes a central concern.[17]

The emergence of Forrester's urban dynamics model may be viewed as part of a recent trend in developing and applying quantitative methods to the study of urban policy problems. This general trend is evident in a number of volumes that discuss the progress and research needs in applying quantitative methods to the analysis of urban problems [18] and that describe quantitative methods useful in the study of urban policy problems.[19] These volumes, as well as periodical literature, often treat the use of simulation modeling as a methodological tool for urban policy analysis. In addition, there are several studies devoted primarily to developing and applying computer simulation models in the study of urban policy.[20]

Immediately after publication, *Urban Dynamics* attracted widespread attention and strong criticism, and the model put forth in the book continues to be the subject of research efforts. The book was reviewed in a wide range of professional and technical journals,[21] and

[17] H. Igor Ansoff and Dennis P. Slevin. "An Appreciation of Industrial Dynamics." *Management Science, 14*:383, 394–395, March 1968.

[18] For example, see Mihajlo D. Mesarovic and Arnold Reisman, eds. *Systems Approach and the City.* Amsterdam, North-Holland, 1972; Stephen B. Sweeney and James C. Charlesworth, eds. *Governing Urban Society: New Scientific Approaches.* Monograph of The American Academy of Political and Social Science. No. 7. Philadelphia, American Academy of Political and Social Science, 1967.

[19] For example, see Anthony J. Catanese. *Scientific Methods of Urban Analysis.* Urbana, Ill., University of Illinois Press, 1972; Ira M. Robinson, ed. *Decision-Making in Urban Planning: An Introduction to New Methodologies.* Beverly Hills, Calif., Sage Publ., 1972.

[20] For example, see Brewer. *Politicians, Bureaucrats and the Consultants;* George C. Hemmens, ed. *Urban Development Models.* Washington, D.C., Highway Research Board, National Academy of Sciences, 1968; Maurice D. Kilbridge, Robert P. O'Block, and Paul V. Teplitz. *Urban Analysis.* Boston, Division of Research, Graduate School of Business Administration, Harvard University, 1970; Douglas B. Lee, Jr. *Models and Techniques for Urban Planning.* Report CAL-VY-2474-G-1. Buffalo, N.Y., Cornell Aeronautical Laboratory, Inc., Cornell University, September 1968.

[21] Thomas A. Barber. "Review of Jay W. Forrester, *Urban Dynamics.*" *Datamation, 15*:452–454, November 1969; Alexander N. Christakis. "Review of Jay W. Forrester, *Urban Dynamics.*" *Technological Forecasting, 1*:427–429, Spring 1970; Herman L. Danforth. "Review of Jay W. Forrester, *Urban Dynamics.*" *Public Management, 53*:20, January 1971; Allan G. Feldt. "Review of Jay W. Forrester, *Urban Dynamics.*" *American Sociological Review, 35*:364–365, April 1970; Aaron Fleisher. "Review of Jay W. Forrester, *Urban Dynamics.*" *Journal of the American Institute of Planners, 37*:53–54, January 1971; Walter Helly. "Review of Jay W. Forrester,

received considerable attention from the news media and popular publications.[22] Reactions to the book and model were mixed. Typical of the more positive reactions is the judgment that the Forrester model is ". . . an important and instructive landmark in society's effort to effect quantitative understanding and efficient planning of its environment." [23] On the negative side, there were many criticisms of particular assumptions and relationships used in the model; moreover, a frequent, broader attack criticized the whole model as being too comprehensive and ambitious. Typical of this point of view is John Kain's assertion that

Such methods have a great deal of potential for the analysis of urban problems and have already demonstrated their value in a number of specific, though limited applications. However, the development of truly useful and trustworthy urban simulation models remains a distant objective.[24]

The model has been the subject of a number of research efforts. In addition to the aforementioned reviews and papers, three collections

Urban Dynamics." Operations Research, 18:749–750, July–August 1970; James A. Hester, Jr. "Systems Analysis for Social Policies." (Review of Jay W. Forrester, Urban Dynamics.) Science, 168:693–694, May 8, 1970; Gregory K. Ingram. "Review of Jay W. Forrester, Urban Dynamics." Journal of the American Institute of Planners, 36: 206–208, May 1970; Eugene E. Kaczka. "Review of Jay W. Forrester, Urban Dynamics." Administrative Science Quarterly, 15:262–264, June 1970; Donald A. Krueckenberg. "Review of Jay W. Forrester, Urban Dynamics." Journal of the American Institute of Planners, 35:353, September 1969; Harold T. Moody. "Urban Dynamics: A Review of Forrester's Model of an Urban Area." Economic Geography, 46:620–626, October 1970; Jerome Rothenberg. "Problems in the Modeling of Urban Dynamics: A Review Article on Urban Dynamics, by Jay W. Forrester." Journal of Urban Economics, 1:1–20, January 1974; Allen Schick. "Five Theories in Search of an Urban Crisis." (Combined review of Urban Dynamics by Jay W. Forrester and five other books.) Public Administration Review, 32:546–552, September–October 1972; Herbert Weinblatt. "Urban Dynamics: A Critical Review." (Review of Jay W. Forrester, Urban Dynamics.) Policy Sciences, 1:377–383, Fall 1970.

[22] "A Daring Look at City Ills." Business Week: 142, 144, 146, June 14, 1969; Haynes Johnson. "Probing Our Future: From the Computer, a Revolution in Values." The Washington Post:C1, C4, June 8, 1975; John F. Kain. "A Computer Version of How a City Works." (Review of Jay W. Forrester, Urban Dynamics.) Fortune, 80:241–242, November 1969; Rebuttal by Jay W. Forrester. "Overlooked Reasons for Our Social Troubles." Fortune, 80:191–192, December 1969; Peter Passell, Marc Roberts, and Leonard Ross. (Combined review of Donella H. Meadows et al., The Limits to Growth, and Jay W. Forrester, World Dynamics and Urban Dynamics.) The New York Times Book Review:1, 10, 12–13, April 2, 1972; William K. Stevens. "Computer Is Used as Guide for Expert Seeking Way Out of Labyrinth of Urban Problems." The New York Times:47, 49, October 31, 1969.

[23] Helly. "Review of Jay W. Forrester, Urban Dynamics," p. 750.

[24] Kain. "A Computer Version of How a City Works," p. 241.

of papers dealing with various aspects of the urban dynamics model have been published. The first of these consists of 16 papers initially published as a special issue of the *IEEE Transactions* [25] and subsequently published in book form. [26] The second collection consists of 20 papers, most of which were authored by researchers connected with the System Dynamics Group at MIT. [27] The third collection also was authored by members of the System Dynamics Group. [28] The model also has been the subject of at least two doctoral dissertations, [29] several master's theses, [30] and a session at the December 1972 annual meeting of the American Association for the Advancement of Science. [31] Some of this model-related research is directed toward the application of the urban dynamics model to a specific area. The most ambitious effort in this direction was undertaken by Leo P. Kadanoff and his associates in the Urban Analysis Group at Brown University in their application of the model to Providence, Rhode Island; [32] similar work includes the Porter and Henley application to the Houston, Texas metropolitan area [33] and the work of Schroeder et al. of the System

[25] "Urban Dynamics: Extensions and Reflections." *IEEE Transactions on Systems, Man, and Cybernetics, SMC-2*:121–298, April 1972.

[26] Kan Chen, ed. *Urban Dynamics: Extensions and Reflections.* San Francisco, San Francisco Press, 1972.

[27] Nathaniel J. Mass, ed. *Readings in Urban Dynamics: Volume I.* Cambridge, Mass., Wright-Allen Press, 1974.

[28] W. Schroeder, L. Alfeld, and R. Sweeney, eds. *Readings in Urban Dynamics: Volume II.* Cambridge, Mass., Wright-Allen Press, 1975.

[29] Daniel L. Babcock. "Analysis and Improvement of a Dynamic Urban Model." Doctoral Dissertation. Los Angeles, University of California, 1970; James A. Hester, Jr. "Dispersal, Segregation, and Technological Change: A Computer Simulation Model of Large Metropolitan Areas During the Twentieth Century." Doctoral Dissertation. Cambridge, Mass., Massachusetts Institute of Technology, 1970.

[30] Albert Mason Harlow, Jr. "Exploring Rent Control with Urban Dynamics." Master's Thesis. Cambridge, Mass., Massachusetts Institute of Technology, 1972; Howell R. Porter III. "Application of a Generalized Urban Model to a Specific Region." Master's Thesis. Houston, Tex., University of Houston, 1971; Walter Warren Schroeder III. "Lowell Dynamics: Preliminary Applications of the Theory of Urban Dynamics." Master's Thesis. Cambridge, Mass., Massachusetts Institute of Technology, 1972.

[31] American Association for the Advancement of Science. "The Central Program of the 1972 AAAS Annual Meeting." *Science, 178*:890–891, November 24, 1972.

[32] Leo P. Kadanoff and Herbert Weinblatt. "Public-Policy Conclusions from Urban Growth Models." *In: Urban Dynamics: Extensions and Reflections,* pp. 87–104.

[33] Howell R. Porter III and Ernest J. Henley. "Application of the Forrester Model to Harris County, Texas." *In: Urban Dynamics: Extensions and Reflections,* pp. 173–210.

Dynamics Group to Lowell, Massachusetts.[34] There also have been reports of plans to apply the model to Minneapolis, Minnesota and Dallas, Texas.[35]

Although a number of the model's aspects have been examined critically, and it has been used to some extent in policy studies, the model has not yet been subjected to a full, systematic evaluation. This is a primary reason for selecting the urban dynamics model as a case study in model evaluation, but there are others. First, the model is well documented by Forrester's book. Working with an already developed, well-documented model greatly facilitates the task of carrying out the case study evaluation. Second, the urban dynamics model is manageable in size and, owing largely to the documentation provided, is relatively easy to understand. Third, the model has aroused considerable controversy, which heightens interest in evaluation findings.

As indicated, the case study of the policymaking usefulness of urban dynamics is a broad, general model evaluation; that is, the utility of the model is examined within the context of existing policy-oriented urban simulation models, and all potential uses of the model are taken into consideration. Adopting this broad orientation for the case study, rather than a narrow one, increases the opportunities to illustrate ways in which the detailed steps within each of the three parts of the evaluative paradigm can be structured and carried out. As mentioned earlier, the analysis required by the evaluative paradigm is equally appropriate for developing a policy model and for evaluating an existing model, as in the case study. Consequently, the details considered in carrying out the evaluative paradigm for the case study provide ideas which can be applied profitably during planning stages for the development of policy models.

There is another interesting area in which the case study evaluation may contribute. The results from the evaluation of the urban dynamics model may provide some insights into the policy usefulness of both the world dynamics model set forth by Forrester [36] and the version of that model used in the study sponsored by the Club of Rome.[37] The modeling methodology and techniques used in the latter are the same as in Forrester's urban model. In general, there is less

---

[34] Mass. *Readings in Urban Dynamics: Volume I,* Chapters 16 and 20; and Schroeder, Alfeld, and Sweeney. *Readings in Urban Dynamics: Volume II,* Chapters 11 and 12.

[35] Stevens. "Computer Is Used as Guide," p. 47.

[36] Forrester. *World Dynamics.*

[37] Meadows et al. *The Limits to Growth.*

existing theory, fewer dependable relationships that are empirically based, and less reliable data available to support the development of world models than to support urban models. This means that any deficiencies in urban dynamics are likely to be magnified in the world models. Of course, any opinion on their policymaking usefulness will be conjectural, since an evaluation of the world models is not being carried out.

CASE STUDY APPLICATION OF EVALUATION PARADIGM: OVERVIEW OF THE BOOK

The case study application of the evaluation paradigm to the urban dynamics model follows this introductory chapter. The next five chapters (2–6) present the analyses and conclusions of examining the model from the in-perspective, in-principle, and in-practice points of view. The final chapter summarizes the implications for model evaluation of the case study and the findings and conclusions from the policy evaluation of the urban dynamics model. The appendixes include a glossary of terms, documentation of the computer programs used in the evaluation, and documentation of the empirical estimation of model parameters used in the evaluation.

Chapter 2 provides a general introduction to the policymaking process, computer simulation modeling, and the relationship between them. The primary focus is on public policymaking involving broad, complex policy questions; the objective is to provide the background and framework for undertaking the case study model evaluation. As initial steps, the adopted view of policymaking is set forth, and a definition of computer simulation is developed. Then, policymaking is examined in terms of the intellectual tasks required and the methodological tools, including computer simulation modeling, available for assisting in carrying out the tasks. The role of simulation modeling in policymaking and the steps required in applying the methodology to policy problems are examined. The chapter concludes with a synthesized view of the developing relationship between public policymaking and computer simulation modeling.

Chapter 3 covers the first phase of the evaluation of the urban dynamics model: an examination of the model's policy perspective. The examination identifies the set of policy questions addressed by the urban dynamics model and compares the policy questions addressed by urban dynamics and other urban simulation models. In the comparison, a description of the principal features of the urban dynamics model is given. The potential utility of urban dynamics is assessed to determine the kinds of policy problems the model can deal with, as compared with other models, and the role urban dynamics can serve in policy analysis.

Examination of the supporting theory and assumptions of the urban dynamics model (i.e., examination of the model in-principle) is undertaken in Chapter 4. For the case study, this phase of the evaluation is organized into seven research tasks which span the process of developing policy-oriented simulation models. The critical review of the theoretical underpinning of the model identifies areas of relative strengths and weaknesses. Also, since the case-study evaluation is intentionally broad in its orientation, model deficiencies and possible improvements are identified so they can be considered in the in-practice phase of the evaluation.

Chapters 5 and 6 address the third phase of the model evaluation, which is concerned with the utility of the model in dealing with policy problems in-practice. Chapter 5 traces the development of an urban dynamics model representation of the District of Columbia by incorporating area-specific parameter values into the model and making a number of modifications. Parameter values are estimated to initialize the model for the 1960 period, and the model's performance is evaluated by comparing model-computed values for the 1960–1970 period with historical data for key model variables. Chapter 6 extends the in-practice examination by using the Washington, D. C. urban dynamics model to analyze a broad, complex policy problem in the area of housing. Several policy alternatives are identified for the selected problem, and modifications are made to adapt the model to the analysis of the problem. The model is then used in the computer projection of the outcomes of alternative policies for the 1980–1985 period. The development of the Washington, D. C. model and the analysis of the housing problem provide a basis for evaluating the utility of the model in dealing with policy problems in-practice; insights into additional research needed to improve the model as a tool for policy analysis also result.

Chapter 7 interprets the case study in terms of the general problem of evaluating the utility of models as tools in policy analysis. Also, the findings from the evaluation of urban dynamics are summarized, and conclusions are presented regarding the current and future utility of urban dynamics in assisting with policy analysis. On the basis of the findings, some conjectures are made regarding the policy usefulness of the methodologically similar world models developed by Forrester and others.

Although the appendix material is not essential to understanding the case study developed in the book, the computer programs and the model parameter estimations will interest those who want to make use of the urban dynamics model. It will be more convenient, generally, to use the model by means of the Fortran-language computer programs presented in the appendixes than to use the Dynamo-language computer programs developed by Forrester.

CHAPTER **2**

Policymaking and Computer Simulation Methodology

It is often said that a particular simulation model is a tool for assisting in policymaking. An illustrative case is the socioeconomic simulation model developed at The Urban Institute, a description of which declares that its "primary purpose . . . is to provide a tool for decision makers that will give them information not previously available about alternative programs within given policy areas." [1] Although typical of researchers who develop models, such statements usually are not accompanied by well-developed justifications. This chapter deals with broad aspects of the problem by delineating the general relationship between the policymaking process and computer simulation modeling. Insights are afforded into the policymaking aspects for which simulation modeling may prove useful, and information is provided on the application of simulation modeling to policy problems. This background defines the context within which evaluations of policy models are undertaken and within which the case-study evaluation is presented.

The relationship between the policymaking process and computer simulation modeling is developed in four sequential stages. First, the

---

[1] Harold W. Guthrie. "Microanalytic Simulation Modeling for Evaluation of Public Policy." *Urban Affairs Quarterly,* 8:403–404, June 1972.

intellectual tasks which policymaking requires and the methodological tools, including computer simulation modeling, available for performing these tasks are examined. Second, computer simulation is defined, and its scope is discussed. Third, the process of applying computer simulation to policy problems is characterized, and some of the considerations and difficulties inherent in this process are examined. The chapter concludes with a synthesis, or broad integrating view, of the emerging relationship between the policymaking process and computer simulation modeling and the implications of this synthesis or view for model evaluation.

ELEMENTS OF POLICYMAKING

Policymaking in this book is viewed as an approximation of an ideal pattern for making rational decisions and is compared with other policymaking views. Next, the policymaking process is structured as a set of constituent intellectual tasks, which are discussed in relation to methodological tools that have proved useful in addressing the tasks. Computer simulation is one of the tools considered, and the discussion assesses the role of computer simulation modeling in policymaking relative to the role of other methodological tools.

View of Policymaking

The ideal pattern of rational policymaking assumes that, for a given policy problem, the following six steps can be carried out:

1. Complete enumeration of goals
2. Complete inventory of resources
3. Complete enumeration of alternative policies
4. Valid prediction of the costs and benefits of each alternative
5. Computation of the net benefit for each alternative
6. Identification and selection of the alternative with the highest net benefit expected

This pattern corresponds to the mode of policymaking that Dror [2] calls the "pure-rationality mode." Although the assumptions of this mode are deeply rooted in modern culture and are consistent with the

---

[2] Yehezkel Dror. *Public Policymaking Reexamined.* Scranton, Pa., Chandler Publ., 1968, pp. 132–133.

tenets of rationalism, positivism, and optimism, Dror admits that, with few exceptions, pure-rationality policymaking is impossible.

The impossibility of achieving pure rationality in policymaking had been recognized by others prior to Dror. For example, both Simon and Lindblom rejected the pure-rationality mode as the first step in developing their approach to policymaking. Simon's satisficing model assumes that the search, evaluation, and selection of alternative policies are carried out only to the extent of achieving a satisfactory quality of policymaking rather than achieving the utopian goal of optimal policy, which is the objective of the pure-rationality model.[3] The satisficing model originally was developed as a behavioral model of policymaking, but it has acquired a normative interpretation. Lindblom's approach to policymaking is one of "muddling through," or of examining and adapting only those policies that represent incremental changes from previous policies.[4] His approach is discussed in more detail later in this chapter.

An "economically rational" model of policymaking has been adopted for this study, wherein the steps of the pure-rationality model are carried out only to the extent that it is effective from an economic point of view; that is, "this model is to be only as rational as is economical . . ."[5] Therefore, the steps that determine goals, resources, alternative policies, and selection of the best alternative are carried out only to the extent that the cost of performing the steps is less than the marginal benefit of improved policy. Because the point at which the net marginal benefit of improved policy becomes negative is a matter of judgment, the economically rational model produces results that only approximate those produced by the pure-rationality model.

The economically rational view of policymaking is sufficiently broad for the purpose of evaluating policy-related simulation models. The economically rational model includes the satisficing model, as a special case, since satisficing corresponds to the case in which the steps of the pure-rationality policymaking process are carried out only to the extent necessary to select a satisfactory policy alternative. As a normative model of policymaking, the satisficing model implicitly assumes that it is not beneficial—in terms of marginal improvement in policy—to continue the search for, and evaluation of, policy alternatives because of the costs imposed by the limitations on the rationality of both

---

[3] Herbert A. Simon. *Administrative Behavior.* 2nd Edition. New York, Macmillan, 1957, pp. xxiv-xxv.

[4] Dror. *Public Policymaking Reexamined,* pp. 144–147.

[5] *Ibid.,* p. 141.

human beings and organizations. Also, the economically rational model of policymaking provides stronger motivation for the improvement of policymaking than is provided by accepting the satisficing view.

The economically rational model also may be regarded as subsuming the sequential-decision model of policymaking. The sequential-decision model addresses the situation in which information essential to fully evaluate policy alternatives can be learned only in the early stages of applying the alternatives. The basic idea is to implement the two or more promising alternatives simultaneously, to gain the information on which to base the selection of the best alternative.[6] This may be regarded as a variant of the economically rational model.

Lindblom's incremental-change model of policymaking is an alternative to the pure-rationality model. From his viewpoint, pure rationality, or any approximation of it, is impossible, because of the difficulties and magnitude of collecting data and identifying and evaluating alternatives, the uncertainties of the consequences of policy actions, and the problems of reconciling policy choices in the sociopolitical situation. Lindblom contends that policy proposals should be confined to small, exploratory alterations of existing policy, asserting that this strategy will assure that the costs of policy analyses are minimized, the consequences of new policies are foreseen, and the new policies are politically acceptable to many groups.[7]

The incremental-change model is entirely suitable for many policy situations, and, in fact, incremental decisions constitute the largest proportion of government decisions. For areas in which incremental policy change is suitable, such change represents a mode very close to economically rational policymaking. Many of the most important policy decisions, however, are not incremental.

The massive tax cut of 1964 was not an incremental decision, nor was the passage of the Elementary and Secondary Education Act of 1965, the adoption of Medicare, the Interstate Highway Program, the poverty program, the shift of defense policy from massive retaliation to reliance on graduated response, the 1961 decision for a manned lunar landing in this decade, or the administration's current proposals for building 6 million low-cost housing units in ten years. . . . Only if the concept of "incremental" is defined as anything short of revolution, would these decisions fit the definition.[8]

[6] *Ibid.,* p. 142.

[7] David Braybrooke and Charles E. Lindblom. *A Strategy of Decision.* New York, Free Press, 1963, pp. 37–57.

[8] Charles L. Schultze. *The Politics and Economics of Public Spending.* Washington, D. C., The Brookings Institution, 1968, pp. 77–78.

In other words, there are many problems for which an effective policy will not be devised, even in the long run, through consideration of only incremental policy changes. An urban example is the New York City housing policy. For years the city followed an incremental policy of improving housing in selected neighborhoods, assuming that this would improve the city's entire housing stock. A study by the New York City Rand Institute, however, found that the critical issue was New York City rent control, which was causing a deterioration and abandonment of existing housing on a scale that completely negated the policy of improving housing in selected neighborhoods.[9] The resulting reform in rent control represented a rather drastic policy change that would not have occurred if only incremental changes had been considered.

Adoption of the economically rational view is not a contention that this view is accepted with any degree of finality. Ultimately, it may prove feasible to develop a broader perspective for policymaking, one that includes extrarational processes which, for experienced policymakers, are essential. Dror has promoted a broad research strategy to develop a policymaking model that is an optimal mix of rational and extrarational processes.[10] An example of basic research that follows Dror's strategy is the work of Marney and Smith,[11] who attempt a philosophical reconstruction that unifies the rational and humane concerns of policymaking.

Tasks and Tools of Policymaking

With the economically rational view as a framework, policymaking may be examined in terms of the intellectual tasks required; methodological tools can then be roughly correlated with the set of tasks. This provides a general perspective on the role of computer simulation modeling in policymaking and leads to the development of a more explicit definition of computer simulation.

Harold Lasswell views the policymaking process in terms of five tasks:

1. Goal clarification
2. Trend description

[9] Ira S. Lowry. "Reforming Rent Control in New York City: The Role of Research in Policymaking." *Policy Sciences*, 3:49–50, March 1972.

[10] Dror. *Public Policymaking Reexamined*, pp. 149, 153.

[11] Milton Marney and Nicholas M. Smith. "Interdisciplinary Synthesis." *Policy Sciences*, 3:299, September 1972.

3. Analysis of conditions
4. Projection of developments
5. Invention, evaluation, and selection of alternatives [12]

These tasks are ordered sequentially as they are performed for a specific problem, but the sequence often varies. Backtracking to reconsider tasks often results from an increased understanding of the problem, gained through performing subsequent tasks. Although many other classifications of the policymaking tasks are possible, this set is suitable for the current purpose. Figure 1 relates each of the five tasks to a set of methodological tools that often help to deal with that task. Listed under each task title are some typical questions that have been formulated to amplify Lasswell's characterization of the tasks.

Two points must be kept in mind when considering the association between the tasks and tools shown in Figure 1. First, each tool is shown only in association with a single task, whereas, in reality, the method may be useful in dealing with several tasks. For example, the regression and correlation method may prove useful in dealing with either the projection-of-developments task or the invention, evaluation, and selection-of-alternatives task, but, in Figure 1, it is associated with the analysis of conditions, because this is probably the area of its most significant usage. Second, a broad array of methods is considered, including systematic methods for dealing with expert opinion and public opinion, as well as more highly quantitative methods.

The goal-clarification task can be dealt with only in small part by systematic methods. Public opinion assessing methods can provide some insight into the importance and desirability of specified goals to society. Expert opinion, especially consensus expert opinion developed through the use of techniques such as the Delphi method, can help determine the desirability and feasibility of proposed goals. Technological forecasting techniques, many of which incorporate the use of expert opinion, can provide assistance through exploratory studies to identify a range of futures that will be possible from a technological point of view, or can provide estimates of the time-phased sequence of technological developments that will be required to support the attainment of a specified goal.

A number of statistical comparison techniques are used in addressing the trend description task. The tools include statistical techniques, such as cross-tabulations of data and the analysis of time series

[12] Harold D. Lasswell. *A Pre-View of Policy Sciences.* New York, American Elsevier Publ., 1971, p. 72.

POLICYMAKING TASKS	METHODOLOGICAL TOOLS

—Goal Clarification
  What are ultimate policy goals?
  What are preferred future states?
  What are the possible future states?
	Individual expert opinion
	Consensus expert opinion
	Public opinion
	Technological forecasting

—Trend Description
  Have past and recent events approximated preferred future states?
  What discrepancies between goals and current states exist?
  What is magnitude of discrepancies?
  Have discrepancies been increasing or decreasing?
	Statistical comparison
	Time series analysis
	Social and performance indicators
	Inequality measures

—Analysis of Conditions
  What factors caused recent trends?
  What is relative importance of factors?
  How have factors been changing in importance?
	Regression and correlation analysis
	Component or factor analysis
	Cluster analysis
	Analysis of variance

—Projection of Developments
  What are possible future states if current policies are continued?
  What are projected discrepancies from preferred future states?
  Are projected discrepancies increasing or decreasing?
	Matrix methods
	Curve extrapolations
	Simple probability models

—Invention, Evaluation, and Selection of Alternatives
  What short term objectives will promote goal realization?
  What are relative resource costs of alternatives?
  What strategy will optimize future goal realization?
	Cost-benefit analysis
	Analytical mathematical model
	Gaming simulation
	Computer simulation

FIGURE 1   Policymaking tasks and the methodological tools for addressing them.

that describe aspects of system behavior. Social indicators are used in describing trends for many social systems. Inequality measures, such as Gini coefficients of inequality, also are useful trend indicators when they can be developed to reflect pertinent aspects of system behavior over time.

When addressing the analysis-of-conditions task of the policymaking process, the identification of causal factors and an assessment of their significance is sought. Regression and correlation, factor analysis, cluster analysis, and analysis of variance methods are among the tools that provide assistance. In all but the simplest systems, variations in behavior will be a function of a number of variables, so multivariate techniques usually will be appropriate. In the analysis-of-conditions task, a beginning is made in establishing the relationships of variables to system behavior. Such analyses often are initial steps in the formulation of a model of the system.

In the projection-of-developments task, the basic tools may be regarded as simple models. They include the representation of a system's behavior as a system of linear equations, or perhaps as a system of nonlinear equations. Projections are then made under the premise that the relationships among the variables represented in the system of equations are static over the period of the projection. An example of this method is the input-output economic model, wherein interrelationships among industries are expressed as a system of linear equations, and projections for future time periods generally are made under the assumption that the technological relationships among industries are static. Other projection methods include statistical curve fitting and simple probability models. The probability models may take the form of sequential decision trees in which estimates of the probabilities of various decision paths are assumed to be known, or such models may take a critical path form which provides probabilistic estimates of the state of future systems.

When dealing with the invention, evaluation, and selection of policy alternatives, more highly developed models of systems are used. Actually, methodological tools provide assistance in the evaluation and selection of alternatives, but they provide little or no assistance with the invention of alternatives. The invention or conception of policy alternatives depends primarily on a broad understanding of the problems by both policymakers and researchers. This understanding includes the ability to judge the degree of policy control to which different variables can be subjected and the relationships among multiple goals which a policy may affect. The use of models and other techniques in the study of policy problems may, of course, suggest new alternative policies.

Cost-benefit analysis is one of the approaches applied to the evaluation and selection of policy alternatives. In this approach, the costs and benefits associated with a range of alternatives are projected for future periods. The costs and benefits attributable to alternative policies are identified; the value of their costs and benefits are assessed, insofar as possible, in common units, usually dollars. The dollar amounts attributed to projected costs and benefits of policy alternatives are discounted to obtain their values in current dollars, and the ratios provide guidance in selection among alternatives. Also, the process of comparing policy alternatives may suggest additional alternatives. Cost-benefit analysis explicitly reflects the economically rational model of policymaking.

A variety of analytical mathematical models exist which can assist in the policy invention, evaluation, and selection process. Analytical mathematical models are those that are completely specified in mathematical terms and have a well-defined mathematical solution. The solution may take the form of an algebraic solution to the general mathematical model, or an algorithm that provides a mathematically assured solution when applied to any specified numerical version of the model. Analytical models include the entire group of mathematical programming models that encompass linear programming, nonlinear programming, dynamic programming, and a variety of related techniques. Other analytical mathematical models are based in part on probability concepts and include inventory models, queuing models, and Markov chain models.

In addition to cost-benefit analysis and a variety of analytical mathematical models, gaming simulation and computer simulation are tools that address the task of studying policy alternatives. This book centers on computer simulation, but both methodologies are conceptually similar. Gaming simulation involves participation by human players who, by their activities of decision making or role playing, are actually a part of the logic of the simulation model. Because of the involvement of human players, the objectives of gaming simulation often are different from those of computer simulation. For example, the training of decision makers or the study of the behavior of decision makers are often primary objectives of gaming simulation. In addition to differences in purpose, gaming simulation has an element of complexity occasioned by the involvement of human players, whereas the entire logic of a computer simulation is incorporated explicitly in the computer program that implements the model.

Computer simulation methodology, because of its potential for supporting comprehensive analyses, is especially attractive for use in addressing the policymaking task of invention, evaluation, and selection of alternatives. There are two related aspects of this potential capability. First, computer simulation, as opposed to other methodologies, can deal with systems of greater complexity. Second, computer simulation is a highly integrative form of model building which can be used to bring together and relate segments of knowledge from several levels. These two characteristics will be examined more closely later in this book, because, although they make computer simulation attractive, they also cause difficulties in applying computer simulation to policymaking.

As previously mentioned, there is a flow of information between the five policy tasks shown in Figure 1, the primary flow being the order in which the tasks are listed. There also are feedback flows, in that a task may have to be redone as a result of information produced in performing a subsequent task. The primary information flow reflects that, in general, the five tasks require an increasingly comprehensive grasp of the problem under study as progress is made from the goal-clarification task to the invention, evaluation, and selection-of-alternatives task. This requirement for increased comprehension is reflected in the sequence in which the methodological tools are ordered. This set of tools forms a methodological hierarchy that progresses from tools that assist in the analysis of parts of a problem to tools that provide comprehensive, holistic approaches for dealing with a problem. In Figure 1, the tools associated with goal clarification and trend description analyze a problem in a rather piecemeal way. With the tools for the analysis-of-conditions task begins the process of relating problem variables and developing a more comprehensive view of the problem. The tools reach their most comprehensive form with the modeling approaches; and the most comprehensive tools often incorporate results from the application of other tools. For example, a computer simulation model for a policy problem may incorporate regression relationships and projection methods developed in the analysis of previous tasks for the problem.

This discussion of the general relationship between the tasks of policymaking and the tools that may assist in the performance of the tasks is based on major simplifications. The methodological tools are merely tactical instruments which a researcher may be able to use to gain some degree of assistance in dealing with a task. The intellectual strategy for attacking the task, however, and the formulation of the context in which the tools can be applied fruitfully are jobs with which the researcher must cope. No methodological tool can do these jobs for him, since they require reliance on supporting theory, not only in the area under study but in related areas as well, combined with the judgment of the researcher. For example, in applying a statistical technique, a researcher will rely on available supporting theory for guidance in selecting relevant variables or in adopting an appropriate functional form for developing a statistical relationship. Similarly, the selection of an appropriate model for a specific policy problem depends upon an evaluation of the theory supporting the model and upon the judgment of the researcher, which is based on his knowledge of the use of the prospective model, as well as of the use of other models for similar problems.

DEFINITION AND SCOPE OF COMPUTER SIMULATION

The aforementioned assessment of the general role of simulation in policymaking was developed without adopting an explicit definition of computer simulation. A more precise definition is desirable, and the formulation of a definition is dealt with in the first part of this section. After a suitable definition has been expressed, the general characteristics of problems for which the methodology is useful are examined, and a brief indication is given of the areas in which the methodology has been applied. This provides the background for the last two sections of this chapter, which give broader consideration to the role of computer simulation in the policymaking process.

When defining simulation, it is necessary to distinguish between simulation and gaming. Current usage of the terms for these two very different, but often intertwined, methodologies is not always consistent. Martin Shubik's definitions indicate the nature of each and the distinctions between them.

Simulation involves the representation of a system or organization by another system or model which is deemed to have a relevant behavioral similarity to the original system. The simulator or model is usually far simpler than the system or organism it represents. It should be far more amenable to analysis and manipulation.[13]

Whereas gaming, according to Shubik,

. . . employes human beings or robots acting as themselves or playing simulated roles in an environment which is either actual or simulated and which

[13] Martin Shubik. "On Gaming and Game Theory." *Management Science, 18*:P37–P39, January 1972.

contains elements of potential conflict or cooperation among the real or simulated players. The players may be experimental subjects whose behavior is being studied or they may be participants in an exercise being run for teaching, training, or operations purposes.[14]

Simulation may be regarded as the more general methodology, because all games may be considered simulations, but all simulations are not games.[15] These definitions are consistent with most definitions used in operations research.

Since the emphasis in this book is on policy-oriented models of social systems, an examination will be made of some definitions from public administration and the social sciences. The General Accounting Office glossary [16] defines a simulation model as

. . . a model which is being used to determine results under each of many specific sets of circumstances rather than one which is being used to determine an optimal solution to a problem.

The *International Encyclopedia of the Social Sciences* [17] characterizes simulation as

. . . a method for analyzing the behavior of a system by computing its time path for given initial conditions, and given parameter values. The computation is said to "simulate" the system, because it moves forward in time step by step with the movement of the system it is describing. For the purpose of simulation, the system must be specified by laws that define its behavior, during any time interval, in terms of the state it was in at the beginning of that interval.

This definition is widely used in the social sciences.

A common characteristic, which is either explicit or implicit in these definitions, is that simulation models are based on mathematical and logical relationships that rest on a conceptual understanding of the behavior of the systems under study. This excludes physical, verbal, and analog models. Another theme in the definitions is that simulation models are of interest because they make it possible to conduct experiments over extended periods of time and under dynamic conditions with models of the systems represented. This ex-

[14] *Ibid.,* p. P37.

[15] *Ibid.,* p. P38.

[16] U.S. General Accounting Office. *Glossary for Systems Analysis and Planning-Programming-Budgeting.* Washington, D.C., U.S. Government Printing Office, 1969, p. 61.

[17] Allen Newell and Herbert A. Simon. "Simulation: Individual Behavior." *In: International Encyclopedia of the Social Sciences.* Vol. 14. Edited by David L. Sills. New York, Macmillan and Free Press, 1968, p. 262.

cludes analytical mathematical models, such as a linear programming model, which are completely specified mathematically and which have analytical solutions that are assured to be optimal. Such analytical models do not readily provide the basis for conducting experiments that simulation models provide. Implicit in these definitions and consistent with the purpose of this study are restrictions in scope to models of social systems and, for the most part, to models of urban systems. Another restriction, which will be assumed, is that the models will be used on digital computers. Although not a logical necessity, as a practical matter, the models of interest will be computer-based, to provide a means of readily exercising the models to study the systems represented.

Because of the heavy reliance on computers in policy-oriented simulations, the term "computer simulation" will be used to denote the primary methodology. With consideration given to the characteristics previously discussed, the following definition is adopted: Computer simulation is a method for conducting experiments on a digital computer by the use of models which are specified by mathematical and logical relationships and which describe the dynamic behavior of a social system over an extended period of time.

The related, but distinct, gaming methodology will be referred to as "gaming simulation." As noted, in gaming simulation, human players participate and provide significant parts of the model logic, either through role-playing activities or by providing expert opinion.

Computer simulation methodology is potentially useful in the study of many policy-oriented problems, but its unique potential is in dealing with complex problems in a more comprehensive manner than is possible by using other methodologies. This view is expressed by Wagner [18] in his assessment that simulation is well suited to studying problems that exhibit

. . . the combined effects of uncertainty, the dynamic interactions between decisions and subsequent events, the complex interdependencies among the variables in the system, and, in some instances, the need to use finely divided time intervals. Such total system problems are too big and too intricate to handle with linear and dynamic programming models, or standard probabilistic models.

Simulation allows almost complete freedom of choice in model structure, which provides a capability for dealing with problems that cannot be formulated readily in the rigid mathematical structures

[18] Harvey M. Wagner. *Principles of Operations Research.* Englewood Cliffs, N. J., Prentice-Hall, 1969, p. 889.

imposed by analytical models, such as linear programming. Simulation models typically incorporate a number of relationships among system variables, based on regression, probabilistic, or other statistical methods. The relationships among variables are tied together by connective logical and mathematical relations to achieve a representation of the system under study. The model representing the system can develop in the form required by the problem being addressed rather than in a preset form. This flexibility of model structure makes computer simulation a highly integrative approach to the study of policymaking problems. In the simulation modeling of a system, the segments of knowledge and understanding—purposes of the model, conceptual understanding of the system, empirical relationships among system variables, and data from the system, to the extent these are known—are woven together into a model representing the system.

The use of simulation methodology in the social sciences has evolved since 1950, and has paralleled the development and increased availability of computer technology for the support of research in the social sciences. An indication of the rapid growth in the application of the methodology during its first decade is provided in Harold Guetzkow's collection of readings,[19] which reports on uses of simulation in psychology, political science, economics and business, education, industrial engineering, and military operations.

In the mid-1960s, a survey conducted for the National Commission on Technology, Automation, and Economic Progress provided further evidence of the increasing use of the methodology. Although the survey [20] was limited to a sample because of time and resource constraints, it included more than 50 major modeling and simulation efforts devoted to the study of social, political, and economic problems. More recently, Guetzkow et al.[21] compiled a volume presenting applications of the methodology in the social and administrative sciences, and critically examining the progress in research and gaps in knowledge regarding the development and application of simulation. In

---

[19] Harold Guetzkow, ed. *Simulation in Social Science: Readings.* Englewood Cliffs, N. J., Prentice-Hall, 1962, pp. xiii–xv.

[20] Abt Associates, Inc. "Survey of the State of the Art: Social, Political, and Economic Models and Simulations." *In: Technology and the American Economy. Appendix Volume V: Applying Technology to Unmet Needs.* Washington, D.C., U.S. Government Printing Office, 1966, pp. V203–V205.

[21] Harold Guetzkow, Philip Kotler, and Randall L. Schultz, eds. *Simulation in Social and Administrative Science.* Englewood Cliffs, N. J., Prentice-Hall, 1972, pp. xiii–xiv.

addition to these three studies, scores of books and articles related to simulation are now published each year. Two journals devoted entirely to the methodology are *Simulation* and *Simulation and Games.*

The nature of the increased interest in simulation methodology is indicated by the three general areas in which it has been applied: research, decision making, and instruction. Simulation, in support of research, is a particular kind of modeling tool and a vehicle for experimentation. As such, it can contribute to theory development, testing, comparison, and communication. In the decision-making or policymaking areas, simulation can provide assistance in four ways: as a tool for increasing the general understanding of a system that supports future policymaking; as an aid in developing alternative policies for a specific decision situation; as a tool for the evaluation of policy alternatives; and as an aid to verification and control by testing results obtained via other methods. For instructional purposes, simulation is a tool for both teaching and training.[22] These areas of application indicate the broad scope of computer simulation.

In the policymaking area of application, which is the focus in this book, there have been many varied uses of simulation. The military were leaders in the early development and application of the methodology. In 1966, it was reported that, in the preceding three years, between 200 and 300 major simulation projects had been conducted in the United States in support of military decisions.[23] Simulation has been applied to a variety of economic problems or problems having significant economic content, including such broad, ambitious efforts as The Brookings Institution's 400-equation macroeconomic model of the U. S. economy and Guy Orcutt's microanalytic, socio-economic simulation of the United States.[24] Economic simulations also include more narrowly oriented efforts, such as the Federal Power Commission's econometric model of the U. S. natural gas supply,[25] a model of the economic impact of dock strikes in Hawaii,[26]

---

[22] Randall L. Schultz and Edward M. Sullivan. "Developments in Simulation in Social and Administrative Science." *In: Simulation in Social and Administrative Science,* pp. 28–31.

[23] *Ibid.,* p. 30.

[24] Irma Adelman. "Economic System Simulations." *In: Simulation in Social and Administrative Science,* pp. 217, 220.

[25] J. Daniel Khazzom. "The FPC Staff's Econometric Model of Natural Gas Supply in the United States." *Bell Journal of Economic & Management Science,* 2:51, Spring 1971.

[26] James E. Jonish and Richard E. Peterson. "The Impact of a Dock Strike on the State of Hawaii: A Simulation." *Simulation,* 20:45, April 1973.

and a housing model in support of New York State policymaking.[27] In the area of urban analysis, a survey of policy-oriented models existing in the late 1960s reviewed more than 20 distinct models dealing with urban problems of land use, transportation, population, and economic activity.[28]

APPLYING COMPUTER SIMULATION TO POLICY PROBLEMS

This section will review the steps usually taken in applying computer simulation modeling to policy problems, followed by a discussion of selected aspects of the application process—aspects that often present difficulties.

Systems analysts, operations researchers, and policy-oriented social scientists are primary promoters of model building, including computer simulation modeling, as an approach to policy studies. The frequent justification for this view is that policymakers rely on conceptual understandings of policy problems which, in reality, are implicit models; the more explicit and clearly structured the models can be made, the better. Wagner [29] expresses this view as follows:

Constructing a model helps you put the complexities and possible uncertainties attending a decision-making problem into a logical framework amenable to comprehensive analysis . . . . In short, the model is a vehicle for arriving at a well-structured view of reality.

From the standpoint of policy analysis, the process of applying computer simulation modeling is a special case in the general process of applying model-building methods to policy problems, often expressed in five stages: formulating the problem, constructing a model, deriving a solution, testing the model and evaluating the solution, and implementing the solution.[30] The process of applying computer simulation modeling consists of these same basic stages, but they often are presented in a more detailed sequence of steps. Thomas Naylor

[27] David W. Sears. "The New York State Regional Housing Model." *Simulation and Games,* 2:131, June 1971.

[28] Maurice D. Kilbridge, Robert P. O'Block, and Paul V. Teplitz. *Urban Analysis.* Boston, Division of Research, Graduate School of Business Administration, Harvard University, 1970, pp. 8–10.

[29] Wagner. *Principles of Operations Research,* p. 10.

[30] Russell L. Ackoff and Maurice W. Sasieni. *Fundamentals of Operations Research.* New York, Wiley, 1968, pp. 6–11.

and his associates,[31] for example, used nine steps to describe the process: formulating the problem, collecting empirical data, formulating a mathematical model or logical representation of the problem, estimating values for model parameters from the data collected, evaluating the model and parameters, formulating and implementing a computer program, validating the model, designing simulation experiments, and analyzing the results from the model. Emshoff and Sisson [32] described the process in 11 steps. In substance, however, both descriptions are the same. They have been presented in two widely used books dealing with the application of computer simulation to policymaking. Agreement on the application process is fairly general in the systems analysis, operations research, and policy analysis literature.

The general strategy in this process is apparent from the steps involved. Computer simulation models are developed as analogs of their referent systems or the systems they purport to represent. This is done in such a way that the models are useful in studying certain questions related to the behavior of the system. The models incorporate representations of the structural relationships of their referent systems, but the level of detail for incorporating these relationships in the model will vary: some aspects of the system may be either omitted or represented only in highly abstract form, and others may be represented in considerable detail. The level of representation depends on the purpose of the model.

The overall process of model development and application is directed toward producing a model that will be useful in policymaking. A step-by-step review of this process will not be undertaken, since the general nature of most of the steps is apparent. Rather, the three aspects which often cause difficulties will be examined. First is model validation, including an examination of the role of model validation in the process of applying computer simulation and the approach taken to validation. This should help clarify the relationship between social science theory and the process of applying computer simulation to policymaking. The second aspect covers the design of experiments for the application of computer simulation models to the study of policy problems. The third aspect deals with the implementation of

[31] Thomas H. Naylor et al. *Computer Simulation Techniques.* New York, Wiley, 1968, pp. 23–26.

[32] James R. Emshoff and Roger L. Sisson. *Design and Use of Computer Simulation Models.* New York, Macmillan, 1970, pp. 49–59.

computer simulation models and the development of high-level computer languages to assist in this task.

All three aspects are incorporated into the three-phase model evaluation paradigm discussed in Chapter 1. Actually, model validation is given attention in both the in-principle and in-practice phases. This becomes apparent in examining the approaches to model validation. The design of experiments and computer implementation aspects are subsumed primarily under the in-practice phase.

Model validation is a crucial step in the application of computer simulation to policymaking. Validation refers to the set of actions directed at ". . . building an acceptable level of confidence that an inference about a simulated process is a correct or valid inference for the actual process." [33] Model validation is closely related to model utility, but each is a distinct concept. Utility refers to the usefulness of a model for some policymaking purpose; that is, model utility is a broader consideration than model validity. An assessment of the utility of a model must consider the potential users of a model, the alternative actions open to the users, and the consequences that are considered by users when evaluating alternatives.[34] Both the model evaluation paradigm set forth in Chapter 1 and the aforementioned sequence of steps in the application of computer simulation to policy problems are strategies for achieving model utility. Utility, of course, requires a degree of model validity; however, validity ". . . is not an end in itself but merely a means of enhancing the utility of a model . . . While validity is the ultimate test of theory, the ultimate test of a model is its utility. Decisions regarding model development should be made on the basis of utility-cost tradeoff." [35] This reflects an economically rational view of policymaking: we are as rational as is economical. Both utility and validity are matters of degree. A model may be valid enough for some purposes, but not for others, and it may have utility for dealing with some policy problems, but not with others.

There are three approaches to the validation of computer simulation models: constructing models that have face validity, testing the assumptions upon which a model is based, and comparing the input-

---

[33] Richard L. Van Horn. "Validation of Simulation Results." *Management Science, 17*:247–248, January 1971.

[34] David W. Sears. "Utility Testing for Urban and Regional Models." *Policy Sciences, 3*:235, June 1972.

[35] Schultz and Sullivan. "Developments in Simulation in Social and Administrative Science," p. 14.

output transformations of the model with those of the referent system. These three approaches reflect the philosophical views of rationalism, empiricism, and positive economics, respectively.[36] The first approach reduces the validation effort to searching for and adopting the general knowledge, basic assumptions, and relevant theory that support the construction of a valid model. For example, if experience has shown that a gravity model relationship has represented accurately the volume of traffic interaction between two population centers, then using this relationship to build a new model contributes to the validity of the model. In the second approach, each assumption in support of the model should be empirically tested; indeed, the extreme form of this approach would reject any assumption that could not be empirically verified. The third approach requires that comparisons be made of the input-output transformations of the model and the referent system. Such comparisons are facilitated by carrying them out within historical periods so the model inputs can be the same as those of the system under study.

The approach taken most often to validation of computer simulation models combines all three approaches because, basically, each ". . . is a necessary procedure for validating simulation experiments but [none] of them is a sufficient procedure for solving the problem of verification." [37] Under the combination of the three approaches—model construction, empirical testing of assumptions, and comparison of input-output transformations—model validation is carried out to the extent practicable under each approach,[38] which varies with the problem considered; it also depends on the availability of related theory and knowledge and on the feasibility of obtaining empirical data. Sensitivity testing of the simulation model often is useful in the empirical testing of assumptions, because it affords insights into the sensitivity of model outputs to alternative empirical assumptions.[39]

It is apparent that the model-evaluation paradigm incorporates all three of the basic approaches to model validation. The in-principle phase encompasses the construction of models having face validity (rationalism) and the testing of model assumptions (empiricism). The in-practice phase includes the comparison of a model's input-output transformations with those of the referent system (positive economics). (Both the in-principle and the in-practice phases of

[36] Thomas H. Naylor and J. M. Finger. "Verification of Computer Simulation Models." *Management Science, 14*:B93–B95, October 1967.

[37] *Ibid.*, p. B95.

[38] *Ibid.*, pp. B95–B97.

[39] Van Horn. "Validation of Simulation Results," p. 251.

evaluation, of course, go beyond the considerations of model validation.)

This discussion of model validation leads to the relationship between models and theory: A model has only to represent its referent system, whereas theory must adequately explain the behavior of the system.[40] Models often make use of simple empirical relationships, such as prediction equations based on fitting curves to observed values, but such relationships do not explain behavior, and, thus, they do not constitute theory.[41] Computer simulation models, however, often are based on theory, which, as previously mentioned, enhances model validity. Usually, where theory is inadequate, computer simulation models that support policymaking are based on both theory and simple empirical relationships. Computer simulation models, then, are not theories in the true sense, although the terms "model" and "theory" sometimes are used interchangeably. Also, while not all theories are models, many are.[42]

The second aspect to be considered in the process of applying computer simulation to policy problems is the design of experiments. Experimental design serves the same overall purpose in this process as it does in the biological and physical sciences. Design provides a structure for the use of a model to study a system, and it can minimize the number of experimental trials or model runs required. Designs for the application of computer simulation models assume that the model is a valid representation of the referent system. Although model validation is never fully achieved, the degree of validation achieved must be kept in mind during the development and use of experimental designs.

Two basic types of simulation experiments are frequently conducted with computer simulation models. The first is exploratory experimentation, wherein the objective is to explore the relationship between a set of factors and a response variable. The factors generally represent controllable system variables through which policies can be expressed by specifying factor levels. The response variable usually is a system variable that measures some aspect of system performance related to policy objectives. In such exploratory experimentations, the emphasis is on mapping system response for a range

[40] Schultz and Sullivan. "Developments in Simulation in Social and Administrative Science," p. 5.

[41] Hubert M. Blalock, Jr. *Theory Construction*. Englewood Cliffs, N. J., Prentice-Hall, 1969, pp. 58–59.

[42] Abraham Kaplan. *The Conduct of Inquiry*. San Francisco, Chandler Publ., 1964, pp. 264–265.

of factor settings to gather information that would point up policy possibilities and limitations. Hunter and Naylor [43] discussed the application of four different designs for conducting exploratory simulation experiments: full factorial design, fractional factorial design, rotatable design, and response-surface design. Many other designs can be used, of course, and the choice of design depends on the cost of model runs and the nature of the analysis to be conducted with the information produced by the runs. For example, if a first-order regression equation is to be fitted to express response in terms of factor levels for a two-level problem, then a full factorial or fractional factorial design would be appropriate; but, to fit a second-order equation, the design would have to provide more design points, and a rotatable design would be appropriate. Optimizing experimentation is another type of simulation experiment often conducted, where the objective is to determine the levels of a set of factors that optimize the value of a response variable. Such experiments use optimum-seeking or search methods, in which successive design points on the response-surface hyperplane are chosen to improve the value of the response variable being optimized. The strategies for selecting successive design points constitute different optimizing methods. Two frequently used search methods are the steepest-descent and the single-factor methods. In the former, the search moves from the current point toward the direction of most rapid improvement in the value of the response variable. When no further improvement can be made, a new direction is chosen. In the latter, a single factor is varied while holding all other factors constant. When no further improvement in the response variable is possible, another factor is selected and varied, while all others are held constant.[44] When using optimum-seeking methods, a test must be conducted to determine when the optimum value of the response variable has been achieved.

A number of problems can arise in the design of experiments for computer simulations, a common one being multiple response; that is, there might be an interest in observing many different response variables. Few design techniques exist for multiple-response experiments, and the problem is often bypassed by treating an experiment with many responses the same as many experiments, each with a single response. This, however, is not always a satisfactory approach.

[43] J. S. Hunter and T. H. Naylor. "Experimental Designs for Computer Simulation Experiments." *Management Science, 16*:425–430, March 1970.

[44] *Ibid.*, pp. 430–431.

Another problem is the convergence of optimum-seeking methods. One aspect of this problem is the speed of convergence, which usually is not known in advance and, hence, may prove costly in terms of computer time. A second aspect is making certain that what appears to be an optimum in the search procedure is not just a local optimum.[45] There are no general answers for many of the problems encountered in experimental design for computer simulations. The problems must be worked out for the particular experiment, utilizing what can be gleaned from the literature and from experience.

The third aspect to be examined in the application of computer simulation methodology is the computer implementation of models. Because computer simulation models do not have a rigidly defined prototype structure, the costs of developing programs to implement them is high in comparison to the computer implementation costs for models that have well-defined mathematical structures. For instance, a single computer program can be used to solve all linear programming problems of a specified size range, but each computer simulation model is, to a great extent, an ad hoc computer programming effort. In reaction to this situation, and as an indication of their significance, more than two dozen high-level computer languages have been developed and are being used to assist in the formulation and translation of models into computer programs. These languages attempt to reduce the computer programming effort, to provide assistance in conceptualizing the models, and to allow flexibility for future modifications of the computer programs as experimental purposes dictate. The more widely used of the simulation languages are languages in the general sense: ". . . they are useful in describing a situation independent of the fact that they can be translated by a computer into machine languages . . . As with other languages, people who use simulation languages tend to think in them." [46] Simscript, General Purpose System Simulator (GPSS), and Dynamo are examples of languages that are particularly useful in describing systems. Simscript and GPSS are the two most widely used; Dynamo is not as widely used, but it has several unique features. Dynamo is of particular interest here, because it was used to implement Forrester's urban dynamics model. Although the development of simulation languages is continuing, progress to date already has eased the problem of computer implementation of simulation models.

[45] Naylor et al. *Computer Simulation Techniques,* pp. 332–340.
[46] Emshoff and Sisson. *Design and Use of Computer Simulation Models,* p. 117.

CONVERGENCE—COMPUTER SIMULATION IN THE POLICYMAKING PROCESS

As noted a number of times in the foregoing discussions, computer simulation modeling is used for, and is potentially applicable to, a wide range of policy problems, which may cover a spectrum extending from narrowly oriented questions to the most broad and complex problems. At one end of the spectrum are questions related to the efficiency or effectiveness of policy alternatives for narrowly oriented organizational or program problems. Examples of such problems include inventory and replacement policies and many resource allocations. These problems usually have clear goals and are readily susceptible to quantification. At the other end of the spectrum are what may be called broad-aim programs: programs designed to cure specific social problems for which only multiple, imperfect measurement criteria exist. Examples of broad-aim programs include a

. . . number of the social action programs launched during the 1960's—the delinquency prevention and grey area programs, portions of the poverty program, and the model cities planning program. These programs attempted to produce increased community competence, increased participation of low-income citizens in community action, and more effective utilization of existing institutions. All these aims could be realized in many alternative ways, and none of these programs could be judged by whether one particular end was achieved.[47]

Many social problems in areas such as urban development, housing, and welfare have characteristics that place them at or near the broad-aim end of the policy-problem spectrum.

The primary purpose of this section is to set forth a strategy for applying computer simulation to broad-aim policy problems. Simulation methodology, however, may be useful in studying policy problems at any point on the spectrum. The decision as to whether the application of simulation modeling will be useful in the policy considerations for a particular problem depends on other characteristics of the problem, as previously indicated. When simulation methodology is applied, however, the context or environment in which the modeling effort is conducted will vary considerably, depending on whether the position of the problem is at the narrow- or broad-aim end of the spectrum. An explicit awareness of the

---

[47] Robert S. Weiss and Martin Rein. "The Evaluation of Broad-Aim Programs: Experimental Design, Its Difficulties, and an Alternative." *Administrative Science Quarterly, 15*:97, March 1970.

different contexts is needed for a broad understanding of the potential of computer simulation methodology in addressing broad-aim policy problems.

The context in which computer simulation typically is applied to narrow-aim policy problems corresponds closely to the context which often is assumed in operations research; it usually is confined to an organization, and often only to a functional area within an organization. This is not to say that operations research is confined to narrow-aim policy problems, but it is the perspective expressed in much of the operations research literature. For example, in one widely used textbook, operations research is characterized as "concerned with the practical management of the organization . . . ," and as adopting "an organizational point of view . . ."[48] Generally, the restricted organizational environment of narrow-aim problems provides fairly explicit goals to guide policymaking activities, which often are related to organizational efficiency and effectiveness in performing the function under study. When such problems are addressed by computer simulation, the conceptual underpinning of models is usually well understood, because the models will be a representation of existing or proposed organizational arrangements and processes. Compared with other social processes, organizational processes tend to be closely controlled, so model building has to incorporate only behavioral processes in which the variables vary over restricted ranges. In the organizational context, such processes often can be directly observed, allowing for development of strong empirical relationships to guide the model-building efforts.

An example of the use of computer simulation to address a problem at the narrow-aim end of the spectrum is the analysis of possible improvements in ambulance service in New York City. In the analysis of policies, the quality of ambulance service was measured by ambulance response time, which is the period of elapsed time between the call for emergency service and the arrival of the ambulance on the scene. The objective of the study was to examine alternative policies to achieve a decreased response time for emergency service in one of the city's largest hospital districts. The simulation model developed represented the geographical distribution of the emergency ambulance service system and the scheduling of calls for service, the number of ambulances available in the hospital district, the location of each hospital, and the location of the ambulance garages. The policy

---

[48] Frederick S. Hillier and Gerald J. Lieberman. *Introduction to Operations Research.* San Francisco, Holden-Day, 1967, p. 5.

alternatives examined included redistributing the existing ambulances in the district, increasing the number of ambulances in the district, and a combination of the two alternatives. The model was used in support of a cost-effectiveness analysis of a number of specific policy alternatives. As a result of the study, the policy adopted required a redistribution of the ambulances by locating some of them at satellite garages rather than at the hospitals, as was previously done.[49] It promised a significant improvement in service for the district at a small increase in cost.

When computer simulation is applied to assist in broad-aim policy problems, the context is much broader in scope and not so well defined as the context for narrow-aim problems. The context of broad-aim problems often encompasses organizations at a number of levels, such as federal, state, and local governments, and often extends into society, generally to the level of individuals or family units. This expanded context makes the delimitation of analysis more difficult with broad-aim problems than with narrow-aim problems. The broader context increases the possibilities of significant inter-actions between the policy problem under study and other policy problems. Simulation models to support the analysis of broad-aim problems tend to have an uncertain conceptual underpinning at some points, often incorporating theories and behavioral relationships that are only partially developed and tested.

For policy problems at the broad-aim end of the spectrum, Donald Campbell [50] has advocated that policymaking be administered as an experimental approach. He characterized this as

. . . an approach in which we try out new programs designed to cure specific social problems, in which we learn whether or not these programs are effective, and in which we retain, imitate, modify, or discard them on the basis of apparent effectiveness on the multiple imperfect criteria available.

A readiness for viewing social reforms as experiments is indicated by provisions for program evaluation in recent social legislation. Campbell's primary concern is the formulation of research designs that are appropriate for such program evaluations and that protect against threats to experimental validity.[51]

The application of computer simulation modeling to the study of

[49] E. S. Savas. "Simulation and Cost-Effectiveness Analysis of New York's Emergency Ambulance Service." *Management Science,* 15:B608–B627, August 1969.

[50] Donald T. Campbell. "Reforms as Experiments." *Urban Affairs Quarterly,* 7:133, December 1971.

[51] *Ibid.,* pp. 136–139.

broad-aim policy problems should be conducted in a manner analogous to Campbells's paradigm of viewing social reforms as experiments. Under this approach, a computer simulation model for assisting in policy studies will be improved by the feedback of information from policy implementations. This will provide for improved evaluation of both the supporting theory and the performance of the simulation model at each iterative stage of policymaking.

The welfare reform issue is an example of a broad-aim policy problem in which computer simulation was used in the contextual view of policymaking as an experimental reform. The problem centered on the welfare reform issues and alternatives considered by the administration and Congress during President Nixon's first term.

The administration made a commitment to implement reforms in welfare policy. The basic dimensions of its proposal were of the negative income tax type: wide coverage, a low guaranteed level of income, and a moderate marginal tax rate. The proposal also was a compromise between the conservative view that spending should be cut and stringent work requirements imposed and the liberal view that the system should be reformed to reduce inequities even though this would require increased spending. This new federal program became known as the family assistance plan.[52]

A computer simulation to assist in examining alternative versions of the plan was developed as a microsimulation model of the population. It worked with a sample file of low-income families, which was based on a Bureau of the Census survey that included size, sex of household head, income by source, employment status, and other relevant characteristics for individuals and families. The model was capable of simulating (estimating) the effects of alternative plans with different guaranteed income levels, different marginal tax rates, and different coverage provisions. It was a tool used by analysts in estimating the costs and benefits under alternative plans and in comparing plans in terms of effectiveness in reducing poverty, effects on work incentives, and costs and other factors. Variations of the plan were analyzed in dozens of runs through a computer programmed with the model. This analysis contributed to the submission to Congress by the administration of a family plan that guaranteed $1,600 for a family of four, and a marginal tax rate of 50 percent.[53]

The model used in the analysis of the administration's program was

---

[52] Alice M. Rivlin. *Systematic Thinking for Social Science.* Washington, D. C., The Brookings Institution, 1971, pp. 27–28.

[53] *Ibid.,* pp. 28–29.

an improved version of a model initially developed in support of the work of the Presidential Commission on Income Maintenance Programs. The model was further extended and improved by both the administration and The Urban Institute,[54] who applied their versions of the model to the analysis of a number of versions of the welfare reform proposal during its consideration by the 91st and 92nd Congresses, including program revisions by the administration and program alternatives for the Senate Finance Committee and members of Congress (including Senators Harris, McGovern, Javits, Goodell, and Ribicoff). The welfare reform finally adopted in 1972 departs significantly from the administration's initial proposal, and may be regarded as an iterative step in evolving a welfare policy. Since that time, The Urban Institute has developed a more advanced version of the model.[55] This new version is expected to assist in the analysis of further welfare reform measures by executive and congressional offices and some state governments.

From a broad perspective, this simulation modeling effort has been and continues to be an evolving model development. Alice Rivlin envisioned the development of a modeling tool for the analysis of welfare and closely related proposals for income maintenance programs as requiring three steps:

. . . *Step One* toward this goal would be to reproduce on a computer tape the characteristics of a sample of low-income families . . ., which could be used to try out different structures and levels of income maintenance. Estimates could be made of those who would benefit and how much each alternative would cost—assuming that no changes in family composition or working behavior took place as a result of changes in income maintenance benefits. *Step Two* would be to draw on research and experimentation for estimates of these behavioral responses and to build these into the calculations . . . *Step Three* would be to incorporate in the model the estimated effects on earnings of investments in people, such as education and training and health programs.[56]

The first of these steps has been accomplished in large part. Progress has been made toward the second step by incorporating into the

[54] John F. Moeller. "Development of a Microsimulation Model for Evaluating Economic Implications of Income Transfer and Tax Policies." Paper read at the Conference on the Computer in Economic and Social Measurement, sponsored by the National Bureau of Economic Research, September 20, 1972, at State College, Pennsylvania, pp. 1–2. For another treatment of this topic, *see* James R. Storey. "Systems Analysis and Welfare Reform: A Case Study of the Family Assistance Plan." *Policy Science*, 4:1–11, March 1973.

[55] Moeller. "Development of a Microsimulation Model," pp. 8, 19–28.

[56] Rivlin. *Systematic Thinking for Social Science*, p. 32.

model the findings from some social experiments funded by the Office of Economic Opportunity. These experiments, begun in 1968, were designed to test several variants of a negative income tax on a sample of families in a number of communities. When the Nixon administration began examining welfare reform alternatives, the Office of Economic Opportunity provided preliminary findings on the effects of the negative income tax on the work incentives of the beneficiaries, and the findings were used in the modeling efforts. In the meantime, several other experiments had been launched ". . . to test other types of income maintenance systems, coordination of income maintenance with other public programs, notably manpower and social services, and the behavior of other kinds of families, especially those headed by a female, and the rural poor." [57] Results from these experiments will contribute to accomplishing steps two and three of the broad-income maintenance model development foreseen by Rivlin. Feedback information from the later income maintenance experiments is being incorporated into The Urban Institute's income maintenance modeling effort.[58]

It is clear from these examples of narrow- and broad-aim policy problems that the development and evaluation of models addressing problems at the broad-aim end of the policy-problem spectrum involve many difficulties not encountered when dealing with more narrowly oriented problems. There are several reasons for this. First, broad-aim problems involve policy in a broad context, and consideration must be given to the interactions of the problem under study with policies in other areas. Second, there usually is greater uncertainty about the conceptual underpinning of models dealing with broad-aim problems, owing to the necessity of using theory and relationships that are not fully developed and tested. Third, broad-aim modeling must accommodate incremental improvements through the incorporation of information feedback from pertinent experiments and the implementation of the initial program involved. Because of these complexities, it is essential that models dealing with broad-aim problems be subject to a broad, systematic evaluation of the type set forth in the model evaluation paradigm described in Chapter 1.

The urban dynamics model selected for the evaluation case study addresses a policy area at the broad-aim end of the policy-problem spectrum. Broad-aim urban policymaking deals with problems for which there are a number of goals that do not and probably can-

[57] *Ibid.*, pp. 94–101.

[58] Jodie T. Allen. Personal interview. May 10, 1973.

not have clearly established priorities. The criteria for the measurement of policy success with respect to goals tend to be multiple and imperfect. The context of such problems is broad, often encompassing a number of governmental units, governmental departments, and government-related planning organizations. The long-term improvement of models for broad urban policymaking, such as the urban dynamics model, will depend on the feedback and analysis of information from policy implementations, as in the model for analyzing welfare policies.

CHAPTER 3

The Urban Dynamics Model Policy Perspective: In-Perspective Evaluation

The approaches to evaluating the policy perspective of a model differ considerably in their comprehensiveness. A narrowly oriented examination is appropriate when it is necessary to determine whether a model can deal with one or more specific policy problems. A broader examination is needed when it is necessary to understand the full range of policy problems a model can accommodate. In either case, it is often useful to compare the capabilities of the model under study or development with the capabilities of other available models.

In the case study of the urban dynamics model, a comprehensive approach is followed, because it illustrates fully how such an evaluation is performed. Using this approach, a comparative analysis is conducted to determine whether urban dynamics has characteristics that give it a perspective distinct from that provided by other urban models. Results from this examination also provide insights into which of the four policymaking roles of computer simulation modeling urban dynamics may possibly serve. In Chapter 2, the four roles were identified as increasing the general understanding of a system in support of future policymaking, developing policy alternatives, evaluating proposed policy alternatives, and verifying results obtained by other models.

The evaluation of the policy perspective of the urban dynamics

47

model is presented in four stages. First, the dimensions of the comparative analysis are set forth by indicating how the models to be included in the comparison are selected and which set of characteristics is to be considered. Second, a descriptive analysis is given of the models to be compared. Third, the general features and principal sectors of the urban dynamics model are described, together with some of the model formulation techniques used. Finally, the evaluation itself is presented.

DIMENSIONS OF COMPARATIVE ANALYSIS

The problems of urbanization in the United States began with population movement to the cities during the late nineteenth and early twentieth centuries. In the 1930s, the Federal Government became actively involved in a series of programs dealing with urban problems in housing, transportation, and other areas. The problems have intensified during recent decades; and continuing federal concern resulted in the establishment, in 1965, of a cabinet-level Department of Housing and Urban Development. A variety of programs have been sponsored and largely funded by the Federal Government, including the model cities and urban renewal programs.

Since 1960, simulation modeling methodology has been applied to a number of urbanization problems. A combination of developments made this possible, primarily the availability of computers, the increasingly complete data on urban physical and population characteristics, and an improved understanding of the determinants of urban land use. These circumstances gradually led to a number of modeling efforts to simulate the operations and interactions of the many variables related to urban planning. At the same time, efforts increased to develop a more coordinated set of programs for dealing with urban problems.

Early simulation models were developed for use in Baltimore, Boston, Detroit, Pittsburgh, and San Francisco, and later in other cities. Several of the early models, such as those developed for Baltimore and Detroit, were related primarily to transportation planning, although the strong interaction of transportation with other aspects of urban development usually was represented to some extent. Models such as those developed for Pittsburgh and San Francisco were more inclusive, because they were oriented toward evaluating broad, urban renewal plans; [1] many were large-scale, complex efforts. For example,

[1] Harry B. Wolfe and Martin L. Ernst. "Simulation Models and Urban Planning."

the original version of the San Francisco model required approximately 35,000 data inputs, many of which had to be changed for each simulation run.[2]

The urban dynamics simulation model was developed by Professor Forrester in 1969. As indicated, an evaluation of the model's policy perspective will compare urban dynamics and other principal urban simulation models. First, the scope of the comparison is indicated by specifying the criteria for selecting the models included. Then, the method of organizing the comparison is described, providing the groundwork for the comparative examination. In many cases, of course, a less comprehensive approach will be appropriate, but the ideas used here also will prove useful in carrying out less comprehensive evaluations of the policy perspective of models.

Selection of Models

There are two primary criteria for selecting models to be included in the comparative analysis. First, the models must be policy-oriented; that is, they must address urban policy questions in terms of variables that are related to public policy. This criterion rules out models such as that of the National Planning Association (for preparing long-range economic and demographic projections for metropolitan areas), which makes no provision for representing and evaluating policy alternatives.[3] Second, the models must have been applied to a specific urban area. It might be said that urban dynamics fails to satisfy this criterion, in that Forrester used the model only in the study of a hypothetical city. Others, however, have applied urban dynamics to specific cities, as discussed in Chapter 4. An additional criterion which should be observed is to exclude models that are specialized and narrow in their orientation. A model developed in 1969 to predict Chicago traffic patterns is thus eliminated, because it provides only a narrow treatment of transportation and no representation of related urban systems.[4]

In: Operations Research for Public Systems. Edited by Philip M. Morse, assisted by Laura W. Bacon. Cambridge, Mass., MIT Press, 1967, pp. 49–50.

[2] Mark Nagelberg and Dennis L. Little. *Selected Urban Simulations and Games.* Working Paper WP-4. Middletown, Conn., Institute for the Future, April 1970, p. 21.

[3] National Planning Association. *Economic and Demographic Projections for States and Metropolitan Areas: Projections to 1975, 1980, and 1985 of Population, Income, and Industry Employment.* Report No. 68-R-1. Washington, D. C., January 1969.

[4] Maurice D. Kilbridge, Robert P. O'Block, and Paul V. Teplitz. *Urban Analysis.* Boston, Division of Research, Graduate School of Business Administration, Harvard University, 1970, p. 125.

The set of models that satisfy these criteria is selected from the relevant literature. The review of 20 urban models published by Kilbridge et al. in 1970 provides a good starting point in the literature examination, because it includes complete coverage of policy-oriented urban models up to its publication.[5] The review includes models presented in the 1959 and 1965 special issues of the *Journal of the American Institute of Planners,* which provide state-of-the-art reports on urban modeling.[6] Kilbridge et al. also cover the seven urban development models that Lowry compared in 1968.[7] More recent reviews, by Babcock[8] and by Nagelberg and Little,[9] have added little to the Kilbridge coverage, except that they both include urban dynamics.

The selection of models for the current comparison begins with the list of 20 models from the Kilbridge review, eliminating those that do not meet the criteria previously discussed and adding those that are described in recent literature; 14 of the models in the Kilbridge review are included in the current comparison. Of the six excluded, four were rejected because they were not applied to specific cities and two others because they were too narrowly oriented. Additions to the list were made by reviewing issues of the *Journal of the American Institute of Planners, Simulation and Games, Urban Affairs Quarterly,* and *Simulation* for the period 1968–1975.

The literature examination produced a set of 16 models for inclusion in the comparison. The names of the models selected are given in Table 1. Two other models mentioned in the recent literature are not included in the comparison because they are still in the process of development, and the published information is insufficient. They are referred to and characterized, however, at the end of the "Comparative Analysis of Models" section in this chapter.

Framework for Comparison

The comparison of the policymaking perspective of urban dynamics with other urban models uses a conceptual framework that represents four basic model characteristics: subject, function, theory, and method.

[5] *Ibid.,* p. 7.

[6] *Journal of the American Institute of Planners, 25,* May 1959; and *31,* May 1965.

[7] Ira S. Lowry. "Seven Models of Urban Development: A Structural Comparison." *In: Urban Development Models.* Edited by George C. Hemmens. Washington, D. C., Highway Research Board, National Academy of Sciences, 1968, pp. 121–163.

[8] Daniel L. Babcock. "Analysis and Improvement of a Dynamic Urban Model." Doctoral Dissertation. Los Angeles, University of California, 1970, pp. 9–30.

[9] Nagelberg and Little. *Selected Urban Simulations and Games.*

TABLE 1 Comparison of Urban Simulation Models

Model	Subject							Function			Theory				Method					
	Population	Housing	Transportation	Employment	Economic Activity	Land Use	Public Finance	Projection	Allocation	Derivation	Behavioral	Gravity	Growth Trend	Input-Output	Linear Equations	Nonlinear Equations	Differential and Difference Equations	Input-Output Matrix Equations	Mathematical Optimization	Markov Processes
Chicago Area Transportation	X		X	X				X		X			X		X					
Baltimore Retail Market Potential			X			XX		X	X	X		X			X					
Urban Detroit Area	X	X	X	X	X			X	X	X		X			X					
Penn-Jersey Regional Growth	X	XX				X		X	X	X					X				X	
San Francisco Housing	X	X	X			X		X	X	X					X				X	
Buffalo Regional Growth	X	X				X		X	X	X	X	X			X				X	X
New York Metropolis	X			XX	XX				X	X	X			X	X	X		X		
Philadelphia Activities Allocation	X		X	X	X	X		X	X	X			X	X	X			X		
Southeastern Wisconsin Land Use	X			X	X	XX		X	X	X			X		X		X			
Polimetric Land Use	X			X	X	XX		X	X	X	X	X	X		X		X			
Empiric Land Use	X			X	XX	XX		X	X	X	X		X		X					
Economic Growth Dynamics	X	X		X		XX		X		X	X				X				X	
Pittsburgh Metropolis	X	X		X	X	XX		X	X	X		X	X	X	X			X	X	
Pittsburgh Urban Renewal	X	X		X	X	XX		X	X	X		X	X		X				X	
Provincial-Municipal	X	X	X	X	X	X	XX	X	X	X		X	X	X	X			X	X	
Urban Dynamics	X	X		X		X	X			X	X		X				X			

X–In aggregate form only.
XX–Detailed form.

The framework is patterned after one developed by Kilbridge et al.[10] The detailed attributes examined under the basic model characteristics as shown in Table 1, however, differ from those used by Kilbridge, in order to construct a framework with a stronger policy orientation.

The subject of a model can be defined as the subsystems or components of an urban system that the model represents. Model subjects are grouped into seven general classes: population, housing, transportation, employment, economic activity, land use, and public finance. These classes are closely interrelated and, to some extent, overlap. Another important aspect of model subjects in policymaking is the level of detail with which the model represents its subjects. For instance, a particular model may represent the transportation subsystem in considerable detail, represent other subsystems only in aggregate form, and omit still other subsystems entirely. The choice of subsystems represented and the degree of detail in their representation depends on the purpose of the model, and the choice relates directly to the policymaking perspective of the model.

Function is the general model-building approach used in estimating the future state of the subjects treated by the model. Models perform one or more of three functions: projection, allocation, and derivation. In projection, estimates of the future are made by using a mathematical or logical relationship to convert inputs into estimates for a future point in time. In allocation, models distribute a subject among subclasses for some specific time period, such as allocating employment to the districts of a city. In derivation, a model transforms one subject into another or derives one subject from another. For example, transportation activity levels may be derived from land-use information within a model. Most models perform one or some combination of these functions; many combine all three.

For purposes of comparison, the term "theory" indicates the general nature of the relationships supporting the model. Many of the supporting relationships for policy-related simulation models are not fully developed theories that can provide an adequate explanation of system behavior; they are merely empirically based relationships which are useful in model development. All modeling relationships, however, will be regarded as theory for purposes of model comparison.

Four categories of supportive theory will be considered: behavioral, gravity, growth trend, and input-output. Behavioral relationships are those based on rational choice or decision-making processes, by individuals or groups of individuals. The other three types are regarded as

---

[10] Kilbridge et al. *Urban Analysis*, pp. 7–19.

growth-trend relationships and depend on rationality and statistical stability in describing collective behavior. Gravity relationships are analogous to Newtonian physics and assert that the social interaction between two population centers, as measured by some variable, is directly proportional to the product of their populations and inversely proportional to some power of the distance between their centers. In growth-trend relationships, equations are developed to represent behavior and growth trends. Equations may be based on historical data, an understanding of system behavior, or a combination of the two. Input-output relationships are used to represent the structural interdependencies between industries in their consuming and producing roles. These four categories of supportive theory consolidate the six categories used by Kilbridge.[11]

Method, the last of the four basic model characteristics, is the technique used in the model to estimate the future state of the model's subject. A computer simulation model often combines several techniques, ranging in complexity from simple equations to highly developed optimizing techniques. To classify the modeling methods, six categories are used: linear equations, nonlinear equations, differential and difference equations, input-output, mathematical optimization, and Markov processes. These categories provide more detail about the forms of equations used in a model than the categories used by Kilbridge.[12]

This framework is more appropriate for comparing models from the policymaking perspective than some of the other comparative approaches which have been used. An approach used by Harris[13] to compare urban models examined six dimensions: descriptive versus analytic, holistic versus partial, macro versus micro, static versus dynamic, deterministic versus probabilistic, and simultaneous versus sequential. Another set of characteristics used as a comparative framework for models is comprehensiveness, disaggregation, treatment of time, abstraction, and descriptive-behavioral-normative.[14] Both emphasize the comparison of model structure and method and, hence, the interest of the model builder rather than that of the model user.

[11] *Ibid.*, pp. 13–16.

[12] *Ibid.*, pp. 16–19.

[13] Britton Harris. "Quantitative Models of Urban Development: Their Role in Metropolitan Policy-Making." *In: Issues in Urban Economics.* Edited by Harvey S. Perloff and Lowdon Wingo, Jr. Baltimore, Johns Hopkins Press, 1968, pp. 366–367.

[14] Douglas B. Lee, Jr. *Models and Techniques for Urban Planning.* Report CAL-VY-2474-G-1. Buffalo, N.Y., Cornell Aeronautical Laboratory, Inc., Cornell University, September 1968, pp. 2.1–2.12.

Neither of the two frameworks, however, provides an explicit representation of the subsystems or subjects of the urban system represented in the model; the framework adopted here, on the other hand, provides an essential, detailed characterization of the subjects treated in the model—a crucial aspect of the policymaking perspective.

COMPARATIVE ANALYSIS OF MODELS

The comparative analysis of selected urban models is summarized in Table 1. The 16 models analyzed have been classified into four groups according to their primary area of policy emphasis. The first three are regarded as transportation models, and the second three deal with housing and residential development. The next six emphasize economic activity, and the final four are general urban development models. This rough classification is useful in discussing the primary characteristics of the models. The four groups are presented in order of increasing comprehensiveness, beginning with models of restricted scope, such as those that emphasize transportation, and proceeding to more comprehensive models that attempt to represent all major subsystems of an urban area.

A full description of each model included in the comparative analysis will not be attempted. The principal features of each will be briefly identified; Table 1 serves both to summarize and supplement the discussion. Moreover, the structured presentation in tabular form supports conclusions related to the policymaking perspective of the models.

In Table 1, an x is entered in the appropriate columns of a row to indicate the characteristics of the model represented. For example, one of the functions of the Chicago-area transportation model is projection. In general, an x indicates that a model has the attribute the column represents. For the seven subject categories in Table 1, however, the cell entries also indicate the degree of detail with which the model treats the subjects; this information is relevant to determining the policymaking perspective of a model. In the subject columns then, an x indicates that the model represents the subject subsystem only in an aggregate form, while xx indicates subject representation in more detailed form. In representing land use, for example, the urban dynamics model provides only an aggregate or gross representation, while the southeastern Wisconsin land-use design model provides a fairly detailed representation.

Transportation Models

As noted previously, transportation planning was one of the early areas in which urban simulation models were applied.

Chicago Area Transportation Study: The first of early transportation models to be examined is the Chicago-area transportation study, wherein the Chicago area is represented by traffic analysis districts. For each district, the model projects future land use from an initially specified inventory of land uses; a set of decision rules and linear relationships is applied, based on the plans of public agencies, zoning policies, and measures of the accessibility and capacity of the traffic districts. Seven types of land use are predicted for each district: residential, commercial, manufacturing, transportation, public buildings, public open space, and streets. Population and employment estimates for each district are derived from the activities implicit in the land-use estimates, and all of these become inputs into the process of forecasting aggregate transportation flows for the area. The Chicago model is less formal in structure than many urban models and readily accommodates judgmental interventions, such as the location of a shopping center. Used in making 20-year projections to help develop a transportation plan for Chicago, the model has influenced the development of most other urban transportation models.[15]

Baltimore Retail Market Potential: The Baltimore retail market potential model was developed to study Baltimore-region transportation. The model, however, was equally concerned with the location of urban activities, especially retail trade centers, on the premise ". . . that the location, intensity, and interaction of urban land uses govern the level of transportation demand and the pattern of intraurban traffic flows." [16]

The Baltimore model is based on a gravity-model framework, wherein the sales of each retail center are directly proportional to the center's size and its proximity to customers and their prosperity, and inversely proportional to the center's proximity to other centers. The model requires data on customer retail expenditures for each small area, location and size of retail centers, and transportation links

[15] Lowry. "Seven Models of Urban Development," pp. 130–131; and Nagelberg and Little. *Selected Urban Simulations and Games,* p. 6.

[16] T. R. Lakshmanan. "An Approach to the Analysis of Interurban Location Applied to the Baltimore Region." *Economic Geography, 40:*348, October 1964.

between customers and centers. The data must be specified for a definite date, say 1990, and the model then estimates the sales for each center for that date. Customer retail expenditures are estimated by an independent econometric model. The designers of the model used it to explore alternative distributions of retail trade centers for the Baltimore metropolitan area. The technique used in the solution of the model involves repeated trials to find a balanced distribution of trade centers, wherein the distribution of retail outlets provides the minimum total customer transportation costs. The solution procedure used is equivalent to a mathematical programming optimization, although the problem was not formally structured in that way.[17]

Detroit Regional Transportation and Land-Use Study: Although the Detroit model is grouped with the transportation models, it is more comprehensive than the Chicago and Baltimore models. The Detroit modeling effort includes a group of related models and analytical procedures. It represents the Detroit area in terms of 297 districts, subdivided into 1,446 zones. The model projects population for the area by use of a regression equation. These population forecasts, exogenous forecasts of employment by industry, and exogenous forecasts of households are distributed among the districts on the basis of accessibility of the population to employment and other factors. Projections of transportation requirements are then made on the basis of the population and employment distributions. The model also provides land-use estimates, but these are largely the result of exogenous inputs on which the model performs bookkeeping. Overall, the Detroit model forecasts only population and transportation needs, although the model spatially distributes several other urban subjects.[18]

Housing and Residential Development Models

The next three models shown in Table 1 are classified as housing and residential development models. Although two of the models were motivated by the study of transportation policy, their primary contribution is in the area of residential development.

Penn-Jersey Regional Growth: The first of these models, Penn-Jersey

---

[17] T. R. Lakshmanan and Walter G. Hansen. "A Retail Market Potential Model." *Journal of the American Institute of Planners, 31:*134–143, May 1965.

[18] H. James Brown et al. *Empirical Models of Urban Land Use: Suggestions on Research Objectives and Organization.* New York, National Bureau of Economic Research, 1972, pp. 53–59.

regional growth, was developed in the early 1960s to study the nine-county region that includes Philadelphia. As initially conceived, the heart of the model was the Herbert-Stevens residential location model, which attempted to build an economic behavior theory of individual households and firms. The initial model was not feasible because of time restrictions and unavailability of data; therefore, an alternative formulation was developed to describe locational behavior in an aggregate manner. This alternative approach established multiple regression relationships that defined residential location for classes of housing as a function of a number of variables. The residential location model was solved as a linear programming problem that maximized the aggregate rent-paying ability of the region's population. Models with the same linear programming structure were proposed for the location of other activities, but these were never implemented. The model is unique in that it attempts to represent market demand for the location of residential development as an optimizing model. The results of this effort contributed directly to the development of the Philadelphia activities allocation model discussed later in this chapter.[19]

San Francisco Housing: The San Francisco housing model simulates the construction, deterioration, and modification of housing in response to both market demand and governmental policies. It provides a more complete representation of the housing market than the Penn-Jersey model, and it is easily the most detailed representation of the current urban housing models. In the San Francisco model, the city is divided into 106 neighborhoods, each containing 500 tracts of approximately two acres each. More than 20 kinds of housing units are classified according to size, type of structure, condition, and neighborhood; and more than 100 types of households are classified according to size, stage in family cycle, race, and income. The model operates for nine two-year periods. For each two-year span, household populations are matched with the stock of housing available at the end of the previous period; characteristics of both housing and residents are considered in the matching process. Housing shortages and surpluses indicated by the matching create market response in the form of changes in rents, modification of properties, and building of new and demolition of old housing. A Markov process is used to represent the

[19] Decision Sciences Corporation. *New Communities. Survey of State of the Art.* Jenkintown, Pa., November 1971, pp. 33–37; and Lowry. "Seven Models of Urban Development," pp. 139–141.

deterioration of housing. The model provides for testing the impacts on residential housing of such policies as zoning changes, building code changes, and rent supplements.[20]

Buffalo Regional Growth: The Buffalo regional growth model is concerned primarily with distributing residents to the 200-square mile Buffalo area. Two of the principal developers of the model helped develop the Chicago-area transportation model, and the Buffalo model is a substantially modified version of the Chicago model. The Buffalo model de-emphasizes transportation and adds the control of activity densities and open spaces. The model spatially distributes growth using a gravity-type relationship that considers the possibility of locating new units of urban activity in each district, as well as the accessibility of the locations to the center of the urban core. The concepts of holding capacity and density of development are constraints on the location of activities. After the main model allocates forecasts of urban activities to small geographic areas, these allocations are then input to the traffic-assignment model that evaluates alternative systems of transportation.[21]

Economic Activity Models

The six models that deal primarily with economic activity differ considerably in their emphasis on the location of activities and in their supporting theories. Two of the models emphasize the forecasting of economic activities for an urban area as a whole; whereas the other four are equally concerned with the spatial distribution of projected activities. Two of the models rely on aggregate economic theory: one is an interindustry input-output model; and the other is an economic-growth model, which is essentially a dynamic version of an economic-base study. Two of the models rely on behavioral concepts that reflect market economics and other factors. The other two models rely on gravity and growth concepts very similar to the gravity concept used in some of the models discussed previously.

[20] Ira M. Robinson, Harry B. Wolfe, and Robert L. Barringer. "A Simulation Model for Renewal Programming." *Journal of the American Institute of Planners,* 31:126–133, May 1965; and Lowry. "Seven Models of Urban Development," pp. 141–145.

[21] George T. Lathrop and John R. Hamburg. "An Opportunity-Accessibility Model for Allocating Regional Growth." *Journal of the American Institute of Planners,* 31:95–103, May 1965; and Nagelberg and Little. *Selected Urban Simulations and Games,* p. 6.

New York Metropolis: The purpose of the New York metropolis model, developed in the early 1960s, was to provide 30-year projections of the important economic measures for a 22-county region that includes New York City. The model represents the economy of the region by an economic input-output model with 42 industry classes. The input-output model projects employment, output, and value added for each of the 42 industries of the region as a whole. Demographic projections, including natural population increase, migration, and age composition of the population, also are made for the entire region. Although the model does not emphasize the distribution of projected economic activities within the region, employment and population changes are estimated for four subregions, including Manhattan, which is the region core, and three concentric circles of counties surrounding the core.[22] The modeling effort emphasizes economic projection rather than policymaking; however, the model can be used to estimate the impact of alternative policies.

Philadelphia Activities Allocation: This modeling effort evolved from the Penn-Jersey regional growth model. Both models were undertaken by the Penn-Jersey transportation study staff, which has become part of the Delaware Valley Region Planning Commission. The activities allocation model is broader in scope, weaker in its behavioral orientation, and simpler in mathematical structure than the earlier Penn-Jersey regional growth model.

The objective of the activities allocation model is to analyze, through the year 1985, the locational patterns of urban activities, with alternative transportation plans for the Philadelphia region. The model consists of a series of seven submodels. Six of the submodels deal with the location of new industrial, commercial, and residential activities and the amount of land each type of activity requires. The seventh submodel deals with the land occupied by new streets. The submodels that locate industrial and commercial activities also estimate the employment these activities generate. Structurally, the submodels are combinations of linear and nonlinear regression equations based on historical data. The model operates by projecting the location of activities in five-year increments through 1985. In so doing, the model allocates activities to 192 subregions of the Philadelphia region. This provides projected spatial distributions of economic activities,

[22] Barbara R. Berman, Benjamin Chinitz, and Edgar M. Hoover. *Projection of a Metropolis; Technical Supplement to the New York Metropolitan Region Study.* Cambridge, Mass., Harvard University Press, 1960, pp. 1–14.

employment, and population. Policy options that could be studied include the impact of alternative mass transit and highway networks on the pattern of urban development.[23]

Southeastern Wisconsin Region: In the mid-1960s, the Southeastern Wisconsin Region Planning Commission undertook a modeling effort to assist in the commission's developmental planning for the Milwaukee metropolitan area. The model emphasizes regional economic development and its impact on land use. The three major submodels deal with the economic simulation of the region and the design and testing of land-use plans. The economic simulation submodel is a dynamic input-output model of the region, and it is used to forecast the economic growth and employment of some 30 industries. These forecasts are used to estimate future population and land-use requirements for the region. The second submodel designs an optimal plan to meet the land-use requirements determined by the economic simulation submodel projections; it is a linear programming formulation that determines land-use distribution to minimize total public and private costs, that meets land requirements, and that satisfies constraints on the location and density of activities. The third submodel simulates the time-phased land development process in the region and is used to test the feasibility of plans produced by the second submodel. A number of iterations between the second and third submodels usually is needed, with intervention by planners, to produce a suitable land-use plan. This modeling effort is a continuing one and is being extended to include transportation planning.[24]

Polimetric and Empiric: The polimetric and empiric models were developed initially by the Boston Regional Planning Project. The objective of both models is to distribute, among 29 Boston-area districts, exogenous metropolitan-area forecasts of blue-collar population, white-collar population, manufacturing employment, trade employment, and other employment. Polimetric is more sophisticated mathematically and attempts a representation that is more behavioral than empiric. The Boston group, however, abandoned polimetric in favor of empiric. Nonetheless, the Delaware Valley Region Planning Commission simplified and applied polimetric for studies of the Phila-

[23] Lee. *Models and Techniques for Urban Planning*, pp. 5.74–5.76.

[24] Brown et al. *Empirical Models of Urban Land Use*, pp. 38–44; and Kenneth J. Schlager. "A Land Use Plan Design Model." *Journal of the American Institute of Planners, 31*:103–111, May 1965.

delphia region.[25] Empiric has been adapted for use in the Minneapolis-St. Paul and Washington, D. C. areas.

Both polimetric and empiric use a set of simultaneous equations—one equation for each activity in each district—to express the allocation of part of an areawide forecast of each activity to each district in terms of the characteristics of the district. The two models differ in regard to the form of these sets of equations. In polimetric, the form is a set of nonlinear differential equations, where the dependent variable in each equation is the rate of change over time in the level of an activity in a district. In each equation, the dependent variable is a function of the regional growth rate for the activity, volume of the activity already in the district, usable space in the district, relative desirability of districts for the activity, and mobility of the activity. Empiric is formulated as a set of simultaneous linear equations, the dependent variable of which is the change in the level of an activity in a district. The dependent variable in each equation is a function of the accessibility and desirability characteristics of the district. In both models, the equations are fitted by regression techniques; the empirical aspects of this job prove to be more manageable with the empiric model because of the simpler mathematical structure of its equations.[26]

Kent County: The last economic-activity model examined was sponsored by the Kent County Planning Commission and is directed toward evaluating the economic growth policies for Grand Rapids, Michigan and surrounding Kent County. The model consists of a population submodel, a job submodel, and linkages between the two. Population is represented in terms of age and occupation groups; and the population submodel simulates the processes of death, aging, migration, labor-force participation, and occupational changes. The job submodel is organized by industries, and the labor, by occupational groups needed to support these industries. The nine industries represented are grouped into manufacturing, domestic, and primary classes. Manufacturing industries are the principal growth stimulant, because they export goods from Kent County. The change in manufacturing industry levels is represented as being dependent on national demand for the product, differential advantage of locating industry in Kent County, labor availability, and other factors. The population and job submodels are linked by their set of common occupational categories

---

[25] Lowry. "Seven Models of Urban Development," pp. 133–137.
[26] *Ibid.*, pp. 134–136.

and by interactions between the submodels in determining migration, occupational changes, and labor-force participation. Mathematically, the model consists of a set of differential equations. Computer implementation in the Dynamo computer language means that the solution to the set of equations is approximated by solving a set of first-order difference equations.[27]

General Urban Development Models Other than Urban Dynamics

The four models included in the general urban development category are more comprehensive than the models previously discussed; they usually represent more urban subjects than models in the other categories, and they attempt to represent more fully the synergistic relationships among the urban subsystems they include. The Pittsburgh metropolis model, for example, is regarded as being more comprehensive than the Chicago-area transportation model. Although both models include the same number of urban subsystems, the Pittsburgh metropolis model provides a sophisticated representation of the location of residential and employment centers. This is accomplished by allowing two-way interactions between employment and residential locations when determining the spatial distribution of these activities. On the other hand, the Chicago model distributes activities to districts by applying decision rules and linear relationships; there are no provisions for the influence that one activity has on the location of other activities.

Pittsburgh Metropolis: This model was developed by Ira Lowry in the early 1960s and is often referred to as the Lowry model or Model of a Metropolis. Treatment of this and the Pittsburgh urban renewal model could be combined, because an improved version of the Pittsburgh metropolis model is a core component of the urban renewal model. The Lowry model, however, deserves separate treatment because of its strong influence on the development of other urban models. Versions of the Lowry model are incorporated in the San Francisco Bay Area Transportation Study, the Cornell Land Use Game, and the Projective Land Use Game,[28] as well as in the Pittsburgh urban re-

---

[27] Carl V. Swanson and Raymond J. Waldmann. "A Simulation Model of Economic Growth Dynamics." *Journal of the American Institute of Planners, 36*:314–322, January 1970.

[28] William Goldner. "The Lowry Model Heritage." *Journal of the American Institute of Planners, 37*:100–105, March 1971.

newal model. In addition, the Lowry model directly influenced the development of the Provincial-Municipal model discussed later in this chapter.

In the Pittsburgh metropolis model, Lowry divides the Pittsburgh region into 420 one-mile-square tracts. Three classes of urban activities are distributed among these tracts: basic industry, retail industry, and housing. Basic industry includes enterprises that export most of their output from the region. The amount and location of basic industry are determined exogenously and input to the model. Then the model applies distribution algorithms alternately to housing and retail industry in an iterative process. First, housing is distributed to each tract in proportion to the tract's accessibility to total employment, which includes employment from basic and retail industry. A maximum density constraint limits the housing assigned to tracts. Second, retail activity is distributed to tracts in proportion to their accessibility to consumer markets, where market size considers both residential population and employment centers. Three types of retail activity are dealt with separately: neighborhood, local, and metropolitan, corresponding to the kind of market served. The iterative execution of these two steps is continued to achieve an equilibrium spatial distribution of housing and retail activity. The novel feature of this approach is that it produces an equilibrium distribution of employment and residential locations by allowing each distribution to enter into the computation of the accessibility of the other. In its initial use in Pittsburgh, the Lowry model represented only a single time period,[29] but later uses extended it to multiple time periods.

Pittsburgh Urban Renewal: The Pittsburgh urban renewal model was built on Lowry's work, but it was a far more ambitious effort. The heart of the model consists of three submodels that operate in sequence. The first is an input-output model for the Pittsburgh region that produces projected employment for the basic industries of the region. The future employment estimates, which are stratified by industry and income, are input to the second submodel, which determines regional locations for the projected increases in the 30 types of basic industry represented in the input-output submodel. This industrial location submodel assigns industries to locations by a combination of techniques that involve the consideration of past industry location patterns and the matching of individual firms and sites. The third submodel uses the information on the location of basic industries

[29] Lowry. "Seven Models of Urban Development," pp. 137–139.

and associated employment to locate housing and retail employment. This submodel is a multiple-time period, improved version of Lowry's Pittsburgh metropolis model. The improved version classifies employment into white collar and blue collar and represents six types of households.[30]

The Pittsburgh urban renewal model was planned as a complex, multistage, multiple-time period, computer simulation. The data requirements alone impose a burdensome job of collection, organization, and analysis. Data include three intensive surveys of Pittsburgh's commercial and other activities; detailed 1950 and 1960 U. S. Census information for blocks and census tracts; and information from the Pittsburgh Department of City Planning on real property for each block and lot of the city.[31] Apparently, the complexity of the modeling effort and the burden of the data requirements have kept the model from being completed according to its initial design,[32] although the Department of City Planning uses some of the submodels and components. Lee's assessment[33] is that the model could provide very useful information once built, but

> Unfortunately, it was too ambitious. In 1963, when the model was designed, there seemed to be some possibility that the detailed problems in constructing the model could be worked out. At the present time, the task of building such a model would correctly be regarded as monumental . . . In fact, computer systems . . . adequate to handle the large storage, the billions of computations, and the accounting and transfer operations necessary for a large simulation, are not yet available. Nor have the data been found.

Although advances in computer technology may have alleviated the computer processing difficulties to some degree since this 1968 assessment, the difficulties of model formulation and data availability remain.

PROMUS: A general urban development model undertaken more recently is the Provincial-Municipal Simulator, or PROMUS, model. Since 1970, this has been an ongoing modeling activity of the city of Toronto and Province of Ontario, Canada. The model, which is a unification of urban developmental planning and financial policy planning for

---

[30] Wilbur A. Steger. "The Pittsburgh Urban Renewal Simulation Model." *Journal of the American Institute of Planners, 31*:144–149, May 1965.

[31] *Ibid.*, p. 146.

[32] Douglas B. Lee, Jr. "Requiem for Large-Scale Models." *Journal of the American Institute of Planners, 39*:167, May 1973.

[33] Lee. *Models and Techniques for Urban Planning*, pp. 5.5, 5.9.

Toronto, more directly addresses the planning needs of the operational management of a city than have been addressed by previous urban simulations.[34]

The objective of PROMUS is to help administrators of city financial, budgeting, and operational departments to evaluate proposed programs before the programs are funded or implemented. The model consists of two main submodels, the community submodel and the financial policy planning submodel. The community submodel provides a detailed representation of the city in terms of population, employment, housing, and transportation in small neighborhood areas. It represents proposed city programs and simulates their impact over time by the characteristics of neighborhoods. A version of the Pittsburgh metropolis model is incorporated in the submodel to deal with the spatial distribution of activities. The financial policy planning submodel performs a financial evaluation of proposed programs, including projected cost by city department, projected revenue by source, and cash flow. This submodel uses program matrices that structure the activities of each department in a way that relates them to budgetary expenditures. Overall, PROMUS is perhaps at least as ambitious as the Pittsburgh urban renewal model. In 1972, two of the developers [35] stated,

> To date, PROMUS is probably the most sophisticated and powerful urban planning and management system which allows urban planning and management administrators to rapidly evaluate alternative action planning in terms of financial implications and effects on community characteristics.

The last of the general urban development models considered, and the last one included in Table 1, is the urban dynamics model. This is the model of primary interest in this book, and it is described in the following major section of this chapter. Worth mentioning, first, however, are two models that are under development.

Other Models

Although these models are not included in the comparison, they merit brief examination, and probably would have been considered if their development and application had been further advanced. The first is a model by the National Bureau of Economic Research, which in-

[34] Dilip R. Limaye and Donald F. Blumberg. "Systems for Urban Planning and Management." *In: Computers and Urban Society: Proceedings ACM Urban Symposium, 1972.* New York, Association for Computing Machinery, 1972, pp. 57–59.
[35] *Ibid.,* pp. 61–72.

corporates features from a number of previous efforts, including treatment of housing development similar to that of the San Francisco housing model and adoption of the Lowry activity location method used in the Pittsburgh models. This model is an ambitious effort, with a coverage of urban subjects and a level of spatial representation at least equivalent to that of the Pittsburgh urban renewal model. Policy applications, however, are not anticipated for several years.[36]

The second modeling activity is underway at the University of Reading to represent the Reading, England area. This effort emphasizes the dynamics of urban development in a model that is structured mathematically as a system of difference equations. The model represents the spatial location of such activities as basic industry employment, retail and service industry employment, and housing. The model's initial uses have been in the generation and testing of hypotheses about the growth trends of cities, but its developers hope to apply the model to planning decisions.[37]

URBAN DYNAMICS MODEL

The urban dynamics model is grouped with the general urban development models because it includes a representation of not only most of the subjects in the comparative framework but also of the interactions among urban subsystems. Urban dynamics, however, is distinct from other general urban development models and from other urban models, largely because its developer, Forrester, is not an economist, an urban planner, nor a social scientist; that is, he is not associated with any of the professional groups that usually deal with urban problems. He brought to urban modeling an approach he had developed and applied for more than a decade to industrial management problems.

As stated in Chapter 1, Forrester, in 1969, set forth the urban dynamics model in his book, *Urban Dynamics*. The book was the result of a coalescing of two factors: Forrester's work on industrial dynamics and exposure to urban problems. He characterizes industrial dynamics as

. . . the investigation of the information-feedback character of industrial systems and the use of models for the design of improved organizational form

[36] Lee. "Requiem for Large-Scale Models," p. 175.
[37] Michael Batty. "Modelling Cities as Dynamic Systems." *Nature, 231*:425–428, June 18, 1971.

and guiding policy. Industrial dynamics grows out of four lines of earlier development—information-feedback theory, automatizing military tactical decision making, experimental design of complex systems by use of models, and digital computers for low-cost computation.[38]

Industrial dynamics, essentially, is a simulation approach based on the view of an organization as a feedback system.

The second factor that influenced the development of urban dynamics was the series of lengthy discussions and the exchange of views between Forrester and a group of people organized by John Collins (see Chapter 1).[39]

Therefore, urban dynamics exhibits no dependency on earlier urban modeling efforts; in contrast, most urban models tend to draw heavily on such efforts. Another indication of the model's independence from other urban models is that only six references are cited in the entire *Urban Dynamics* volume, and none of the references is to urban literature; in fact, Forrester is the author of five of them.[40]

Urban dynamics is comprehensive in its coverage of urban subjects, considering that, excepting transportation, the model represents all the subsystems included in Table 1. Urban dynamics, however, provides only a very summary representation of some of its subjects. For instance, land-use accounting is performed for the urban area as a whole, providing no spatial detail and only two categories of land use. Public finance, also, is represented at a summary level. Each of the population, housing, and economic activity subsystems is stratified into three types (see "Description of Model Sectors"). The model provides a behavioral-oriented representation for these three aggregates by including concepts that express economic and social preferences. Concepts of economic attractiveness and perceived attractiveness, for example, are included as factors in the determination of migration to and from the city by the three population groups (manager-professional, labor, and underemployed). Although subsystems are represented at a summary level, urban dynamics gives considerable attention to the representation of interactions among subsystems. The representation of the synergistic relationships of subsystems in the model is enhanced by its mathematical structure—a set of simultaneous first-order difference equations. The set of equations is solved successively for each year to be simulated, and many of the equations include lagged variables that permit values computed in the preceding

---

[38] Jay W. Forrester. *Industrial Dynamics.* Cambridge, Mass., MIT Press, 1961, p. 13.
[39] Jay W. Forrester. *Urban Dynamics.* Cambridge, Mass., MIT Press, 1969, p. ix.
[40] *Ibid.,* p. 281.

time period to influence the computations for the period immediately following. The simultaneity of solutions for all subsystems for each time period permits a strong representation of the interactions among subsystems.

Description of Model Sectors

As developed by Forrester, urban dynamics attempts to model an urban area in terms of "those system components that are always to be found interacting in urban growth and stagnation," the focus being "in the broad sweep of how an urban area evolves." [41] The model is a representation of a general, rather than a specific, urban area. In the model, the city is assumed to have a fixed land area and a closed-system boundary. By a closed-system boundary, Forrester means that the urban system under study incorporates all the system interactions that determine its characteristic behavior. It is recognized that the system under study exists within a broader environment and that, accordingly, this outside environment is represented implicitly in the model. Interactions between the system and its environment are regulated by measures of attractiveness. The model computes these measures and uses them as determinants in the movement of population and industry to and from the area under study. [42]

The urban dynamics model assumes that three subsystems—industry, housing, and population—and the interactions among them are the key to modeling urban growth processes. As Forrester asserts,

These three subsystems are chosen because they appear to be the dynamic framework of urban structure. The changes in housing, population, and industry are the central processes involved in growth and stagnation. They are more fundamental than city government, social culture, or fiscal policy. [43]

This assumption is reflected in the structure of the model, which consists of 11 sectors, 9 of them dealing with industry, housing, and population. Industry, which encompasses the entire range of industrial and business enterprises, is stratified into three types according to the age and condition of the enterprise: new enterprise, mature business, and declining industry. The housing subsystem also is stratified on the basis of age and condition into three types: premium housing, worker housing, and underemployed housing. Population is divided into three groups, primarily on the basis of occupational level: the

[41] *Ibid.*, p. 14.
[42] *Ibid.*, pp. 17–18.
[43] *Ibid.*, pp. 15, 17.

manager-professional group includes the highly trained and entrepreneurial elements of the population, the labor group includes skilled workers, and the underemployed group includes unskilled workers and unemployed persons. The model has two other sectors, which primarily tie together the nine principal sectors. The tax sector computes tax collections and tax effectiveness measures, and the job sector computes employment measures. The values computed by the tax and job sectors influence population migration, construction, and other activities at a number of points in other sectors.[44]

Figure 2 is a diagram of the primary relationships in the industry, housing, and population subsystems of the urban dynamics model. Before examining the subsystems, it is necessary to explain the conventions and symbols used in the diagram. In Forrester's modeling concepts, the two principal types of variables are "level" and "rate" variables. Level variables represent accumulations at some point in a system, such as the number of people or number of housing units in a city. Rate variables control system flows; for example, annual births per 1,000 people is a rate variable. Under Forrester's conventions, the same type of variables do not interact directly, but the two variables interact with each other; levels are changed only by rates, and rates depend on information from levels. Because of this process, paths through the system structure show alternate level and rate variables, depicted in Figure 2.[45]

In the diagram, the level variables are represented by rectangle symbols, and rate variables are represented by valve symbols. No attempt is made to show the interrelationships among subsystems in the diagram. The "cloud" symbol represents the outside environment in which the system is embedded. In some cases, the cloud represents the source of flows from the environment into the system, and, in other cases, it represents flows from the system into the environment.

The first portion of Figure 2 indicates the relationship of the three major level variables and the four major rate variables of the industry subsystem. A unit of industry represents a standard building unit on a standard land area. The model views the life cycle of an industrial establishment from its beginning as a new enterprise, gradually filtering down from this status to that of a mature business, and, finally, to a declining-industry status. The transitions from one status level to the next lower one depend on the age of the establishment and the general condition of the entire urban area. As Figure 2 shows, rate

[44] *Ibid.*, pp. 19–20.
[45] *Ibid.*, pp. 13–14.

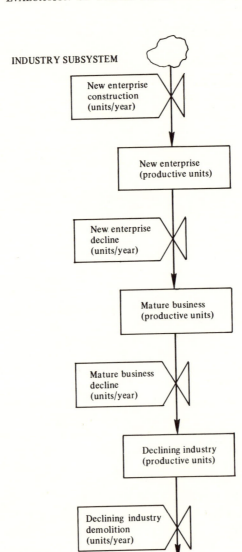

FIGURE 2   Urban dynamics model subsystems.

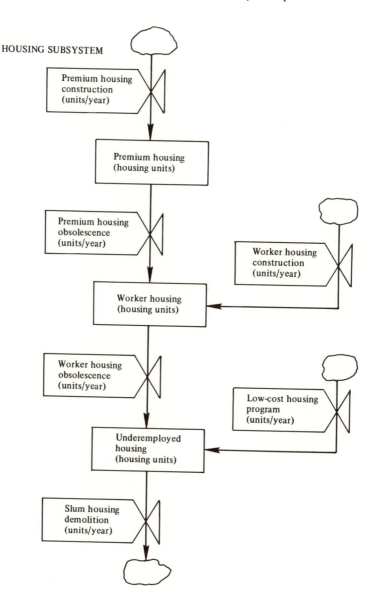

HOUSING SUBSYSTEM

FIGURE 2 (continued)

POPULATION SUBSYSTEM

FIGURE 2   (continued)

Source: Adapted from Jay W. Forrester. *Urban Dynamics.* Cambridge, Mass., MIT Press, 1969, p. 16.

variables control the construction of new enterprise units, the transition of new units to mature ones, the transition of mature units to declining ones, and the demolition of declining units. These rates are affected by information flows from the housing and population subsystems, but these flows do not appear in the diagram.[46]

The second part of Figure 2 deals with the housing subsystem. Construction and deterioration processes operate to change the number of units for each type of housing. Each may be constructed according to rates that are controlled by the demand for that type of housing and the availability of construction labor. Premium and worker housing units age and decline and become units of the next lower type. The rates controlling the decline of housing units depend on the age of, and demand for, housing units of each type. In addition, underemployed housing units are destroyed in accordance with the slum housing demolition rate, which depends on the age of underemployed housing and the rate of occupancy.[47]

The last section of Figure 2 presents the population subsystem. The model assumes a general relationship among the three categories of population and the three categories of housing; that is, manager-professionals live in premium housing, laborers in worker housing, and underemployeds in underemployed housing. The 12 primary rate variables that determine the population levels are shown in Figure 2. In addition to people born into the three population categories, others may enter the urban area from the outside environment, or they may leave the area; the controlling rates depend on the relative attractiveness of the area. In addition, rates represent the population mobility between classes. Upward mobility is represented from the underemployed to the labor class, and from the labor to the manager-professional class; downward mobility, from labor to underemployed. Migration and mobility population flows depend on the availability of housing and jobs and population mix.[48]

This description of the 9 major level variables and 22 major rate variables of urban dynamics provides only an overview of the model structure. In its full detail, the model requires a much larger number of variables, as indicated by Forrester's computer computations with the model, in which he printed 124 model values.[49] These 124 values include the 86 model parameters and initial values of level variables

[46] *Ibid.*, p. 19.

[47] *Ibid.*

[48] *Ibid.*

[49] *Ibid.*, pp. 42–43.

that are estimated in Appendix c to develop an urban dynamics model of the District of Columbia; in addition, the 124 values include a number of intermediate values.

Modeling Techniques

To complete the description of the urban dynamics model, some of the techniques used in developing the model are examined. These techniques have been used for some time by Forrester and others who follow his approach to model development, but have been used very little in urban modeling. Some are embodied in the special Dynamo computer language developed by Forrester and his associates. Appendix B discusses the principal characteristics of the Dynamo language and provides a complete description of the computer-program representation of urban dynamics used in this book, whereas the emphasis here is on general modeling techniques.

As previously mentioned, the urban dynamics model is a set of first-order difference equations. The Dynamo language assists in the formulation and computer implementation of models with this mathematical structure, and it was used by Forrester to represent urban dynamics. The Dynamo version of the model consists of some 300 language statements. Forrester used the model to perform simulations for a hypothetical city for a period of 250 years and to test some alternative policies for dealing with urban problems over a 50-year time span.[50] The Dynamo computational procedure is to solve the set of first-order difference equations for each successive time period. Computed results from each period can influence results in subsequent periods, because many model equations include model values from the previous period. Such dependencies make it necessary to estimate values of a number of model quantities in order to initialize the computational procedure. The unit time period in urban dynamics is one year, and computed results can be printed for each year or for some desired multiyear interval.

One of the basic techniques of urban dynamics equations is the use of multipliers to modify rate variables. All rate variables "are stated in terms of a 'normal' set of conditions. This normal rate flow is then modified by a multiplier that represents the deviation of the actual urban-area conditions from the normal."[51] Multipliers are useful in representing the impact of factors from other sectors of the model and usually are defined as the product of several components.

[50] *Ibid.*, pp. 1–11.
[51] *Ibid.*, p. 23.

The components of a multiplier are combined by multiplication rather than addition for two reasons: First, multiplication makes the effect of the components mutually enhancing; and, second, it is possible for one component to become zero and dominate the entire group of components.[52]

Illustrating the multiplier concept are the computations related to the mobility of the labor population group in achieving manager-professional status. As with most other flow rates in the model, this one is described normally as a fraction of the level to which it applies. The flow rate is modulated by a multiplier that embodies the influence of economic and social conditions represented in other sectors of the model. In computational terms

$$\text{LTM.KL} = (\text{LMN}) \; (\text{L.K}) \; (\text{LMMP.K}) + \text{LTPG.K}$$

LTM = labor to manager (men/year)
LMN = labor mobility normal (fraction/year)
L = labor (men)
LMMP = labor mobility multiplier perceived (dimensionless)
LTPG = labor training program (men/year).

This is expressed in Dynamo notation and indicates that the labor-to-manager flow during period KL is the product of the normal rate, the labor population level at time K, and the perceived values of the labor mobility multiplier at time K. Forrester set the normal labor mobility rate at 2 percent in his computations. The labor training program in the equation is nonzero only when a government job-training program is in operation, and it may be ignored in this discussion.[53] The appearance of a perceived multiplier in this example introduces another technique used in the model. The perceived multiplier, LMMP, is a delayed value of the actual multiplier, LMM. The multiplier and the computation of its perceived value will be examined.

The labor mobility multiplier is computed as follows:

$$\text{LMM.K} = (\text{MSM.K}) \; (\text{MLM.K}) \; (\text{LEM.K}) \; (\text{LMF})$$

LMM = labor mobility multiplier (dimensionless)
MSM = manager supply multiplier (dimensionless)
MLM = manager/labor multiplier (dimensionless)
LEM = labor educational multiplier (dimensionless)
LMF = labor mobility factor (dimensionless).

[52] *Ibid.*, pp. 25–26.
[53] *Ibid.*, p. 154.

It is the product of three multipliers that measure the influence of the supply of managers on labor-to-manager mobility, the ratio of manager-professional population to labor population, and tax expenditures on education. These factors represent influences from other model sectors. The labor mobility factor is a technical factor, set equal to one, and included for use in sensitivity testing experiments with the model.[54]

As indicated, the perceived multiplier, LMMP, represents a delayed value of the actual labor mobility multiplier, LMM. In some ways, the term "effective multiplier" might be more appropriate, because the delay includes the time needed to obtain training and the experience required to advance, as well as the time necessary for labor population to perceive the opportunity for advancement. The perceived multiplier is computed as:

$$\text{LMMP.K} = \text{LMMP.J} + (\text{DT}/\text{LMMPT})(\text{LMM.J} - \text{LMMP.J})$$

LMMP   = labor mobility multiplier perceived (dimensionless)
LMMPT = labor mobility multiplier perception time (years)
LMM   = labor mobility multiplier (dimensionless).

In Dynamo notation, time K is the current time period, J is one time period earlier, and DT denotes the unit time interval equal to one year in urban dynamics. According to the equation, the perceived multiplier is equal to the perceived multiplier one period earlier, plus an adjustment which is a fraction of the difference between the multiplier and its perceived value in the previous period. Since Forrester takes the labor mobility multiplier perception time, LMMPT, to be 15 years, the fraction of the difference taken in the adjustment is one-fifteenth.[55] The use of this form of delay function means that the perceived or effective value of the mobility rate is always moving toward the rate indicated by current conditions. This functional form is called a first-order exponential delay and has been used for some time by Forrester in his modeling efforts; it is used in the urban dynamics model to represent delayed values of rates at a number of points.

Another technique frequently used in urban dynamics is called tabular functions. It provides a means for expressing the relationship between two variables by a table of values; the relationship may be nonlinear between two variables. The use of such tables is a principal way of introducing nonlinearities into the model. The table must be

[54] *Ibid.*, p. 156.
[55] *Ibid.*

specified, and must provide values of the two variables for a series of points on the function curve; these pairs of values may be considered as actually specifying a piecewise linear approximation to a continuous nonlinear function. The Dynamo language has features that provide for easily creating tables to define functions and for performing table lookups and interpolations to produce function evaluations.[56] In Appendix B, tabular functions are discussed in more detail, and examples are provided of their use.

ASSESSMENT OF URBAN
DYNAMICS POLICY PERSPECTIVE

Assessing the policymaking perspective of urban dynamics, which is the motivation of this chapter, will be considered next. The comparison of urban models and the description of urban dynamics already presented have provided the background for dealing with the assessment, which is only tentative, because the model is assumed to be a valid representation of an urban area. Essentially, the assessment is an evaluation of the model's potential for dealing with policy problems.

Among urban models, urban dynamics is regarded as a general urban development model, because it deals with a wide range of subjects and the interrelationships among them; thus, it is set apart from urban models that emphasize a single subject such as transportation, housing, or economic activity. Urban dynamics has several additional characteristics that distinguish it from other general urban development models; these characteristics have important implications for the role of the model in policymaking.

One of the most distinctive of these characteristics is that urban dynamics provides a summary or aggregate representation of its subsystems. A key to developing its aggregate representation is that, unlike other general urban development models, urban dynamics does not try to deal with the spatial distribution of activities. In contrast, in the Pittsburgh models and PROMUS, a significant part of the modeling effort is related to developing a detailed spatial distribution of activities and associated measures of land utilization. The inclusion of the spatial location of activities increases both the size and complexity of models. Not only must the model incorporate relationships to determine the location of the activities, but often the activities need to be represented in greater detail to conform with the relationships used

---

[56] *Ibid.*, pp. 26–27.

to locate them. The aggregate, nonspatial nature of urban dynamics has implications for policy application. For instance, a model that does not locate urban activities cannot deal effectively with many questions related to transportation policy. On the other hand, the data collection and computation costs of such a model are lower than those of models that deal with the spatial location of activities.

Another characteristic of urban dynamics is its strong representation of the interrelationships among model sectors. As Catanese [57] concluded in his review of urban simulations, one of the chief contributions of the urban dynamics model is that the "breadth and scope . . . are much greater and more synergistic than previous attempts at simulation." The strong representation of interactions among sectors is made possible by the mathematical structure of urban dynamics, which is a system of simultaneous, first-order difference equations. The simultaneity of interactions in urban dynamics contrasts with the one-directional interactions provided by the sequential computational approach used in many models. In the Pittsburgh urban renewal model, for example, sequential steps estimate basic industry levels, assign basic industry to locations, and locate housing and retail businesses. No feedback occurs from each step to the earlier steps, although Lowry's iterative computational approach, which achieves an equilibrium spatial distribution of housing and retail trade, does provide for two-directional interaction in the location of these activities.

A third important characteristic of urban dynamics is that it attempts to incorporate behavioral relationships. Although the model deals with aggregates of population, housing, and industry, behavioral responses to many situations are represented. For instance, the behavioral response to conditions and to perceived conditions influences migration, mobility, and construction of housing and business units. As indicated in Table 1, the urban dynamics model is the only one of the general urban development models that depends on behavioral concepts in an explicit way; and urban dynamics includes more behavioral concepts than any of the 16 models included in Table 1, except the San Francisco housing model and the southeastern Wisconsin land-use model.

These characteristics of the policy perspective of urban dynamics make it a tool for dealing with strategic policy issues, including the broad questions of setting system objectives and related general resource usage. Strategic policy questions are distinct from operational policy questions. The latter are narrower in scope and focus on effec-

---

[57] Anthony J. Catanese. *Scientific Methods of Urban Analysis.* Urbana, Ill., University of Illinois Press, 1972, p. 248.

tiveness and efficiency in system management, as well as on policy execution, to accomplish specified goals.[58] The aggregate representation of subsystems in urban dynamics makes the model suitable for dealing with policy related to strategic issues; whereas addressing urban policy questions on the operational level often requires more detail, including the spatial distribution of activities. Moreover, the urban dynamics stress on modeling-sector interactions is important for the study of strategic policy, because the analysis of strategic policy must emphasize capturing the behavior of the whole system; this requires representation of the interactions among the primary components of the system.

Also, urban dynamics is a relatively low-cost modeling tool. The low cost is attributable largely to the absence of the spatial distribution of activities and the aggregate nature of the model representation. Although estimating modeling costs is difficult, "a rule-of-thumb estimate for a full-scale land-use model is probably at least $500,000." [59] This cost includes original model development and initial data collection, but does not include continuing costs of maintaining computer programs and updating data files. The data-collection costs for urban dynamics are modest compared to those of most large-scale models that include spatial distribution of activities. For instance, the San Francisco housing model represents 84 population groups and requires 61 items of information for each group; its data base consists of approximately 35,000 input numbers.[60] The data requirements for the Pittsburgh urban renewal model are even greater, and are considered to be "unmanageable without large-scale, full-time data collection." [61] In contrast, the data requirements of urban dynamics consist of approximately 500 numbers that include initial values, parameters, and the tables used in the model's tabular functions. Furthermore, computation costs for the urban dynamics model are low. For a computer run of models such as the San Francisco housing model or the Pittsburgh urban renewal model, the cost is several hundred dollars; for urban dynamics, a computer run costs less than 10 dollars.

This evaluation of the policy perspective of urban dynamics shows

[58] Robert N. Anthony. *Planning and Control Systems: A Framework for Analysis.* Boston, Division of Research, Graduate School of Business Administration, Harvard University, 1965, pp. 16–18.

[59] Lee. "Requiem for Large-Scale Models," p. 168.

[60] San Francisco Department of City Planning. "The San Francisco Community Renewal Simulation Model." *In: Decision-Making in Urban Planning: An Introduction to New Methodologies.* Edited by Ira M. Robinson. Beverly Hills, Calif., Sage Publ., 1972, p. 592.

[61] Nagelberg and Little. *Selected Urban Simulations and Games,* p. 21.

that the model has considerable potential as a low-cost modeling tool for addressing strategic urban policy questions. In addition to this advantage, the model can serve four roles in the policymaking process: increasing general system understanding, developing policy alternatives, evaluating proposed policy alternatives, and verifying results obtained by other methods.

Urban dynamics perhaps is most useful in the role of evaluating proposed policy alternatives. Forrester's uses of the model are directed at testing policies that deal with several urban development problems. Kadanoff [62] and his associates at Brown University, for example, regard urban dynamics as a tool for the "comparison of different public policy alternatives." Applications of the model to particular urban areas, reviewed in Chapter 4, concentrate primarily on the role of the model in testing alternatives. Policy alternatives can be incorporated readily into the model by introducing additional equations and by modifying equations, as Chapter 6 illustrates.

Beyond testing policy alternatives, urban dynamics may be useful in conjunction with other models, particularly to supplement the results obtained from models that deal with a specific policy area such as housing or transportation. Urban dynamics could provide a broader framework for the more narrowly oriented model; that is, the specialized policy model could be used to test alternative policies and, tentatively, to choose the most desirable of these. Then urban dynamics might test the desirable policies and evaluate the broader impacts of each. This procedure would often be very useful, because many specialized policy models do not represent some of the subsystems that are included in urban dynamics.

Because of its low operating costs, urban dynamics can help develop policy alternatives. Once the data collection has been completed to develop an urban dynamics model of an urban area, the model may be used to evaluate many policy alternatives to help select those worthy of further consideration.

To summarize, urban dynamics offers a different perspective for the study of urban policy than that provided by other urban models. Like them, urban dynamics is designed primarily to test policy; however, the model also can help develop policy alternatives. The distinctive aspect of the model's perspective is that it provides a low-cost tool for addressing strategic urban policy problems. It must be kept in mind, however, that this evaluation of the model's perspective only

---

[62] Leo P. Kadanoff. "From Simulation Model to Public Policy: An Examination of Forrester's *Urban Dynamics*." *Simulation,* 16:263, June 1971.

indicates the kinds of policy problems and questions with which urban dynamics purports to deal. The following two phases of the case study evaluation examine the model in-principle and in-practice, and determine how adequately the model addresses particular policy questions.

CHAPTER 4

Research Information on the Urban Dynamics Model: In-Principle Evaluation

The in-principle evaluation of the case study model examines the model's supporting theory and assumptions. How adequate are they for supporting a model that purports to deal with the range of strategic policy questions encompassed by the urban dynamics policy perspective? By its nature, the in-principle examination is critically oriented, because the evaluation of the research foundation attempts to detect faults and defects that would reduce the policy usefulness of the model. The orientation of the in-perspective evaluation, in contrast, centers on the questions the model addresses. Both the in-principle evaluation and the in-practice evaluation, which are presented in subsequent chapters, critically evaluate the adequacy of the model to deal with the questions it addresses.

All the model sectors and their interactions are analyzed, rather than only a narrow area such as housing for the poor. The analysis also identifies possible modifications that must be considered when applying Forrester's model to policy problems. A number of these modifications also are considered during the in-practice evaluation.

This chapter consists of five sections. The first indicates the approach that was taken in examining the supporting research for the urban dynamics model. Actual analysis of the theory and assumptions on which the model is based is presented in the following three sections. The final section provides an overall evaluation of the research foundation of urban dynamics.

ORGANIZATION FOR EXAMINATION OF RESEARCH FOUNDATION

Before the supporting research for the urban dynamics model can be examined, it is necessary to adopt an explicit structure for the examination and to indicate its scope. The general organizing structure for the in-principle examination of the case study model could be used for the in-principle examination of most policy models. Many model evaluations, of course, will be restricted to an examination of the theory and assumptions related to a model's capability to deal with very specific policy questions. In such cases, the in-principle examination will be more brief and more sharply focused than the one presented in this case study evaluation.

Structure of Examination

The structure adopted for examining the supporting research for the case study model parallels the process of developing and applying policy simulation models, which was described in Chapter 2. That process is characterized by three general stages. First, the real-world policy situation of interest is examined: The general scope is defined by selecting the real-world elements to be represented in the model and by identifying the general concepts to be used in the representation; that is, determining the basic dimensions of the model and the general conceptual basis of the model. The second stage of the process builds on the results of the first stage by developing a manageable set of relationships that provide the basis for an operational model and by developing a computer-based version of the model. In the third stage, the model is validated and used to address policy problems. In all three stages, the policy questions to be addressed by the model must be kept clearly in mind. Overall, the first two stages are directed toward developing an abstract representation of the real-world situation. The abstraction process seeks to develop a model that is conceptually clear and computationally manageable; but, in the process, parts of the real-world situation are simplified or ignored. The third stage returns to focus on the real-world situation, first, by testing the validity of the model representation and, second, by applying the model.

The three stages of the research process are used to organize the review of research and development related to the urban dynamics model. Table 2 expands this structure by identifying research tasks within the three stages. Each of the first two stages is divided into two research tasks, and the third stage is divided into three tasks. This means that the total research process has seven tasks: establishing the scope of the model, adapting model concepts, formulating model relationships, testing model relationships, collecting data and developing model parameters, validating the model, and applying the model. Research related to urban dynamics is viewed in terms of these seven tasks, and Table 2 indicates research activity by listing the principal contributors for each task.

This set of seven research tasks does not differ in content from the set of tasks usually regarded by the operations-research or systems-analy-

TABLE 2 Contributors to the Research Foundation of the Urban Dynamics Model

RESEARCH STAGES AND TASKS	CONTRIBUTORS OF SUPPORTING RESEARCH
Conceptualization of Problem and Model	
—Establishing Scope of Model	Forrester, Weinblatt, Gibson, Kadanoff and Weinblatt, Kain, Garn and Wilson
—Adapting Model Concepts	Gray et al., Jaeckel, Babcock, Weinblatt
Development of Model	
—Formulating Model Relationships	Forrester, Gibson, Garn and Wilson
—Testing Model Relationships	Babcock, Pack, Gray et al., Jaeckel
Validation and Application of Model	
—Collecting Data and Developing Model Parameters	Porter and Henley, Bartos and Tsai, Schroeder
—Validating Model	Porter and Henley, Bartos and Tsai, Kadanoff, Schroeder
—Applying Model	Kadanoff and Weinblatt, Harlow, Gray et al.

sis disciplines as necessary to develop and apply simulation models. As indicated in Chapter 2, a typical systems-analysis view of the research steps required consists of nine tasks: formulating the problem, collecting empirical data, formulating the model, estimating values for model parameters, evaluating the model and parameters, implementing the computer program, validating the model, designing simulation experiments, and analyzing results from the model. The seven-task version, however, is better suited to the review of research for a model such as urban dynamics, which addresses a policy area at the broad-aim end of the policy-problem spectrum (described in Chapter 2); the systems-analysis version is directed toward more narrowly oriented problems.

In neither of these views of the process of applying simulation to policymaking must the set of tasks be performed strictly in the order listed. In fact, the tasks are intertwined and interact in many ways. Data collection, for example, occurs in conjunction with several other tasks or strongly influences the way other tasks are carried out. Model validity, as indicated in Chapter 2, depends on adapting supporting concepts that have face validity, on testing the relationships that are the basis of model development, and on comparing model results with the actions of the referent systems.

Scope of Examination

The review of research encompasses both published and unpublished materials related to the model. Forrester's *Urban Dynamics* and his related published writings are a starting point for the review. Other published sources include more than a dozen reviews of *Urban Dynamics* and brief descriptions of the model that appeared in news and professional publications, some 20 articles from the professional literature, and a number of books and articles that deal with urban dynamics or some aspect of the model in another context. Unpublished materials include dissertations and theses on urban dynamics, papers presented at professional meetings, working papers made available by researchers, and discussions with researchers working with the model.

The review places primary emphasis on research related to the development of the model as a policymaking tool, which is consistent with the structure adopted for the review. Under the policymaking emphasis, there are two subjects related to the model, and often discussed in the research included in the review, that are of little importance, largely because the subjects are not relevant to the research foundation of the model. The first is Forrester's philosophy of modeling; the second is his findings on the effectiveness of certain urban policies in dealing with public problems. The following brief discussion merely places these subjects into the perspective of the research review.

Although Forrester's philosophy of systems and modeling developed over a long period of time, it is basically the same as that presented in his *Industrial Dynamics* in 1961; in his more recent books, *Urban Dynamics* and *World Dynamics,* he has argued for the relevance of his philosophy to broader social systems. His philosophy centers on the concept of "complex systems" that generally have the following characteristics:

(1) are counterintuitive; (2) are remarkably insensitive to changes in many system parameters; (3) stubbornly resist policy changes; (4) contain influential pressure points, often in unexpected places . . .; (5) counteract and compensate for externally applied corrective efforts . . .; (6) often react to policy change in the long run in a way opposite to how they react in the short run; (7) tend toward low performance.[1]

Forrester maintains that complex systems have a fundamental structure and that, in order to model the dynamic behavior of such systems, four hierarchies of structure must be recognized:

1. Systems should have a closed boundary around them.
2. Feedback loops are the basic structures within the system boundary.
3. There are two kinds of system variables: level or state variables and rate-of-flow variables.
4. The determinants of rate variables in the system should include goals, conditions, discrepancies, and actions based on discrepancies.[2]

Forrester's basic assumption in applying his philosophy is that a complex system provides a structure that is sufficiently general to model a wide variety of problems. He regards many phenomena as complex systems.

All social systems belong to this class. The management structure of a corporation has all the characteristics of a complex system. Similarly, an urban area, a national government, economic processes, and international trade all are complex systems.[3]

[1] Jay W. Forrester. *Urban Dynamics.* Cambridge, Mass., MIT Press, 1969, p. 109.
[2] *Ibid.,* p. 12.
[3] *Ibid.,* p. 107.

Forrester regards his philosophy of systems and modeling—which he invokes at many points in support of his developmental decisions in the urban dynamics model—as a heuristic theory of system behavior. His attitude is not surprising, since he viewed his industrial dynamics philosophy as a "systems theory" of a firm in the same way cybernetics is regarded as a theory of social behavior. His current philosophy is essentially the same as industrial dynamics, except that it is called system dynamics and is applied to a broader class of problems. One objective evaluation of industrial dynamics concluded "that little evidence to date qualifies ID [industrial dynamics] to be viewed as a distinctive body of theory about behavior of firms." [4]

This is the position taken here on Forrester's philosophy of systems and modeling. Although the philosophy provides motivation for developing models that embody certain concepts, it does not justify the choices made in model development. For example, information-feedback loop structures of the type Forrester uses frequently may have heuristic appeal for representing certain behavior, but may be inappropriate for use in an empirically based model.

Forrester's philosophy of systems and modeling contributes little to the research foundation of the urban dynamics model, and will be given little attention. In the review of research, however, the related but distinct subject of simulation modeling techniques based on system dynamics ideas is discussed. Chapter 3 described the simulation modeling approach in terms of the modeling techniques it embodies, and Appendix B presents the essential features of the Dynamo language that assist in the computer implementation of models based on this approach. The review of research will consider these techniques, with the assumption that a model based on such techniques is tested for validity and utility in the same way as any other model.

Forrester's policy interpretations, based on his analysis of the effectiveness of certain urban policies, also are given little attention in the review of research. He used the urban dynamics model to examine urban programs that provide jobs, training, tax subsidies, and housing for the underemployed. From a series of model runs, Forrester concludes that these traditional programs for dealing with urban problems are entirely ineffective or even destructive. These policy interpretations are a focus of much of the negative reaction to urban dynamics; as one evaluation of the model noted, the "severest criticism . . . has not been as much about its methods and assumptions as

---

[4] H. Igor Ansoff and Dennis P. Slevin. "An Appreciation of Industrial Dynamics." *Management Science, 14*:383, March 1968.

about its interpretations." [5] It must be clearly recognized, however, that, in his computer runs, Forrester uses entirely hypothetical data. The model, as developed by Forrester, "floats free of any empirical evidence. Every structural relation and number in the model is an assumed one without any justification based on data from the real world." [6] Because the policy interpretations are without empirical basis, neither Forrester's recommendations nor the criticisms of them contribute to the research foundation of the model.

CONCEPTUALIZATION OF PROBLEM AND MODEL

The first of three stages of model development, as previously indicated, is divided into two tasks: establishing the scope of the model and adapting model concepts. The scope of the model is determined by asking which aspects of the real-world problem are to be included in the model and which excluded, and what the general rationale is for these decisions. Adapting model concepts means developing the general conceptual basis for representing the behavior of the entities included in the model; this implies the review and evaluation of relevant theory and modeling concepts.

Establishing the Scope of the Model

Forrester includes a representation of the following features of an urban system in his urban dynamics model:

1. Three categories of people: the manager-professional, labor, and underemployed.
2. In each category, people are born, they die, and they migrate to or from the urban area, or move from one population level to another.
3. For each population category, there is a corresponding housing category.
4. Each housing category may be constructed, and all housing ages and deteriorates to a lower category and is eventually destroyed.

[5] Anthony J. Catanese. *Scientific Methods of Urban Analysis.* Urbana, Ill., University of Illinois Press, 1972, p. 247.

[6] Harvey A. Averch and Robert A. Levine. *Two Models of the Urban Crises: An Analytical Essay on Banfield and Forrester.* RM-6366-RC. Santa Monica, Calif., The RAND Corporation, September 1970, p. 43.

5. Business/industry is divided into three categories: new, mature, and declining.

6. As units of business/industry age, the units deteriorate and become units of a lower category.

The model contains mechanisms that govern the migration of each category of people to and from the urban area and that govern the construction and aging of housing and business/industry units.[7]

The choice of three subsystems—industry, housing, and population—and the interactions among them set the basic scope of the model. There has been almost no criticism by other researchers of Forrester's choice of these subsystems to model the broad sweep of urban growth processes, although there has been criticism of the conceptual representation of these subsystems. Other assumptions made by Forrester, however, related to the scope of urban dynamics, have been questioned by researchers. These assumptions are examined by considering the normative orientation of the model and the basic structural choices made in developing the model.

Normative orientation: All models imply a normative position, because there are no objective models of systems. The normative position often has significant influence on the results obtained with the models and, hence, has implications for the models' policymaking uses. It is, therefore, desirable to understand the normative orientation of the urban dynamics model.

In the urban dynamics model, primary emphasis is on the economic development of the urban area. This emphasis is evident in the model structure and in many of Forrester's statements. For example, "urban growth and stagnation do not appear to require changes in the world environment as a cause . . . The behavior of a city is much more directly dependent on its own economic merit . . .,"[8] is a view that oversimplifies by ignoring intercity competition in economic development of the type discussed by Thompson.[9] When discussing taxes, however, Forrester's emphasis on economic development goals is very clear:

---

[7] Forrester. *Urban Dynamics*, pp. 14–20.

[8] *Ibid.*, p. 15.

[9] Wilbur Thompson. "Internal and External Factors in the Development of Urban Economics." *In: Financing the Metropolis, Public Policy in Urban Economics.* Edited by John P. Crecine. Beverly Hills, Calif., Sage Publ., 1970, pp. 41–42.

People are the fundamental generator of municipal expenditure. People require welfare. People require police and fire departments. People require transportation. People use schools. People demand city services. Unless the people are economically able to support these services and politically responsible for authorizing them, the urban system is almost sure to be self-defeating . . . . Only if cost and revenue are closely coupled will the city be responsible in its expenditure. Only if the revenue is highly correlated with the people who require the expenditure will the city have a self-regulating system which generates a population able to sustain a healthy city and to pay for the urban services they desire.[10]

Another aspect of this economic orientation of the model is a set of values held by Forrester. Gibson's [11] analysis of the implicit-value system reflected in the urban dynamics model found at least partial adherence to the following values:

1. Dedication to the world of work, in that people are attracted to and depart from the city on the basis of perceived personal economic well-being, people accept a work-centered world, and people desire to move upward through a work-centered hierarchy.

2. A concept of progress in which people expect to improve their economic well-being.

3. A frontier concept that seeks trade with the "outside world," which provides advantage to the city.

4. An impersonal, economic imperialism without primacy of individual welfare, in which upward mobility is provided for the good of the economic system rather than of the individual.

5. Defensive territorial imperative under which the city neither expands nor contracts.

6. Permanence of value structure, in that the value system is assumed to be static for 250 years.

While the model's economic orientation restricts its scope, more restrictions and possible bias result from the influence of Forrester's view of economics in developing a model for dealing with urban economic development. Following publication of *Urban Dynamics*, Forrester's understanding of economics was characterized as rather simplistic by Paul Yivisaker,[12] then Commissioner of Community

---

[10] Forrester. *Urban Dynamics*, pp. 123–124.

[11] J. E. Gibson. "A Philosophy for Urban Simulations." *In: Urban Dynamics: Extensions and Reflections*. Edited by Kan Chen. San Francisco, San Francisco Press, 1972, pp. 33–34.

[12] William K. Stevens. "Computer Is Used as Guide for Expert Seeking Way Out of Labyrinth of Urban Problems." *The New York Times:* 47, October 31, 1969.

Affairs for the state of New Jersey and an adviser to Forrester in the development of the urban dynamics model. A direct, far-reaching consequence of this simplistic view is the development of an economic model of a city that is entirely uncoupled from the economy of the regional and national environment in which the city functions. Such a restriction in scope, although often acceptable for a model dealing with a particular functional area such as transportation, is open to question for a model that attempts to portray the economic development of an urban area.

There are indirect, pervasive consequences of Forrester's simplistic view of economics, in that he favors a restricted set of urban policies that conform to his economic view, and this influences model development at many points. For example, Kadanoff [13] observed that Forrester's "normative scheme seems to be one in which a 'healthy' city contains relatively few unskilled workers." Kain [14] found that this policy bias serves the dominant emphasis placed by the model on balancing the budget. The emphasis on budget balancing is combined with bias toward a central city viewpoint. As Lee [15] remarks, "Forrester learned what he knows about cities from John Collins, a former mayor of Boston, and it is not too surprising that a major public official in a large central city should hold these views."

Overall, the simplistic economic view, applied from a central city perspective, restricts the scope of urban dynamics. Efforts to apply the model to policy problems must consider these biases, which may be reflected in the numerical values of parameters and initial levels, as well as in the structure of the model relationships.

Structural assumptions: Some of the basic simplifying assumptions made by Forrester in developing urban dynamics have been criticized by other researchers. Of course, it is always necessary to simplify, because the aim of model development is to produce a tool for studying a system and not to reproduce reality. It is fundamental, however, that the features of reality that are ignored or given only cursory treatment are not essential, and that simplifications are not made merely for the sake of ease or elegance of modeling.

In the urban dynamics model, three structural assumptions that

[13] Leo P. Kadanoff. "From Simulation Model to Public Policy: An Examination of Forrester's *Urban Dynamics.*" *Simulation, 16*:262, June 1971.

[14] John F. Kain. "A Computer Version of How a City Works." (Review of Forrester's *Urban Dynamics.*) *Fortune, 80*:241, November 1969.

[15] Douglas B. Lee, Jr. "Requiem for Large-Scale Models." *Journal of the American Institute of Planners, 39*:174, May 1973.

limit the scope of the model have been questioned by other researchers. The first of these assumptions is that the urban system represented by the model is a closed system that functions within a limitless environment. The second is that a central city can be represented without including its suburbs. Both assumptions simplify the interactions between the urban system being modeled and its environment. The second assumption is a particular aspect of the first one, but merits special attention. The third assumption is that the city's land area is fixed, and that the density of construction is constant over time.

The urban area represented by the model is assumed to be within a closed boundary that exists in a limitless environment.

> The closed boundary and the limitless environment are two sides of the same coin. Certain components interact to create the kinds of responses being studied. These, by definition, lie within the boundary. Anything that is not essential to creating the behavior of interest is, by lack of essentiality, on the outside in the unspecified environment. . . . The environment can affect the system, but the system does not significantly affect the environment.[16]

The fact that the environment can affect the system, however, is somewhat disturbing, because the model provides no representation of the environment except that it is an unlimited, unspecified entity. As Catanese [17] observed,

> . . . the limitless environment and closed boundary of the urban system result in a closed system which draws freely upon the resources of the environment without constraint and which interacts with other urban systems solely by attracting their migrants and investment dollars.

In his examination of urban dynamics, Rothenberg [18] found that Forrester's treatment of an urban area as a self-contained system was a serious weakness, and "it results in grave difficulties" in the model.

Regarding the policymaking consequences of this closed boundary and limitless environment assumption, Weinblatt [19] observed that it "may be justified for certain policy-evaluation purposes as long as any significant changes in the environment are independent of the changes which occur in the city." For many policy situations,

---

[16] Forrester. *Urban Dynamics*, p. 17.

[17] Catanese. *Scientific Methods of Urban Analysis*, p. 246.

[18] Jerome Rothenberg. "Problems in the Modeling of Urban Development, A Review Article on *Urban Dynamics*, by Jay W. Forrester." *Journal of Urban Economics*, 1:5, January 1974.

[19] Herbert Weinblatt. "*Urban Dynamics:* A Critical Review." (Review of J. W. Forrester, *Urban Dynamics*.) *Policy Sciences*, 1:379, Fall 1970.

however, changes in the environment are not independent of the urban area under study. Many researchers have pointed out that, if the policies adopted by several major cities are the same or are part of a national program, those policies will alter significantly the environment of the city under study, and the capability of the model to deal with such cases will be limited severely.[20] In work supporting this idea, Kadanoff and Weinblatt [21] compared the results for three models: the original urban dynamics model, an extension to include all the central cities of the nation with migration between them, and a further extension that models the national economy, including both cities and suburbs. Their analysis indicates clearly that the focus of the model affects the policy conclusions reached.

The second questionable assumption in the structure of urban dynamics is the lack of suburban representation. According to Forrester, the model should represent either a suburban or a core city area, but not an area including both. The orientation of the model, however, leans heavily toward representing a central city area. If this is true, then the suburbs are not included, because "all other urban areas, even those that are part of the same city, are part of the outside environment"; [22] that is, the suburbs are not represented but are included in the limitless, unspecified environment of the city.

There has been considerable criticism of this failure to include a specific representation of the suburbs.[23] As one critique noted, "the most common criticism of Forrester's work is that it does not model the suburbs." [24] Kain [25] reflects the same opinion in saying that the "model's most serious weakness is that the suburbs never explicitly

---

[20] For example, see Harvey A. Garn and Robert A. Wilson. *A Critical Look at Urban Dynamics: The Forrester Model and Public Policy.* Washington, D. C., The Urban Institute, December 1970, pp. 80–82; Richard Rochberg. "Some Questionable Assumptions in the Model and Method of Urban Dynamics." *In: Urban Dynamics: Extensions and Reflections,* p. 275; and Weinblatt. "Urban Dynamics: A Critical Review," p. 379.

[21] Leo P. Kadanoff and Herbert Weinblatt. "Public-Policy Conclusions from Urban Growth Models." *In: Urban Dynamics: Extensions and Reflections,* p. 87.

[22] Forrester. *Urban Dynamics,* p. 18.

[23] For example, see Daniel L. Babcock. "Assumptions in Forrester's Urban Dynamics Model," p. 69, Leo P. Kadanoff. "A Modified Forrester Model of the United States or a Group of Metropolitan Areas," p. 105, Gibson. "A Philosophy for Urban Simulations," p. 31, and J. Gray, D. Pessell, and P. Varaya. "A Critique of Forrester's Model of an Urban Area," p. 52. *In: Urban Dynamics: Extensions and Reflections.*

[24] Gray, Pessell, and Varaya. *Ibid.*

[25] Kain. "A Computer Version of How a City Works," p. 242.

appear in it." Omission of the suburbs excludes an integral part of the problem. As Garn and Wilson [26] assessed it, "in Forrester's model there is no commuting across the boundary. . . . One of the most interesting and difficult problems, therefore, is lost in his formulation." Weinblatt's [27] analysis shows that the omission of suburbs in the model interacts with the model's assumption of a constant density of construction. He found that Forrester's simulated city exhibited some behavior similar to that of many central cities with recently expanded suburbs. The processes that caused the behavior in the real cities and in the model's city, however, were substantially different.

In real cities, the increased availability of the private automobile has made possible a movement of both people and industry to the suburbs, thus tending to discourage further expansion of the total amount of housing and industry in many central cities. In the model's city, the assumption that density of construction must remain constant tends to prevent increases in the amount of housing and industry when most of the city's limited land supply has been occupied.

Weinblatt's general assessment is that urban dynamics attempts to compensate for its omission of suburbs by exaggerating other problem-causing processes; although the model may produce symptoms typical of real cities, the processes that cause the symptoms differ from those in real cities. Hence, the results of the model's evaluation of policies are likely to be distorted.

The assumption, in urban dynamics, of a constant density of construction for the fixed-land area represented has led to an exaggeration of "the effect of land availability on the city's potential for expansion and, consequently, on its ability to attract new industry." [28] This assumption completely disregards the fact that capital can substitute for land. Densities do change over time. For example, the population density in Washington, D. C. increased by about 0.8 percent per year during the period 1940–1965. Many central cities will increase in density as the proportion of the population housed in multifamily housing units rises.[29] The same trend applies to business/industry density. The assumption of constant density, therefore, imposes a constraint on the model's capability to represent urban economic development.

[26] Garn and Wilson. *A Critical Look at Urban Dynamics*, p. 74.
[27] Weinblatt. *"Urban Dynamics*: A Critical Review," p. 382.
[28] *Ibid.*, p. 379.
[29] National Industrial Conference Board, Inc. *Economic Dimensions of Major Metropolitan Areas*. Technical Paper No. 18. New York, 1968, p. 18.

Adapting Model Concepts

Usually, in the development of models to support policy studies, theory and concepts having a degree of acceptance and/or relationships based on empirical analysis become a conceptual basis for the model. Forrester disregarded these in the development of urban dynamics. "We are presented with a model which seems intuitively reasonable, and which was developed through consultation with 'experts' who, we can only assume, responded intuitively." [30] Forrester is in the strange position of having developed a model which he claims can help policymakers cope with problems that cannot be dealt with on an intuitive basis, but that can be addressed by his model, which is based largely on intuition.

Forrester made no attempt to relate the results of previous research to the development of urban dynamics, which might have provided conceptual support for his model. Not only was there no attempt to use existing concepts and theory, but there is the suspicion that such an effort was regarded as not very important. One examiner of the model wrote,

One may criticize Forrester for his *ad hoc* approach. He does not explicitly present any underlying theory for his model. The implicit theory appears to be too primitive for such an ambitious model . . . . In sum, we get the overall impression that the theoretical foundations of the model received minimal attention.[31]

Such lack of explicit attention to conceptual and theoretical support may be excusable in modeling problems that are characteristic of the narrow-aim end of the policy problem spectrum discussed in Chapter 2. But the conceptual underpinning of such models is often well understood and often represents processes that are conceptually simple and dependent on relationships wherein the range of the variables is rather restricted. For the kind of broad-aim problems urban dynamics attempts to deal with, however, this attitude is not appropriate. Nevertheless, Forrester treated the conceptual basis of urban dynamics in the same way he had previously treated the development of models of industrial organizations.

Since Forrester's publication of *Urban Dynamics*, other researchers have examined some of the model's concepts from the standpoint of

[30] Edward Berger, Harvey Boulay, and Betty Zisk. "Simulation and the City: A Critical Overview." *Simulation and Games, 1*:425, December 1970.

[31] Gray, Pessell, and Varaya. "A Critique of Forrester's Model of an Urban Area," pp. 54–55.

how well these concepts reflect understandings from previous research. These examinations, however, have not been systematic, but in the nature of comments and observations on the use of particular concepts in the model. The review of the supporting concepts of urban dynamics is organized according to the three model subsystems: business/industry, housing, and population. Because the work undertaken in this area is sketchy in covering the model, attempts are made to identify pertinent concepts and to provide a preliminary assessment of the model in terms of these concepts. It also must be noted that researchers have given little attention to examining the relationships that tie together these three model subsystems.

Business/industry subsystem: As mentioned earlier, in urban dynamics, business/industry units are categorized as new, mature, and declining. Units follow a life cycle, beginning as new units and deteriorating over time to the next lower category. The rates at which business/ industry units deteriorate vary somewhat with general economic conditions. The rate of new business/industry formation depends on the attractiveness of the city to business/industry and to the population groups that supply labor. Two very basic but questionable aspects of the business/industry subsystem representation will be examined. The first is the model's treatment of the interrelationship of the urban area economy represented by the model and the economy of the regional and national environment within which the city functions. This fundamental aspect of model structure has ramifications for the population and housing subsystems, as well as for the business/ industry subsystem. The second aspect is the representation of business/industry in terms of a three-level life cycle, wherein the units are assumed to filter down to successively lower levels. Although a similar concept of filtering has been applied to housing, the concept apparently has not been applied to business/industry, perhaps because it is not altogether suitable for such application.

Two approaches often used in urban models to represent the economic interrelationship of the urban area and its environment attempt to represent the economic activity of the area in a manner consistent with the economic activity of the environment. The more advanced conceptual approach is generally called export-base theory. In this approach, industries that export or sell a significant amount of their products outside the area are identified; and a technique is developed for estimating the external demand for the products of these industries. Because an urban area is seldom self-sufficient, an export base is necessary to provide the means to purchase many of the area's requirements that are produced elsewhere; and, further, the demand for the area's products are a major determinant of the economic vitality of the area. The other industries of the area, which operate at levels related to the levels of the export-oriented industries, often are classified as those serving industries and those serving households. Although this export-base concept is the more advanced of the concepts usually used in urban models, it is regarded as too simplistic to explain many aspects of urban economic growth.[32] The economic growth dynamics model, described in Chapter 3, includes an implementation of the export-base concept by incorporating a representation of national demand on the manufacturing industries of Grand Rapids, Michigan. Probably more urban models use the second approach; that is, to specify exogenously the projected levels of economic activity for the urban area rather than to incorporate techniques into the model to implement an export-base concept. The exogenously specified levels may be based on export-base or other concepts. The Pittsburgh urban renewal, Provincial-Municipal, and empiric models use this approach. There are many variations of both approaches, but it is important that the economic activity of the area be represented in a way that reflects the influence of the environment.

Forrester's formulation of urban dynamics uses neither of the foregoing approaches to relate the urban area to its environment. As Ingram[33] noted, "the economic submodel ignores demand factors in determining the rate of economic growth." The Brown University group found it necessary to append a demand sector to urban dynamics "to represent how consumer and governmental demand for privately produced goods and services is distributed among businesses and industries in the various districts of the metropolitan areas of the nation."[34] This approach is a version of export-base theory. Forrester relies on his concept of limitless, unspecified environment and the relative attractiveness of the urban area to industry and population to govern economic activity and growth. It is doubtful that this representation is adequate for a model emphasizing urban economic development.

[32] Thompson. "Internal and External Factors in the Development of Urban Economics," pp. 27–30.

[33] Gregory K. Ingram. "Review of Jay W. Forrester, *Urban Dynamics*." *Journal of the American Institute of Planners*, 36:207, May 1970.

[34] Herbert Weinblatt. "The Demand Sector." Research Note 18. Providence, R. I., Urban Analysis Group, Brown University, March 1972, p. 1. Mimeographed.

The second unusual aspect of the business/industry representation that is questionable is the life-cycle representation used. Jaeckel,[35] in his analysis of urban dynamics, felt that the business/industry representation was

. . . a central structural assumption in Forrester's model, but one which we question on substantive grounds. . . . Industrial productivity depends primarily on the technological level of the means of production, which are renewable at a rate several times faster and relatively independent of that of the structures housing them. . . . Perhaps Forrester has simply happened to map the aging process and its concomitants from the housing sector into that of industry.

The fact that production technology is, in practice, independent of plant structure is supported by estimates of the length of plant and equipment life for various industries. These estimates show that plant life is nearly always at least twice, and often up to five or six times, that of equipment life.[36]

Forrester's classification of business/industry units in terms of age and condition is based on a concept entirely different from the classifications generally used in urban models. The Standard Industrial Classification, or S.I.C., often is used. For example, the Metropolitan Washington Council of Governments' empiric model of the Washington, D. C. area uses a five-industry classification;[37] the New York Metropolis model uses a 43-industry classification.[38] Both are based on the S.I.C. system. Other models use an industry classification based on the size of the market area served by the industry. In fact, at Brown University, a system of this type, which classifies industries as local, metropolitan, and export, has been incorporated into urban dynamics, and Forrester's aging concept is applied to each class. This approach to classifying industries, used in a number of urban models, is directly related to the export-base concept. Forrester's life-cycle concept is different from either the S.I.C. or market-area classification concepts.

[35] Martin Jaeckel. "Forrester's Urban Dynamics: A Sociologist's Inductive Critique." In: Urban Dynamics: Extensions and Reflections, p. 255.

[36] Graham Cecil Scott. "Industrial Production and Investment in a Dynamic, Multiregional, Interindustry Model of the United States." Doctoral Dissertation. Durham, N.C., Duke University, 1972, pp. 136–137.

[37] Metropolitan Washington Council of Governments. "Empiric" Activity Allocation Model, Application to the Washington Metropolitan Region. Washington, D. C., December 1972, p. 84.

[38] Barbara R. Berman, Benjamin Chinitz, and Edgar M. Hoover. Projection of a Metropolis; Technical Supplement to the New York Metropolitan Region Study. Cambridge, Mass., Harvard University Press, 1960, p. 12.

Forrester presents no conceptual or empirical evidence to support his representation of the business/industry subsystem, and most researchers who have commented on it doubt its appropriateness. One assessment concludes that

> Although it is generally agreed that filtration (and construction) are the essential dynamics of the housing sector, this decomposition of business is orthogonal to the classical decomposition into administration, service, retail, wholesale, and manufacturing. One suspects that the former decomposition was chosen because of its simplicity rather than for technical reasons . . . . We therefore reject this model of the business sector.[39]

Rothenberg [40] similarly concludes that the model's "life-cycle business hypothesis is highly vulnerable" and that the heavy reliance "on the life-cycle hypothesis for determining business levels is a very serious defect."

Housing subsystem: In urban dynamics, the housing stock of the urban area is classified in three levels: premium, worker, and underemployed; and housing at each level is assumed to be occupied by families of the corresponding labor-force level. Housing units, as they age, filter from the premium-to-worker level and from the worker-to-underemployed level. The model uses both family-size and housing-density parameters for each population group, so an increase in families per housing unit can be represented as units deteriorate. The normal housing market constructs premium and worker housing units to meet demand. Underemployed units are constructed only for a low-cost urban development program.[41]

The concept of filtering has been used for some time to explain changes in housing stock over time. Basically, "the filtering process is viewed . . . as a change in home values and rents. . . . It is frequently either assumed or specifically stated that the shift in values is accompanied by a change in occupancy." In examining many aspects of the filtering concept, Grigsby [42] concludes that "broadly speaking, it is the principal dynamic feature of the housing market." A number of urban models, including the San Francisco housing model in which housing is classified in terms of five condition levels, have used the filtering concept.

---

[39] Gray, Pessell, and Varaya. "A Critique of Forrester's Model of an Urban Area," p. 50.

[40] Rothenberg. "Problems in the Modeling of Urban Development," p. 9.

[41] Forrester. *Urban Dynamics,* pp. 140–141, 214–215.

[42] William G. Grigsby. *Housing Markets and Public Policy.* Philadelphia, University of Pennsylvania Press, 1963, pp. 98–99.

The formulation of the housing subsystem of urban dynamics is in general agreement with the concept of filtering, which most observers find appropriate. A disadvantage of the subsystem's formulation is the lack of distinction between single- and multifamily units, which use land differently and probably filter at different rates. It also may be desirable to distinguish between rental and owner-occupied housing units, because of the occupants' differing behavior. A number of relationships could be considered for possible inclusion in the subsystem; overall, however, its basic concepts seem adequate.

Population subsystem: As discussed earlier, urban dynamics classifies population in terms of three labor-force groups: manager-professional, labor, and underemployed. The level for each group represents only the labor-force population. To obtain total population of the urban area, the level of each labor-force group is multiplied by the family-size parameter for the group, and the three products are summed. The population for each group changes as a result of births, deaths, migration, and intergroup mobility. Births and deaths actually are handled together by defining a net birth rate; each of the three groups has its own net birth rate. For all three population groups, incoming migration depends on factors such as job and housing availability, tax rates and expenditures, and potential for upward mobility. The structure of the relationship for the migration or arrival rate is somewhat different for each group. The inverse of each group's arrival rate is taken as a departure rate which, in effect, assumes that the same factors which are associated with inward migration operate in a negative way to produce outward migration. Upward and downward mobility occur in the model at normal rates, and the actual rates at any given time deviate from the normal rates according to the influence of such factors as job availability. Interestingly, downward mobility for the manager-professional group is not represented in the model, because Forrester regards it as too small to be significant.[43]

The basic concepts of the population subsystem have not been overly criticized, although selected aspects have been questioned. One aspect of the overall formulation deserves examination, however, because it ignores one of the essential elements of population growth dynamics, namely, an age distribution of its population groups. Many activities that cause significant changes in population occur at rates that are strongly dependent on age; these activities interact to pro-

[43] Forrester. *Urban Dynamics,* pp. 31–36.

duce an amplified effect on population change. For instance, migration rates, highest among the young-adult population, fall rapidly for ages beyond that.[44] The sharp variation in these rates is shown in the migration rates between states in the United States in 1960: they ·were nearly seven times as high for those in the 20–24 year age group as for those 45 and older.[45] The young-adult age group has a very low death rate and is responsible for most births. Because of the interaction of these rates, migration from an urban area will draw heavily on the young-adult population; this will tend to reduce the birth rate and increase the death rate of the area's population. The result is a compound decrease in the net birth rate of the area. In the same manner, the net birth rate will show a compound increase from migration into the urban area.

Because of these dynamic aspects of population change, the need for an age distribution of the population in urban dynamics should be examined closely. Many models have used such a distribution to simulate the demographic processes included in urban dynamics. The economic growth dynamics model examined in Chapter 3, for instance, divides the population into 15 age groups for the purpose of simulating the birth, aging, death, and migration processes. Developers of the Susquehanna River Basin model used Forrester's system dynamics methodology and, after careful analysis, adapted a population representation with six age groups, which exhibited relatively homogeneous birth, death, and migration characteristics.[46]

The aspects of the population subsystem most frequently criticized have been those dealing with individual relationships, especially migration. Criticisms center on the relative influence of various factors in determining migration, particularly Forrester's strong emphasis on housing as a factor promoting inward migration. These criticisms, together with those of other model relationships, are examined in the following section.

DEVELOPMENT OF THE MODEL

The second of the three stages of model development transforms the conceptual model into a manageable set of relationships and an opera-

---

[44] John B. Lansing and Eva Mueller. *The Geographic Mobility of Labor.* Ann Arbor, Mich., Institute for Social Research, University of Michigan, 1967, p. 335.

[45] H. R. Hamilton et al. *Systems Simulation for Regional Analysis: An Application to River-Basin Planning.* Cambridge, Mass., MIT Press, 1969, p. 138.

[46] *Ibid.,* p. 126.

tional model. This stage has two tasks: The first formulates model relationships, emphasizing the mathematical and logical structure of the model and the computer implementation of an operational model. The second task is an aspect of overall model validation, and tests model relationships from a substantive viewpoint.

Formulating Model Relationships

As mentioned in Chapter 3, the mathematical structure of the urban dynamics model consists of a set of first-order difference equations. Actually, the model relationships are specified in the Dynamo language in differential equation form, but, with the choice of the solution-interval unit length, the relationships become a set of first-order difference equations. Forrester selected one year as the solution interval for his work with the model, because this is short enough not to influence the simulated behavior of the system; [47] other researchers also have used this one-year interval. The rules of the Dynamo computer language used by Forrester to implement the model (described in Appendix B) assure that the system of difference equations will be solvable and that the Dynamo software can carry out the solution. The computational procedure consists of solving the set of equations for each successive time period to be simulated. Some variables computed for each period become input for the next period, and initial values for many of these variables are stipulated to initialize the computational procedure.

The basic formulation and computer implementation techniques developed by Forrester and used in urban dynamics are discussed in Chapter 3 and Appendix B. They include the basic features of the Dynamo language, as well as the multiplicative relationships and tabular functions used extensively in the model. Generally, the computer implementation and model formulation techniques have been subject to neither major criticisms nor efforts to modify Forrester's techniques. The use of multiplicative relationships and tabular functions, however, which are the principal means of introducing nonlinear relationships into the model, have been subject to scattered criticisms. Although a comprehensive evaluation of these techniques is lacking, it is apparent from the criticisms and the extensive use of the techniques that a systematic examination is needed.

Forrester provides only a brief, general argument to justify the multiplier concept used in the model. He favors multiplicative rather

---

[47] Forrester. *Urban Dynamics*, p. 146.

than additive forms, because they mutually enhance the components in a relationship and make it possible for one component to become zero, or approach zero, and dominate a relationship. Forrester's justification for tabular functions also is on general grounds. The model structure contains 10 major multiplicative relationships, several of which combine five or six variables by multiplication. Furthermore, the model makes use of more than 50 tabular functions which are nonlinear in form. The multiplicative relationships and tabular functions are often closely intertwined in the model structure.[48] These relationships constitute a very strong nonlinear structure, which is not justified by Forrester and which has been questioned but not thoroughly examined. Gibson's assessment of the use of these nonlinearities is that, although most of Forrester's assumptions are generally plausible, they are not beyond doubt, and that linking dozens of these assumptions together, each of which has a degree of uncertainty, raises serious questions. With respect to Forrester's affinity for nonlinearities of the multiplicative form, Gibson [49] notes that the model's extensive use of this nonlinear form presents a grave analytical difficulty. Because Forrester deals with neither the validation of the model nor the application of the model to an urban area, he never faces up to these problems. Garn and Wilson [50] note this in observing that: "It is one thing to make the methodological point that . . . functions should be nonlinear. It is quite another to know what the critical functions are, as well as their range and shape." A comprehensive evaluation of the appropriateness of the nonlinear structure of the model clearly needs to be undertaken.

Testing Model Relationships

The second task of model development is testing the substantive relationships of the model. As previously noted, this empiricist view of model validation focuses on empirically testing the individual relationships upon which the model is based. Forrester's work is not empirically based, although he assumes parameter values for his model representation of a hypothetical city. In doing so, he makes empirical assumptions regarding the relative contribution of various factors in determining the behavior of particular aspects of the urban system. Many of these assumptions have been examined by researchers who, in a number of cases, have suggested alternative assumptions. The

[48] *Ibid.*, pp. 274–280.
[49] Gibson. "A Philosophy for Urban Simulations," pp. 38–40.
[50] Garn and Wilson. *A Critical Look at Urban Dynamics*, p. 83.

concern here is the testing of model relationships rather than Forrester's choice of parameter values, although the distinction between
these concerns is not always sharp. The relationships dealing with
migration are discussed first, because this is the most frequently
criticized aspect of the formulation. Other relationships include those
dealing with the obsolescence multipliers for business and housing, and
those used in the tax structure.

Of the researchers who have examined Forrester's migration relationships, Janet Pack has performed the most comprehensive analysis. She
compared the relationships in urban dynamics with migration equations, which she estimated by applying regression techniques to data on
U. S. migration for the 1955–1960 period. Although the estimated
equations are not identical to Forrester's, they are similar enough to
afford a general comparison. For the model's manager-professional and
worker population groups, both relationships place job and housing
availability as the first and second variables, respectively, in terms of
explanatory power. Taxes also have the same general effect in both
relationships, since in-migration for these two population groups is
correlated negatively with tax rates; however, Pack finds a relationship
between the types of expenditures financed by taxes and migration.
Specifically, she finds that migration into central cities by these groups
is correlated positively with increased per capita education expenditures and correlated negatively with increased per capita welfare
payments. Forrester's formulation, however, cannot represent this
refinement. For the underemployed population group, the comparison
indicates that urban dynamics places too much emphasis on housing
as a factor in migration.[51]

In addition to Pack, other researchers, including Babcock,[52] Garn
and Wilson,[53] and Averch and Levine,[54] have found that urban
dynamics overemphasizes housing as a determining factor in migration,
especially for the underemployed group. Forrester was aware of this
general deficiency, because he notes that some social scientists who
reviewed his book manuscript objected to the housing multiplier on
the basis that other studies have shown that housing is not a strong
determinant of urban migration of the underemployed.[55] He chose to

[51] Janet Rothenberg Pack. "Models of Population Movement and Urban Policy."
In: Urban Dynamics: Extensions and Reflections, pp. 214–222.

[52] Daniel L. Babcock. "Analysis and Improvement of a Dynamic Urban Model."
Doctoral Dissertation. Los Angeles, University of California, 1970, pp. 70–73.

[53] Garn and Wilson. *A Critical Look at Urban Dynamics,* p. 75.

[54] Averch and Levine. *Two Models of the Urban Crises,* p. 24.

[55] Forrester. *Urban Dynamics,* p. 140.

publish the volume, however, without modifying the model formulation.

Another factor related to migration is job availability. Babcock compared the impact of job availability in urban dynamics with that in two other empirically based studies and found that the effect of jobs on migration is not given sufficient influence in the model.[56] Belkin made the same observation, based on his analysis of two studies that suggested economic opportunity as a dominant influence in migration. Belkin further argues that, because the factors influencing migration are not of equal weight, the relationship should not be formulated in a multiplicative form. Under such a formulation, a percentage change in any factor causes the same percentage change in migration.[57] This argument is supported implicitly by migration studies such as those by Pack [58] and Lowry,[59] wherein the factors governing migration are combined additively.

A second set of relationships supporting the urban dynamics model is the formulation related to the obsolescence rates for business/industry and housing units. The rates governing business/industry and housing deterioration interact with the fixed land area and fixed land per business/industry and housing unit assumptions to control the equilibrium state of the model. As one analysis of this interaction concluded

The equilibrium of the system stems from the fact that it has a fixed land area, thus constraining each of the variables from divergence, and from the fact that the "filtration" model of business and housing strongly constrains their populations by fixing their ratios.[60]

Jaeckel performed a series of runs with the model that led to the same general conclusion. His experiments varied the normal yearly rates of industry decline or obsolescence and computed the equilibrium ratios of the three types of industry. Forrester assumed the normal fraction that would decline for premium, mature, and declining industry units as .08, .05, and .03, respectively. This implicitly assumes an average lifetime in each industry stage of 12, 20, and 33 years in the premium, mature, and declining stages, respectively, because the average lifetimes

[56] Babcock. "Analysis and Improvement of a Dynamic Urban Model," pp. 65–70.

[57] Jacob Belkin. "Urban Dynamics: Applications as a Teaching Tool and as an Urban Game." In: *Urban Dynamics: Extensions and Reflections*, pp. 126–127.

[58] Pack. "Models of Population Movement and Urban Policy," pp. 211–222.

[59] Ira S. Lowry. *Migration and Metropolitan Growth: Two Analytical Models.* San Francisco, Chandler Publ., 1966.

[60] Gray, Pessell, and Varaya. "A Critique of Forrester's Model of an Urban Area," p. 50.

are the reciprocals of the decline rates. For Forrester's rates and a number of alternative normal decline rates, each model run computed equilibrium ratios of the three types of industry, which closely approximated the ratios of the average industry lifetimes that were implicit in the normal decline rates used in the run. There was always a persistent bias, however, in the direction of overrepresenting the number of declining units of industry. With respect to housing, the model did not exhibit so strong a bias toward overrepresenting underemployed housing at equilibrium. Jaeckel concludes from this that

In the sequences of employment and housing densities and of basic obsolescence rates which Forrester assumes, we have located the sources of certain system pressures and/or major determinants of the over-all equilibrium ratios, and therewith factors that influence the situation of the underemployed.[61]

Babcock also analyzed the formulation of business and housing obsolescence rates and set forth a modified formulation. He found that the effective obsolescence rates, as computed in the model, were a significant factor in increasing the availability of underemployed housing which, in turn, made the city more attractive to the underemployed. The impact on the city was reinforced, because the model overstates the influence of housing on the in-migration of the underemployed, as mentioned previously. Babcock identified two key objections to the formulation. First, he felt that the relationships in the model, whereby a shortage of land or higher taxes caused an increase in the effective rate of decline for business and industry, were not justified on the basis of urban experience. To correct this, he deleted the land and tax multipliers that compute the effective rates of decline for business and housing from the model equations. Second, he thought the rate of decline in housing should depend not only on the demand for housing at its current level of usage, as Forrester formulated it, but also on the demand at the next lower level of usage. He modified the equations which computed the effective housing decline rates to include this idea. These fairly simple changes were very effective in reducing the overrepresentation of declining industry and underemployed housing, according to the model runs made by Babcock. Although his tests were conducted with a model representation of a hypothetical city, he had made many changes in parameter values to bring them into agreement with available data sources. Parameter changes included birth rates, in-migration and out-migration rates, and perception times.[62] This

---

[61] Jaeckel. "Forrester's Urban Dynamics: A Sociologist's Inductive Critique," p. 247.

[62] Babcock. "Analysis and Improvement of a Dynamic Urban Model," pp. 124–139.

alternative formulation of obsolescence relationships appears to be a significant improvement in model formulation.

Another set of urban dynamics relationships, that of the tax sector, also has been examined. The model's tax sector is very simple: its equations compute the total assessed value of the city's business and housing units, taxes collected, taxes needed by the city, and tax effectiveness measures. Forrester used taxes per capita to compute a public-expenditure multiplier and an underemployed-education multiplier, which are factors in computing the attractiveness of in-migration for the underemployed and the effect of educational expenditures on upward mobility, respectively. The assumption that educational expenditures affect mobility is open to question, in view of a recent assessment.[63] Babcock argues that a tax-adequacy ratio would be a more appropriate measure of public expenditures than taxes per capita, since the tax-adequacy ratio measures the extent to which the need for tax-supported services is being met. Babcock introduced an equation into the model to compute the tax-adequacy ratio. He modified the two equations that compute the public-expenditure multipliers and the under-employed-education multipliers to use the tax-adequacy ratio rather than the taxes per capita. Based on test runs with the model, Babcock [64] judged this change to be an improvement in producing a mix of labor that more nearly matched the demand for labor and a more favorable tax structure.

Modification of the tax sector of urban dynamics also was suggested by Schroeder,[65] as a result of his work with an urban dynamics representation of Lowell, Massachusetts. Schroeder found that a more detailed tax sector was needed to represent adequately Lowell's current and proposed alternative tax-assessment policies. In particular, it was desirable to apply different assessment rules for business and residential properties. Although the necessary model modifications were not made, Schroeder recommended that they be made and tested when his work is extended to make it a policymaking tool for use in Lowell.

As has been noted, researchers have examined model relationships in areas that include migration, obsolescence rates, and the tax sector. On the whole, however, examination of the model's supporting relation-

[63] Christopher Jencks et al. *Inequality: A Reassessment of the Effect of Family and Schooling in America.* New York, Basic Books, 1972, pp. 188–195.

[64] Babcock. "Analysis and Improvement of a Dynamic Urban Model," pp. 73–74, 131–133.

[65] Walter Warren Schroeder III. "Lowell Dynamics: Preliminary Applications of the Theory of Urban Dynamics." Master's Thesis. Cambridge, Mass., Massachusetts Institute of Technology, 1972, pp. 86–87.

ships appears to be far from systematic and complete. Other related work that has been undertaken deals primarily with estimating model parameter values rather than with testing the structure of model relationships. Babcock's work,[66] for example, is directed largely to estimating more realistic parameter values of a hypothetical U. S. city than Forrester's are. Probably one reason relationships in some areas have not been tested is that researchers have rejected the conceptual basis of a model sector and, therefore, regard the substantive relationships of the sector as not worth testing. For instance, neglect in examining the relationships supporting the business/industry sectors may stem from lack of acceptance of the conceptual basis of these sectors.

VALIDATION AND APPLICATION OF MODEL

The third stage of the model development process focuses on validation of the model and its application to policy problems. Review of the research related to this stage is organized into three supporting tasks: collecting data and developing model parameters, validating the model, and applying the model. From an overview of model development, this stage concerns the adequacy of the model—developed in the first two stages—for policymaking: how well it uses available sources of data, how good the model representation is of the system under study, and how well it represents policymaking problems.

Collecting Data and Developing Model Parameters

As noted previously, in the development of urban dynamics, Forrester made no use of urban data sources. In addition, he did nothing to assure that the data requirements of the model could be satisfied by the data sources usually available for an urban area. In brief, the empirical practicability of the model was not considered. A number of researchers recognized this shortcoming. Dennis Meadows, for example, suggested that Forrester should have spelled out the precise operational meaning of the variables used in the model and should have provided verbal descriptions from existing data sources to permit easy use of the model.[67] As these are efforts of considerable magnitude, very little progress has been made in this direction.

[66] Babcock. "Analysis and Improvement of a Dynamic Urban Model," pp. 131–133.
[67] Dennis L. Meadows. "Forrester-Type Urban Growth Models." Comments in a panel discussion at the American Association for the Advancement of Science Annual Meeting, Washington, D. C., December 26, 1972.

Collecting data and estimating initial values and parameter values for the urban dynamics model are sizeable tasks. Forrester suggests that a total of 41 model values should be estimated to develop a model representation of a particular urban area. There are more than 80 model values, however, that are possibly area dependent and which should be considered. Furthermore, a complete empirical implementation of the model requires an examination of the values of the more than 50 tabular functions that appear in the model. Researchers who have developed model representations of particular cities have undertaken the estimation of only selected model values. In fact, most researchers have estimated only a few. It is evident, therefore, that little has been accomplished on the broader task, envisioned by Meadows, of operationalizing the model variables so that existing data sources can be used readily to develop a model representation of a particular city.

Some researchers, such as Kadanoff, who have developed urban dynamics models of particular urban areas, have not reported on the supporting empirical work for their efforts. Other studies, such as Babcock's, deal with estimating model values for a hypothetical city, whereas here the interest is in representing specific urban areas. There are three studies of specific urban areas, however, that have reported on the approach taken in estimating model values. In his work with Lowell, Massachusetts, Schroeder [68] estimated values for nine model parameters, including the total land-area parameter, land area per housing unit and per building unit parameters, three family-size parameters, and three housing-density parameters. Bartos and Tsai,[69] in their work with four U. S. cities, estimated only the initial values for the three labor-force groups, three types of housing, and three types of business units for each of the four cities. Porter and Henley,[70] in their development of a model of Harris County, Texas, reported on examining 53 initial values and parameters and estimating area-dependent values for 37 of them. All three of these studies explicitly report the procedures used in estimating model values.

The Bartos-Tsai and Porter-Henley studies do the best job of operationalizing variables and estimating model values. These studies also illustrate some of the difficulties involved in the process. For instance,

[68] Schroeder. "Lowell Dynamics," pp. 38–45.

[69] Otomar J. Bartos and Yung-Mei Tsai. "Forrester's Model and Four U. S. Cities." Paper read at the American Association for the Advancement of Science Annual Meeting, Washington, D. C., December 26, 1972, pp. 10–14.

[70] Howell R. Porter III and Ernest J. Henley. "Application of the Forrester Model to Harris County, Texas." In: *Urban Dynamics: Extensions and Reflections*, pp. 175–179.

the two studies define the nine basic level variables of the model differently, particularly the three levels for business/industry units. On the one hand, Porter and Henley rely on business failure and new business establishment statistics. They define new enterprises as those which have existed for two years or less, and declining enterprises as those expected to fail in two years or less. All others are mature business units.[71] On the other hand, in their study, Bartos and Tsai define the three types of business/industry units in terms of the mix of personnel that the units employ: manager-professional, labor, and underemployed groups; the groups are defined by average weekly pay. Although there are differences in the way these two studies define housing levels and population levels, the differences are not as sharp as their definitions of business/industry units. Bartos and Tsai [72] sum up the situation by stating that "the manner in which the sectors of labor, housing, and industry are operationalized is open to wide interpretations." The ambiguity in the development of operational definitions for the model's basic variables causes further variations in the definitions of the many other variables dependent on the basic ones.

It is probably neither desirable nor realistic to expect that all model values be defined operationally in sufficient detail so they can be mechanically evaluated from data sources available for every urban area. Available sources vary for different areas, and the purpose of developing models of areas also will vary. Such differences affect the way variables are operationalized. It would be useful, however, to develop fairly standard definitions for the principal model variables and to evaluate the effectiveness of the definitions for use in developing models of particular urban areas. The more basic problem of establishing model validity, however, must be dealt with first.

Validating the Model

The model validation task tests the model by comparing computed results with observed system behavior or with independent projections of system behavior. Tests are conducted with model representations of specific urban areas, rather than with a generalized or hypothetical city. Four research efforts have developed significant results in this area.

One of the validation efforts for the urban dynamics model is the work of Porter and Henley in developing a model representation of

[71] *Ibid.*, p. 180.
[72] Bartos and Tsai. "Forrester's Model and Four U. S. Cities," p. 9.

Harris County, Texas, which includes the city of Houston. As noted previously, area-dependent values for 37 initial values and parameters were developed; these estimates were made so that model computations could be initialized for the year 1950. Two types of tests were conducted with the model representation of Harris County. First, computed results of 10 model values for 1960 and 1970 were compared with values from Census Bureau and local government agency data sources. The values were the total population and three levels each of labor, housing, and business. For 1960, the model's estimate of the total for the three labor-force groups was 7 percent low, the estimate of total housing was 27 percent high, and the estimate of total businesses was 11 percent high. The model's 1960 total population figure was high by 15 percent. For 1970, the total labor-force estimate was 14 percent low, total housing was 17 percent high, total business establishments was 1 percent low, and total population was 7 percent high. In both years, the variations between the computed and actual levels of the labor, housing, and business categories were significantly greater in many cases than those for the category totals. From these results, Porter and Henley concluded that, for the major model variables, the model results were fairly close to reality.[73] Many researchers would probably say that the results cited do not support this conclusion. Porter and Henley made no effort to explain the discrepancies between actual and computed values, nor to explain why the model estimates were good in some areas but very poor in others.

The second test by Porter and Henley was to compare model results for 1980 with projections made by the Houston Chamber of Commerce through the application of regression techniques. No details are given of the variables used or the form of the relationship for the Chamber of Commerce projection method. The comparison was made for total labor force, housing, business, and population. For all four of these values, the model estimates were somewhat lower than the Chamber of Commerce projections; model results were 3 percent lower for the labor force, 5 percent for housing, 8 percent for business, and 13 percent for population.[74] Although, at first glance, these results are generally encouraging, some basic information for evaluating them is missing. In particular, the model results in this comparison apparently were computed by initializing the model for the year 1950; the model results, therefore, constitute a 30-year projection. For the regression

---

[73] Porter and Henley. "Application of the Forrester Model to Harris County, Texas," pp. 179–181.

[74] *Ibid.,* pp. 180–182.

projection, however, the initializing point in time for making the 1980 projections is not given.

The work of Leo P. Kadanoff and his associates at Brown University is related, to some extent, to the model validation task. As already mentioned, the empirical aspects of the Brown University group's work have not been reported on, so it is not known which model values were estimated or how variables were operationalized; but Kadanoff has reported in general terms on their validation effort. The test was carried out for Providence, Rhode Island, using a version of the urban dynamics model which was modified to include a representation of the suburbs. Census data were used for estimating values to initialize the model for the year 1950, and model estimates for 1960 and 1970 were compared with actual results. The computed and actual results for each of the labor, housing, and business levels generally agreed within 5 to 10 percent.[75]

In their work with the urban dynamics model, Bartos and Tsai conducted validation tests for four cities: Chicago, New Orleans, Detroit, and Philadelphia. For each city, the model was initialized for the year 1940 by estimating values for the nine model levels representing each of the three types of labor, housing, and business. The model was used to compute results for each city for 1950 and 1960. The results for the same nine-level variables were compared with actual data. Overall, the model exhibited a strong tendency to overestimate the levels of the labor force and housing and to underestimate the number of businesses. At the more detailed level of estimating the categories of labor, housing, and business, the model was found to be very pessimistic: the underemployed, underemployed housing, and declining industry were consistently and substantially overestimated. Only one exception to this pessimistic bias occurred in the 24 comparisons of these categories. Such a bias is perhaps largely due to Forrester's use of hypothetical parameter values. Bartos and Tsai [76] conjecture that, if they had estimated additional parameter values for the four cities in their study, the results would have been much improved.

The fourth study related to model validation is Schroeder's work with the urban dynamics representation of Lowell, Massachusetts. As mentioned in the discussion of data collection and model value esti-

[75] Leo P. Kadanoff. "Uses and Misuses of Urban Growth Models." Address at the Applied Physics Laboratory, The Johns Hopkins University, Laurel, Maryland, March 24, 1972; and "Forrester-Type Growth Models." Comments in a panel discussion at the American Association for the Advancement of Science Annual Meeting, Washington, D. C., December 26, 1972.

[76] Bartos and Tsai. "Forrester's Model and Four U. S. Cities," pp. 2–7.

mation, Schroeder estimated nine parameter values in developing his Lowell model. He initialized computations for the year 1820—the year in which Lowell was established—and computed results through 1970. He performed some general comparisons of the model results with actual results. The computed population growth pattern over time compared closely with Lowell's actual growth. As Schroeder [77] points out, for the 1900–1970 period, computed model results and observed results agree fairly well. Also, the level of underemployed and the extent of land utilization computed for 1970 correspond closely to the actual situation in Lowell.

Despite the shortcomings mentioned in the Porter and Henley validation effort, it is probably the best of those made, because their model incorporates a reasonably large number of area-dependent parameters. Their test results, nonetheless, probably should be considered inconclusive. As to the other validation efforts, it is not known what empirical work supports Kadanoff's test with Providence; the tests conducted by Bartos and Tsai and by Schroeder probably estimate too few model parmeters to be regarded as model representations of specific urban areas.

Applying the Model

Model application means using a model representation of a specific urban area to test and evaluate a set of alternatives in some particular policy area. Were this definition of model application applied stringently, there would be no research to be reviewed under this topic. Most efforts to develop urban dynamics models of specific urban areas have stopped short of evaluating policy questions. The few efforts that have used urban dynamics to examine policy problems have done so in terms of a general or hypothetical city and, hence, have not developed models of specific urban areas. Nevertheless, three research efforts did make a contribution in this area.

Two of the research efforts used urban dynamics to examine rent control policy problems. One of these, by Gray and his associates,[78] was an examination of rent control in New York City. Actually, they used Forrester's model of a hypothetical city with one minor change. This change introduced rates to increase the downward filtering of housing, beginning in the 200th simulated year, to reflect what the researchers conjecture would be the impact of rent control. In dis-

---

[77] Schroeder. "Lowell Dynamics," pp. 44-47.
[78] Gray, Pessell, and Varaya. "A Critique of Forrester's Model of an Urban Area," pp. 47–49.

cussing the results from computer runs of this slightly modified version of Forrester's model, a loose analogy is drawn between the computed results and the spread of Harlem in New York City since rent control was imposed during World War II. The principal contribution of this work illustrates what might be a useful way to incorporate policy alternatives for rent control into the model structure.

The second study dealing with rent control was conducted by Harlow.[79] It also uses Forrester's model of a hypothetical city rather than an urban dynamics representation of a specific area. The impacts of rent control are introduced into the model by changing nine parameter values, including lowering housing construction rates, increasing housing downward filtration or obsolescence rates, and increasing the attractiveness for in-migration rates. The choice of the parameters modified are justified by references to the literature on urban housing and rent control, but the parameter values selected are not based on empirical analysis. Several simulation runs were made and examined to assess the impact of these parameter changes over a 25-year period. Harlow's contribution from a policymaking point of view is in the same area as the other rent control study; his study illustrates ways in which the impacts of rent control policies can be reflected in the urban dynamics model.

The third model application study was conducted by Kadanoff and Weinblatt.[80] They developed the National Metropolitan model, an extension of Forrester's model, which represents the nation's cities and suburbs as well as the national economy. Kadanoff and Weinblatt used their model to evaluate the impacts of several combinations of urban programs. The National Metropolitan model apparently is not supported by any substantial empirical analysis. The interesting aspect of the study is that its analysis of urban programs provides much different results than Forrester's analysis of the same programs with his model. In fact, with their National Metropolitan model, Kadanoff and Weinblatt found that a combination of programs providing public service jobs, training of the underemployed, and urban renewal were effective in most respects. The researchers warn, however, that the National Metropolitan model does not provide a compelling case for this set of policy actions. In fact, uncalibrated models such as the National Metropolitan model cannot provide definitive answers to policy questions.

[79] Albert Mason Harlow, Jr. "Exploring Rent Control with Urban Dynamics." Master's Thesis. Cambridge, Mass., Massachusetts Institute of Technology, 1972, pp. 9–39.

[80] Kadanoff and Weinblatt. "Public-Policy Conclusions from Urban Growth Models," pp. 99–102.

EVALUATION OF RESEARCH FOUNDATION

The foregoing review of the research foundation of the urban dynamics model can be drawn on to provide an overall evaluation of the adequacy of the model's supporting theory and assumptions. Although an evaluation of a model's research foundation in terms of an absolute standard is not possible, areas of relative strength and weakness can be identified. The point of view in the evaluation is that the objective of the model-building process is to develop a tool that will increase understanding of policy issues.

Table 2 lists the principal contributors of supporting research, according to the significance of their contribution, for each of the seven tasks of the model development process. The tasks are organized under the three stages into which the research process was structured. Although a subjective element enters into the listing and ordering of contributors, such a listing may add information that is perhaps only implicit in the review of research. Using the structure of the review given in Table 2 as a basis, the evaluation is made by examining, first, the three stages of model-building research and, then, the individual tasks involved in the process.

In the three-stage structure of the review of model-related research, the last stage has been neglected; that is, the conceptualization and development stages appear to have received relatively more research attention than the model validation and application stage. Although some efforts related to the third stage have been undertaken, the total results are weak. This is unfortunate, because the third stage validates the entire model development process.

There are four reasons for this neglect of the validation-application stage. First, the traditional orientation in social science is more closely associated with the examination of underlying assumptions than with the examination of models in terms of their predictive performance. Second, researchers may have judged that efforts in this area would not be fruitful, therefore, have been reluctant to invest resources in this stage. For example, if researchers have no confidence in the conceptual underpinning of the model, they are apt to believe that work in the validation-application area will not be productive. They may therefore choose to examine and improve the model concepts or to channel their efforts elsewhere. Third, undertakings in the model validation-application stage are expensive, because they generally require substantial empirical analysis and computer-related costs. The fourth factor contributing to the neglect of the model validation-application stage is bias in the model-related research. Published research offers many criticisms of urban dynamics, but few research efforts have undertaken significant model reconstructions to eliminate model deficiences.

The task of establishing model scope has received considerable attention within the model and problem conceptualization stage of research, but the task of adapting model concepts has been rather neglected. As noted in the review, Forrester established the basic scope of the model. Others called attention to the model's strong normative orientation and to a number of structural assumptions that tended to limit the model's scope in undesirable ways. These limitations in scope, however, are not fatal flaws, because model modifications that can overcome these limitations are feasible. For example, model concepts and relationships must be examined to determine whether the influence of normative values might reduce the model's usefulness; and it might be necessary to improve the model's relationships between the urban area represented and its environment. The task of analyzing the supporting concepts of the model has been neglected to the extent that no systematic treatment has been given to any one of the three major subsystems. Based on the foregoing review of model concepts, it can be concluded that the housing subsystem appears to follow acceptable concepts of filtering; that there are some significant problems with the concepts of the population subsystem; and that there are major problems with the business/industry subsystem. Although the life-cycle concept used in the business/industry subsystem appears, at first glance, to have some face validity, Rothenberg found the concept seriously inadequate in representing economic activity, and the concept fails to incorporate considerations Thompson regards as important in understanding urban economic development. The relationships that tie together the three model subsystems have been given almost no attention by researchers. There is a clear need for considerable research to evaluate fully the model's supporting concepts.

With respect to the second stage of model development, the task of formulating model relationships is more adequately supported by research than is the task of testing model relationships. Nevertheless, one aspect of the model formulation is open to question and has potentially far-reaching consequences: the appropriateness of the form of the nonlinear functions that are used extensively in the model. The question should be analyzed; but it is intertwined with the testing of model relationships, because the functional forms used are likely to be appropriate for the representation of some phenomena, although not for others.

In support of testing model relationships, some very pertinent research has been undertaken, particularly by Babcock and Pack. The research thus far, however, constitutes only a beginning, because most of the supporting relationships of the model remain untested from a substantive point of view. No effort has been made to examine the research from the areas of urban economics and urban sociology to determine whether or not such research contributes to developing the urban dynamics model.

CHAPTER 5

Urban Dynamics Model Representation of an Urban Area: In-Practice Evaluation

The case study now examines the urban dynamics model from the in-practice point of view, which assesses the utility of the model for dealing with actual policy problems. The evaluation is organized into two sequential parts: The first, covered in this chapter, develops and evaluates an urban dynamics representation of a specific urban area; the second, discussed in Chapter 6, uses the model representation of the urban area to analyze an illustrative policy problem. These developments provide the basis for the in-practice evaluation of the model.

In conducting model evaluations, the extensiveness of the in-practice evaluation will vary. It often will not be justifiable or feasible to conduct an in-practice evaluation as extensive as the one undertaken here; however, by proper planning, many of the tests may be undertaken in conjunction with the normal model development process, thereby reducing the costs of model evaluation.

The first section of this chapter outlines the approach used in developing an urban dynamics representation of a specific area and explains the reasons for selecting Washington, D. C. as the area. In the second section, the model representation is developed and evaluated. Chapter 6 shows how the model of Washington, D. C. is used to analyze a relevant policy problem for the city; the final section of that chapter evaluates the utility of the model for dealing in-practice with policy problems for a specific urban area.

APPROACH TO IN-PRACTICE EVALUATION

As noted earlier, many of the assumptions of the urban dynamics model are restrictive and questionable in light of previous modeling efforts. Nevertheless, the application of the urban dynamics model to real problems is worthwhile. In fact, this strategy recognizes that often it is necessary and useful to make restrictive and unrealistic assumptions in model construction and that models should be judged on their performance rather than solely on the basis of the reality of their assumptions. Furthermore, in using the model, many assumptions will prove to be not crucial to model results. The in-practice evaluation of the urban dynamics model is undertaken under this general strategy.

The urban area selected for the application of the model is the District of Columbia, or Washington, D. C., which is the highly urbanized center of the Washington Standard Metropolitan Statistical Area, including large suburban areas in Virginia and Maryland, with a total population of nearly three million.

The District's 1970 population was approximately 757,000,[1] and its total land area is 61 square miles.[2] Washington is a good area for application of the model for two reasons. First, the city has had, for some time, stable legal boundaries that are not subject to change due to expansion, as is the case in many cities; this conforms to Forrester's concept of an urban system as a fixed-size area. The land area of the city is slightly less than one-half of Forrester's hypothetical city. The second reason is that sources of statistical data for the District are relatively good, because many statistical compilations treat the city as a state, thereby providing information not readily available for some other cities.

Washington has many of the problems common to the central portion of most major metropolitan areas. These include population losses to the suburbs, increasing numbers of people holding jobs in the city and commuting from the suburbs, increasing racial imbalance due to

[1] U. S. Bureau of the Census. *Census of Population and Housing: 1970, Census Tracts.* Final Report PHC(1)–226, Washington, D. C.-Md.-Va. SMSA. Washington, D. C., U. S. Government Printing Office, 1972, p. 1.

[2] U. S. Bureau of the Census. *County and City Data Book, 1962* (A Statistical Abstract Supplement). Washington, D. C., U. S. Government Printing Office, 1962, p. 52.

a higher proportion of Blacks, and relatively large numbers of families at both ends of the income stratum. For example, while the Washington metropolitan area grew rapidly between 1950 and 1970, the District's population decreased. The city's maximum census-year population was 802,000 in 1950, and it had successive counts of approximately 764,000 and 757,000 in 1960 and 1970; [3] that is, the city was a net exporter of people during the 1950–1970 period. Another trend of the 1960–1970 period was the change in the racial composition of the city from 54 percent to 70 percent Black.[4] Income discrepancies are illustrated by the fact that, in 1970, approximately 13 percent of the families had a mean income of $23,848, while another 13 percent had a mean income of only $1,960.[5]

These trends, of course, create many difficult policy problems for the city government. Following the development of the urban dynamics representation of the city, a policy question related to some of these problems is selected for analysis using the model.

URBAN DYNAMICS REPRESENTATION OF WASHINGTON, D. C.

Previous attempts to develop an urban dynamics representation of a specific urban area estimated area-specific values of only a few of the model's initial values and parameters. As discussed in Chapter 4, in developing their urban dynamics model of Houston, Porter and Henley estimated 37 initial values and parameters. Bartos and Tsai, in their work with four cities, estimated only nine initial values; and Schroeder estimated only nine parameters in developing a model of Lowell, Massachusetts. This lack of strong emphasis on the empirical estimation of model values probably is due to Forrester's opinion that empirical implementation is not of primary importance. The estimation of some 40 model values, he believes, is sufficient to achieve a model representation of a specific urban area.

An empirical implementation of the model requires the estimation

[3] U. S. Bureau of the Census. *Current Population Reports: Population Estimates and Projections*. Series p-25, No. 477. Washington, D. C., U. S. Government Printing Office, 1972, p. 3.

[4] U. S. Bureau of the Census. *Census of Population and Housing: 1960, Census Tracts*. Final Report phc(1)–166, Washington, D. C.-Md.-Va. smsa. Washington, D. C., U. S. Government Printing Office, 1962, p. 15; and U. S. Bureau of the Census. *Census of Population and Housing: 1970, Census Tracts*, p. 10.

[5] "nw Tract Is Richest in Area." *The Washington Post*: C1, C8, December 5, 1972; and U. S. Bureau of the Census. *Census of Population and Housing: 1970, Census Tracts*, p. 151.

of approximately 80 initial values and parameters. In addition, there are more than 50 tabular functions that should be based on empirical estimates. A complete empirical implementation of the model is a sizable and difficult undertaking, because data are not available to support many of the parameter estimations. For instance, the model uses the concept of perceived values to influence behavior at a number of points. The attractiveness-for-migration multiplier perceived influences migration and is a time-lagged value of the attractiveness-for-migration multiplier; the perceived multiplier's value depends on the parameter that specifies the length of the lag. Parameters such as these, however, are difficult to estimate because of the lack of suitable data. A number of similar concepts in the model call for parameter estimates that cannot be made readily from available sources of data.

In developing an urban dynamics model of Washington, D. C., a fairly complete set of model values is estimated, and selected model modifications are introduced. Development is performed in four stages, with each successive stage incorporating the results of the previous stages. Initially, area-specific values of a limited set of parameters are incorporated into the computer model, replacing those used by Forrester. The second stage extends the set of area-specific values to include a broader set. In the third stage, the model structure is extended to incorporate a limited representation of the Washington suburbs and the city-suburb interactions. In the final stage, additional changes are made in the model, which include minor modifications and empirical adjustments of some of its tabular functions. These changes are based on the analysis of model results. The model resulting from the fourth stage of development serves as the tool for analyzing a policy problem in Chapter 6.

In developing the Washington, D. C. model, area-specific values are estimated to initialize the model at the beginning of 1960, which is used to simulate the decade of the 1960s, and computed results are compared with historical data for the period. The assessment of the Washington model is made in two ways. First, by computing results for the 1960s with the model at each of its four stages of development, some light may be shed on the question of what level of effort is appropriate in developing an urban dynamics representation of a specific urban area. In other words, is the payoff from the successive stages of development worth the additional effort of producing an improved model? Second, the Washington model is evaluated on the basis of how good a representation it provides of the city in the 1960s. This evaluation is made by comparing the computed and historical values of key quantities.

Discussion of the urban dynamics model of Washington is in two parts. First, the empirical estimates and model modifications undertaken in each of the four stages of development are described. Then, the adequacy of the model representation for the support of policy studies is evaluated.

Sequential Stages of Model Development

The modifications made in each stage of model development are described hereafter, and reasons for the changes are explained. In order to provide a full, precise record of the modifications made, Appendix D lists the Fortran computer program for the model. The listing can be used to reconstruct the computer program used for each stage in the development of the Washington model.

Stage 1 – Basic area-specific parameters: The initial stage of development incorporates area-specific values of 41 model values that Forrester [6] regards as adequate to represent a specific urban area. These include nine initial values that specify the level of each of the three types of population, housing, and industry at the beginning of 1960. Six initial values that specify perceived values of multipliers related to population migration and mobility are initialized at unity, which is their normal value. Another estimated initial value specifies the perceived level of movement from the underemployed to the labor population group during 1960. Estimated parameter values include three that specify family sizes for each of the three population groups, three that specify the population density in each type of housing, three that are related to land utilization, four that are related to taxes, six that are related to the assessed values of the three types of housing and three types of industry, and six that specify the labor requirements for the three types of industry for the manager-professional and labor groups. Details on the sources of data, the basic assumptions made in relating data used to the concepts of the model, and the approach used in carrying out the estimations, as well as the 41 basic area-specific model values introduced in the first stage, are provided in Appendix C.

Stage 2 – Extended area-specific parameters: In the second stage of model development, the set of area-specific model values is extended to include 82 model values discussed in Appendix C, depending on whether data are available to support estimates. The set of model values introduced in stage 2 consists of 9 related to general-population

---

[6] Jay W. Forrester. *Urban Dynamics*. Cambridge, Mass., MIT Press, 1969, pp. 36–37.

characteristics, 14 related to population-migration behavior, 8 related to population-mobility characteristics, 20 related to the housing sector, 22 related to business/industry, 3 dealing with land utilization, and 6 related to taxes. This stage represents a full empirical implementation of the model, except that area-specific tabular functions are not estimated. Again, Appendix c provides details regarding the estimation of model values introduced in this stage.

Stage 3 – Suburb representation: The third stage introduces a representation of the suburbs into the Washington model. As pointed out in Chapter 4, the lack of suburb representation is one of the most widely criticized structural assumptions of the urban dynamics model. There are several ways of extending the model to include a representation of the suburbs. In his work with a hypothetical city, Babcock [7] coupled two urban dynamics models—one of the urban center and the other of the suburbs of a metropolitan area—to represent urban-suburban interactions. Kadanoff [8] also introduced a simple representation of both the suburban and rural areas beyond the central city in his modifications of urban dynamics. The approach adopted here is patterned after one formulated by Graham,[9] which has never been applied to a specific urban area. It gives a very aggregate representation of the suburbs and the primary impacts of the suburbs on the city and generally agrees with Forrester's basic philosophy.

Under the extension of the model to include the suburbs, a representation of the suburban labor groups and their growth over time is introduced. The four ratios in the model relating labor availability and demand are redefined in terms of the labor supply and demand in the metropolitan area. Because, in the model, these ratios influence activities such as business/industry growth and population migration, defining them on the basis of a metropolitan area is indicative of the central city being modeled in the context of its metropolitan area. In more specific terms, representation of the suburbs takes the following form. First, projected estimates of the three labor groups in the metropolitan area surrounding the city are introduced as exogenous inputs. These labor groups are denoted as manager-professional surrounding,

[7] Daniel L. Babcock. "Analysis and Improvement of a Dynamic Urban Model." Doctoral Dissertation. Los Angeles, University of California, 1970, pp. 219–220.

[8] Leo P. Kadanoff. "A Modified Forrester Model of the United States as a Group of Metropolitan Areas." In: *Urban Dynamics: Extensions and Reflections.* Edited by Kan Chen. San Francisco, San Francisco Press, 1972, p. 105.

[9] Alan K. Graham. "Modeling City-Suburb Interactions." *IEEE Transactions on Systems, Man, and Cybernetics,* SMC-2:157–158, April 1972.

MPS, labor surrounding, LS, and underemployed surrounding, US. The manager/job ratio for time K is defined in the original model as

$$MR(K) = MP(K)/MJ(K)$$

where

MR = manager/job ratio, dimensionless
MP = manager-professional, men
MJ = manager jobs, men.[10]

In the modified model, the manager/job ratio is redefined as

$$MR(K) = (MPS + MP(K))/(MPS + MJ(K))$$

where

MR   = manager/job ratio, dimensionless
MP   = manager-professional, men
MJ   = manager jobs, men
MPS = manager-professional surrounding, men.

MPS represents the manager-professional surrounding workers at time K, although it does not carry an explicit subscript as do the other quantities. The labor/job ratio, LR, the underemployed/job ratio, UR, and the labor/job ratio perceived, LRP, are redefined similarly to reflect the metropolitan area labor supply. Redefining these ratios recognizes the nature of the metropolitan area labor force and is intended to reduce sudden model responses to changes in the demand for labor within the city.

Redefining labor-force ratios in this way has an influence on a number of model relationships. The nature of these influences is seen by examining the model relationships in which the manager/job ratio, MR, has a direct effect. MR appears in model relationships that determine the manager arrival job multiplier, MAJM, the manager supply multiplier, MSM, and the enterprise manager/job multiplier, EMM. For example, the relationship that determines MAJM is

MAJM(K) = TABLE(MAJMT,MR(K),0,2.,.25)
DATA MAJMT /2.7,2.6,2.4,2.,1.,.4,.2,.1,.05/.[11]

MAJMT is expressed as a tabular function, in which the ratio MR is the

---

[10] Forrester. *Urban Dynamics,* p. 157.
[11] *Ibid.,* p. 167.

independent variable. This tabular function states that MAJM values of 2.7, 2.6,....,0.05 correspond to MR values of 0, 0.25,....,2.0; and, if necessary, an interpolation is made in the table to determine an intermediate value of MAJM corresponding to a specified value of MR. Appendix B fully discusses tabular functions.

In the model, MAJM is a key factor in determining the manager arrival multiplier, MAM, which governs manager-professional migration. The values of MSM and EMM also are formulated in terms of tabular functions, with MR as the independent variable. Through these quantities, MR influences population mobility and development of new business/industry. The four labor-force ratios that are redefined to reflect metropolitan area values are used directly in relationships that determine 11 other model quantities; these quantities, in turn, influence migration, mobility, and the building of new business/industry units.

Estimates of the suburban labor force for 1960 are developed from census data that give the labor force by occupational categories. Census occupations are grouped into the three labor components used in the urban dynamics model. The manager-professional group corresponds to two census categories: professional, technical, and kindred workers; and managers, officials, and proprietors. The labor group includes the census categories of clerical, sales, craftsmen and foremen, operatives, household workers, and service workers. The underemployed group includes the laborer category plus the unemployed. This correspondence between the model's labor components and census occupations was used in estimating model values in Appendix C, which depicts 1960 estimates for labor levels in the Washington Standard Metropolitan Statistical Area, excluding the District of Columbia, as 181,304, 300,612, and 21,128 for the manager-professional, labor, and underemployed worker groups, respectively. An annual growth rate for the three surrounding labor components is taken at 2.2 percent, which is the projected growth rate given by the National Planning Association through 1985.[12]

In the representation of the suburbs for the Washington model, only the labor force is represented. The concepts of this formulation could be extended to include a representation of suburban population and housing as well. The labor force is selected as the most essential component for inclusion, because it has a much greater influence than

[12] National Planning Association. *Economic and Demographic Projections for States and Metropolitan Areas: Projections to 1975, 1980, and 1985 of Population, Income, and Industry Employment.* Report No. 68-R-1. Washington, D. C., January 1969, p. S-149.

population or housing on other activities represented in the model. In fact, the labor force includes that portion of the suburban population which contributes most in economic terms.

As mentioned earlier, the four labor-force ratios that are redefined to reflect metropolitan area values directly influence the computation of 11 model quantities, which, in turn, influence population migration, population mobility, and construction of housing and business/industry units. The introduction of suburban housing and population would have a less pervasive influence. For instance, including suburban housing would call for redefining the three ratios that reflect the availability of each type of housing. These ratios directly influence the computation of only six model quantities, and their influence is confined primarily to determining the level of construction for premium and worker housing. Representation of suburban population would have less influence than the introduction of housing, because the labor-force representation already subsumes economic and some other influences of the suburban population. Therefore, if the representation of the suburbs is extended, it would be desirable next to introduce a representation of suburban housing. Because the labor force is potentially more important in improving the overall model representation, however, and because there is an interest in limiting the number of model modifications, the representation of suburban housing is not included.

In his experimentation with representation of the suburbs by introducing a representation of the suburban labor force for a hypothetical city, Graham [13] judged it a significant improvement in terms of introducing into the model the influences of the suburban environment on the city. As Graham indicates, the concept lends itself to an explicit representation of employment commuting, which may be important in many policy problems.

Assessment of stages 1, 2, and 3: Before undertaking the final stage of model development, the first three stages are assessed. This examination indicates how well model development is progressing in terms of representing Washington, D. C. during the selected test period of the 1960s. It also indicates whether a fourth stage of development is desirable and reveals areas of possible improvement.

In the assessment, a comparison of the model with the city being modeled is performed by comparing computed model results for three basic time series with historical data. The quantities chosen for comparison represent the three principal subsystems of the model—popula-

---

[13] Graham. "Modeling City-Suburb Interactions," pp. 157–158.

tion, housing, and industry. Although many other model quantities could be compared with historical data, these three provide a comprehensive measure of the model's representation of Washington during the 1960s.

To facilitate the comparison, a statistical measure developed by Theil [14] is adopted. In his approach, the values of a time series are expressed in terms of the percent which they deviate from the initial value of the series. For example, the series 100, 95, 117, 82 is expressed as 0, -5, 17, -18. Given pairs of values, (C_i, A_i), for computed and actual time series expressed in terms of the percent which they deviate from an initial true value, Theil's inequality coefficient U is computed as

$$U = (\sum_i (C_i - A_i)^2 / \sum_i A_i^2)^{\frac{1}{2}}.$$

U provides a ratio of the root mean square error for the computed series and the root mean square error associated with a no-change extrapolation from the initial actual value. From inspection, it is clear that the $U = 0$ if, and only if, $C_i = A_i$ for all i, and $U = 1$ when the computed series gives the same root mean square error as an assumption of no-change from the initial value of the series. The interpretation of $U = 0.62$, for example, is that the computed result contains 62 percent of the error that would have been observed if the no-change extrapolation had been made. The measure U has no upper bound, so its range extends to computed projections that are much worse than the no-change assumption.

There are no widely accepted techniques for establishing the goodness of fit of the results of a simulation model with historical data, and all too often social scientists have restricted themselves to graphical techniques of comparison. Theil's U coefficient has appeal over graphical methods because it provides a quantitative measure, and the measure has a degree of intuitive appeal because it is defined relative to an assumption of no-change. Of course, the U coefficient has not been widely used with policy-oriented models, so there are no standards of model acceptability for policy purposes in terms of U coefficients. Also, a sampling distribution apparently has not been derived for the U statistic. As a general standard, however, it might be expected that a model acceptable for policymaking will represent a set of key quantities over a historical test period with a smaller error than results from

[14] Henri Theil. *Applied Economic Forecasting.* Amsterdam, North-Holland Publ., 1966, pp. 26–29.

a no-change assumption. With this general notion of an acceptable model, results produced by the first three stages of the urban dynamics model of Washington are examined. U coefficients must be interpreted carefully, because low coefficient values for a number of key model quantities may occur by chance or from compensating errors; therefore, they should not be taken as conclusive evidence that the model is an adequate representation.

Tables 3, 4, and 5 represent comparisons of computed results from the first three stages of the Washington model and observed results for population, housing, and employment. Total population, in Table 3, is a summary output from the model's labor subsystem, because population is computed by summing the product of each labor-group level and its family-size parameter. The housing levels presented in Table 4

TABLE 3   Comparison of Computed Estimates from Stages 1, 2, and 3 of Washington Model and Historical Estimates for 1960–1970: Population

| Year | Computed Population Estimates | | | Historical Population Estimate (thousands) |
	Stage 1 Model (thousands)	Stage 2 Model (thousands)	Stage 3 Model (thousands)	
1960	764	764	764	763
1961	813	780	791	770
1962	859	726	751	778
1963	875	721	762	789
1964	877	702	744	797
1965	870	694	743	798
1966	858	685	732	794
1967	844	679	725	791
1968	829	674	717	785
1969	815	670	710	770
1970	803	666	703	759

U coefficients: Stage 1 = 2.68
Stage 2 = 3.84
Stage 3 = 2.19

Source: Historical population estimates for July 1 of each year were obtained from the U.S. Bureau of the Census, *Statistical Abstract of the United States*, editions 87, 91, 92, 93, and 94, Washington, D. C., U. S. Government Printing Office, 1966, 1970, 1971, 1972, and 1973. The July 1 estimates for pairs of successive years were averaged to obtain estimates for the beginning of each year.

TABLE 4 Comparison of Computed Estimates from Stages 1, 2, and 3 of Washington Model and Historical Estimates for 1960–1970: Housing

Year	Computed Housing Estimates			Historical Housing Estimate (thousands)
	Stage 1 Model (thousands)	Stage 2 Model (thousands)	Stage 3 Model (thousands)	
1960	263	263	263	263
1961	259	247	247	264
1962	258	246	246	265
1963	257	244	244	266
1964	256	242	243	269
1965	255	240	241	273
1966	254	237	239	276
1967	253	235	237	278
1968	252	232	235	279
1969	250	229	233	280
1970	248	227	231	280

U coefficients: Stage 1 = 1.74
Stage 2 = 3.08
Stage 3 = 2.93

Source: Historical housing estimates were obtained by assuming that the net increase in units per year is distributed in the same way as the net units authorized. Net housing units authorized each year were obtained from the District of Columbia, Office of Assistant to the Mayor for Housing Programs, *Housing Construction and Demolition, Compilation of Permit Data, 1960–1972*, Washington, D. C., December 1972, p. 5. The number of units as of the beginning of 1960 and the net increase during the 1960s were obtained from U. S. Bureau of the Census, *1970 Census of Housing: Components of Inventory Change*, HC(4)–16, Washington, D. C.-Md.-Va. SMSA, Washington, D. C., U. S. Government Printing Office, 1973, p. 9.

are the sum of the three classes of housing represented in the urban dynamics housing subsystem. In Table 5, total employment estimates of the city's resident population are compared. Employment is computed in the model's business/industry subsystem and is taken as a measure of the level of business/industry activity projected by the model. In addition to providing an overall indicator of the quality of the model's representation of the city, historical values of these three quantities are estimated readily from available data sources.

In the comparisons presented in Tables 3, 4, and 5, *U* coefficients are provided for the computed time series. Two general conclusions

TABLE 5 Comparison of Computed Estimates from Stages 1, 2, and 3 of Washington Model and Historical Estimates for 1960–1970: Employment

Year	Computed Employment Estimates			Historical Employment Estimate (thousands)
	Stage 1 Model (thousands)	Stage 2 Model (thousands)	Stage 3 Model (thousands)	
1960	381	378	390	325
1961	373	363	368	328
1962	363	359	357	336
1963	352	356	348	341
1964	341	352	340	343
1965	330	348	332	352
1966	320	345	326	358
1967	310	342	321	365
1968	299	340	318	371
1969	289	337	314	361
1970	278	335	311	356

U coefficients: Stage 1 = 1.67
Stage 2 = 0.74
Stage 3 = 1.20

Source: Historical employment estimates for each year were obtained from U. S. Bureau of Labor Statistics, *Employment and Earnings: States and Local Areas: 1939–1971*, Bulletin 1370-9, Washington, D. C., U. S. Government Printing Office, 1972, pp. 133–135. These estimates, reduced by Federal Government employment of nonresidents, were obtained from Metropolitan Washington Council of Governments, *Statistics—Washington Metropolitan Area*, Washington, D. C., January 1968; and U. S. Bureau of the Census, *County Business Patterns, District of Columbia*, CBP-68-10, CBP-69-10, and CBP-70-10, Washington, D. C., U. S. Government Printing Office, 1969, 1970, and 1971.

emerge from these comparisons. First, there is little to choose from among the three stages of development—all are equally bad. Overall, the computed projections have significantly more errors than a no-change extrapolation of the three variables compared. Second, there is a clear need to extend model development to a fourth stage. Additional development efforts should attempt to explain why the stage 2 and stage 3 development efforts show no improvement over stage 1. Furthermore, the fourth-stage effort should attempt to bring the development of the Washington model to a point where it is potentially useful in the study of policy.

From these comparisons, an obvious aspect to be examined in the fourth stage of development is that the initial levels of employment in all three stages are significantly higher than the 1960 historical employment level. This contrasts with the 1960 computed levels for population and housing, which essentially agree with historical values. The employment series actually has relatively better U coefficients than the population and housing projections, but the employment projections are far from satisfying. Not only are the U coefficient values poor, but there is a suspicion that something is amiss in the model's initialization process.

This experience with the Washington model does not support the idea expressed by Forrester, Porter and Henley, and others that an urban dynamics model of a specific area can be developed by providing area-specific values of 40 or fewer parameters and initial values. Although the stage 2 and stage 3 models contain more area-specific values than other attempts to represent a specific area with the model, the representation is judged to be poor. It must be remembered, however, that the stage 3 model makes additional assumptions in introducing a representation of the suburbs, which makes it impossible to make a clear comparison of stage 3 with stages 1 and 2. The conclusion must be that further development is required to have an urban area model representation that is potentially useful in policymaking.

Stage 4: Other modifications for final Washington, D. C. model: In the fourth stage, additional model modifications and adjustments are made as a result of an analysis of model relationships and computed results for the test period of the 1960s. Can the model developed in the first three stages be improved by minor modifications and adjustments so that it is a reasonably good representation of Washington?

The modifications made in stage 4 fall into four groups. The first group is related to land use, which exerts a critical influence on the construction of housing and industry and the demolition of housing in the model. The second group of changes modifies the household-size parameters so they can vary over time rather than having to remain fixed, as in Forrester's formulation. The third group makes minor modifications to the relationships that influence migration in the model. The final changes adjust several tabular functions to make them reflect the specific urban area being represented.

1. LAND USE: The modifications related to land use include changing the land-use parameters for housing and industry to allow them to vary over time to reflect the increase in density; modifying construction

multipliers for housing and industry to eliminate the influence of land use and taxes; and reducing the influence of land use on the demolition of housing.

The model's two land-use parameters are the land per productive unit, LPP, and the land per house, LPH. Because Washington is a mature city, in that most of its land is used, its growth is accommodated by increased density of land use. To reflect this, LPP and LPH are made variable over time. The parameter values are based on data which the Metropolitan Washington Council of Governments [15] used in its empiric model of Washington. Based on these data, the average land per housing unit will decrease from 0.088 acres per unit in 1960, to 0.082 in 1970, to 0.079 in 1975, and continue at the 1975 rate through 1990. The LPP parameter is estimated to change from 0.37 acres per business/ industry unit in 1960, to 0.295 in 1970, and to remain constant thereafter.

The second change related to land use modifies the computation of the construction multipliers PHM (premium housing), WHM (worker housing), and EM (business enterprises). The change actually involves the influence of taxes, as well as land use, on these three multipliers. The role of these multipliers is to modify the normal rates of construction for the type of unit to which they apply. Also, each construction multiplier determines the value of an obsolescence or decline multiplier that governs the downward filter rate for the type of unit it represents. Each decline multiplier is inversely proportional to the corresponding construction multiplier. The two housing construction multipliers are formulated as the product of six factors, and the business enterprise multiplier is the product of five factors. Among the factors entering into the computation of each multiplier is one reflecting the influence of the fraction of the city's occupied land and one reflecting the tax rate.[16]

Under this formulation, if a high proportion of the city's land is occupied or if taxes are high, a constriction of construction activity results. Because the decline multipliers are inversely related to the construction multipliers, these conditions also cause an acceleration in the decline of units. Two objections to this formulation have been discussed by Babcock. First, the factors for the proportion of occupied land and for taxes cause unwarranted restrictions in the level of construction. For example, Babcock found that, when the land fraction

[15] Metropolitan Washington Council of Governments. "COG Estimates Derived from Local Forecasts." Empiric Alt. 6.2. Washington, D. C., March 1974, p. 1. Mimeographed.

[16] Forrester. *Urban Dynamics*, pp. 172, 181, 192.

occupied approaches 0.8, a slow growth rate near equilibrium occurs. This does not represent a mature city like Washington, where the land fraction occupied is more than 90 percent as measured in the model.

The second objection is to the assumption implicit in the decline multipliers that a shortage of land and high taxes accelerate the decline of housing and industry. Babcock observed that areas such as the Georgetown section of Washington contradict this assumption. He found no real empirical evidence to support the idea that high land occupancy or taxes either retards or accelerates construction or filtering, and regards it as prudent to eliminate the land-use and tax factors from the multiplier equations. In his test of this change with an urban dynamics model of a hypothetical city, Babcock [17] found the change produced a dramatic improvement in the balance of housing, population, and employment. Eliminating the land-use and tax factors from the three construction multipliers in the Washington model produced similar results.

The third change related to land use adjusts the relationship between the fraction of the city's occupied land and the rate of housing demolition. In the model, only underemployed-level housing units are lost through demolition; and the number of demolitions each year is determined by applying a normal demolition rate, which is adjusted upward or downward by a multiplier. One of the two factors that determine the value of this adjusting multiplier is the slum housing land multiplier, SHLM, which is a function of the occupied land fraction. Forrester's tabular function, which specifies the relationship between SHLM and the land occupied fraction, sets $SHLM = 1.0$ when the fraction of occupied land is 0.8 and $SHLM = 2.2$ when the fraction occupied is 0.95.[18] This causes an excessive number of housing demolitions in the Washington model, because the fraction of occupied land in 1960 was approximately 0.95 and, hence, demolitions were occurring at 2.2 times the normal rate. Because the estimated demolition rate parameter used to initialize the model for 1960 is assumed to be the normal rate, it is necessary that $SHLM = 1.0$ when the fraction of land occupied is 0.95. To achieve this, Forrester's slum housing land multiplier tabular function, SHLMT, is modified. The same general form of the functional relationship used by Forrester is retained. This change, when incorporated into the Washington model, reduces the number of demolitions to approximately the level experienced during the 1960s.

[17] Babcock. "Analysis and Improvement of a Dynamic Urban Model," pp. 96–97, 105–108, 135–137.

[18] Forrester. *Urban Dynamics*, pp. 188–189.

2. HOUSEHOLD SIZE: The second group of modifications is related to the three household-size parameters PHPD, WHPD, and UHPD, which specify the average number of persons living in premium-, worker-, and under-employed-level housing, respectively. There is a need for these parameters to vary over time rather than to remain fixed, as they are in Forrester's model. This need is evidenced by the 1970 census data, which indicates that the average household size throughout the United States declined during the 1960s and that the decline was even greater in metropolitan Washington. Data from the Metropolitan Washington Council of Governments' empiric model,[19] together with comparisons of the 1960 and 1970 census data for Washington,[20] are used to estimate the decline in household size from 1960 to 1980. For instance, the premium housing density parameter is initialized at 3.05 persons per household in 1960 and gradually reduced each year to 2.85 in 1970, 2.65 in 1980, and held constant thereafter. The WHPD and UHPD parameters are reduced in the same way over time.

3. MIGRATION: The third set of changes in this stage of model development deals with minor modifications to migration relationships. The first of these is related to the model equation of underemployed in-migration or underemployed arrivals. In Forrester's model,

$$UA(K) = (U(K) + L(K)) * UAN * AMMP(K)$$

where

UA   = underemployed arrivals, men/year
U   = underemployed, men
L   = labor, men
UAN = underemployed arrivals normal, fraction/year
AMMP = attractiveness-for-migration multiplier perceived, dimension-
       less.[21]

Underemployed arrivals are represented as a fraction of the sum of the current underemployed and labor groups, with the fraction adjusted by an attractiveness multiplier. The relationship for underemployed arrivals is different in one aspect of its structure from the comparable relationships for manager and labor arrivals. Whereas manager and

[19] Metropolitan Washington Council of Governments. "COG Estimates," p. 2.
[20] U. S. Bureau of the Census. *General Demographic Trends for Metropolitan Areas, 1960 to 1970.* Final Report PHC(2)–10. Washington, D. C., U. S. Government Printing Office, 1971, pp. 5, 10.
[21] Forrester. *Urban Dynamics,* p. 135.

labor arrivals are expressed as a fraction of their own group level, the underemployed arrivals depend on the sum of the current level of underemployed and labor groups. Attention initially focused on this relationship, because the underemployed arrivals parameter, UAN, was estimated in relation to the size of the underemployed population level. This resulted in excessive underemployed in-migration, because the parameter was being applied to the sum of the two groups, which is more than eight times the size of the underemployed group. It was necessary either to scale the UAN parameter or to modify the relationship. It was decided to modify the relationship by making the underemployed arrivals depend only on the size of the underemployed group. Forrester presents no particular reason why the structure of the relationship governing underemployed in-migration should be different; with the modification, the three relationships have the same structure.

The other aspect of the changes related to migration deals with mobility between classes. The urban dynamics model represents interclass mobility from the labor group upward to the manager and downward to the underemployed groups. Also, mobility of the underemployed to the labor group is represented.[22] Forrester's values of the parameters that govern interclass mobility were used in the previous stages of the Washington model because data sources for estimating area-specific parameter values were not available. The rates for labor-class mobility, however, both upward and downward, produce excessive flows from labor to manager and underemployed groups; this, in turn, causes very high levels of in-migration and out-migration. Babcock made the same observation, noting that Forrester's mobility parameters produced excessive interclass flows from the labor group, primarily because the group is several times the size of the other two groups. To deal with this, the parameters governing the mobility of the labor class were reduced to half the values Forrester used. Although this adjustment is arbitrary, in the same sense that Forrester's values are arbitrary, it is instrumental in reducing migration in the model to a level that corresponds more closely to that observed in the 1960s. Incorporating this change into the Washington model involves reducing the values of the LMN parameters and the values of the LLFT tabular function by one-half.

4. AREA-SPECIFIC VALUES: The final set of changes adjusts five tabular functions to reflect area-specific values. These fall into two groups. The first group involves the adjustment of two tabular functions to corre-

---

[22] *Ibid.*, pp. 152–154.

spond more closely to observed conditions in Washington in 1960. The second group involves three tabular functions that use ratios of the model's population groups as independent variables, and are modified so they reflect the range of ratios between population groups in Washington rather than in Forrester's hypothetical city.

The first of these groups involves modifying the underemployed/labor job ratio table, ULJRT, and the enterprise growth multiplier table, EGMT. The ULJRT table determines ULJR according to the relationships

$$ULJR(K) = TABLE \ (ULJRT, LR(K),.0,2.,.5)$$
$$DATA \ ULJRT/1.15, .8, .5, .25, .1/$$

where

ULJR   = underemployed/labor job ratio, dimensionless
ULJRT = underemployed/labor job-ratio table
LR   = labor/job ratio, dimensionless.[23]

These relationships indicate that the underemployed/labor job ratio, ULJR, is a function of the labor/job ratio, LR, which is the ratio of labor workers to labor jobs. As the tabular function indicates, ULJR takes on the values $1.15, 0.8, \ldots, 0.1$ corresponding to values of LR of $0.0, 0.5, \ldots, 2.0$, respectively. The number of jobs for the underemployed group is computed as a function of the number of jobs for the labor group by multiplying the quantity ULJR by the number of labor jobs. The problem in the Washington model is that the values of ULJR are too high, resulting in too many underemployed jobs. This is the reason for the wide discrepancy noted in the first three stages of model development between the computed and observed levels of employment for 1960. To correct this problem, the values of the table, ULJRT, are scaled down so a value of LR of unity results in ULJR$=0.09$, which corresponds to the 1960 ratio of underemployed to labor jobs. In adjusting ULJRT, Forrester's functional form is retained, and values are scaled down. The table, EGMT, which governs the rate of new enterprise growth, is adjusted in the same way, because its values were significantly different from those observed for 1960.

A second group of tabular functions was modified because of the dependency on ratios between population groups. One of these is the manager arrival population multiplier, MAPM, which is a function of the ratio of the manager population to the sum of the labor and underemployed populations. MAPM is one of the factors in determining

[23] *Ibid.*, p. 209.

the multiplier for manager migration. The other two tabular functions determine values of the worker housing underemployed multiplier, WHUM, and the labor arrival underemployed multiplier, LAUM, both of which are a function of the ratio of the labor and underemployed population groups, LUR. WHUM is one of the factors in determining the worker housing multiplier, which regulates construction, and LAUM is a factor in determining the labor migration multiplier. The adjustment to WHUM illustrates the problem. In Forrester's model, LUR, the ratio of the labor to the underemployed population group, is defined with a range of 0 to 5. For the Washington model, however, LUR=7.3 for 1960, which is outside the defined range and causes WHUM to be set at the maximum possible value. This is corrected by redefining the range of LUR and retaining Forrester's values for the tabular function table, WHUMT. Similar modifications were made to the equations for MAPM and LAUM.

As the results discussed hereafter indicate, the fourth stage modifications significantly improve the model with respect to the three quantities examined earlier. These modifications were selected through the analysis of model relationships as well as through computed results. For the most part, they are minor empirical adjustments or minor alterations of model relationships. Although arguments are advanced that provide general justifications for most of the modifications, other modifications might provide as much or more improvement. This set of modifications, however, brings the model to a state of development wherein it can support the analysis of an illustrative policy problem and to a point whereat some insight can be gained into the difficulties inherent in significantly improving the Washington model over the fourth stage of development.

Evaluation of Washington, D. C. Model

As observed earlier, experience gained through the development of the Washington model does not support the contention by Forrester and others that a useful urban dynamics model of a city can be developed by incorporating approximately 40 area-specific values. No pattern of gradual improvement is apparent in the first three stages of development. Perhaps if some of the modifications introduced in the fourth stage had been made first, there would have been a pattern of improvement in the first three stages. Although this is an interesting conjecture, the emphasis is on examining the final result of the four stages of development in order to understand the implications of the model's use in policy studies of a specific urban area. The first part of the examination assesses the model that resulted from the fourth stage of development. The second part assesses the potential for improvement of the Washington model by examining the difficulties inherent in making significant further improvements.

Assessment of final model representation for 1960–1970: Table 6 presents a comparison of computed results from the fourth stage of the Washington model with historical results. The same three quantities as examined for previous stages of development—population, housing, and employment—are shown. As measured by Theil's U coefficient, of the three quantities compared, a substantial improvement is shown over the preceding stages. While the computed population estimates for the comparison period show a root mean square error more than twice that of a no-change extrapolation from 1960, the computed esti-

TABLE 6   Comparison of Computed Estimates from Stage 4 of Washington Model and Historical Estimates

Year	Population		Housing		Employment	
	Computed Estimate (thousands)	Historical Estimate (thousands)	Computed Estimate (thousands)	Historical Estimate (thousands)	Computed Estimate (thousands)	Historical Estimate (thousands)
1960	763	763	263	263	324	325
1961	755	770	265	264	325	328
1962	747	778	268	265	328	336
1963	739	789	270	266	331	341
1964	734	797	272	269	335	343
1965	730	798	273	273	339	352
1966	727	794	275	276	344	358
1967	726	791	276	278	349	365
1968	727	785	277	279	354	371
1969	728	770	279	280	358	361
1970	730	759	280	280	363	356

U coefficients: Population $= 2.19$
Housing $= 0.15$
Employment $= 0.37$

Source: See Tables 3, 4, and 5.

mates for housing and employment conform fairly closely to the observed estimates. Keeping this overall fourth-stage performance of the model in mind, it is useful to examine the three model subsystems in more detail.

As noted, results from the model subsystem representing population are poor; and an examination of the results offers no clear, simple explanation. The model generates 95,000 net births during the 1960–1969 period, which corresponds reasonably well to the observed estimate of 93,000. For the same period, the model computed a net migration loss of 125,000, which corresponds to an observed loss of 100,000.[24] Not only is the computed net migration loss 25 percent too high, but the model estimates that 65 percent of the loss would be in the first half of the decade, whereas the higher loss should be in the latter half. Also, the model's estimate that nearly 40 percent of the net migration loss occurs in the underemployed group is suspect, because that group represents only approximately 12 percent of the city's population. The model computes the distribution of the 1970 population among the three population groups as 27 percent manager-professional, 64 percent labor, and 9 percent underemployed. This corresponds reasonably well to the estimates of 22, 68, and 10 percent, respectively, from 1970 census data.[25]

Tracking Washington population over the decade of the 1960s is an exacting test for any model. As shown in the historical population estimates used in the comparative tables, the population increased from 763,000 in 1960 to 798,000 in 1965 and then declined sharply to 759,000 by the end of the decade. There is a possibility of error, however, in the Bureau of the Census figures for the years between the decennial censuses of 1960 and 1970. These figures are estimates, and the methodology used for obtaining them has been questioned. The Bureau of the Census has conceded that there are special difficulties in preparing population estimates for the District of Columbia, because the city is the densely settled core of a large metropolitan area and may have a population close to its practical maximum. This is supported by the fact that Washington had its maximum census-year population of 802,000 in 1950, followed by counts of 764,000 and 757,000 in 1960 and 1970, respectively.[26] During the 1960s, the Bureau initially applied to the District the method used to compile state estimates for the years

[24] U. S. Bureau of the Census. *General Demographic Trends*, p. 8.

[25] U. S. Bureau of the Census. *Census of Population and Housing: 1970, Census Tracts*, p. 101.

[26] U. S. Bureau of the Census. *Current Population Reports: Population Estimates and Projections*, p. 3.

between the decennial censuses, but abandoned this as unsuitable. A combination of two other estimating methods [27] was deemed more favorable. All of this indicates the possibility of error in the estimates used in the comparison for the years 1961–1969. Even in the event of substantial error in the historical estimates for these years, however, the computed estimates would still be poor and would probably have a U coefficient value in excess of 1.

The fourth-stage model projects the longer term population trends more accurately than it tracks the population during the 1960s. This is based on a comparison of the model's projections with those of the Council of Governments' empiric model of the Washington metropolitan area. The urban dynamics model of Washington estimates its population as 774,000 in 1980 and 799,000 in 1985, compared to the empiric estimates of 771,000 for 1980 and approximately 776,000 for 1985,[28] and these are in close agreement. There are, of course, any number of population projections that may be used for comparison, and many will differ widely from the estimates of the urban dynamics Washington model. The empiric estimates are interesting, because they are produced by a fairly well-developed urban model.

The model computations of the yearly housing inventory during the 1960s are reasonably close. The root mean error is only 15 percent of the error in a no-change extrapolation from 1960. Computed values of the two general components of housing inventory change are also close to the observed values. According to the model, the total housing units constructed during the 1960–1969 period was 46,000. This compares closely to the observed estimate of 47,000 units added to the inventory, although nearly 7 percent of these were conversions and gains by means not represented by the model. During this period, the model computations showed 28,000 units lost through demolition, compared to an observed loss of 29,000 units.[29] Again, the computed and observed losses are not exactly comparable, because the model represents only the loss of units through demolition, while the observed loss includes units lost through mergers and other means. Over the longer term, the model estimates of housing units in the city are 296,000 units in 1980 and 308,000 in 1985. This compares reasonably well with the empiric model

[27] U. S. Bureau of the Census. *Current Population Reports: Estimates of the Population of States: July 1, 1967*. Series P-25, No. 414. Washington, D. C., U. S. Government Printing Office, January 28, 1969, p. 5.

[28] Metropolitan Washington Council of Governments. "COG Estimates," p. 1.

[29] U. S. Bureau of the Census. *1970 Census of Housing: Components of Inventory Change*. Report HC(4)–16, Washington, D. C.-Md.-Va. SMSA. Washington, D. C., U. S. Government Printing Office, 1973, p. 9.

projections of 289,000 units in 1980 and approximately 291,000 in 1985.[30]

Employment, which is the measure adopted for the model's business/industry subsystem, is represented only moderately well by the model. The projection contains more than one-third of the error in a no-change extrapolation. The distribution of 1970 employment is computed by the model as 25, 68, and 7 percent, respectively, in the manager-professional, labor, and underemployed job levels. This corresponds closely to the estimated distribution from the 1970 census [31] of 26, 69, and 5 percent, respectively, in the three employment levels. Because the Washington model reflects only the employment of the city's population, and the empiric estimates cover total employment, comparison of the longer term employment estimates with estimates from the empiric model is not possible.

The general conclusion regarding the Washington model is that it may be of some use in the analysis of policy-related questions, but it is far from being a trustworthy tool for use with policy problems. A substantial further improvement is needed, as is apparent in the population estimates for the 1960s. The need for improvement, however, goes beyond the population subsystem itself. Equally as disappointing as the population estimates for the 1960s is the seeming lack of sensitivity of other model subsystems to these poor population estimates. This lack of sensitivity again raises the suspicion that the interrelationships among the three primary model subsystems are not well represented by the model.

Potential for improvement: In view of this general conclusion, are further improvements possible in the model? One of the primary tasks that this would require is an estimate of empirical values for the model's tabular functions, which is unavoidable in light of their frequent use. More than 50 tabular functions appear, so a high proportion of the model equations involve such functions. Tabular functions also are important because of their frequent use in the model representation of the interrelationships among model subsystems. Typically, a tabular function is used to represent the influence of housing or job availability on population. The role of tabular functions and the work involved in estimating values for them can be seen by examining the model relationships that govern a particular

[30] Metropolitan Washington Council of Governments. "cog Estimates," p. 1.
[31] U. S. Bureau of the Census. *Census of Population and Housing: 1970, Census Tracts,* p. 101.

kind of behavior. For this purpose, the relationships representing the in-migration behavior of the manager-professional group are examined.

In the urban dynamics model, in-migration of manager-professionals is computed each year as a function of the manager-professional population level, a normal migration rate, and the perceived value of a manager arrival multiplier. In equation form,

$$MA(K) = MAN*MP(K)*MAMP(K),$$

where

MA   = manager arrivals, men/year
MAN   = manager arrivals normal, fraction/year
MP   = manager-professional, men
MAMP = manager arrival multiplier perceived, dimensionless.[32]

The manager arrival multiplier perceived, MAMP, is a time-delayed value of the manager arrival multiplier, MAM, to allow for the perception time delay of arriving manager-professional persons in perceiving true conditions in the city. For the purpose at hand, the multiplier, MAM, is the quantity of most interest.

MAM is the product of four factors that indicate conditions in the city and a factor for use in sensitivity testing. The model relationships determining these four factors and MAM are

MAJM(K) = TABLE(MAJMT,MR(K),.0,2.,.25)
DATA MAJMT/2.7,2.6,2.4,2.,1.,.4,.2,.1,.05/
MAPM(K) = TABLE(MAPMT,MPR(K),.0,.1,.02)
DATA MAPMT/.3,.7,1.,1.2,1.3,1.3/
MATM(K) = TABLE(MATMT,1.44*ALOG(TR(K)),−2.,4.,2.)
DATA MATMT/1.4,1.,.7,.3/
MAHM(K) = TABLE(MAHMT,MHR(K),.0,3.,.5)
DATA MAHMT/1.3,1.2,1.,.5,.2,.1,.05/
MAM(K) = MAJM(K)*MAPM(K)*MATM(K)*MAHM(K)*MAF,

where

MAJM   = manager arrival job multiplier, dimensionless
MAJMT = manager arrival job multiplier table
MR   = manager/job ratio, dimensionless
MAPM   = manager arrival population multiplier, dimensionless

---

[32] Forrester. *Urban Dynamics,* p. 166.

MAPMT = manager arrival population multiplier table
MPR = manager/population ratio, dimensionless
MATM = manager arrival tax multiplier, dimensionless
MATMT = manager arrival tax multiplier table
TR = tax ratio, dimensionless
MAHM = manager arrival housing multiplier, dimensionless
MAHMT = manager arrival housing multiplier table
MHR = manager/housing ratio, dimensionless
MAM = manager arrival multiplier, dimensionless
MAF = manager arrival factor, dimensionless.[33]

Each of the four factors is computed by a tabular function relationship in which a measure of the condition influencing migration appears as the independent variable. For instance, in computing the housing multiplier, MAHM, the ratio of the manager population's demand for housing and the capacity of the available premium housing, MHR, appears as the independent variable. If MHR is unity, indicating a balance of demand and supply for manager housing, then MAHM = 1. If MHR is less than 1, then MAHM assumes a value greater than 1, which encourages in-migration. Conversely, if MHR is greater than 1, there is a shortage of housing, and MAHM takes on a value less than 1, which discourages in-migration. The other three multipliers that enter into the equation for MAM are determined in a similar manner.

The problems inherent in estimating empirical values for model relationships, such as the one for MAM, are considerable. They include obtaining sufficient data, as well as computing statistical estimates given the data. Although the comparison is only a general one, an idea of the difficulty of the estimation problem is seen by comparing it with a linear regression estimation problem. Ignoring MAF, Forrester's equation for MAM states that,

$$\text{MAM}(\text{K}) = \text{MAJM}(\text{K}) * \text{MAPM}(\text{K}) * \text{MATM}(\text{K}) * \text{MAHM}(\text{K}).$$

The equation may be transformed into

$$\log \text{MAM}(\text{K}) = \log \text{MAJM}(\text{K}) + \log \text{MAPM}(\text{K}) \\ + \log \text{MATM}(\text{K}) + \log \text{MAHM}(\text{K}).$$

By using these tabular function relationships, the equation for MAM becomes

[33] *Ibid.*, pp. 166–169.

$$\log \text{MAM}(\text{K}) = \log t_1(\text{MR}(\text{K})) + \log t_2(\text{MPR}(\text{K}))$$
$$+ \log t_3(1.44 * \log \text{TR}(\text{K}))$$
$$+ \log t_4(\text{MHR}(\text{K}))$$

where t_1, t_2, t_3, and t_4 represent the tabular functions in the model relationships. For example, t_2 represents the tabular function and its associated table, MAPMT, which determines the value of MAPM. With the equation in this form, the analogy to linear regression is apparent. The estimation problem for MAM is, given sets of observations (MAM, MR, MPR, TR, MHR), to determine the functional relationships t_1, t_2, t_3, and t_4, which correspond to the four independent variables that determine MAM. In a linear regression estimation problem, this corresponds with determining a coefficient, rather than a nonlinear function, for each independent variable in the relationship. If it is assumed, as Forrester does, that the tabular functions are nonlinear, then the estimation problem for MAM is much more difficult than a linear regression estimation; in addition, it demands considerably more data.

It will be possible, of course, to obtain sufficient data to estimate the functions for some of the 50 tabular functions in the model, but there will be many for which sufficient data cannot be obtained. From recent studies of urban migration, for example, available data are not adequate to support the model's requirement for estimating migration parameters for each of the three population groups. In his regression-analysis study of migration, Lowry[34] developed equations for migration between cities by pooling data for 90 large metropolitan areas. Pack,[35] in her study of New Haven, Connecticut, developed separate linear regression relationships for the migration of whites and nonwhites. In neither case are the data adequate to support the development of the nonlinear migration relationships formulated in urban dynamics. As Garn and Wilson[36] observed in their analysis of tabular functions in the model, "It is one thing to make the methodological point that the . . . functions should be nonlinear. It is quite another to know what the critical functions are, as well as their range and shape."

In addition to the data availability and statistical estimation prob-

[34] Ira S. Lowry. *Migration and Metropolitan Growth: Two Analytical Models*. San Francisco, Chandler Publ., 1966, p. 20.

[35] Janet Rothenberg Pack. "Models of Population Movement and Urban Policy." *In: Urban Dynamics: Extensions and Reflections*, pp. 216–220.

[36] Harvey A. Garn and Robert H. Wilson. "A Look at *Urban Dynamics*: The Forrester Model and Public Policy." *In: Urban Dynamics: Extensions and Reflections*, p. 83.

lems inherent in dealing with tabular functions, there is the more general question of whether Forrester has included the appropriate explanatory variable in the model relationships. In the manager population in-migration equations, the four variables included— job availability, population balance, taxes, and housing availability —are pertinent to explaining migration behavior. There are other variables, however, some of which Pack identified, that should be tested empirically for significance and considered for inclusion. This same observation applies to more than a dozen relationships in the model that display the same multiplicative structure, combined with the use of tabular functions, as the manager in-migration relationship displays.

In view of these difficulties in the Washington model, a significant improvement over the fourth-stage version would involve a major research undertaking rather than merely developing estimates for a few dozen more parameters. Such a research effort probably would include the following: estimation of values for Forrester's tabular functions, wherever possible; reformulation of some model relationships as linear regression equations, or a form simpler than Forrester's nonlinear tabular function form; and reformulation of behavioral relationships wherever Forrester's choices of explanatory variables prove to be inappropriate. It is not likely that this set of research tasks will be resolved quickly.

A related conclusion is that, because tabular functions are a key element in the model representation of interactions among subsystems, the model's representation of such interactions probably is not reliable. This idea is supported by the results from the fourth stage of the Washington model, in which very poor results from the population subsystem appear to have little or no effect on the results produced by the other two principal model subsystems. Such a conclusion has strong negative implications regarding the model's utility, because, in the assessment of the policymaking perspective presented in Chapter 3, it was indicated that the stress in urban dynamics on modeling subsystem interactions was a key feature in realizing the model's potential as a tool for dealing with strategic policy problems. With the lack of a reliable representation of the interaction among subsystems, much of this potential remains unrealized.

Chapter 6 applies the Washington model to a specific policy problem to complete the in-practice evaluation of the urban dynamics model. The concluding section of that chapter returns to the problem of the need for further improvement in the model and sets forth a strategy for undertaking the required research.

CHAPTER 6

Urban Dynamics Model Analysis
of a Housing Policy Problem:
In-Practice Evaluation

The second half of the in-practice evaluation of the urban dynamics model, presented in this chapter, analyzes a specific policy problem using the final version of the model developed in Chapter 5.

ANALYSIS OF A WASHINGTON, D.C. HOUSING PROBLEM

The policy problem examined is illustrative only, and the results are necessarily limited by the model's shortcomings; but the analysis indicates the kinds of problems for which the model has potential and contributes to an overall evaluation of the model. The evaluation is divided into three steps: The selected problem is discussed in general conceptual terms; the problem is defined in an operational form, and the model is modified for adaptation to the study of the problem; and the model is used to compute information to support the analysis of alternative policies.

Selection of Policy Problem

Housing is selected as the general area of policy consideration for

146

two reasons. First, District officials regard housing policy as essential to achieving improved housing and increased economic stability. Second, the urban dynamics model is well suited to housing problems, because the conceptual basis of the model's housing subsystem is considerably stronger than that of the other two subsystems; housing results for the 1960s with the Washington model are reasonably good. The particular policy problem considered is related to a housing policy developed by the District government. Considered from the city's point of view, the general question is whether the strategy can be expected to achieve certain projected objectives for 1980–1985.

As background, the city's housing and population trends are examined, and the relationships among the principal organizations involved in housing policy are delineated. The city's housing policy is then described, and the particular problem selected for analysis is defined.

Housing and population trends: The general population and housing trends in the District since 1960 indicate some of the problems related to housing policy. During the 1960s, considerable new housing was constructed: 43,934 new units were built, while 31,910 units were lost through demolition. The net gain of approximately 12,000 units represented a 6 percent increase in the housing stock.

There were, however, significant trends not visible in these overall figures. First, the number of new units produced each year after 1965 has decreased: in 1970 only 1,947 new units were built, and in 1971, only 836. These figures represent a very sharp downturn in housing production from the 8,459 units built in 1965. Second, only 6 percent of the units built during the 1960s were single-family units.[1] Single-family units, which are usually owner occupied, promote greater economic stability than multifamily units, which generally are rental units. Third, housing conditions actually worsened in major parts of the city, as indicated by the number and percentage of families living in overcrowded conditions, the number and percentage of occupied housing units classified as dilapidated,[2] and the availability of housing for families of moderate income.[3]

[1] District of Columbia Government, Office of Assistant to the Mayor for Housing Programs. *Housing Construction & Demolition, Compilation of Permit Data, 1960–1972*. Washington, D. C., 1972, pp. 1, 5.

[2] U. S. Bureau of the Census. *1970 Census of Housing: Components of Inventory Change*. Report HC(4)–16, Washington, D. C.-Md.-Va. SMSA. Washington, D. C., U. S. Government Printing Office, 1973, p. 39.

[3] James G. Banks. "Growth Statement." Washington, D. C., Office of Housing Programs, District of Columbia Government, September 21, 1973, p. 2. Mimeographed.

These trends occurred in the 1960s, during which time the city experienced a net population loss of 7,466, or 1 percent. The population loss continued into the 1970s, with the two-year, 1970–1972 net loss estimated at 7,400,[4] approximately the same as the loss during the 1960s. These population losses were disproportionately high among the over 18- and under 65-year age groups and sharply increased the proportion of the city's population in the dependent age ranges of under 18 and over 65.[5]

District officials regarded the lack of appropriate housing as a primary factor in the city's population loss from the productive over-18 and under-65 age groups. It was the opinion of the Assistant to the Mayor for Housing Programs that the city had already lost much of its white middle class and now also was losing its black middle class. Many upwardly mobile blacks in the productive, young age groups leave for the suburbs because they cannot afford city housing.[6]

Housing policymaking structure: The responsibility for housing policy in the District of Columbia is dispersed among a number of agencies. The National Capital Planning Commission (NCPC), a federal agency, exercises the most pervasive influence on housing, and it is responsible for comprehensive planning for the development of the District as a whole. Two other federal agencies are more directly involved in housing: the D. C. Redevelopment Land Agency (RLA) and the National Capital Housing Authority (NCHA). Both RLA and NCHA are corporate-type federal agencies. In 1972, RLA,[7] the public agency for urban-renewal programs in the District, was involved in 10 project areas that included approximately 7 percent of the city's land area and 18 percent of its population. NCHA [8] is the housing authority for the District's federally subsidized, low-rent, public housing programs and manages the more than 11,000 units of public housing built in the city since 1940. Within the District government, the Office of Housing Programs, Zoning Commission, Board of Zoning Adjustment, Office of the Sur-

[4] Kirk Scharfenberg. "City Population Drops 7,400 in 2-Year Period." *The Washington Post:* C1, September 19, 1972.

[5] John B. Willmann. "City's Problems Seen Magnified with Age Gaps." *The Washington Post:* C7, May 27, 1972.

[6] *Ibid.*, p. C3.

[7] District of Columbia, Redevelopment Land Agency. *Annual Report 1972.* Washington, D. C., 1972, pp. i–ii.

[8] National Capital Housing Authority. *Annual Report for the Fiscal Year Ending June 30, 1972: Public Housing in Crisis.* Washington, D. C., U. S. Government Printing Office, 1973, pp. 14–15.

veyor, Department of Economic Development, and several other agencies are involved in various aspects of housing.

Organizational changes during the late 1960s and early 1970s increased the authority of District government executives in the housing area. These changes provided more coherence to the organizational structure and increased the District's control of housing policies and programs. The most significant change created the position of Assistant to the Mayor for Housing Programs as a focal point for housing policy in the municipal government. The assistant heads the Office of Housing Programs, a staff office of approximately 24 professionals. He represents the mayor in coordinating the policies and activities of RLA, NCHA, and other departments and agencies. In the centralizing changes,[9] the mayor was granted authority to appoint the executive director of NCHA as well as members of the RLA board of directors. The Office of Housing Programs, RLA, and NCHA constitute the three central agencies responsible for housing policy and project implementation in the District. Through the aforementioned organizational developments, the mayor increased his authority to promote a unified housing policy for the city.

Washington housing policy strategy: The organizational changes, coupled with the need to deal with the District's housing and related population problems, produced a new strategy for coping with housing problems—a strategy initiated by the Assistant for Housing Programs and the Office of Housing Programs. As background to the discussion, the range of possible strategies and their implications are examined.

Formulation of a housing strategy requires some basic questions to be answered: Should the government concern itself with new housing, existing housing, or both? What quality standards should be imposed on housing? Should subsidies be directed to the poor or other income groups? Should policies operate within, or independently of, the competitive housing market? [10] A number of possible answers to these questions and, hence, a number of strategies may be narrowed down to four major strategies: filtering, low-income subsidy, minimal standards, and mixes of the three. Filtering strategies produce good-quality

[9] District of Columbia Government, Office of Planning and Management. *Government of the District of Columbia Organization Handbook.* Washington, D. C., 1972; and U. S., Congress, Senate, Subcommittee on Appropriations. *District of Columbia Appropriations for Fiscal Year 1973, Hearings.* 92nd Congress, 2nd Session, March 16, 1972, pp. 417–420.

[10] Henry J. Aaron. *Shelter and Subsidies: Who Benefits from Federal Housing Policies?* Washington, D. C., The Brookings Institution, 1972, p. 159.

housing with subsidies and incentives focused on middle- and high-income households. Theoretically, under filtering, as new units are occupied by the nonpoor, the poor receive decent housing through the filtering of older units from those with higher incomes. Low-income subsidy strategies allocate subsidies to lower income households, usually through landlords. Minimal standard strategies only partially enforce housing quality standards.[11] Such strategies are regarded as unacceptable in the United States, although in many urban areas the legally adopted standards are not fully enforced.

In theory, both filtering and low-income subsidy strategies are expected to stimulate housing production and to generally improve housing stock and housing conditions. If the supply of housing for the group subsidized is insufficient, however, then the subsidy may raise housing prices as demand for the limited housing increases. The effects of public subsidies for high- and middle-income groups and for lower income groups differ, because the subsidy required to put a household into a decent housing unit will be larger for lower income households. Consequently, a given-size public subsidy can generate more new housing units if concentrated in higher income households than in lower income groups. By subsidizing higher income groups, the lower income groups benefit through the filtering process; but the total benefit to the lower income households will be less than if they had been subsidized directly.[12] How well filtering actually works is open to some debate. The benefits of filtering are supported by a number of studies, including a 1970 study conducted in Columbus, Ohio, that traced the impacts of a rent supplement program for low-income households and a home-ownership assistance program for moderate-income households. Taking filtering into consideration, the program for moderate-income households "affected more than three times as many households and more than one and a half times as many poor households as did the rent supplement program per dollar spent."[13] To obtain the potential benefits of filtering for improving the quality of housing, however, subsidies must be accompanied by programs that actually increase the supply of housing to meet demand. Otherwise, subsidies will have a tendency to raise housing prices.[14]

By 1972, the District government had adopted a filtering strategy to

---

[11] Anthony Downs. "Housing the Urban Poor: The Economics of Various Strategies." *The American Economic Review*, 49:649, September 1969.

[12] *Ibid.*, pp. 647–648.

[13] Aaron. *Shelter and Subsidies*, p. 143.

[14] Herbert J. Gans. "A Poor Man's Home Is His Poorhouse." *New York Times Magazine:* 54, 58, March 31, 1974.

deal with the city's housing and related economic problems, which promoted an increased supply of housing for middle-income families. The strategy reflected the views of both city and federal officials; namely, that the District's policy must concentrate on establishing economic stability rather than on serving its dependent residents and that less effort be directed toward serving the large, poor urban family and more effort be directed toward attracting and retaining small families and single persons who could help revitalize the city economically.[15] The lack of economic stability was evidenced by the dramatic rise in the District's budget and taxes, despite a population decline since 1960. City officials attributed this to the marked change in the population effected by a greater proportion of low-income families. Both the mayor and his Assistant for Housing Programs advanced the filtering strategy in an effort to achieve the desired economic stability. In a 1973 meeting on future growth, the Assistant for Housing Programs summed up for District officials the rationale for the strategy. He reported that statistical data clearly showed that the city was losing many upwardly mobile black and white families and that steps had to be taken to regain that population. Study results indicated that public policies had discouraged the development of the moderate-cost housing these upwardly mobile families wanted and needed, and that by providing such housing this population loss would be reversed.[16]

The primary thrust of the filtering strategy was contained in two projects in the Office of Housing Programs. The first was Project Rehab, a program to rehabilitate sound, but run-down, housing units and make them available to low- and moderate-income families. The Department of Housing and Urban Development (HUD) approved the District's Rehab program in 1971, designating the District as one of 28 Project Rehab cities. Under this program, the Federal Government subsidizes bank loans to non- and limited-profit developers who purchase, renovate, and rent or sell the units. HUD pledged subsidy funds for a minimum of 4,000 units of rehabilitated housing through 1976. The District government would identify units suitable for rehabilitation, assist developers in gaining HUD approval, and improve public facilities in the affected areas.[17] Rehabilitation is an appealing idea, because if most cities are to meet their future housing needs, it must

[15] Thomas W. Lippman. "Report Asks City to Attract New Families." *The Washington Post:* D1, February 10, 1974.

[16] Kirk Scharfenberg. "Officials Optimistic on City's Future Growth." *The Washington Post:* B5, September 9, 1973.

[17] Eugene L. Meyer. "HUD Subsidizes Inner City Plan." *The Washington Post:* D1, D4, July 9, 1972.

be done, at least in part, through rehabilitation of existing housing stock.[18]

The second project, Project Home, started in 1972. Its objective is to encourage and assist private investors to develop moderately priced housing in the District. A part of the Office of Housing Programs, the project staff helps builders by developing a detailed inventory of potentially available land, by expediting plan reviews and zoning actions through District government offices, and by bringing developers together with landowners and financial institutions. HUD supported the staff activities of Project Home with a grant of $95,000.[19] During the first year, builders and developers submitted approximately 2,200 units for approval. The project was considered one of the keys to economic stability in the District and an effort to disprove the prediction that "by 1985 the population of Washington, D. C. will be predominantly senior citizens and impoverished large families." [20]

The District's strategy was aligned generally with Federal Government housing policy. Project Home housing, under conventional financing, did not depend on federal subsidies. Project Rehab was dependent on HUD subsidies, principally under Sections 235 and 236 of the Housing and Urban Development Act of 1968. These sections authorized interest subsidies on mortgages for home ownership and rental housing development, respectively. These provisions of the act were designed to help low- and moderate-income families achieve improved housing and to reach the heretofore neglected group situated between those eligible for public housing and the higher income groups with adequate access to financing.[21]

The District's strategy complements the activities of NCHA and RLA. The development of new low-income public housing was deemphasized in the early 1970s because of a dearth of federal funds, and because public housing was expected to expand at the rate of only 200 to 300 units a year.[22] This leaves NCHA with the role of managing the available stock of approximately 11,000 units of public housing. RLA has

[18] Michael A. Stegman. *Housing Investment in the Inner City: The Dynamics of Decline.* Cambridge, Mass., MIT Press, 1972, pp. 2–3.

[19] "HOME Receives HUD Grant." *Housing & Community Development Newsletter,* 2:2, August 1973.

[20] Banks. "Growth Statement," pp. 2–3.

[21] District of Columbia, Office of Assistant to the Mayor for Housing Programs. *F-NE, Washington's Far Northeast 1972: Housing.* Washington, D. C., 1972, pp. 23–24.

[22] Cathe Wolhowe. "Phillips Blasts City, Quits Housing Unit." *The Washington Post:* C1, January 23, 1974.

several urban renewal projects that should contribute a substantial number of housing units. In the urban-renewal activities, the Federal Government bears at least two-thirds of the project costs, and the District bears the rest, which may consist of expenditures in cash or in kind for public improvements that benefit project areas.[23] RLA's urban renewal objectives agree in general with the District's housing strategy, as noted by RLA's executive director:

. . . the renewal program must be evaluated in terms of the City's fundamental problems including taxes, employment, racial and economic integration, as well as housing, and this means making the City attractive to middle income black families in addition to white families, as well as providing for families of low and moderate income.[24]

The basic question is whether the District's filtering strategy will achieve the desired general objectives—improved housing conditions and increased economic stability. As seen in the foregoing discussion, two premises underlie the strategy. First, the moderate-income housing generated under the strategy will benefit not only the moderate-income group but, through the filtering process, the lower income group as well. Second, the moderate-income housing generated will increase the proportion of productive population and improve the city's financial balance.

In more specific terms, if Project Home and Project Rehab are continued for several years, will their impact significantly improve housing conditions and economic stability in the District, say, by 1980 or 1985? It will be assumed that the efforts of these projects will have produced new and rehabilitated housing over and above the housing generated by RLA, NCHA, and normal market forces. Inherent in the general question of whether the filtering strategy is effective is the question of what activity levels of the two projects and what combination of these levels are effective in achieving the desired objectives. In analyzing the policy question, measures of policy impact are adapted to relate the impacts of alternative policies to the general policy objectives. The urban dynamics model is adapted to this analysis by minor modifications to the previously developed Washington, D. C. model.

[23] Metropolitan Washington Council of Governments. *Housing Policies and Programs for Metropolitan Washington–1972.* Washington, D. C., October 1972, pp. 128–131.

[24] Melvin A. Mister. "Twenty Years of Urban Renewal." Washington, D. C., District of Columbia Redevelopment Land Agency, January 8, 1970, p. 10. Mimeographed.

Operationalization of the Problem

To apply the urban dynamics model of Washington to the study of Project Home and Project Rehab, it is necessary to relate the problems to the concepts of the model. To accomplish this, first, minor modifications must be made to incorporate representations of both project operations into the model. This provides a means of specifying the policy alternatives to be examined in terms of assumed levels of operation for each of the projects. Second, policy outcomes or consequences, appropriately considered in evaluating policy for the problem under study, must be identified.

Representation of policy alternatives: The preceding discussion indicates that the housing program based on Projects Home and Rehab is intended to complement housing production from other sources. To represent this realistically in the model, the Home and Rehab operations are assumed to compete with other housing production; that is, the projects' levels of operation are conditioned by the demand for housing, constraints on construction, and other factors. In this way, desired levels of operation for Home and Rehab activities can be indicated by policy variables, but actual levels of operation may be constrained during the course of the program by conditions in the city. Other sources of housing are assumed to include the activities of NCHA and RLA as well as market forces.

The objective of Project Home is to promote the production of single-family housing units in the $30,000–$40,000 price range (in 1972 dollars),[25] regarded appropriately in the urban dynamics housing classification as premium housing units occupied by manager-professional persons. An important factor governing the number of units constructed under Project Home is the availability of suitable land. Private builders prefer tracts on which eight or more units can be built. Because such tracts are difficult to obtain in a mature city like Washington, the project staff devotes considerable resources to locating suitable land. Therefore, an estimate of land availability for Project Home building activity is a suitable variable to indicate a planned level of policy action. A convenient form for specifying such a policy variable is the fraction of the city's unused land which can be assumed to be available for Project Home development. Although there is always some land available, only a small fraction of it can be acquired for building the single-family units promoted by Project Home. As an indication of available land, consider that, according to model computations, approximately

---

[25] Deborah Lyons. Personal interview. February 26, 1974.

8 percent, or more than 3,000 acres, of Washington's land was unused at the beginning of 1975. In the model's land accounting, this 8 percent includes land made available by the demolition of housing and business units during 1974. If, say, 10 percent of this land is obtained for Project Home activities, however, it could accommodate approximately 4,000 housing units.

For Project Home, the policy-control variable is referred to as the Project Home land fraction, PHLF. The policymaker's setting of PHLF determines a planned level of project activity called Project Home planned construction, PHPC. The planned-construction level is constrained by the demand for premium-level housing units to obtain a Project Home desired construction level, PHDC. In terms of model equations, these relationships take the form

PHPC(K) $=$ PHLF $*$ AREA $*$ $(1.-$ LFO(K) $)$ /LPH
PHDM(K) $=$ TABLE(PHDMT,MHR(K),.0,2.,.25)
DATA PHDMT / .0,.1,.25,.5,1.,1.,1.,1.,1./
PHDC(K) $=$ PHDM(K) $*$ PHPC(K)

where

PHPC $=$ Project Home planned construction, housing units/year
PHLF $=$ Project Home land fraction, dimensionless
AREA $=$ land area, acres
LFO $=$ land fraction occupied, dimensionless
LPH $=$ land per house, acres/housing unit
PHDM $=$ Project Home demand multiplier, dimensionless
PHDMT $=$ Project Home demand multiplier table
MHR $=$ manager/housing ratio, dimensionless
PHDC $=$ Project Home desired construction, housing units/year

The quantities PHPC, PHLF, PHDM, PHDMT, and PHDC are introduced to achieve the representation of Project Home, whereas the other quantities are already part of the model. From these relationships, it can be seen that the planned construction for year K is equal to the number of housing units that the fraction, PHLF, of available land can accommodate. The demand multiplier, PHDM, is a function of the ratio, MHR, of premium housing demand and supply, which is used at several points in the model. The value PHDM is determined through a tabular function relationship. The values assigned to the table, PHDMT, reflect an assumption that, to some extent, Project Home units are constructed in advance of the demand for premium housing. For instance, if MHR $=$ .75, which indicates a 25 percent oversupply of premium housing, then

50 percent of the planned construction level, PHPC, is taken as the desired construction level, PHDC. If MHR = 1, then the desired construction level is set equal to the planned level. This tabular function reflects the Project Home premise that, if units of the type promoted are built, then the manager-professional families will not leave the city or they will be attracted into the city and occupy them.

In addition to being constrained by demand for premium housing, the Project Home activity level may be further constrained by a shortage of labor for construction support, which is the same constraint applied by the model to all construction activity. In the model, this is done by computing a labor construction ratio, LCR, which is the fraction of the desired construction achievable during the current year. This fraction is applied to reduce the desired housing and industry construction to a level actually achieved. Two minor changes in model equations are made to apply this constraint to Project Home construction. First, the equation for construction labor requirements is modified to include labor for Project Home desired construction, PHDC, for the year. The labor requirements for these housing units are assumed to be the same as those required for other premium housing units. It is essential to incorporate these labor requirements, because they must be reflected in the computation of the model's labor construction ratio, LCR. Second, the Project Home desired construction level, PHDC, is constrained by the supply of labor to obtain a Project Home actual construction level, PHAC. In equation form

$$\text{PHAC}(\text{K}) = \text{PHDC}(\text{K}) * \text{LCR}(\text{K})$$
$$\text{PH}(\text{NXT}) = \text{PH}(\text{K}) + \text{DT} * (\text{PHC}(\text{K}) - \text{PHO}(\text{K}) + \text{PHAC}(\text{K}))$$

where

PHAC = Project Home actual construction, housing units/year
PHDC = Project Home desired construction, housing units/year
LCR = labor construction ratio, dimensionless
PH   = premium housing, housing units
DT   = solution interval, one year
PHC = premium housing construction, housing units/year
PHO = premium housing obsolescence, housing units/year.

The first equation computes the Project Home actual construction level, PHAC. The second modifies the model relationship for the premium housing level for the next year by incorporating the Project Home actual construction during the current year.

The representation of the Project Rehab operation follows the same general approach. In Rehab, however, the objective is to rehabilitate sound, but rundown, housing units for occupancy by low- and moderate-income families. In terms of the model's classification of housing, the candidate units for the project are assumed to be the underemployed level, upgraded by rehabilitation to the level of worker units. The policy control variable adopted for Rehab is the Project Rehab rehabilitation fraction, PRRF, which is the policymaker's estimate of the fraction of underemployed units that are suitable for rehabilitation and that can be promoted by the project. The value of PRRF also must take into consideration the expected availability of federal funds to support rehabilitation.

The Project Rehab planned construction level, PRPC, and desired construction level, PRDC, are determined by the following equations introduced into the model:

PRPC(K) = PRRF*UH(K)
PRDM(K) = TABLE(PRDMT,LHR(K),.0,2.,.25)
DATA PRDMT / .0,.1,.25,.5,1.,1.,1.,1.,1./
PRDC(K) = PRDM(K)*PRPC(K)

where

PRPC = Project Rehab planned construction, housing units/year
PRRF = Project Rehab rehabilitation fraction, dimensionless
UH   = underemployed housing, housing units
PRDM = Project Rehab demand multiplier, dimensionless
PRDMT = Project Rehab demand multiplier table
LHR   = labor/housing ratio, dimensionless
PRDC = Project Rehab desired construction, housing units/year.

The planned construction level, PRPC, is the product of the policy variable, PRRF, and the level of underemployed housing, UH. The desired construction level, PRDC, is the planned level reduced in accordance with the demand multiplier, PRDM. In this case, the demand multiplier is a function of the labor housing ratio, LHR, which is the ratio of worker housing demand and supply used elsewhere in the model. As with Project Home, the demand function for Rehab assumes that rehabilitation of units under the project is undertaken in advance of demand, on a graduated scale.

The labor supply also may restrict Project Rehab construction. Again, the equation for construction labor requirements is modified to include the labor for Project Rehab desired construction, PRDC; the labor required to rehabilitate a unit is assumed to be half that required to build a new worker unit. These labor requirements are incorporated into the labor construction ratio, LCR, which is used to constrain the desired construction level, PRDC, to obtain the actual construction level, PRAC. As shown in the last two of the model equations that follow, the equations for worker housing, WH, and underemployed housing, UH, are modified to take into account the Project Rehab actual construction level, PRAC, in determining the worker and underemployed housing levels for the next model year.

$$\text{PRAC}(\text{K}) = \text{PRDC}(\text{K})^* \text{LCR}(\text{K})$$
$$\text{WH}(\text{NXT}) = \text{WH}(\text{K}) + \text{DT}^*(\text{PHO}(\text{K}) + \text{WHC}(\text{K}) - \text{WHO}(\text{K}) + \text{PRAC}(\text{K}))$$
$$\text{UH}(\text{NXT}) = \text{UH}(\text{K}) + \text{DT}^*(\text{WHO}(\text{K}) - \text{SHD}(\text{K}) + \text{LCHP}(\text{K}) - \text{PRAC}(\text{K}))$$

where

PRAC = Project Rehab actual construction, housing units/year
PRDC = Project Rehab desired construction, housing units/year
LCR = labor construction ratio, dimensionless
WH = worker housing, housing units
DT = solution interval, one year
PHO = premium housing obsolescence, housing units/year
WHC = worker housing construction, housing units/year
WHO = worker housing obsolescence, housing units/year
UH = underemployed housing, housing units
SHD = slum housing demolition, housing units/year
LCHP = low-cost housing program, housing units/year.

This representation of Project Home and Project Rehab, which is adopted and incorporated into the Washington model, is intended to be consistent with the level of detail and general approach that Forrester used in the original model. Although this rather summary representation does not make provision for addressing many of the pertinent questions about these two housing projects, it does provide a means for evaluating their strategic impacts. This is consistent with the basic policymaking perspective of the urban dynamics model. The representation of the two projects also is deficient in empirically based support. For example, the values of the tabular functions used to determine the demand multipliers for housing promoted by the projects is not supported by empirical data. More generally, the representation of these housing projects suffers from the same shortcomings in empirical implementation as does the model as a whole. Clearly, then, the representation of the project operations is adopted as a plausible, rather than a highly accurate, representation of how the projects operate.

Measurement of policy impacts: As modified to incorporate a representation of Projects Home and Rehab, the model provides for specifying alternative housing policies in terms of the two projects' levels of operation. It also provides for carrying out model simulations over time to furnish information on the policy outcomes associated with alternatives. Several measures of policy outcomes are of potential interest, because the two projects interact with each other, with other aspects of housing, and with other subsystems. For example, the two projects compete with each other and with other construction projects for labor. Housing promoted by the projects affects the city's population level by influencing migration; it affects the level of business/industry activity by competing with business for land. Because all policy outcomes cannot be considered, a limited set of consequences should be selected that would be of interest to policymakers examining alternatives for the Washington housing problem. Measures of the selected outcomes or consequences are defined in terms of the outputs provided by the model. Although the set of outcomes considered is limited, it is sufficient to use in analyzing the illustrative problem and to provide some insight into the utility of the model in supporting the analysis of policy problems.

Two kinds of policy outcomes are considered in examining the problem: The first consists of policy outcomes or consequences directly related to the housing subsystem, including the impacts of housing policy actions on the quality and quantity of housing in the city. The second deals with the more direct impacts of policy actions, such as impacts on subsystems other than housing. For example housing policy may influence the population level, the distribution of the population among income classes, the level of business/industry activity, and the fiscal aspects of city government.

Four policy outcomes directly related to the housing subsystem will be examined. Two are related to the direct impact of the two projects that constitute the housing program under study. The other two are related to the impacts of policy alternatives on the quantity and condition of the city's housing stock. As previously indicated, policy alternatives are specified in terms of the policy control variables for Project Home and Project Rehab; and a policy is assumed to be in effect for some specified period of years. The measure of the direct impact of Project Home and Project Rehab is taken as the net production of the type of housing promoted by the project as a consequence of the project operation during the period of the policy. For Project Home, the measure of the net production of premium housing attributable to the project operation is the difference between the total production of premium units during the period the project was in effect and the production of premium units for the same period when the project was not operational. The model results for the policy period with a zero level of Project Home operation are taken as a base or benchmark case; the net increase in the production of premium units over the base case production is attributed to the Project Home operation. This approach is necessary, because Project Home competes with other premium housing production, thus inflating the production ostensibly attributable to Project Home with housing which, in fact, would have been produced in any event. Since the same considerations apply, the net production of worker-level housing attributed to Project Rehab is defined in the same way.

Two measures of the outcome of policy actions on the overall housing situation are used in analyzing the policy problem: the total number of housing units, and the distribution of these units among the model's three classes of housing. These measures may be examined for various points in time, both during and following the period in which the policy is in effect. In this way, both the near-term and longer range consequences of policy actions may be assessed. The policymaker usually will be interested in comparing these measures with similar measures from the base case, which does not include a policy action, and from model results for other levels of policy actions.

To help assess the impact of alternative policy actions on subsystems other than housing, four other policy outcomes are selected. Two deal with the city's population, providing an estimate of the total population and of the distribution of the population among the three labor-force classes represented in the model. The other two are both related to the city's tax base, although one is closely related to the level of business/industry activity. The first is the assessed value of all business/ industry property; the second is the assessed property value per capita. Taken together, these two measures provide information on the city's ability to obtain tax revenue, as well as on the distribution of taxable property between business/industry and housing. It generally will be interesting to examine these measures at various points in time.

Admittedly, the selection of a set of policy outcomes and the measures of the outcomes limit the scope of the problem analysis. The policy outcomes adopted were chosen to reflect the strong emphasis in the District's housing policy on improving both the city's economic stability and its housing stock. The measures of these policy outcomes are dependent on the level of representation and the outputs provided by the model. The model's outputs are limited, of course, by its basic macroeconomic orientation.

Analysis of Policy Alternatives

With the urban dynamics model of Washington modified to incorporate the operationalization of Projects Home and Rehab, a set of alternative policies is identified and examined through the use of the model. A policy alternative is a combination of Project Home and Project Rehab operation levels examined in terms of the eight (direct and indirect) measures of policy outcome outlined in the foregoing paragraphs.

Nine policy alternatives, consisting of the combinations of low, medium, and high levels of operation of each of the two housing projects, are considered. Both projects are assumed to be implemented at least at a low level of operation. Parameter settings for the Project Home land fraction, PHLF, policy control variable are .05, .10, and .15, respectively, for the low, medium, and high levels of operation. The Project Rehab rehabilitation fraction, PRRF, policy variable is set as .025, .050, and .075 for the low, medium, and high options, respectively. For a clearer meaning of these project levels, note that a 10 percent land fraction, or medium level of Project Home operation for 1975, results in a planned construction level of nearly 4,000 units, but this is constrained to an actually achieved level of 3,000 units. For Project Rehab, a medium level of operation for 1975 produces a planned rehabilitation of approximately 1,500 units, which is constrained to approximately 1,100 units actually rehabilitated. In addition to these nine policy alternatives, the benchmark case, which represents a zero level for both housing projects, is included for comparative purposes.

In the model simulations, the policy alternatives are assumed to be in effect for the six-year period 1974–1979. By performing model computations for each alternative through 1985, the policy alternatives are simulated for 1974–1979, and the policy impacts are measured through 1985 from the model results. The performance of the two projects is measured in terms of their net production of housing units during the six-year policy implementation period. Other policy outcome measures are obtained for 1980 and 1985 in order to compare the impacts of alternatives.

The results of the model computations for the nine alternative policies and the benchmark case are presented in Table 7. Policy out-

TABLE 7 Washington Model Results for Alternative Housing Policies

Policy Alternatives		Policy Outcomes			
Project Home Level	Project Rehab Level	Project Home Net Construction 1974–1979 (thousands)	Project Rehab Net Construction 1974–1979 (thousands)	Total Housing Units 1980/1985 (thousands)	Distribution of Housing 1980/1985 (percent PH:WH:UH)
Zero	Zero	0	0	296	26:63:11
				308	28:62:10
Low	Low	7.2	3.5	304	28:63:9
				316	28:62:10
Low	Medium	7.1	6.6	305	28:63:9
				318	28:63:9
Low	High	7.1	9.5	306	28:64:8
				320	28:63:9
Medium	Low	12.5	3.5	310	29:62:9
				321	29:62:9
Medium	Medium	12.4	6.6	310	29:62:9
				323	29:62:9
Medium	High	12.3	9.5	311	29:63:8
				324	29:63:8
High	Low	16.6	3.4	314	30:61:9
				324	30:61:9
High	Medium	16.4	6.6	314	29:62:9
				326	29:62:9
High	High	16.4	9.5	315	29:63:8
				328	29:62:9

come measures for the housing subsystem are given in the first half of the table, and those related to the other subsystems appear in the second half. The results indicate that the net construction for Project Home increases as the level of project activity increases from low, to medium, to high, corresponding to Project Home land fraction settings of .05, .10, and .15 percent, respectively. The increases in construction for successive levels of project activity, however, are less than the proportional increases in the land fraction parameter, indicating the increasing influence of the demand and labor constraints on higher levels of the Project Home operation. The same effect is apparent in the net

TABLE 7   (continued)

Policy Alternatives		Policy Outcomes			
Project Home Level	Project Rehab Level	Total Population 1980/1985 (thousands)	Distribution of Population 1980/1985 (percent MP:L:U)	Business Assessed Value 1980/1985 (billion $)	Assessed Value Per Capita 1980/1985 (thousand $)
Zero	Zero	774	27:63:10	1.054	3.99
		779	28:62:10	1.044	4.01
Low	Low	775	27:63:10	1.049	4.12
		801	28:62:10	1.029	4.09
Low	Medium	774	27:63:10	1.048	4.13
		801	29:62:9	1.026	4.10
Low	High	773	27:63:10	1.047	4.15
		800	29:62:9	1.023	4.11
Medium	Low	777	27:63:10	1.042	4.19
		803	29:61:10	1.020	4.13
Medium	Medium	776	27:63:10	1.041	4.20
		802	29:62:9	1.017	4.15
Medium	High	774	27:63:10	1.040	4.22
		801	29:62:9	1.015	4.16
High	Low	778	27:63:10	1.035	4.24
		803	29:61:10	1.014	4.17
High	Medium	777	27:63:10	1.034	4.25
		803	29:62:9	1.011	4.18
High	High	776	27:63:10	1.033	4.27
		802	29:62:9	1.009	4.20

construction for Project Rehab, but there the effect is less pronounced. Because Project Home activity increases the housing stock, the level of project activity is correlated positively with changes in the total housing units. Increases over the base case of approximately 8,000, 14,000, and 18,000 units by 1980 are associated, respectively, with the low, medium, and high levels of Project Home activity. Increases in Project Rehab levels also are correlated positively with small net increases in the total number of units. As expected, there is a shift in the housing distribution in the direction of a higher proportion of premium units with increasing levels of project operations.

Concerning the relationship between policy alternatives and the population level, increased project levels are associated with rather modest population increases, compared with housing unit increases. In fact, although increased Project Home activity levels are associated with modest increases in total population, increased Project Rehab levels appear to be associated with slight population decreases. For example, the low-low policy alternative for the Home-Rehab levels shows a 1980 population increase of 1,000 over the base case; on the other hand, the population decreases by 1,000 for the low-medium alternative and by another 1,000 for the low-high option. The examination of more detailed model results indicates that housing promoted by the program produces a substantial increase in unoccupied housing. The extent of this increase is revealed in the base case, where premium housing is 100 percent occupied in 1980, but, in the same year, for the low-low, medium-low, and high-low alternatives, the premium housing is occupied at the 94, 89, and 86 percent levels, respectively. Similar results hold for 1985, although the levels of occupancy increase somewhat over the 1980 levels.

If the model results are accepted, then one of the supporting premises of the Washington housing program is contradicted or, at least, the premise is weaker than assumed. In other words, manager-professional and worker-labor classes do not remain in the city (nor do they migrate to the city in significant numbers) to occupy available housing as was assumed. On the other hand, the model population results may be bad, because the weak response to the available premium-level housing appears to be unrealistic given the metropolitan Washington housing market. The model's conceptual formulation and empirical implementation of population responses to the substantial increases in housing promoted by the policy alternatives considered may well be faulty. This is a problem reminiscent of those encountered earlier in testing the final Washington model. For the 1960s, the model gave creditable housing estimates, but very poor population results, indicating a poor representation of the relationship between the housing and population subsystems. The problem, of course, must be resolved if the model is to produce useful results.

The last two measures of policy alternative outcomes depicted in Table 7 are related to assessed property values. The first is the assessed value of all business/industry enterprises for 1980 and 1985. With increased operation levels of Projects Home and Rehab, the assessed value of business declines. Project Home has a more pronounced effect, because it competes with business for available land; whereas Rehab competes only indirectly with business by reducing the number of underemployed units for demolition which, in turn, reduces the possibility that land will become available. The total assessed value per capita provides a tax-base measure relative to the population to be served by the government. Assessed value per person increases more sharply for increased Project Home activity levels because of the higher assessed value of premium housing units, as compared with the worker units produced by the Rehab Project.

Given the information on the policy outcomes shown in Table 7, the policymaker must select a preferred alternative from the set. The approach, which applies a utility formulation, permits the policymaker to select the policy attributes of interest to him, to combine his judgments about policy outcomes, and to select a preferred policy alternative. In the formulation developed by Shapiro,[26] the policymaker's utility-loss function for n policy alternatives available is represented by

$$L_1 = (X - V_1)' A (X - V_1)$$
$$L_2 = (X - V_2)' A (X - V_2)$$
$$\vdots \qquad \vdots$$
$$L_n = (X - V_n)' A (X - V_n).$$

This quadratic loss function is an inverse of the standard utility-loss function. It expresses the expected loss for each alternative in terms of m policy attributes that the policymaker regards as important. The elements of the vector X specify the policymaker's preferred outcomes of the policy attributes, with each of the m attributes rated on, say, a seven-point scale. The entries of the vector V_i carry the policymaker's rating of the ith policy with respect to the m attributes selected for the analysis, again on a seven-point scale. The elements of the diagonal matrix A indicate the relative weights of each of the m policy attributes to the policymaker. The policymaker will select the alternative that gives the minimum loss. This utility-loss formulation is open-ended: each policymaker can consider the attributes he regards as important, and, in addition, can specify the relative importance of the attributes selected.

In the problem under study, a policymaker may regard the total number of housing units and the assessed value of business enterprises as the most important policy attributes. Assume that the policy-

[26] Michael J. Shapiro. "Rational Political Man: A Synthesis of Economic and Social-Psychological Perspectives." *American Political Science Review, 63*:1106–1119, September 1969.

maker desires both the largest number of housing units possible and a high level of assessed value for business enterprises and their associated job-providing activity. The *A* matrix values for both of these attributes will be high, indicating the high utility placed on obtaining the desired outcomes for the policy attributes. The outcomes of the two attributes compete, in that each policy alternative that gives desirable outcomes for one of the attributes gives less-desirable outcomes for the other. The utility function merely permits the policy-maker's judgments on the desirability of the outcomes for the two dominant policy attributes and other attributes of interest to be combined with his judgments on the performance of policy alternatives. This is only one of many approaches which can be used to combine criteria related to policy alternatives and to select a preferred alternative. This systematic, open-ended approach relates information, provided by a model such as urban dynamics, to policy decisions.

Because of the questions raised about the model's results, there is little motivation here to extend the analysis of the problem through to the computation of the utility loss for the alternatives. As previously noted, the model's representation of the population response to available housing is questionable; it produces results that are at variance with a key premise of the housing program. Therefore, instead of following the analysis through to the selection of a specific policy alternative, some additional model results are presented and examined. These results are related to the second key premise of the housing program, namely, that the moderate-income housing generated will benefit not only the higher income groups but, through the filtering process, it also will benefit the lower income groups.

The filtering premise in the Washington housing program assumes that the production of new premium and worker housing loosens the housing market and eventually improves housing for even the city's poorest group. The frictions of the housing market, however, restrict the benefits of filtering that are actually obtained. The extent to which the city expects its poorest group to benefit from the housing program depends, therefore, on the housing demand and supply in the entire metropolitan area. The volume of filtering in the Washington model is indicated by the observation that, in 1980, for the base case heretofore discussed, 432 units filtered from premium to worker housing status, and 2,551 units dropped from worker to underemployed housing status. For the policy alternative with a high level for both Projects Home and Rehab, 942 units filtered from premium to worker status and 2,727 from worker to underemployed status in 1980; that is, according to the model, the volume of filtering increased under the housing program. Since the model does not represent all of the market forces that influence filtering, the volume of filtering may be either too high or too low. Therefore, it might be of interest to ask: What are the differences in policy outcomes for different assumptions about filtering?

Table 8 presents model results for the same set of policy alternatives presented in Table 7, but this time the filtering rates for premium- and worker-level housing are arbitrarily reduced by one-half for the period 1974–1985. A comparison of these results with the earlier ones reveals that construction promoted by the housing program projects is somewhat lower with the decrease in filtering, but that the 1980 and 1985 levels of total housing are significantly higher. With the reduced filtering levels, a shift occurs in the distribution of housing, resulting in an increase in the proportion of premium and worker housing and a decrease in underemployed housing. Also, there is a decrease in the assessed value of business enterprises and an increase in the assessed value of property per capita.

The most interesting aspect of these results is the change in the population level. Whereas the total number of housing units is higher with the reduction in filtering, the total population level is lower. Detailed results indicate that the increased numbers of premium and worker units are not attracting additional population to the city. This is a recurrence of the previously observed lack of population response to additional premium and worker housing, except that this time the housing levels are higher. The change in population is caused almost entirely by a reduction in underemployed. According to the model results, this population group is being forced out of the city by the reduction in the class of housing available to them. This occurs to some extent in the results previously presented, but these results are much more pronounced with reduced filtering. Thus, the choice of policy and the results obtained appear to be sensitive to the rate of filtering, especially with respect to housing the underemployed group. The sensitivity of policy results to filtering is probably valid. Model results with other assumptions on filtering are obtained readily, but such results have limited value in view of the model's other problems.

Because of these difficulties, the treatment of this problem adds very little that is helpful to policymakers. Two aspects of the model, however, provide some insights that are important in dealing with specific problems. First, the model readily accommodates modifications required to incorporate the representation of specific policy problems because of the open-ended, simple mathematical structure inherent in a set of first-order difference equations. For the problem examined, new parameters and equations were introduced easily, and equations were

TABLE 8   Washington Model Results for Alternative Housing Policies with Reduced Filtering Rates for Housing

Policy Alternatives		Policy Outcomes			
Project Home Level	Project Rehab Level	Project Home Net Construction 1974–1979 (thousands)	Project Rehab Net Construction 1974–1979 (thousands)	Total Housing Units 1980/1985 (thousands)	Distribution of Housing 1980/1985 (percent PH:WH:UH)
Zero	Zero	0	0	298	26:65:9
				315	28:65:7
Low	Low	7.1	3.2	306	28:64:8
				322	29:64:7
Low	Medium	7.1	6.1	307	28:65:7
				324	29:65:6
Low	High	7.1	8.7	308	28:66:6
				325	28:66:6
Medium	Low	12.3	3.1	311	29:63:8
				327	29:64:7
Medium	Medium	12.2	6.1	312	29:64:7
				328	29:65:6
Medium	High	12.2	8.7	313	29:65:6
				330	29:65:6
High	Low	16.3	3.1	315	30:63:7
				330	30:63:7
High	Medium	16.2	6.1	316	30:63:7
				332	30:64:6
High	High	16.1	8.7	317	30:64:6
				333	30:64:6

modified readily to obtain a representation of the problem. Second, although the model provides some latitude in selecting measures of policy outcome, it is limited in the measures it provides by its basic macroeconomic orientation. For instance, policymakers may want to know the impacts on neighborhood social conditions of Project Home's promotion of single-family housing units which are for sale rather than of multifamily rental units. The model cannot provide such information, however, because no distinction is made between rental and owner-occupied housing or single- and multifamily housing. No representation of neighborhoods, and only the most summary representation

TABLE 8 (continued)

Policy Alternatives		Policy Outcomes			
Project Home Level	Project Rehab Level	Total Population 1980/1985 (thousands)	Distribution of Population 1980/1985 (percent MP:L:U)	Business Assessed Value 1980/1985 (billion $)	Assessed Value Per Capita 1980/1985 (thousand $)
Zero	Zero	771	27:63:10	1.054	4.05
		794	29:63:9	1.036	4.11
Low	Low	771	27:63:10	1.048	4.18
		793	29:63:8	1.021	4.21
Low	Medium	768	28:63:9	1.047	4.21
		790	29:63:8	1.019	4.24
Low	High	765	28:63:9	1.046	4.24
		787	29:63:8	1.016	4.26
Medium	Low	772	28:63:9	1.040	4.25
		794	29:63:8	1.013	4.27
Medium	Medium	770	28:63:9	1.039	4.28
		791	29:63:8	1.011	4.29
Medium	High	766	28:63:9	1.038	4.31
		788	29:63:8	1.009	4.32
High	Low	774	28:63:9	1.033	4.31
		794	29:63:8	1.007	4.31
High	Medium	771	28:63:9	1.032	4.33
		791	29:63:8	1.005	4.33
High	High	767	28:63:9	1.032	4.36
		788	29:63:8	1.003	4.36

of social conditions, is included in the model. In general, the model does not provide measures for quality-of-life indicators such as level of crime, traffic congestion, and air pollution, although the model can be modified to incorporate some of these measures.

ASSESSMENT OF URBAN DYNAMICS IN-PRACTICE PERFORMANCE

The application of urban dynamics to represent Washington, D. C. and to address a housing policy problem for that city clearly shows that the model is inadequate for dealing with a specific, urban area policy problem. The most positive consequence of this undertaking for policymaking is that it provides some insight into the research needed to develop an improved model. This evaluation discusses the magnitude of the research task and suggests a strategy for attacking that task. One area previously suggested was the incorporation of more detail into the model's housing subsystem to provide separate identification of rental and owner-occupied units and single- and multifamily units. There are similar opportunities to introduce additional, useful details for each of the model's subsystems, but in so doing, the macro-orientation of the model should be retained. Another possible improvement is the extension of suburb representation to include suburban housing and population, as well as the labor-force representation introduced into the Washington model. Labor force was incorporated because it was basic to the representation of the city, but the possibility of introducing other components of the suburbs should be considered. Many other modifications of the type introduced in the final stage of the Washington model development could be examined and incorporated, but no attempt was made to be exhaustive.

A clearer idea of the number of supporting assumptions and relationships of the urban dynamics model and the difficulty of dealing with them emerges from an examination of the overall model structure. The total structure of the urban dynamics model consists of nearly 300 Dynamo-language statements, which may be divided into three groups of almost equal size. One-third of the statements set values for constants and parameters used in model computations. These statements essentially perform housekeeping functions rather than express underlying model relationships. Another one-third of the model statements may be referred to as structural, in that they tie together the entities represented in the model. Many of the structural statements specify relationships of the accounting type. Examples of these include the computation of total population by summing the products of each labor-force group's level by the group's family-size parameter, and the computation of the level of premium housing by starting with the previous-year level, adding gains from construction, and subtracting losses from downward filtering. Once the model's concepts are adopted in terms of the entities to be represented and the level of their detail, the structural relationships are fairly obvious. The remaining one-third of the model statements are regarded as behavioral relationships. These are related to the computation of the quantities referred to as multipliers in the model, such as the manager arrival multiplier. As mentioned in Chapter 5, the manager arrival multiplier is the product of four other multipliers; establishing an empirical basis for such relationships presents considerable difficulty.

Several of the structural relationships of the urban dynamics model were questioned in the review of model-related research in Chapter 4, including the lack of suburb representation, the assumption of constant density of urban activities, and aspects of the supporting concepts of the three model subsystems. There is even greater need, however, for examining the model's behavioral assumptions and relationships. Concerning the structural assumptions and relationships, experience in urban modeling provides some guidance as to the fruitfulness of using various structural concepts. For the behavioral relationships, there is much less knowledge to draw from and little actual experience in modeling the macrolevel behavior of urban systems, especially the interactions among urban subsystems as attempted in urban dynamics. Because the behavioral aspects are more difficult, this part of the problem will be discussed more fully hereupon.

Altogether, there are 58 multipliers in the urban dynamics model, and more than 100 of the model's Dynamo-language statements are involved in computing these multipliers. The multipliers are regarded as the model's primary behavioral assumptions and relationships. It is not possible, of course, to separate precisely the behavioral and structural relationships. The multipliers, however, are strongly behavioral, because they are determined by functional relationships purporting to describe the behavior of the entities of the model. Examples of multipliers are the worker-housing multiplier, which governs the deviation of the worker housing rate of construction from the normal rate, and the business-decline multiplier, which modifies the normal rate at which mature businesses decline. Multipliers are used in the model to relate the influence of such variables as public expenditures, housing availability, demand for labor, and opportunities for social mobility to the migration behavior of each of the model's labor-force groups.[27] Multipliers also are used extensively to relate the influence of activities in one of the model subsystems—population, housing, and business/industry—to activities in the other two subsystems.

The model's multipliers may be divided into two types, according to the method of determining their value. The largest group of multipliers is computed by tabular functions. As mentioned previously, in tabular functions, a value of a dependent variable is computed by linear interpolation in a table of pairs of corresponding values of dependent and independent variables. A multiplier thus determined is the declining-industry land multiplier, which is a function of the independent variable that specifies the fraction of the city's occupied

[27] Jay W. Forrester. *Urban Dynamics*. Cambridge, Mass., MIT Press, 1969, pp. 135–137, 159, 166–167, 181, 197–198.

land.[28] Nearly 50 of the model's multipliers are determined by tabular functions. There are 10 multipliers in the second group, determined by multiplying from two to six factors. In many cases, the factors themselves are multipliers, such as the manager arrival multiplier discussed in Chapter 5, which is the product of four factors. Establishing valid, empirically based relationships for tabular functions involves obtaining data for a tabular correspondence between the values of two variables. Although Forrester used hypothetical nonlinear functions for nearly all tabular functions, the functional form should be based on the analysis of data. Multipliers determined as the product of factors present more difficult nonlinear forms than tabular functions. The appropriateness of such multiplicative relationships also must be investigated empirically.

The total research task required to develop adequate behavioral assumptions and relationships for the urban dynamics model is, essentially, to start with the preliminary, tentative set of behavioral assumptions and relationships provided by Forrester and go on to develop an empirically based theory of the macrolevel behavior of an urban system. It means relating statistical data to the behavioral relationships, testing assumptions and relationships, and modifying and reformulating relationships, as appropriate, to develop valid ones. The research task may be divided by sometimes concentrating on a single relationship and, other times, on a group of interacting relationships. The relationships always should be kept conformable, however, so that they fit together and constitute a coherent, consistent model. The lack of supporting theory and the inadequacy of data related to many of the behavioral relationships make the task a difficult one.

Obviously, the total task of improving the model's structural and behavioral assumptions and relationships cannot be accomplished at one time. A research strategy is needed, therefore, to identify the parts of the task having a high payoff. The strategy proposed is to use the model to undertake the analysis of policy problems for specific urban areas and, within that context, to perform sensitivity tests to identify those behavioral assumptions and relationships to which model results are sensitive. It will be necessary also to test combinations of assumptions, because, in some cases, model results may be insensitive to changes in single assumptions but may prove sensitive to simultaneous changes in two or more assumptions. The identified assumptions and relationships become the subject of empirically based analyses, resulting in the development of more realistic assumptions and relationships, which are then incorporated into the model. Several rounds of sen-

[28] *Ibid.*, p. 201.

sitivity testing, developing improved relationships, and incorporating them into the model may be required to ensure that the model has policy utility for the problem under study. Those model assumptions to which results are insensitive for a particular policy problem are, of course, not necessarily valid; it is just that they are not important in the problem under study.

This strategy can be pursued with the Washington housing policy problem analyzed heretofore. In fact, in that analysis, the model run that introduced the reduced filtering rate for housing constitutes an initial step in the sensitivity testing of the model's filtering assumption for housing. From the one alternative filtering assumption considered there, it appears that the computed policy outcomes related to population levels, the level and distribution of housing, and the assessed value of property are sensitive to the filtering assumption. Additional test runs may determine whether the filtering relationships should be subject to empirical analysis. From the model results for the problem, it is clear that migration relationships should be tested, particularly the assumptions related to the influence of housing availability on migration behavior. Extension of this sensitivity testing will identify the set of assumptions and behavioral relationships that are important for this policy problem and will become the focus of empirical research.

There are a number of interrelated considerations in the research process related to a set of model relationships that are important for a policy problem. These include identifying related research and data sources, testing the explanatory power of independent variables involved in relationships, examining the mathematical structure of relationships, and developing statistical estimates of the parameters of relationships. The model relationship for the manager arrival multiplier, discussed in Chapter 5, illustrates some of these considerations. First, although the research of Lowry and of Pack is relevant (see Chapter 4), there are indications that adequate data are not available to support the statistical implementation of the relationship as formulated in the model. Another question is whether the proper explanatory variables are included in the urban dynamics model relationship, because Pack found that some significant variables do not appear in the model's relationship. Also, is the multiplicative structure of the model relationship for the manager arrival multiplier the appropriate mathematical form, or would a linear regression form be better? These questions indicate that the empirical analysis may result in changes in the model, in both the variables included and the mathematical structure.

It is recommended that a series of research problems in the housing policy area be undertaken. This approach will concentrate research attention on a subset of the model's behavior relationships; by so doing, it will promote maximum development of the model as a policy tool. Unless research attention is concentrated, the development of the model's policy utility will be prolonged, because developing a set of reasonably valid structural and behavioral relationships is a long-term job. Concentration of research attention on those aspects of the model required to support the analysis of problems in a single policy area, such as housing, will enhance the development of an urban dynamics model that is useful in-practice in policy studies.

CHAPTER 7

Summary, Conclusions,
and Implications

Examination of two topics will complete this model evaluation study. First is a concise assessment of the current and possible future usefulness for policy studies of urban dynamics and related models. Drawn from the findings of the case study evaluation of the model from the three points of view called for in the evaluation paradigm, the assessment of urban dynamics is extended by observing the likely policy usefulness of the world dynamics model developed by Forrester and used by Meadows and his associates. The second topic concerns the broader implications for policymaking gleaned from the case study, from both the policymaking and the research points of view.

ASSESSMENT OF URBAN DYNAMICS

The urban dynamics evaluation undertaken in this volume followed the guidelines of the model evaluation paradigm formulated within the general context of the relationship between modeling methodology and policymaking. The paradigm is directed particularly to the evaluation of models, such as urban dynamics, which address problems at the broad-aim end of a policy-problem spectrum ranging from narrow-aim problems dealing with specific questions of effectiveness and efficiency to broad-aim problems dealing with broad questions involving complex interactions. As observed previously, narrow-aim problems often arise in organizational contexts, usually have clear goals, and are quantified readily. On the other hand, broad-aim problems often encompass several organizations, are difficult to quantify, and involve a number of goals without explicit priorities among them. The set of problems addressed by the urban dynamics model usually involves interactions among a number of subsystems, has multiple goals, and requires consideration of a number of policy outcome measures.

In the following pages, the findings from the case study evaluation of urban dynamics are summarized; both the current policy usefulness of the urban dynamics model and the long-term possibilities of its usefulness are assessed; and some observations are made on the policy usefulness of the world dynamics model, which was Forrester's principal modeling effort after his urban dynamics work.

Findings from the Case Study Evaluation

In accord with the model evaluation paradigm, the urban dynamics model was examined from three points of view. First, the model's policy perspective was analyzed to determine what policy problems the model purports to deal with. Second, the adequacy of the model's theoretical support was examined. In this in-principle examination, the basic question was: How well are the supporting theory and concepts of the model buttressed by relevant research? Third, the model's capability to deal with policy problems in-practice was explored to determine how well the model as a whole tied together theory, assumptions, and data to deal with real-world policy problems.

In examining the model's policy perspective in Chapter 3, a comparative analysis was made of what urban dynamics and other urban simulation models offer from a policymaking point of view. The analysis compared urban dynamics and 15 other policy-oriented models, all of which have been applied to specific urban areas. The comparative framework contained four basic characteristics of models —subject, function, theory, and method—represented in terms of detailed model attributes. The models were grouped into transportation, housing and residential, economic activity, and general urban development categories. Each model was described briefly, analyzed, and classified in terms of the 20 model attributes used in the comparison. The principal features of the urban dynamics model were described, as well as the modeling techniques used. The comparison of urban dynamics with the other models was summarized in Table 1.

The comparative analysis concluded that urban dynamics provides a perspective for the study of urban policy problems different from that of previously developed models. It is potentially useful as a low-cost tool for addressing urban policy problems of a broad, strategic nature, rather than for more detailed and operational problems. Three characteristics set the model apart from other urban models and give it a distinctive policy perspective. First, urban dynamics is a very comprehensive, aggregate representation of an urban area. The model represents population, housing, employment, economic activity, land use, and public finance sectors at a very macrolevel. Key considerations in achieving such a representation are that the model represents few attributes of its housing, population, and industry entities, and no spatial distribution of activities. The second distinctive characteristic of the model is its bold representation of the interrelationships among model sectors; it is more synergistic than previous comprehensive urban models. The third special characteristic is the model's representation of behavioral relationships for the aggregates of population, housing, and industry. As indicated in the comparison, behavioral relationships have been incorporated to a significant degree only in models providing far less comprehensive representations of urban areas.

The in-principle examination of urban dynamics reviewed and evaluated prior research related to the model. This review of the model's conceptual and theoretical underpinning was based on seven research tasks regarded as essential in the development and application of policy models. The tasks were grouped into three steps: conceptualization of the problem and model, development of an operational model, and validation and application of the model. The scope of the review included Forrester's *Urban Dynamics* and other publications, more than a dozen review items on *Urban Dynamics*, more than 20 articles from the professional literature, a number of books and articles dealing in whole or in part with the urban dynamics model, a number of dissertations and theses, and papers presented at professional meetings.

Serious deficiencies were found in the supporting research for the model. The areas most lacking in research support were the adaptation of supporting concepts for the three model subsystems and for the interactions among subsystems, the empirical testing of model relationships, and model validation and application. In the first of these areas, it was found that no systematic analysis has been conducted for any of the model subsystems to ensure that the most valid concepts known were used. The tentative conclusion regarding this area was that the housing subsystem followed concepts generally aligned with urban literature, that there were significant problems with the concepts used in the population subsystem, and that there were major questions on the concepts of the business/industry subsystem. No research attention was devoted to the analysis of the conceptual support of the interactions among the three model subsystems, perhaps because little is known about this area. The second area is related to the first, but focuses more on the lack of empirically based research in support of testing the model's underlying assumptions and relationships. In the third area, although some validation-application efforts had been undertaken, the results were inadequate.

The in-practice examination of urban dynamics tested the capability of the model to represent a specific city and to deal with an actual policy problem for that city. Washington, D. C. was selected to be represented, and a housing problem relevant to Washington became the specific policy problem. In Chapter 5, the urban dynamics model representation of Washington was developed, and the performance of the model was evaluated by comparing computed model results with historical data for the 1960–1970 period. The model development was carried out in four stages: The first two incorporated area-specific values of model parameters into Forrester's model, and the third stage extended the model to include a limited representation of the interactions of Washington with its suburbs. In the fourth stage, a number of additional minor modifications and empirical adjustments were introduced. An evaluation of model results failed to support the contention by Forrester and others that a model of a specific city can be developed by incorporating approximately 40 area-specific values into urban dynamics. It was concluded that much more improvement was needed to make the Washington model a useful policy tool. The estimation of empirical values for the model's tabular functions and related relationships was identified as one of the primary jobs required; and some of the difficulties inherent in this job were discussed.

Chapter 6 analyzed a housing policy problem by using the urban dynamics model of Washington. The problem involved two policy initiatives taken in Washington, one promoting construction of new housing and the other promoting the rehabilitation of existing housing. The question posed was: What will the impact be of alternative levels of these two policy initiatives on housing conditions and economic stability in the city in 1980–1985? Although the model readily accommodated the modifications to represent the policy problem and to provide useful measures of policy outcome, the need for substantial improvement in the model was reinforced. A strategy was put forth for model improvement by using sensitivity testing within the context of applying the model to policy problems in a selected policy area. Research attention could thus be concentrated on a subset of the model relationships that require empirically based research.

The in-practice examination emphatically refuted the idea that the urban dynamics model has utility as a tool for policy studies related to a specific urban area. Based on the application of the model to Washington and to the housing policy problem, it was concluded that a large research effort would be required to develop the model to a point of policy usefulness.

Assessment of the Urban Dynamics Model

As the study has shown, urban dynamics is a comprehensive representation of an urban area, which offers a distinctive policy perspective for dealing with urban problems. The potential utility of the model, however, has not been realized, because many of the model's supporting assumptions and relationships are open to question, and insufficient research has been devoted to developing valid assumptions and relationships. This general conclusion is supported by the review of model-related research and the application of the model to a policy problem for a specific urban area.

At its present stage of development, the urban dynamics model is perhaps less useful in analyzing a policy problem than some less sophisticated tools. For instance, in regard to the housing policy problem analyzed in Chapter 6, if the research effort required to apply the model to the housing problem were expended working on the problem with regression analysis and simple projection techniques, this effort would produce considerably more results useful for policy. Under these conditions, there is no justification for choosing the urban dynamics model over simpler policy analysis tools. This poses the more difficult question of whether the model can be improved so it is competitive with, or preferential to, other techniques and, if so, whether it will be worth the effort.

Although the evaluation reasonably concludes that urban dynamics is inadequate for policy analysis use, the evaluation is far less satisfying in pinpointing a concise reason why the model is unsatisfactory. Basically, this is because the model is inadequate for a very broad reason: It floats free of the real world. The model makes no use of theoretical constructs, such as the gravity principle, market theory, or input-output theory, which, although limited in scope and power, have proved useful in other urban policy models. Neither does the model incorporate the results from empirically based research on urban problems. This does not mean that if the model were to incorporate available theory and empirical research it would be a good model. In fact, theory for urban systems is in a primitive state of development and is still inadequate to provide organizing concepts for model building. Because of the lack of theory, empirical research is both poorly developed and organized. In urban dynamics, the problems are compounded, because the limited knowledge available about urban systems is ignored.

This lack of correlation of the urban dynamics model with relevant urban research was observed in the study. The review of model-related research in Chapter 4 concluded that there was a failure to examine systematically the model subsystems and the interactions among subsystems to evaluate the conceptual structure of the model in terms of the concepts used in other research. The application of the model in Chapters 5 and 6 reinforced the conclusion that the model's supporting assumptions and relationships also had been neglected in terms of incorporating existing research and of conducting empirical research.

All of these findings reinforce the basic idea that the urban dynamics model floats free of the real world. It fails to incorporate, to be consistent with, and even to be aware of the knowledge social scientists have assimilated about urban systems. Under these conditions, there can be no confidence in the use of the model's results in policy analyses. Although the model has little or no connection with reality, Forrester uses it as a basis for developing strong recommendations against a number of urban programs which have been used. For example, Forrester's analysis indicates that increasing the supply of low-income housing has the negative effect of increasing the in-migration of low-income population and of discouraging the development of new industry by depleting available land. Another example is that job-training programs tend to increase the out-migration of skilled workers, increase the in-migration of low-income workers, and retard upward mobility in the labor force.[1] Forrester may be absolutely right in these and his other policy conclusions. In its current state of development, however, urban dynamics has nothing useful to offer regarding these matters.

More constructively, can existing urban research be incorporated

---

[1] Jay W. Forrester. *Urban Dynamics.* Cambridge, Mass., MIT Press, 1969, pp. 51–70.

into the model and empirical research conducted to develop urban dynamics into a useful policy model? While the evaluation provides no clear answers, it does suggest some research tasks that can be undertaken toward developing a policy-useful model. After these tasks are undertaken, the conclusion may be that urban systems are not well-enough understood to produce a policy-useful macromodel such as urban dynamics. Nevertheless, such effort may result in a useful model and suggest further research.

In addressing the question posed, the bottom-up approach can be applied to identify a sequence of research tasks that may be undertaken successfully. This approach coincides with the way prospective research is envisaged. Unfortunately, it cannot tell when a policy-useful model might evolve, since the initial research tasks probably will be extended into a succession of research projects. A better time perspective for the development of a useful urban dynamics type model perhaps is provided by drawing a loose analogy with the development of national macroeconomic models. These models, initiated in the 1950s, have become a moderately useful policy tool, although far from completely adequate. During the developmental period, macroeconomic models were supported by a substantial body of theory. In contrast, only fragments of theory support the development of an urban system macromodel. If the analogy holds, it may take two or three decades to bring urban macromodels to the point of moderate usefulness. It might be argued, however, that the urgency of the problem, the quickening pace of research, and other factors will telescope the time required to accomplish this.

Observations on World Dynamics Model

In 1971, Professor Forrester undertook another major extension in the application of his system dynamics modeling methodology to broader problems by setting forth a world dynamics model. The model represents the structure of the world in terms of five principal variables: population, capital investment, natural resources, fraction of capital devoted to agriculture, and pollution. The premise is that these variables and their interactions govern the dynamics of change in the world system.[2] Although Forrester admits that the model is a tentative one, he apparently feels that policy conclusions can be based

---

[2] Jay W. Forrester. *World Dynamics.* Cambridge, Mass., Wright-Allen Press, 1971, pp. 1–2.

on it. As Forrester states in his introductory remarks in *World Dynamics:*

Having defined with care the model contained herein, and having examined its dynamic behavior and implications, I have greater confidence in this world system model than in others that I now have available. Therefore, this is the model I should use for recommending actions.[3]

Forrester applies his world dynamics model to projecting the world's future population, quality of life, natural resource levels, and other characteristics. He examines what he regards as the conventional policy responses to coping with the world and future economic and social problems—increasing capital investment to achieve increased industrialization, birth-control programs, pollution control, increased agricultural productivity, and combinations of these measures. The model-based examination of these policies through the year 2100 indicates that a world crisis will result from a sharp reduction in population and a deterioration in the quality of life. Model results show the global disaster as certain, with the policy alternatives examined altering only somewhat the route taken to disaster and its timing.[4] Forrester, however, formulates one set of policy actions that reduce resource usage, pollution generation, capital investment, and the birth rate, each by prescribed percentages, and, under this set of actions, population is stabilized slightly below the 1970 level, and the quality of life is improved.[5]

Based on these assumptions, Forrester suggests that "a global equilibrium is conceptually possible," [6] but he is concerned that such a set of restrictive actions will not be accepted easily.

The world dynamics model uses the same techniques as the urban dynamics model. It is stated in approximately 115 Dynamo language statements, and is approximately one-third the size of urban dynamics. More than one-third of the 115 statements are used to set the values of constants for the model, and 22 additional statements specify data for the model's 22 tabular functions.[7] As with urban dynamics, Forrester does not incorporate existing research into the model, and he makes only casual use of empirical data. In specifying parameter values and the numerical data for the nonlinear relationships implicit in the tabular functions, Forrester depends on his intuitive powers to

[3] *Ibid.,* p. ix.
[4] *Ibid.,* pp. 93–111.
[5] *Ibid.,* pp. 112–122.
[6] *Ibid.,* p. 122.
[7] *Ibid.,* pp. 132–134.

determine values. He makes no attempt to validate the model as a whole by comparing its results closely with historical results. These facts are strongly reminiscent of the findings from the evaluation of the urban dynamics model and lead to the suspicion that world dynamics also floats free of the real world and is useless in policy studies.

Although reception of Forrester's *World Dynamics* was mixed, the model was the target of even more scathing criticism from leading scientists identified closely with policy modeling than urban dynamics had been. Thomas Naylor [8] of Duke University, in a paper presented at a national meeting, questioned the feasibility of world models, as well as Forrester's approach to such a model. He gibed at Forrester by remarking that, with the appearance of *World Dynamics*, "we and the inhabitants of the other planets in our universe are now anxiously awaiting the publication of a 'Universe Dynamics.'" Martin Shubik [9] of Yale University also was sharply critical of the model and attacked its lack of connection with the real world. In his review of *World Dynamics*, which appeared in *Science*, Shubik stated that "the book is blatant and insensitive advocacy for unsubstantiated model building on a very large scale." He sums up his assessment of the world dynamics model and Forrester's approach to modeling as follows:

> With his three books Forrester has succeeded in publicizing the concept of the applicability of large computer models and feedback systems to human affairs. . . . If his next book deals successfully with how to identify the key variables and parameters in these large systems, and with an example or two with more than casual empirical content, perhaps the value of such models can be accepted as more than an article of faith. In the meantime, he has demonstrated how to approach the understanding of human affairs in an energetic, simplistic, and superficially attractive but nonetheless dangerously wrong manner.[10]

Although Forrester's *World Dynamics* received considerable attention, there was much wider interest in his world model after the publication of a closely related book entitled *The Limits to Growth*.[11] The

---

[8] Thomas Naylor. "Up, Up and Away." (Abstract of paper read at the National Computer Conference, sponsored by the American Federation of Information Processing Societies, June 1973, New York, N. Y.) *Computing Reviews*, 15:267, August 1974.

[9] Martin Shubik. "Modeling on a Grand Scale." Review of Jay W. Forrester, *World Dynamics*. *Science*, 174:1014, December 3, 1971.

[10] *Ibid.*, p. 1015.

[11] Donella H. Meadows et al. *The Limits to Growth*. New York, Universe Books, 1972.

latter, by Donella and Dennis Meadows et al., builds on Forrester's world dynamics model. Both books are linked with the Club of Rome, an informal, international association of private citizens, whose purpose is to promote, through improved understanding, policy actions for dealing with global economic and social issues. Forrester's attendance at a Club of Rome meeting in 1970 led to his development of the world dynamics model. The focus of that meeting was planning the Club of Rome's Predicament of Mankind project. The objective of the project was to develop the understanding of options available to mankind as the world makes the transition from a state of growth to one of equilibrium. The world dynamics model was devised as a basis for discussions at a later meeting with the Club of Rome at MIT, which resulted in a decision by the Club of Rome that the system dynamics approach to world modeling was a suitable methodology for their project. They sponsored research to extend the development of the world dynamics model, to improve its underlying assumptions and empirical support, and to apply the model to gain further understanding of world social and economic behavior.[12] This research effort was led by Dennis Meadows and resulted in the publication of *The Limits to Growth*.

The Limits to Growth, written for a general, nontechnical audience, received immediate and widespread attention in news items, book reviews, and critiques. The general conclusions presented in the book are based on an improved version of the world dynamics model and are essentially the same as Forrester's: If present policies related to world growth are continued, there will be a sudden, irreversible change within the next 50 to 100 years consisting of a decline in population due to starvation, illness, and other causes, and a decline in the quality of life due to reduced levels of industrial production. To avert this disaster, fundamental shifts in government policies are necessary.[13] The primary question from the policymaking point of view is whether the world dynamics model, as improved by Meadows et al., is a trustworthy tool for supporting the policy recommendations made in *The Limits to Growth*.

No final answer is presently available, despite widespread publicity and numerous written commentaries provoked by the model and the model-supported analysis of global growth policies. Nor is an attempt made here to answer the question. Rather, a few published items that

---

[12] Forrester. *World Dynamics*, pp. vii–ix.
[13] Meadows et al. *The Limits to Growth*, pp. 17–24.

are particularly relevant to this question are mentioned, and their tentative conclusions are given.

Two books by Meadows et al. purport to provide technical documentation for the supporting research for *The Limits to Growth*— *Toward Global Equilibrium: Collected Papers*[14] and *Dynamics of Growth in a Finite World*.[15] The first is a set of 13 papers dealing with the flow of DDT, the supply and consumption of natural gas, population control among a primitive people in New Guinea, the role of churches in the world transition from growth to equilibrium, and other topics. Some of these papers were published previously, and some reiterate material from *The Limits to Growth*. Although interesting, this collection of papers does little or nothing to support the assumptions nor to justify the methodology for the world model used by Meadows and his colleagues. The second volume is directly relevant to evaluating the world model. It deals with each of the principal model sectors and provides a report on the research undertaken to justify the methodology and the assumptions used.

The other published items related to the usefulness of Meadows' world model appear in the February 1973 issue of *Futures*. A set of nine articles presents the most complete evaluation undertaken to date of the world model used in *The Limits to Growth*. These articles comprise a research report on the model evaluation effort by the members of the Science Policy Research Unit of the University of Sussex in England. The Sussex group had prepublication access to the primary technical documentation for the Meadows model for use in their work. This documentation appeared as *Dynamics of Growth in a Finite World*. The Sussex group, which consists of an interdisciplinary mix of European academics, provided extensive, detailed criticisms of the world model. The criticisms are sometimes severe, but the study appears to be an objective, constructive effort. Its fundamental conclusion is that, although the Forrester and Meadows models are useful steps toward world modeling, they "should in no sense be used now as a basis for policymaking."[16] This clearly indicates that the model is not regarded as a suitable tool for supporting the categorical conclusions and recommendations made in *The Limits to Growth*. The Sussex group found the major assumptions of the Meadows model

---

[14] Dennis L. Meadows and Donella H. Meadows, eds. *Toward Global Equilibrium: Collected Papers*. Cambridge, Mass., Wright-Allen Press, 1973.

[15] Dennis L. Meadows et al. *Dynamics of Growth in a Finite World*. Cambridge, Mass., Wright-Allen Press, 1974.

[16] Guy Streatfeild. "World Dynamics Challenged." *Futures*, 5:4, February 1973.

to be the same as those of Forrester's world model. Furthermore, the added complexity included in the Meadows model "contributes little to its utility as a forecasting device and tends to give a false air of sophistication and exactitude." [17]

From these observations, the tentative answer to the question previously posed, supported by the work of the Sussex group, is that the modified world dynamics model used by Meadows is not a trustworthy tool for supporting policy analysis. In addition, many of the problems observed in the evaluation of the urban dynamics model discussed in this volume and also inherent in the world model are not dealt with by the Meadows team. For example, as was evident in urban dynamics, the lack of theory and empirically based relationships preclude a sound basis for the world model sectors and the interactions between the sectors. Also, as with the urban dynamics model, estimating empirical values for the tabular functions and other relationships of the world model embodies difficulties in data availability and statistical estimation.

IMPLICATIONS OF THE CASE STUDY

An assessment of the utility of urban dynamics and related models through the findings from the case study leads to an examination of the broader implications of the case study from two points of view: policymaking and research. These points of view are closely intertwined, but it is useful to make a distinction for this discussion. The policymaking view is concerned with identifying broad research needs, establishing organizational procedures, and general research planning to ensure that modeling efforts contribute as much as possible to policy deliberations. The research view is more directly concerned with model development, including the detailed planning and activities associated with model building. The premise in discussing both points of view is that improved understanding, procedures, and techniques for model evaluation will increase the use of policy modeling.

Implications for Policymaking

The implications of model evaluation for policymaking relate primarily to two areas of interest. The first area is that of organizational adapta-

---

[17] H. S. D. Cole and R. C. Currow. "The Evaluation of the World Models." *Futures,* 5:132, February 1973.

tions that may be required when an organization adopts any comprehensive approach to model evaluation, such as the one advanced in this study. The second area is how the information developed by model evaluation efforts is used. Such information is helpful for planning from the policymaking point of view and for advancing the incorporation of modeling into the policymaking process.

The organizational procedures required to relate modeling research to policy needs are similar to the procedures for relating any type of policy-oriented research to policy. As mentioned in Chapter 1, it is more difficult to evaluate modeling research than policy-related research undertaken by other methodologies, because models that address broad-aim policy problems usually integrate theory, empirically based relationships, and data from a number of sources. The evaluation is also more difficult because of the uncertainties inherent in policy models that provide explicit representations of the future and the impact of various policies on the future. As a result, a different emphasis may be placed on certain procedures, but the same procedures generally apply to policy modeling research as apply to other policy-related research.

Organizational procedures to guide policy modeling efforts are devised primarily to establish effective two-way communication between the policymaking and research points of view. The gap between these two viewpoints occurs as a result of differences in the pragmatic view of policymakers and the theoretical view of model researchers. As indicated in Chapter 1, this difference motivates more systematic, structured model evaluations. Organizational procedures cannot, of course, provide communication between policymaking and research in a highly quantitative, analytic form, but they can be used to ensure a continuing, systematic, and comprehensive effort to relate policy needs and modeling research.

To relate modeling research to policy, organizational procedures must promote three essential activities. First, the major policy issues emanating from organizational goals must be identified. In addition to current issues, future issues must be anticipated. This is not always possible, however, as shown, for example, by the energy crisis, which presented many unexpected issues. The second activity must assess the extent to which modeling efforts can possibly address aspects of the policy issues identified. The specific, relevant modeling projects may be ongoing, or they may be projects to be considered and possibly undertaken. Some projects may be in-house efforts; others may be conducted by other organizations through contract arrangements. Some policy issues can be addressed only in part, and perhaps not at all, by modeling research. The result of this assessment will be a set of potential modeling research projects relevant to organizational policy needs. The third activity in the process brings together the results from the first two activities to estimate the extent to which ongoing and planned modeling research actually is meeting policy needs. This includes estimates of how well research is capitalizing on opportunities to contribute to various issues, as well as the identification of neglected and overemphasized policy areas.

Establishing organizational procedures of this kind to fashion a framework for the broad planning of modeling research is a complex matter. But, to conduct the activities outlined, an organizational mechanism is essential to provide guidance. In fact, the planning procedures are aptly regarded as a means for reconciling within an organization the pragmatic and theoretical points of view associated with policymaking and research, respectively. These planning activities depend directly on information derived from the evaluation of existing and proposed models. Often, the model evaluations in support of planning activities need not be as extensive as the case study evaluation of urban dynamics, because questions in support of planning often will be specific with regard to a model's capability and probable usefulness in studying a particular issue.

From the evaluation of urban dynamics, it is evident that information from model evaluations may contribute in a number of ways to the planning process previously outlined. For example, the in-perspective examination of urban dynamics showed it to be a potentially useful tool for addressing broad, strategic problems because of its highly aggregate, synergistic, behavioral representation of an urban area. It is also evident that urban dynamics will not be useful for policy questions requiring a spatial representation of activities or a detailed representation of the transportation system of an urban area. As another example, the in-principle and in-practice examinations showed that urban dynamics presently is not useful for analyzing policy problems—a clear warning against reliance on the model in its current state of development for conducting policy studies.

In addition to indicating whether a model will be useful in dealing with specific policy issues, the information from evaluations helps to identify research tasks and to formulate strategies for approaching these tasks. For example, information from the case study suggests additional research that could be undertaken for the urban dynamics model. In spite of the low probability of near-term payoff, an organization may consider that the urban dynamics model has sufficient potential use to be worth an investment of resources. Two areas of model-related research motivated by the information from the case study merit special discussion.

1. The research task most strongly suggested by the model evaluation is the examination and restructuring of the urban dynamics model to incorporate relevant results from urban research. The pertinent aspects of urban research, or urban analysis, include such areas as urban economics, urban sociology, population studies, housing studies, urban social indicators, and urban information systems. This is a sizable body of research, as indicated by two bibliographies.[18] One of these bibliographies contains more than 800 items in the area of urban analysis. This body of research, however, was merely touched on in the model evaluation undertaken.

The findings from the in-principle examination of urban dynamics strongly suggest the need to examine the structural and behavioral relationships of the model and to reformulate the model appropriately in light of available research. It may be desirable to concentrate on the population, housing, and business/industry subsystems individually, perhaps in separate projects. Model concepts and relationships must be examined against available research results in terms of the appropriateness of the variables included in model relationships; the validity of model relationships and assumptions; the appropriateness of the level of detail included in the relationships; the availability of data to test model relationships empirically and estimate parameter values; and the compatibility of the representations of the model subsystems. A problem encountered in the evaluation, and one that this research can help resolve, is whether the model's business/industry subsystem should be restructured as an input-output model or in some other way that differs from Forrester's life-cycle concept. Another problem is whether the population subsystem should be modified to include age groups for the population, thereby affording a richer demographic representation at the expense of increasing the amount of information the model carries. Still another problem is whether the housing subsystem should be modified to represent rental and owner-occupied units and single- and multifamily units.

Even when this large research task suggested by the model evaluation

[18] Maurice D. Kilbridge, Robert P. O'Block, and Paul V. Teplitz. *Urban Analysis.* Boston, Division of Research, Graduate School of Business Administration, Harvard University, 1970, pp. 127–330; and A. Lee Fritschler, B. Douglas Harman, and Bernard H. Ross. *Urban Affairs Bibliography: A Guide to Literature in the Field.* 2nd Edition. Washington, D. C., School of Government and Public Administration, The American University, 1970.

is completed, the model will still be inadequate, because existing research will not provide support for many aspects of the model. The resulting model, however, will be an urban macromodel generally consistent with urban research. Of course, the final model probably will be so substantially modified as a result of this undertaking that it may be regarded as distinct from urban dynamics.

2. The second area of model-related research suggested by the model evaluation is the application of the model to policy problems for specific urban areas. This should be undertaken only after incorporating urban research into the model as previously discussed. In applying the model to problems for specific areas, the sensitivity testing strategy explained in Chapter 6 should be used. Under this strategy, sensitivity tests are performed within the context of applying the model to policy problems for identification of model assumptions and relationships to which model results for the problem are sensitive. Such assumptions and relationships become the subject of empirically based research to develop more realistic relationships and to incorporate them into the model. As mentioned in Chapter 6, the model's behavioral assumptions and relationships probably will require much of the attention, because existing urban research does not adequately support many of those aspects of the model. Concentration on policy problems in a single area, such as housing, probably will ensure the most rapid progress toward a policy-useful model.

Implications for Research

The case study evaluation also has implications for the research point of view concerned directly with model development. The two examples of research tasks given in the preceding paragraphs and motivated by the case study are of strong interest to researchers as well as to policymakers. In addition to those examples, the case study points to the need for research to improve the model development and evaluation process. Two examples of such research follow.

The first is concerned with the problem of model validation, or determining the degree of correspondence between a model and the system under study. Model validation is the key to the whole process of making useful policy inferences from a model, and is one of the thorniest problems in the development and evaluation of models. Validation was discussed in general terms in Chapter 2, where three approaches to validation were mentioned: constructing a model that has face validity, testing the assumptions upon which the model is based, and comparing the performance of the model with the system being modeled. Each of these approaches was referred to at various points in the case study.

The particular aspect of validation of interest here is the statistical comparison of model results and observed data. A number of measures may be used in comparing computed and observed time series. These include number of turning points, direction of turning points, amplitude of fluctuations, average amplitude, and average values of variables.[19] One of the more elaborate measures, devised by Theil,[20] was used in Chapter 5 to compare computed and historical time series for the city of Washington. In addition, sophisticated statistical techniques can be used to test the goodness of fit of a computed and observed time series. These include analysis of variance, regression analysis, chi-square test, and spectral analysis. It should be noted that different measures and techniques are appropriate according to the policy questions being addressed; the error in policymaking will be a consequence of different types of errors in a computed time series. Consider a policy question, for example, in which there is a need for average yearly costs, distribution of costs by year, and maximum yearly costs for a program. The importance and relative importance of errors or discrepancies to policy results in these three types of costs should be considered in the choice of statistical measures and techniques for comparing the computed and historical time series for the variables that measure these costs. Also, the assumptions underlying the use of the various statistical techniques must be considered. The proposal is to identify the principal types of errors that can occur in model projections and to develop a rationale for the choice of appropriate statistical measures and techniques for testing each type of error. This aspect of validation will become increasingly important as simulation models improve.

The second problem in the use of policymaking simulation is concerned with the extent to which policymakers actually use available simulation models in policy decisions. In which policy areas are models most used by policymakers? What are the characteristics of simulation models that determine whether they will be used by policymakers?

[19] Thomas H. Naylor. "Methodological Considerations in Simulating Social and Administrative Systems." *In: Simulation in Social and Administrative Sciences.* Edited by Harold Guetzkow, Philip Kotler, and Randall L. Schultz. Englewood Cliffs, N. J., Prentice-Hall, 1972, p. 657.

[20] Henri Theil. *Applied Economic Forecasting.* Amsterdam, North-Holland Publ., 1966, pp. 15–30.

What institutional and organizational arrangements for developing simulation models are instrumental in producing models that policymakers actually use?

In response to these questions, computer simulation has advanced to the point where ways of developing models can be identified so they are more useful in policymaking. Recent studies mentioned in Chapter 1 provide some preliminary insight into these questions. One survey suggests that organizational proximity of model developer and policymaker promote the use of models. Also, models were found to be used least when separate organizations representing the policymaker, funding agency, and model developer were involved.[21] Such insights as these will provide direction for the development of models having increased policymaking utility.

[21] Gary Fromm, William L. Hamilton, and Diane E. Hamilton. *Federally Supported Mathematical Models: Survey and Analysis. Volume I: Analysis and Conclusions.* Boston, Data Resources, Inc. and Abt Associates, Inc., 1974, pp. 3–5.

CHAPTER 8

Bibliography

BOOKS

Aaron, Henry J. *Shelter and Subsidies: Who Benefits from Federal Housing Policies?* Washington, D. C., The Brookings Institution, 1972.

Abt, Clark C. *Serious Games.* New York, Viking Press, 1970.

Ackoff, Russell L., and Sasieni, Maurice W. *Fundamentals of Operations Research.* New York, Wiley, 1968.

Anthony, Robert N. *Planning and Control Systems: A Framework for Analysis.* Boston, Mass., Division of Research, Graduate School of Business Administration, Harvard University, 1965.

Babrow, Davis B., and Schwartz, Judah L., eds. *Computers and the Policymaking Community: Applications to International Relations.* Englewood Cliffs, N. J., Prentice-Hall, 1968.

Berman, Barbara R.; Chinitz, Benjamin; and Hoover, Edgar M. *Projection of a Metropolis; Technical Supplement to the New York Metropolitan Region Study.* Cambridge, Mass., Harvard University Press, 1960.

Black, Guy. *The Application of Systems Analysis to Government Operations.* New York, Praeger, 1968.

Blalock, Hubert M., Jr. *Theory Construction.* Englewood Cliffs, N. J., Prentice-Hall, 1969.

Braybrooke, David, and Lindblom, Charles E. *A Strategy of Decision.* New York, Free Press, 1963.

193

Breshers, James M. *Computer Methods in the Analysis of Large-Scale Social Systems.* Cambridge, Mass., MIT Press, 1968.

Brewer, Garry D. *Politicians, Bureaucrats and the Consultants: A Critique of Urban Problem Solving.* New York, Basic Books, 1973.

Brown, H. James, et al. *Empirical Models of Urban Land Use: Suggestions on Research Objectives and Organization.* New York, National Bureau of Economic Research, 1972.

Catanese, Anthony J. *Scientific Methods of Urban Analysis.* Urbana, Ill., University of Illinois Press, 1972.

Chen, Kan, ed. *Urban Dynamics: Extensions and Reflections.* San Francisco, San Francisco Press, 1972.

Churchman, C. West. *Challenge to Reason.* New York, McGraw-Hill, 1968.

Coplin, William D., ed. *Simulation in the Study of Politics.* Chicago, Markham Publishing, 1968.

Crecine, John P. *Government Problem Solving: Computer Simulation of Municipal Budgeting.* Chicago, Rand McNally, 1969.

Creighton, Roger L. *Urban Transportation Planning.* Urbana, Ill., University of Illinois Press, 1970.

Downs, Anthony. *Urban Problems and Prospects.* Chicago, Markham Publishing, 1970.

Dror, Yehezkel. *Public Policymaking Reexamined.* Scranton, Pa., Chandler Publishing, 1968.

Emshoff, James R., and Sisson, Roger L. *Design and Use of Computer Simulation Models.* New York, Macmillan, 1970.

Forrester, Jay W. *Industrial Dynamics.* Cambridge, Mass., MIT Press, 1961.

———. *Urban Dynamics.* Cambridge, Mass., MIT Press, 1969.

———. *World Dynamics.* Cambridge, Mass., Wright-Allen Press, 1971.

Grigsby, William G. *Housing Markets and Public Policy.* Philadelphia, University of Pennsylvania Press, 1963.

Guetzkow, Harold, ed. *Simulation in Social Science: Readings.* Englewood Cliffs, N. J., Prentice-Hall, 1962.

Guetzkow, Harold; Kotler, Philip; and Schultz, Randall L., eds. *Simulation in Social and Administrative Science.* Englewood Cliffs, N. J., Prentice-Hall, 1972.

Hamilton, H. R., et al. *Systems Simulation for Regional Analysis: An Application to River-Basin Planning.* Cambridge, Mass., MIT Press, 1969.

Hemmens, George C., ed. *Urban Development Models.* Washington, D. C., Highway Research Board, National Academy of Sciences, 1968.

Hillier, Frederick S., and Lieberman, Gerald J. *Introduction to Operations Research.* San Francisco, Holden-Day, 1967.

Jencks, Christopher, et al. *Inequality: A Reassessment of the Effect of Family and Schooling in America.* New York, Basic Books, 1972.

Kaplan, Abraham. *The Conduct of Inquiry.* San Francisco, Chandler Publishing, 1964.

Kilbridge, Maurice D.; O'Block, Robert P.; and Teplitz, Paul V. *Urban*

Analysis. Boston, Mass., Division of Research, Graduate School of Business Administration, Harvard University, 1970.

Klerer, Melvin, and Korn, Granino A., eds. *Digital Computer User's Handbook.* New York, McGraw-Hill, 1967.

Lansing, John B., and Mueller, Eva. *The Geographic Mobility of Labor.* Ann Arbor, Mich., Institute for Social Research, The University of Michigan, 1967.

Lasswell, Harold D. *A Pre-View of Policy Sciences.* New York, American Elsevier Publishing, 1971.

Lowry, Ira S. *Migration and Metropolitan Growth: Two Analytical Models.* San Francisco, Chandler Publishing, 1966.

Mass, Nathaniel J., ed. *Readings in Urban Dynamics: Volume I.* Cambridge, Mass., Wright-Allen Press, 1974.

McLeod, John, ed. *Simulation; the Dynamic Modeling of Ideas and Systems.* New York, McGraw-Hill, 1968.

Meadows, Dennis L., and Meadows, Donella H., eds. *Toward Global Equilibrium: Collected Papers.* Cambridge, Mass., Wright-Allen Press, 1973.

Meadows, Dennis L., et al. *Dynamics of Growth in a Finite World.* Cambridge, Mass., Wright-Allen Press, 1974.

Meadows, Donella H., et al. *The Limits to Growth.* New York, Universe Books, 1972.

Mesarovic, Mihajlo D., and Reisman, Arnold, eds. *Systems Approach and the City.* Amsterdam, North-Holland Publishing, 1972.

Naylor, Thomas H. *Computer Simulation Experiments with Models of Economic Systems.* New York, Wiley, 1971.

Naylor, Thomas H., et al. *Computer Simulation Techniques.* New York, Wiley, 1968.

Perloff, Harvey S., and Wingo, Lowdon, Jr., eds. *Issues in Urban Economics.* Baltimore, Md., Johns Hopkins Press, 1968.

Pool, Ithiel de Sola, et al. *Candidates, Issues, and Strategies: A Computer Simulation of the 1960 and 1964 Presidential Elections.* Cambridge, Mass., MIT Press, 1964.

Pugh, A. L., III. *DYNAMO User's Manual.* Cambridge, Mass., MIT Press, 1963.

———. *DYNAMO User's Manual.* 2nd Edition. Cambridge, Mass., MIT Press, 1967.

———. *DYNAMO User's Manual.* 3rd Edition. Cambridge, Mass., MIT Press, 1970.

Raser, J. R. *Simulation and Society.* Boston, Mass., Allyn and Bacon, 1969.

Rivlin, Alice M. *Systematic Thinking for Social Science.* Washington, D. C., The Brookings Institution, 1971.

Robinson, Ira M., ed. *Decision-Making in Urban Planning: An Introduction to New Methodologies.* Beverly Hills, Calif., Sage Publications, 1972.

Sammet, Jean E. *Programming Languages: History and Fundamentals.* Englewood Cliffs, N. J., Prentice-Hall, 1969.

Schroeder, W.; Alfeld, L.; and Sweeney, R., eds. *Readings in Urban Dynamics: Volume II.* Cambridge, Mass., Wright-Allen Press, 1975.

Schultze, Charles L. *The Politics and Economics of Public Spending.* Washington, D. C., The Brookings Institution, 1968.

Simon, Herbert A. *Administrative Behavior.* 2nd Edition. New York, Macmillan, 1957.

Stegman, Michael A. *Housing Investment in the Inner City: The Dynamics of Decline.* Cambridge, Mass., MIT Press, 1972.

Sweeney, Stephen B., and Charlesworth, James C., eds. *Governing Urban Society: New Scientific Approaches.* Monograph of the American Academy of Political and Social Science, No. 7. Philadelphia, The American Academy of Political and Social Science, 1967.

Theil, Henri. *Applied Economic Forecasting.* Amsterdam, North-Holland Publishing, 1966.

Tocher, K. D. *The Art of Simulation.* Princeton, N. J., Van Nostrand, 1963.

Wagner, Harvey M. *Principles of Operations Research.* Englewood Cliffs, N. J., Prentice-Hall, 1969.

PERIODICALS

Abelson, Robert P., and Bernstein, Alex. "A Computer Simulation Model of Community Reference Controversies." *Public Opinion Quarterly, 1*:93–122, 1963.

American Association for the Advancement of Science. "The Central Program of the 1972 AAAS Annual Meeting." *Science, 178*:886–913, November 24, 1972.

American Institute of Planners. *Journal of the American Institute of Planners, 25,* May 1959.

American Institute of Planners. *Journal of the American Institute of Planners, 31,* May 1965.

Ansoff, H. Igor, and Slevin, Dennis P. "An Appreciation of Industrial Dynamics." *Management Science, 14*:383–397, March 1968.

Barber, Thomas A. "Review of Jay W. Forrester, *Urban Dynamics.*" *Datamation, 15*:452–454, November 1969.

Batty, Michael. "Modelling Cities as Dynamic Systems." *Nature, 231*:425–428, June 18, 1971.

Bell, Daniel. "Twelve Models of Prediction—A Preliminary Sorting of Approaches in the Social Sciences." *Daedalus, 93*:845–880, Summer 1964.

Bell, Daniel, et al. "The Nature and Limitations of Forecasting." *Daedalus, 96*:936–947, Summer 1967.

Berger, Edward; Boulay, Harvey; and Zisk, Betty. "Simulation and the City: A Critical Overview." *Simulation and Games, 1*:411–428, December 1970.

Berlinski, David J. "Systems Analysis." *Urban Affairs Quarterly, 6*:104–126, September 1970.

Berry, Brian J. L. "The Retail Component of the Urban Model." *Journal of the American Institute of Planners, 31*:150–155, May 1965.

Blumberg, Donald F. "The City as a System." *Simulation, 17*:155–167, October 1971.

Boyce, David E., and Cote, Roger W. "Verification of Land Use Forecasting Models: Procedures and Data Requirements." *Highway Research Record, 126*:60–65, 1966.

Campbell, Donald T. "Reforms as Experiments." *Urban Affairs Quarterly, 7*:133–171, December 1971.

Chapin, F. Stuart, Jr. "A Model for Simulating Residential Development." *Journal of the American Institute of Planners, 31*:120–125, May 1965.

Christakis, Alexander N. "Review of Jay W. Forrester, *Urban Dynamics.*" *Technological Forecasting, 1*:427–429, Spring 1970.

Churchill, Betty C. "State Distribution of Business Concerns." *Survey of Current Business, 34*:14–24, November 1954.

Cole, H. S. D., and Currow, R. C. "The Evaluation of the World Models." *Futures, 5*:108–134, February 1973.

Crecine, John P. "A Computer Simulation Model of Municipal Budgeting." *Management Science, 13*:806–815, July 1967.

Danforth, Herman L. "Review of Jay W. Forrester, *Urban Dynamics.*" *Public Management, 53*:20, January 1971.

"A Daring Look at City Ills." *Business Week*:142, 144, 146, June 14, 1969.

Deutsch, Karl W. "On Theories, Taxonomies, and Models as Communication Codes for Organizing Information." *Behavioral Science, 11*:1–17, January 1966.

Downs, Anthony. "Housing the Urban Poor: The Economics of Various Strategies." *The American Economic Review, 49*:646–651, September 1969.

Duke, Richard D., and Meier, Richard L. "Gaming Simulation for Urban Planning." *Journal of the American Institute of Planners, 32*:3–17, January 1966.

Feldt, Allan G. "Review of Jay W. Forrester, *Urban Dynamics.*" *American Sociological Review, 35*:364–365, April 1970.

Fleisher, Aaron. "Review of Jay W. Forrester, *Urban Dynamics.*" *Journal of the American Institute of Planners, 37*:53–54, January 1971.

Forrester, Jay W. "Counterintuitive Behavior of Social Systems." *Technological Forecasting and Social Change, 3*:1–22, Winter 1971.

———. "Industrial Dynamics—After the First Decade." *Management Science, 14*:398–415, March 1968.

———. "Market Growth as Influenced by Capital Investments." *Industrial Management Review:* 83–105, Winter 1968.

———. "Overlooked Reason for Our Social Troubles." Rebuttal to John F. Kain review of Jay W. Forrester, *Urban Dynamics. Fortune, 80*:191–192, December 1969.

———. "Systems Analysis as a Tool for Urban Planning." *IEEE Transactions on Systems Science and Cybernetics, SSC-6*:258–265, October 1970.

Gans, Herbert J. "A Poor Man's Home Is His Poorhouse." *New York Times Magazine*: 20–21, 49–58, March 31, 1974.

Garrison, W. L. "Urban Transportation Planning Models in 1975." *Journal of the American Institute of Planners, 31*:156–158, May 1965.

Gillette, Robert. "The Limits to Growth: Hard Sell for a Computer View of Doomsday." *Science, 175*:1088–1092, March 10, 1972.

Goldner, William. "The Lowry Model Heritage." *Journal of the American Institute of Planners, 37*:100–110, March 1971.

Graham, Alan K. "Modeling City-Suburb Interactions." *IEEE Transactions on Systems, Man, and Cybernetics, SMC-2*:156–158, April 1972.

Guthrie, Harold. "Microanalytic Simulation Modeling for Evaluation of Public Policy." *Urban Affairs Quarterly, 8*:403–417, June 1972.

Harris, Britton. "New Tools for Planning." *Journal of the American Institute of Planners, 31*:90–95, May 1965.

———. "The Uses of Theory in the Simulation of Urban Phenomena." *Journal of the American Institute of Planners, 32*:258–272, September 1966.

Helly, Walter. "Review of Jay W. Forrester, *Urban Dynamics*." *Operations Research, 18*:749–750, July–August 1970.

Hermann, Charles F. "Validation Problems in Games and Simulations with Special Reference to Models of International Politics." *Behavioral Science, 12*:216–231, May 1967.

Hester, James, Jr. "Systems Analysis for Social Policies." (Review of Jay W. Forrester, *Urban Dynamics*.) *Science, 168*:693–694, May 8, 1970.

Hill, Donald M. "A Growth Allocation Model for the Boston Region." *Journal of the American Institute of Planners, 31*:111–120, May 1965.

"HOME Receives HUD Grant." *Housing & Community Development Newsletter, 2*:2, August 1973.

Hunter, J. S., and Naylor, T. H. "Experimental Designs for Computer Simulation Experiments." *Management Science, 16*:422–434, March 1970.

Ingram, Gregory K. "Review of Jay W. Forrester, *Urban Dynamics*." *Journal of the American Institute of Planners, 36*:206–208, May 1970.

Jantsch, Erich. "Forecasting and the Systems Approach: A Critical Survey." *Policy Sciences, 3*:475–498, December 1972.

Johnson, Haynes. "Probing Our Future: From the Computer, a Revolution in Values." *The Washington Post*:C1, C4, June 8, 1975.

Jonish, James E., and Peterson, Richard E. "The Impact of a Dock Strike on the State of Hawaii: A Simulation." *Simulation, 20*:45–48, April 1973.

Kaczka, Eugene E. "Review of Jay W. Forrester, *Urban Dynamics*." *Administrative Science Quarterly, 15*:262–264, June 1970.

Kadanoff, Leo P. "From Simulation Model to Public Policy: An Examination of Forrester's *Urban Dynamics*." *Simulation, 16*:261–268, June 1971.

Kain, John F. "A Computer Version of How a City Works." (Review of Jay W. Forrester, *Urban Dynamics*.) *Fortune, 80*:241–242, November 1969.

Khazzom, J. Daniel. "The FPC Staff's Econometric Model of Natural Gas Supply in the United States." *Bell Journal of Economic & Management Science, 2*:51–93, Spring 1971.

Krueckenberg, Donald A. "Review of Jay W. Forrester, *Urban Dynamics.*" *Journal of the American Institute of Planners, 35:*353, September 1969.

Lakshmanan, T. R. "An Approach to the Analysis of Interurban Location Applied to the Baltimore Region." *Economic Geography, 40:*348–362, October 1964.

Lakshmanan, T. R., and Hansen, Walter C. "A Retail Market Potential Model." *Journal of the American Institute of Planners, 31:*134–143, May 1965.

Laska, Richard M. "City Models Challenge Urban Managers." *Computer Decisions, 4:*5–10, February 1972.

Lathrop, George T., and Hamburg, John R. "An Opportunity-Accessibility Model for Allocating Regional Growth." *Journal of the American Institute of Planners, 31:*95–103, May 1965.

Lee, Douglas B., Jr. "Requiem for Large-Scale Models." *Journal of the American Institute of Planners, 39:*163–178, May 1973.

Lindsay, William. "Saul Gass Addresses WORC Banquet on Model Evaluation." *Washington Operations Research Council, WORC Newsletter, 13:*4, July 1974.

Lippman, Thomas W. "Report Asks City to Attract New Families." *The Washington Post:* D1, D4, February 10, 1974.

Lowry, Ira S. "Reforming Rent Control in New York City: The Role of Research in Policymaking." *Policy Sciences, 3:*47–58, March 1972.

———. "A Short Course in Model Design." *Journal of the American Institute of Planners, 31:*158–165, May 1965.

Marney, Milton, and Smith, Nicholas M. "Interdisciplinary Synthesis." *Policy Sciences, 3:*299–323, September 1972.

McLeod, John. "Social Simulation: Validation, Assumptions and Credibility." *Simulation, 17:* Inside Back Cover, August 1971.

Meyer, Eugene L. "HUD Subsidizes Inner City Plan." *The Washington Post:* D1, D4, July 9, 1972.

Moody, Harold T. "Urban Dynamics: A Review of Forrester's Model of an Urban Area." *Economic Geography, 46:*620–626, October 1970.

Morris, William T. "On the Art of Modeling." *Management Science, 12:* B707–B717, August 1967.

Nagelberg, Mark, and Little, Dennis L. "Selected Urban Simulations and Games." *Simulation and Games, 1:*459–481, December 1970.

Naylor, Thomas. "Up, Up and Away." (Abstract of paper read at the American Federation of Information Processing Societies National Computer Conference, June 1973, New York, N. Y.) *Computing Reviews, 15:*267, August 1974.

Naylor, Thomas H., and Finger, J. M. "Verification of Computer Simulation Models." *Management Science, 14:*B92–B106, October 1967.

"NW Tract Is Richest in Area." *The Washington Post:*C1, C8, December 5, 1972.

Orcutt, Guy H. "Simulation of Economic Systems." *The American Economic Review, 50:*893–907, December 1960.

Passell, Peter; Roberts, Marc; and Ross, Leonard. (Combined review of Donella H. Meadows et al., *The Limits to Growth*, and Jay W. Forrester, *World Dynamics* and *Urban Dynamics*.) *New York Times Book Review*:10, 12–13, April 2, 1972.

Regional Economic Division Staff. "State Personal Income, 1948–65." *Survey of Current Business*, 46:11–14, August 1966.

"The Rocky Road to Low Income Rehabilitation for the Private Investor." *Journal of Housing*, 27:76–89, February 27, 1970.

Robinson, Ira M.; Wolfe, Harry B.; and Barringer, Robert L. "A Simulation Model for Renewal Programming." *Journal of the American Institute of Planners*, 31:126–133, May 1965.

Rothenberg, Jerome. "Problems in the Modeling of Urban Development, A Review of *Urban Dynamics*, by Jay W. Forrester." *Journal of Urban Economics*, 1:1–20, January 1974.

Savas, E. S. "Simulation and Cost-Effectivenes Analysis of New York's Emergency Ambulance Service." *Management Science*, 15:B608–B627, August 1969.

Scharfenberg, Kirk. "City Population Drops 7,400 in 2-Year Period." *The Washington Post*:C1, C3, September 19, 1972.

———. "Officials Optimistic on City's Future Growth." *The Washington Post*:B1, B5, September 9, 1973.

Schick, Allen. "Five Theories in Search of an Urban Crisis." (Combined review of Jay W. Forrester, *Urban Dynamics*, and five other books.) *Public Administration Review*, 32:546–552, September–October 1972.

Schlager, Kenneth J. "A Land Use Plan Design Model." *Journal of the American Institute of Planners*, 31:103–111, May 1965.

Schroeder, Walter W., III. "System Dynamics: A Unique Tool for Analyzing Data-Deficient Social Systems." *IEEE Transactions on Systems, Man, and Cybernetics*, SMC-2:217–220, April 1972.

Sears, David W. "The New York State Regional Housing Model." *Simulation and Games*, 2:131–148, June 1971.

———. "Utility Testing for Urban and Regional Models." *Policy Sciences*, 3:235–247, June 1972.

Shapiro, Michael J. "Rational Political Man: A Synthesis of Economic and Social-Psychological Perspectives." *American Political Science Review*, 63:1106–1119, September 1969.

Shubik, Martin. "On Gaming and Game Theory." *Management Science*, 18:P37–P53, January 1972.

———. "Simulation of the Industry and the Firm." *The American Economic Review*, 50:908–919, December 1960.

———. "Modeling on a Grand Scale." Review of Jay W. Forrester, *World Dynamics*. *Science*, 174:1014–1015, December 3, 1971.

Starr, Martin K. "Planning Models." *Management Science*, 13:B115–B141, December 1966.

Steger, Wilbur A. "The Pittsburgh Urban Renewal Simulation Model." *Journal of the American Institute of Planners*, 31:144–150, May 1965.

————. "Review of Analytical Techniques for the CRP." *Journal of the American Institute of Planners, 31*:166–171, May 1965.

Stevens, William K. "Computer Is Used as Guide for Expert Seeking Way Out of Labyrinth of Urban Problems." *The New York Times*:47, 49, October 31, 1969.

Storey, James R. "Systems Analysis and Welfare Reform: A Case Study of the Family Assistance Plan." *Policy Sciences, 4*:1–11, March 1973.

Streatfeild, Guy. "World Dynamics Challenged." *Futures, 5*:4, February 1973.

Swanson, Carl V., and Waldmann, Raymond J. "A Simulation Model of Economic Growth Dynamics." *Journal of the American Institute of Planners, 36*:314–322, January 1970.

Sweeney, Robert E., ed. *System Dynamics Newsletter, 11*:1–74, December 1973.

"*Urban Dynamics*: Extensions and Reflections." *IEEE Transactions on Systems, Man, and Cybernetics, SMC-2*:121–298, April 1972.

Van Horn, Richard L. "Validation of Simulation Results." *Management Science, 17*:247–258, January 1971.

Weinblatt, Herbert. "*Urban Dynamics*: A Critical Review." (Review of Jay W. Forrester, *Urban Dynamics*.) *Policy Sciences, 1*:377–383, Fall 1970.

Weiss, Robert S., and Rein, Martin. "The Evaluation of Broad-Aim Programs: Experimental Design, Its Difficulties, and an Alternative." *Administrative Science Quarterly, 15*:97–109, March 1970.

Willmann, John B. "City's Problems Seen Magnified with Age Gaps." *The Washington Post*:C3, C7, May 27, 1972.

Wolfe, Harry B. "Models for Condition Aging of Residential Structures." *Journal of the American Institute of Planners, 33*:192–196, May 1967.

Wolhowe, Cathe. "Phillips Blasts City, Quits Housing Unit." *The Washington Post*: C1, C6, January 23, 1974.

GOVERNMENT AND OTHER ORGANIZATION PUBLICATIONS

Abt Associates, Inc. "Survey of the State of the Art: Social, Political, and Economic Models and Simulations." *In: Technology and the American Economy. Appendix Volume V: Applying Technology to Unmet Needs.* Washington, D. C., U. S. Government Printing Office, 1966.

Averch, Harvey A., and Levine, Robert A. *Two Models of the Urban Crises: An Analytical Essay on Banfield and Forrester.* RM-6366-RC. Santa Monica, Calif., The RAND Corporation, September 1970.

Baran, Paul, and Greenberger, Martin. *Urban Node in the Information Network.* P-3562. Santa Monica, Calif., The RAND Corporation, April 1967.

Brewer, Garry D. *Evaluation and Innovation in Urban Research.* P-4446. Santa Monica, Calif., The RAND Corporation, August 1970.

Crecine, John P. *A Time-Oriented Metropolitan Model of Spatial Location.* Technical Bulletin No. 6. Pittsburgh, Department of City Planning, 1964.

———. *Computer Simulation in Urban Research.* P-3734. Santa Monica, Calif., The RAND Corporation, November 1967.

Decision Sciences Corporation. *New Communities. Survey of the State of the Art.* Jenkintown, Pa., November 1971.

District of Columbia, Office of Assistant to the Mayor for Housing Programs. *F-NE, Washington's Far Northeast 1972: Housing.* Washington, D. C., May 1972.

———. *Housing Construction & Demolition, Compilation of Permit Data, 1960–1972.* Washington, D. C. District of Columbia Government, December 1972.

District of Columbia, Office of Planning and Management. *Government of the District of Columbia Organization Handbook.* Washington, D. C., District of Columbia Government, July 1972.

District of Columbia, Redevelopment Land Agency. *Annual Report 1972.* Washington, D. C., 1972.

Duke, Richard D. *Gaming-Simulation in Urban Research.* East Lansing, Mich., Institute for Community Development and Services, Michigan State University, 1964.

Duke, Richard D., and Bukhalter, Barton R. *The Application of Heuristic Gaming to Urban Problems.* East Lansing, Mich., Institute of Community Development, Michigan State University, 1966.

Envirometrics, Inc. *The State-of-the-Art in Urban Gaming Models.* Washington, D. C., July 1971.

Fishman, G. S., and Kiviat, P. J. *Spectral Analysis of Time Series Generated by Simulation Models.* RM-4393-PR. Santa Monica, Calif., The RAND Corporation, February 1965.

Flax, Michael J. *A Study in Comparative Urban Indicators: Conditions in 18 Large Metropolitan Areas.* Paper 1206–4. Washington, D. C., The Urban Institute, April 1972.

Fritschler, A. Lee; Harman, B. Douglas; and Ross, Bernard H. *Urban Affairs Bibliography: A Guide to Literature in the Field.* 2nd Edition. Washington, D. C., School of Government and Public Administration, The American University, 1970.

Fromm, Gary; Hamilton, William L.; and Hamilton, Diane E. *Federally Supported Mathematical Models: Survey and Analysis. Volume I: Analysis and Conclusions.* Boston, Mass., Data Resources, Inc. and Abt Associates, Inc., June 1974.

Garn, Harvey A., and Wilson, Robert A. *A Critical Look at Urban Dynamics: The Forrester Model and Public Policy.* Washington, D. C., The Urban Institute, December 1970.

Gass, Saul I., and Sisson, Roger L., eds. *A Guide to Models in Governmental Planning and Operations.* Washington, D. C., Office of Research and Development, Environmental Protection Agency, August 1974.

Hemmens, George C. *The Structure of Urban Activity Linkages.* Chapel Hill, N. C., Center for Urban and Regional Studies, Institute for Research in Social Science, University of North Carolina, 1966.

————. *Urban Development Modeling.* Monograph No. 6. Washington, D. C., Program of Policy Studies in Science and Technology, The George Washington University, April 1970.

Lee, Douglas B., Jr. *Models and Techniques for Urban Planning.* Report CAL-VY-2474-G-1. Buffalo, N. Y., Cornell Aeronautical Laboratory, Inc., Cornell University, September 1968.

Lowry, Ira S. *A Model of Metropolis.* RM-4035-RC. Santa Monica, Calif., The RAND Corporation, August 1964.

————. *Seven Models of Urban Development: A Structural Comparison.* P-3673. Santa Monica, Calif., The RAND Corporation, September 1967.

Metropolitan Washington Council of Governments. *Areawide Population and Employment Forecasts.* Washington, D. C., March 1972.

————. *"Empiric" Activity Allocation Model, Application to the Washington Metropolitan Region.* Washington, D. C., December 1972.

————. *"Empiric" Activity Allocation Study, Study Design.* Washington, D. C., April 1969.

————. *Housing Gap Quantification: A Methodology.* Washington, D. C., 1968.

————. *Housing Policies and Programs for Metropolitan Washington—1972.* Washington, D. C., October 1972.

————. *Statistics—Washington Metropolitan Area.* Washington, D. C., January 1968.

Nagelberg, Mark, and Little, Dennis L. *Selected Urban Simulations and Games.* Working Paper WP-4. Middletown, Conn., Institute for the Future, April 1970.

National Capital Housing Authority. *Annual Report for the Fiscal Year Ending June 30, 1972: Public Housing in Crisis.* Washington, D. C., U. S. Government Printing Office, 1973.

National Industrial Conference Board, Inc. *Economic Dimensions of Major Metropolitan Areas.* Technical Paper No. 18. New York, 1968.

National Planning Association. *Economic and Demographic Projections for States and Metropolitan Areas: Projections to 1975, 1980, and 1985 of Population, Income, and Industry Employment.* Report No. 68-R-1. Washington, D. C., January 1969.

————. *Input-Output Analysis: Two Reports on Its Scope and Application.* Report No. 65-A. Washington, D. C., September 1965.

Pack, Janet Rothenberg, et al. *The Use of Urban Models in Urban Policy Making: Report on Research to Refine the Relevant Questions and to Provide an Appropriate Research Design.* Philadelphia, The Fels Center of Government, University of Pennsylvania, January 1974.

Shryock, Henry S.; Siegel, Jacob S.; and associates. *The Methods and Ma-*

terials of Demography. Vol. 2. Washington, D. C., U. S. Government Printing Office, 1971.

U. S. Bureau of the Census. *Census of Governments: 1962. Vol. II. Taxable Property Values*. Washington, D. C., U. S. Government Printing Office, 1963.

————. *Census of Housing: 1960. Vol. I. States and Small Areas—District of Columbia*. Final Report HC(1)–10. Washington, D. C., U. S. Government Printing Office, 1962.

————. *1970 Census of Housing: Components of Inventory Change*. Report HC(4)–16, Washington, D. C.-Md.-Va. SMSA. Washington, D. C., U. S. Government Printing Office, 1973.

————. *Census of Population and Housing: 1960, Census Tracts*. Final Report PHC(1)–166, Washington, D. C.-Md.-Va. SMSA. Washington, D. C., U. S. Government Printing Office, 1962.

————. *Census of Population and Housing: 1970, Census Tracts*. Final Report PHC(1)–226, Washington, D. C.-Md.-Va. SMSA. Washington, D. C., U. S. Government Printing Office, 1972.

————. *Census of Population: 1960, General Social and Economic Characteristics, United States Summary*. Final Report PC(1)–1C. Washington, D. C., U. S. Government Printing Office, 1962.

————. *Census of Population: 1960, Subject Reports. Mobility for States and State Economic Areas*. Final Report PC(2)–2B. Washington, D. C., U. S. Government Printing Office, 1963.

————. *Census of Population: 1960, Subject Reports. Women by Number of Children Ever Born*. Final Report PC(2)–3A. Washington, D. C., U. S. Government Printing Office, 1964.

————. *County and City Data Book, 1962* (A Statistical Abstract Supplement). Washington, D. C., U. S. Government Printing Office, 1962.

————. *County Business Patterns, District of Columbia*. CBP–68–10, CBP–69–10, and CBP–70–10. Washington, D. C., U. S. Government Printing Office, 1969, 1970, 1971.

————. *Current Population Reports: Estimates of the Population of States: July 1, 1967*. Series P-25, No. 414. Washington, D. C., U. S. Government Printing Office, 1969.

————. *Current Population Reports: Population Estimates and Projections*. Series P-25, No. 477. Washington, D. C., U. S. Government Printing Office, 1972.

————. *General Demographic Trends for Metropolitan Areas, 1960 to 1970*. Final Report PHC(2)–10. Washington, D. C., U. S. Government Printing Office, 1971.

————. *Housing Construction Statistics: 1889–1964*. Washington, D. C., U. S. Government Printing Office, 1966.

————. *Statistical Abstract of the United States*. Editions 77, 82, 83, 87, 91, 92, 93, and 94. Washington, D. C., U. S. Government Printing Office, 1956, 1961, 1962, 1966, 1970, 1971, 1972, 1973.

U. S. Bureau of Labor Statistics. *Employment and Earnings: States and Local Areas 1939–1971.* Bulletin No. 1370–9. Washington, D. C., U. S. Government Printing Office, 1972.

———. *Employment and Earnings Statistics for the United States: 1909–67.* Bulletin No. 1312–5. Washington, D. C., U. S. Government Printing Office, 1967.

U. S., Congress, House. *Report of the Commission on the Organization of Government of the District of Columbia.* 92nd Congress, 2nd session. Doc. 92–317, Vol. 2, August 17, 1972.

U. S., Congress, Senate, Subcommittee on Appropriations. *District of Columbia Appropriations for Fiscal Year 1973.* Hearings. 92nd Congress, 2nd Session. March 16, 1972.

U. S. General Accounting Office. *Glossary for Systems Analysis and Planning-Programming-Budgeting.* Washington, D. C., U. S. Government Printing Office, 1969.

U. S. Office of Business Economics. *The National Income and Product Accounts of the United States, 1929–1965. Statistical Tables.* Washington, D. C., U. S. Government Printing Office, 1966.

ARTICLES IN COLLECTIONS

Adelman, Irma. "Economic System Simulation." *In: Simulation in Social and Administrative Science.* Edited by Harold Guetzkow, Philip Kotler, and Randall L. Schultz. Englewood Cliffs, N. J., Prentice-Hall, 1972.

———. "Simulation: Economic Processes." *In: International Encyclopedia of Social Sciences.* Edited by David L. Sills. New York, Macmillan and Free Press, 1968.

Babcock, Daniel L. "Assumptions in Forrester's Urban Dynamics Model." *In: Urban Dynamics: Extensions and Reflections.* Edited by Kan Chen. San Francisco, San Francisco Press, 1972.

Barney, Gerald O. "Understanding *Urban Dynamics.*" *In: P. oceedings of Fall Joint Computer Conference.* Montvale, N. J., American Federation of Information Processing Societies, Inc., 1971.

Belkin, Jacob. "Urban Dynamics: Applications as a Teaching Tool and as an Urban Game." *In: Urban Dynamics: Extensions and Reflections.* Edited by Kan Chen. San Francisco, San Francisco Press, 1972.

Chen, Kan, and Garrison, W. L. "Urban Modeling." *In: Urban Dynamics: Extensions and Reflections.* Edited by Kan Chen. San Francisco, San Francisco Press, 1972.

Davis, Otto A. "Notes on Strategy and Methodology for a Scientific Political Science." *In: Mathematical Applications in Political Science.* Vol. 4. Edited by Joseph L. Bernd. Charlottesville, Va., University Press of Virginia, 1969.

Eckstein, Harry. "Political Science and Public Policy." *In: Contemporary*

Political Science: Toward Empirical Theory. Edited by Ithiel de Sola Pool. New York, McGraw-Hill, 1967.

Garn, Harvey A., and Wilson, Robert H. "A Look at *Urban Dynamics:* The Forrester Model and Public Policy." *In: Urban Dynamics: Extensions and Reflections.* Edited by Kan Chen. San Francisco, San Francisco Press, 1972.

Gibson, J. E. "A Philosophy for Urban Simulations." *In: Urban Dynamics: Extensions and Reflections.* Edited by Kan Chen. San Francisco, San Francisco Press, 1972.

Gray, James N. "A FORTRAN Version of Forrester's Urban Dynamics Model." *In: Urban Dynamics: Extensions and Reflections.* Edited by Kan Chen. San Francisco, San Francisco Press, 1972.

Gray, J.; Pessell, D.; and Varaya, P. "A Critique of Forrester's Model of an Urban Area." *In: Urban Dynamics: Extensions and Reflections.* Edited by Kan Chen. San Francisco, San Francisco Press, 1972.

Guetzkow, Harold. "Simulations in the Consolidation and Utilization of Knowledge About International Relations." *In: Theory and Research on the Causes of War.* Edited by Dean G. Pruitt and Richard C. Snyder. Englewood Cliffs, N. J., Prentice-Hall, 1969.

Harris, Britton. "Quantitative Models of Urban Development: Their Role in Metropolitan Policy-Making." *In: Issues in Urban Economics.* Edited by Harvey S. Perloff and Lowdon Wingo, Jr. Baltimore, Md., Johns Hopkins Press, 1968.

Jaeckel, Martin. "Forrester's Urban Dynamics: A Sociologist's Inductive Critique." *In: Urban Dynamics: Extensions and Reflections.* Edited by Kan Chen. San Francisco, San Francisco Press, 1972.

Kadanoff, Leo P. "A Modified Forrester Model of the United States as a Group of Metropolitan Areas." *In: Urban Dynamics: Extensions and Reflections.* Edited by Kan Chen. San Francisco, San Francisco Press, 1972.

Kadanoff, Leo P., and Weinblatt, Herbert. "Public-Policy Conclusions from Urban Growth Models." *In: Urban Dynamics: Extensions and Reflections.* Edited by Kan Chen. San Francisco, San Francisco Press, 1972.

Lasswell, Harold D. "Strategies of Inquiry: The Rational Use of Observation." *In: The Human Meaning of the Social Sciences.* Edited by Daniel Lerner. New York, Meridian Books, 1959.

————. "The Transition Toward More Sophisticated Procedures." *In: Computers and the Policy-Making Community: Applications to International Relations.* Edited by Davis B. Bobrow and Judah L. Schwartz. Englewood Cliffs, N. J., Prentice-Hall, 1968.

Limaye, Dilip R., and Blumberg, Donald F. "Systems for Urban Planning and Management." *In: Computers and Urban Society: Proceedings, ACM Urban Symposium, 1972.* New York, Association of Computing Machinery, 1972.

Lowry, Ira S. "Seven Models of Urban Development: A Structural Comparison." *In: Urban Development Models.* Edited by George C. Hemmens. Washington, D. C., Highway Research Board, National Academy of Sciences, 1968.

Millikan, Max F. "Inquiry and Policy: The Relation of Knowledge to Action." *In: The Human Meaning of the Social Sciences.* Edited by Daniel Lerner. New York, Meridian Books, 1959.

Naylor, Thomas H. "Methodological Considerations in Simulating Social and Administrative Systems." *In: Simulation in Social and Administrative Science.* Edited by Harold Guetzkow, Philip Kotler, and Randall L. Schultz. Englewood Cliffs, N. J., Prentice-Hall, 1972.

Newell, Allen, and Simon, Herbert A. "Simulation: Individual Behavior." *In: International Encyclopedia of the Social Sciences.* Vol. 14. Edited by David L. Sills. New York, Macmillan and Free Press, 1968.

Pack, Janet Rothenberg. "Models of Population Movement and Urban Policy." *In: Urban Dynamics: Extensions and Reflections.* Edited by Kan Chen. San Francisco, San Francisco Press, 1972.

Porter, Howell R., III, and Henley, Ernest J. "Application of the Forrester Model to Harris County, Texas." *In: Urban Dynamics: Extensions and Reflections.* Edited by Kan Chen. San Francisco, San Francisco Press, 1972.

Rochberg, Richard. "Some Questionable Assumptions in the Model and Method of Urban Dynamics." *In: Urban Dynamics: Extensions and Reflections.* Edited by Kan Chen. San Francisco, San Francisco Press, 1972.

Sagner, James S. "Refining the Urban Dynamics Model: An Approach Toward Improving the Specification of City Goals." *In: Urban Dynamics: Extensions and Reflections.* Edited by Kan Chen. San Francisco, San Francisco Press, 1972.

San Francisco Department of City Planning. "The San Francisco Community Renewal Simulation Model." *In: Decision-Making in Urban Planning.* Edited by Ira M. Robinson. Beverly Hills, Calif., Sage Publications, 1972.

Schultz, Randall L., and Sullivan, Edward M. "Developments in Simulation in Social and Administrative Science." *In: Simulation in Social and Administrative Science.* Edited by Harold Guetzkow, Philip Kotler, and Randall L. Schultz. Englewood Cliffs, N. J., Prentice-Hall, 1972.

Thompson, Wilbur. "Internal and External Factors in the Development of Urban Economics." *In: Financing the Metropolis, Public Policy in Urban Economics.* Edited by John P. Crecine. Beverly Hills, Calif., Sage Publications, 1970.

Whithed, Marshall H. "Urban Dynamics and Public Policy." *In: Urban Dynamics: Extensions and Reflections.* Edited by Kan Chen. San Francisco, San Francisco Press, 1972.

Wolfe, Harry B., and Ernst, Martin L. "Simulation Models and Urban Planning." *In: Operations Research for Public Systems.* Edited by Philip M. Morse, assisted by Laura W. Bacon. Cambridge, Mass., MIT Press, 1967.

UNPUBLISHED MATERIALS

Allen, Jodie T. (Assistant Vice President, The Urban Institute.) Personal interview. May 10, 1973.

Babcock, Daniel L. "Analysis and Improvement of a Dynamic Urban Model." Doctoral Dissertation. Los Angeles, University of California, 1970.

Banks, James G. "Growth Statement." Washington, D. C., Office of Housing Programs, District of Columbia Government, September 21, 1973. Mimeographed.

Bartos, Otomar J., and Tsai, Yung-Mei. "Forrester's Model and Four U. S. Cities." Paper read at the American Association for the Advancement of Science Annual Meeting, Washington, D. C., December 26, 1972.

Harlow, Albert Mason, Jr. "Exploring Rent Control with Urban Dynamics." Master's Thesis. Cambridge, Massachusetts Institute of Technology, 1972.

Hester, James A., Jr. "Dispersal, Segregation, and Technological Change: A Computer Simulation Model of Large Metropolitan Areas During the Twentieth Century." Doctoral Dissertation. Cambridge, Massachusetts Institute of Technology, 1970.

Hunt, Arch William, III. "Statistical Evaluation and Verification of Digital Simulation Models Through Spectral Analysis." Doctoral Dissertation. Austin, University of Texas, 1970.

Kadanoff, Leo P. "Forrester-Type Growth Models." Comments in a panel discussion at the American Association for the Advancement of Science Annual Meeting, Washington, D. C., December 26, 1972.

――――. "Uses and Misuses of Urban Growth Models." Address at the Applied Physics Laboratory, The Johns Hopkins University, Laurel, Maryland, March 24, 1972.

Lyons, Deborah. (Urban Planner, Project Home Staff. Office of Assistant to the Mayor for Housing Programs, District of Columbia.) Personal interview. February 26, 1974.

Marvin, Keith E. "Getting Involved in Analysis Needed by the Congress of the United States." Paper read at the ORSA/TIMS Joint National Meeting, October 16, 1974, San Juan, Puerto Rico.

Meadows, Dennis L. "Forrester-Type Growth Models." Comments in a panel discussion at the American Association for the Advancement of Science Annual Meeting, Washington, D. C., December 26, 1972.

Metropolitan Washington Council of Governments. "COG Estimates Derived from Local Forecasts." Empiric Alt. 6.2. Washington, D. C., March 1974. Mimeographed.

――――. "Empiric Model Calibration Data File: 1960 and 1968." Washington, D. C., June 1973. Computer listing, unnumbered.

Mister, Melvin A. "Twenty Years of Urban Renewal." Washington, D. C., District of Columbia Redevelopment Land Agency, January 8, 1970. Mimeographed.

Moeller, John F. "Development of a Microsimulation Model for Evaluating Economic Implications of Income Transfer and Tax Policies." Paper read at the Conference on the Computer in Economic and Social Measurement, sponsored by the National Bureau of Economic Research, September 20, 1972, at State College, Pennsylvania.

National Planning Association. "Capital Stock by Industry and Region, 1947–1963." Washington, D. C., 1969. Computer listing, unnumbered.

Porter, Howell R., III. "Application of a Generalized Urban Model to a Specific Region." Master's Thesis. Houston, Tex., University of Houston, 1971.

Schroeder, Walter Warren, III. "Lowell Dynamics: Preliminary Applications of the Theory of Urban Dynamics." Master's Thesis. Cambridge, Massachusetts Institute of Technology, 1972.

Scott, Graham Cecil. "Industrial Production and Investment in a Dynamic, Multiregional, Interindustry Model of the United States." Doctoral Dissertation. Durham, N. C., Duke University, 1972.

Weinblatt, Herbert. "The Demand Sector." Research Note 18. Providence, R. I., Urban Analysis Group, Brown University, March 1972. Mimeographed.

———. "The Industrial Sector." Research Note 15. Providence, R. I., Urban Analysis Group, Brown University, February 28, 1972. Mimeographed.

———. Personal correspondence with author. Providence, R. I., Department of Urban Studies and Planning, Brown University, April 21, 1972.

Glossary

ANALYSIS OF VARIANCE—A statistical technique for computing the degree of significance in the variations of a particular characteristic among comparable groups or classes of data; more precisely, whether differences among the means of two or more groups are greater than the variability which can be expected to result from differences between elements within the groups.

ANALYTICAL MATHEMATICAL MODEL—A broad group of models which are expressed in terms of mathematical functions such as equations and probability distributions. Analytical mathematical models are those that are specified completely in mathematical terms and that have mathematical solutions, including linear and dynamic programming models, inventory models, queuing models, input-output models, and Markov chain models. The complete mathematical representation of such models contrasts with the usual structure of computer and gaming simulation models, which usually have mathematical components as well as many logical relationships to tie the mathematical components together. Simulation models generally do not have mathematical solutions but are used to conduct experiments to study the behavior of the simulated system. (*See also* DYNAMIC PROGRAMMING, INPUT-OUTPUT MODEL, INVENTORY MODEL, LINEAR PROGRAMMING, MARKOV CHAIN MODEL, and QUEUING MODEL.)

CLOSED-SYSTEM BOUNDARY—The assumption that, for a system being modeled, a closed boundary, within which lie the behavioral components of the system, can be identified. Although components outside the system can affect it, the components within the boundary do not affect the environment outside the system; that is, no feedback loops run from the system to the outside environment and back into the system. This is a principal assumption of Jay Forrester's urban dynamics model. (*See also* FEEDBACK LOOPS.)

CLUSTER ANALYSIS—A body of statistical techniques for the analysis of data, wherein the general aim is to determine and describe some simple structure within a complex mass of data. The techniques are used in the analysis of data units, each with a number of measurements—one measurement for each of a number of characteristics or variables. Geometrically, cluster analysis may be described as the mapping of data units into a multidimensional space, wherein each dimension represents a variable and the classes in each dimension represent the values of those variables. In this mapping, the data units may cluster into groups, and the characteristics of the clusters and the relationships between clusters may be computed. In some cases, the clusters may divide the units into groups that are explained by some hypothesis or theory; in others, clusters may provide useful insights into appropriate data-reduction techniques to be applied to the data units. In statistical terms, cluster analysis attempts to find a classification system for the data units that reduces the unexplained variation among units. (*See also* FACTOR ANALYSIS.)

COMPLEX SYSTEM—A concept developed by Jay Forrester to indicate system structures having multiple, interacting feedback loops. Such systems have many system levels, and rates of flow often are controlled by nonlinear relationships. Forrester postulates that complex systems are counterintuitive and deceptive, because people are conditioned to deal with simple systems. The high degree of time correlation between variables in complex systems causes individuals to make cause-and-effect associations among variables that are simply moving together as a part of the dynamic behavior of the total system. In addition to being counterintuitive, complex systems have other behavioral characteristics, such as resisting policy changes, reacting to policy changes in the long run opposite to the way they react in the short run, and tending toward low performance. (*See also* FEEDBACK LOOPS.)

COMPUTER SIMULATION—A methodology for studying systems by conducting experiments on a digital computer, using mathematical and logical models that describe the behavior of the system over an extended period of time. Computer simulation has been applied in many areas of the natural and social sciences, the latter including psychology, political science, economics, and management.

CORRELATION ANALYSIS—A statistical technique that determines a functional relationship which expresses a single variable (regarded as the dependent variable) in terms of one or more other variables (regarded as independent variables). The relationship is determined through empirical observations of the variables. The analysis is a simple correlation if a single independent variable is involved, and a multiple correlation if more than one independent variable is involved.

COST-BENEFIT ANALYSIS—An approach to analyzing problems of choice by emphasizing the quantification of costs and benefits associated with alternative choices. Generally applied to the analysis of governmental programs, the approach requires definition of program objectives, identification of alternative ways to achieve objectives, and measurement and comparison of costs and benefits associated with each alternative. Economic and noneconomic costs and benefits for some projected period of time are quantified and reduced to a single unit of measure, usually dollars, and discounted to obtain the current value of the costs and benefit streams for the life of the program. The computation and comparison of the cost-benefit ratios for the program alternatives provide guidance in selecting from among the alternatives. The analysis may take different forms, such as selecting the program alternative that provides the greatest benefit for a specified cost, or selecting the alternative that produces a specified level of benefit at the lowest cost. Cost-benefit analysis is a specialization of the general systems analysis or operations-research paradigm to address program analysis problems associated with the programming-planning-budgeting processes. (See also SYSTEMS ANALYSIS and OPERATIONS RESEARCH.)

DELPHI METHOD—A means of reaching a consensus about an issue under study by a panel of experts. It consists of a series of repeated interrogations, usually via questionnaires, of the individuals on the panel. Each interrogation after the initial one is accompanied by information on the replies from the previous rounds. The written replies are not attributed to individual panel members; after every round, each member reconsiders his own reply in the light of the replies of other panel members. After several rounds, the replies generally converge.

DYNAMIC PROGRAMMING—A type of mathematical programming model representing problems that require many sequential, interdependent decisions, where an optimal solution is sought to the entire decision process. Such problems are structured as multistage problems: At each stage, a decision must be made among a number of alternatives. The objective is to determine the optimal decision at each stage, where optimality is measured relative to the outcome of the whole process, rather than with respect to the decisions at each stage. Dynamic programming problems have a different formulation rationale and a different solution algorithm from other types of mathematical programming problems. (See also MATHEMATICAL PROGRAMMING.)

DYNAMO—A simulation language that was designed specifically to assist in the computer implementation of models developed according to the concepts of industrial dynamics. The Dynamo language is algebraic in form and provides for a representation of rate and level variables and equations in feedback-loop structures. The language has a number of features to simplify setting model parameter values, setting initial variable values, and creating tables for specifying tabular functions. Dynamo will provide a time series of output values for any model variable in either numerical or graphical form. (*See also* INDUSTRIAL DYNAMICS and SIMULATION LANGUAGE.)

FACTOR ANALYSIS—A statistical technique for the analysis of data units to determine whether a large number of variables can be replaced with a smaller number of conceptual variables. The data units generally have a large number of indices or measurements, one for each of a number of variables characterizing the unit. The object is to replace the large number of variables by a smaller number, which may provide insight into the underlying theory of the system in which the data unit observations were taken. In statistical terms, factor analysis attempts to find a few independent variables such that the regression relationship among those variables fits all the observed data. Factor analysis may be regarded as a generalization of regression analysis. There is overlap between factor and cluster analysis, in that both techniques seek to define and describe structures for multivariate data collections. Factor analysis, however, seeks a more specific type of structure, corresponding to a linear subspace of the full multivariate space over which observations were taken. (*See also* CLUSTER ANALYSIS and REGRESSION ANALYSIS.)

FEEDBACK LOOPS—The basic structural components of industrial or system dynamics models. Feedback loops are composed of related level and rate variables; in feedback-loop structures, a decision point—the rate equation—controls a flow or action stream. The flow or action stream is accumulated to generate a system level; information about the level is a basis for the control of the flow rate. The simplest possible feedback loop contains one level variable and one rate variable. A thermostat-furnace system is a feedback loop: the thermostat receives temperature information and starts the furnace, which raises the temperature that stops the furnace. Another example is where available jobs in a city generate information resulting in in-migration that increases the available labor supply and fills the jobs. Feedback loops also are referred to as information-feedback loops or feedback-control loops. (*See also* INDUSTRIAL DYNAMICS, LEVEL VARIABLE, and RATE VARIABLE.)

GAMING SIMULATION—A methodology for the study of systems, in which computer simulation is used together with human players who participate as decision makers or who play other roles. Computer simulation generally is used in gaming simulation to provide a convincing environment for the players' actions. Gaming simulation has been used to study situations such as international conflicts, military conflicts, business strategy, and urban-development strategy. In some uses, the objectives are to study system behavior under alternative policies; in others, the focus is on providing training to decision makers or to executives. (*See also* COMPUTER SIMULATION.)

INDUSTRIAL DYNAMICS—An approach developed by Jay W. Forrester for simulating the dynamic behavior of industries as reflected in and affected by managerial policies. The application of the approach has been extended to the study of other systems, including urban systems. Under the approach, dynamic behavior is represented in terms of feedback loops composed of level variables (status variables) and related rate variables (rate-of-flow variables). Models of systems under study are developed with feedback loops as the basic structural components. Feedback loops are developed to represent the flows of people, resources, and information; the loops are interconnected to develop a representation of the behavior of the system under study. (*See also* FEEDBACK LOOPS, LEVEL VARIABLE, and RATE VARIABLE.)

INPUT-OUTPUT MODEL—A matrix model structure that may be used to represent an economy in terms of a number of industrial sectors, the inter-industry relationships among the sectors, and the interaction of the sectors in their production and consumption of economic goods and services. The model structure may represent a few or several hundred sectors, depending on the kinds of questions to be addressed. The model structure also has been used to represent other kinds of systems, such as a single industrial organization, in terms of system components and the relationships and interactions among the components. The input-output model often is referred to as an interindustry model, or a Leontief model, after its originator, the economist, Wassily Leontief.

INVENTORY MODEL—A class of prototype mathematical models for determining optimal policies to deal with inventory problems or situations in which a stock of items is held for future use. The various costs associated with inventory problems include item acquisition, storage, inventory shortages, revenues, salvage for damaged or leftover items, and money invested in inventory being held. Model solutions determine the trade-offs among the relevant costs to provide the least cost or most profitable inventory policy. Inventory models differ in the kinds of costs they represent; whether they provide a single time period or multiperiod representation of the problem; and whether the demand for items is deterministic and known, or stochastic and, hence, subject to random variations.

LEVEL VARIABLE—A type of variable that is introduced into a model to assume values representing the state of some aspect of the system being modeled at a particular time. Level variables represent the accumulations within a system. Some examples of level variables are the inventory of an item, goods in transit, amount of residential land, and population. (*See also* VARIABLE.)

LINEAR PROGRAMMING—A type of mathematical programming model in which the objective function and constraining functions are all linear. The linearity of the functions means that a unit change in the value of any variable will produce a constant change in the value of the functions in which the variable appears throughout the range of the variable. In spite of the limitations of the linear programming model due to its linearity, it has been widely applied. The model frequently is applied to a class of problems dealing with the optimal allocation of resources when the limitations on available resources are expressible in terms of a system of linear equations or inequalities. The solution techniques for linear programming models are highly developed, so that computer programs are available for solving problems with several hundred variables. (*See also* MATHEMATICAL PROGRAMMING.)

MARKOV CHAIN MODEL—A class of models based on probability theory and applicable to the study of the behavior of systems with respect to their transitions from one state to another. The Markovian property that is usually assumed for the models assumes that the probabilities governing a system's movement to its next state depend only on the current state of the system—system behavior is assumed to be independent of its past transitional behavior. In Markov chain models, systems are described in terms of a set of states, and the probabilities of movement between states are organized into matrices in which the rows and columns represent the system states. These matrices of probabilities are called transition matrices. The transition probabilities are defined relative to some unit period of time. The transition matrices are applied to a system-state vector to generate the system state at one unit time period later; successive applications of the matrix generate a chain of system states. Markov chain modeling techniques can provide a number of useful statistics describing system behavior such as the steady-state behavior of the system.

MATHEMATICAL PROGRAMMING—A class of prototype mathematical models that have the same general structure, consisting of a single objective function and one or more constraining functions. The model solutions optimize, that is, either maximize or minimize, the value of the objective function while simultaneously satisfying all constraining functions. The models are classified according to the mathematical form of the objective and constraining functions. If all the functions for a model are linear, then the model is a linear programming model. If some of the functions are nonlinear, then the model is a nonlinear programming model; such models may be further classified into subtypes. Many variations of the mathematical programming model have been developed, including integer programming models that restrict the solution values of variables to integer values. The dynamic programming model is another variety developed for dealing with problems involving many sequential decisions, where an optimal solution is sought to the entire decision process rather than merely to the separate decisions. The mathematical programming models have been given a number of problem-related interpretations, including an interpretation as a model of an economic process in which the objective function represents the profits, which are to be maximized, resulting from producing items; the constraining functions represent production relationships and constraints on the production of the items. Numerical solution techniques have been developed for a number of these types of mathematical programming models, and the procedures are readily

available in general-purpose computer programs. (*See also* DYNAMIC PRO-
GRAMMING and LINEAR PROGRAMMING.)

MODEL—A representation of the relationships that define a system under
study. The relationships may be expressed mathematically and logically.
The objective in developing models is to achieve a sufficiently valid representation of the system under study to support inferences concerning the
behavior of the system under alternative conditions by use of the model.
To achieve this, models must be tested against reality for the validity of
their representation.

OPERATIONS RESEARCH—The discipline that applies the scientific method to
problems involving the control of organized systems in order to provide
recommendations that serve the objectives of the entire organization. An
interdisciplinary approach, often by using interdisciplinary teams, is
stressed. Studies often are viewed in five stages: formulating the problem,
constructing a model, deriving a solution, testing the model and evaluating
the solution, and implementing the solution. A number of prototype
models are frequently applied in studies, including inventory models,
Markov chain models, queuing models, and mathematical programming
models. (*See also* SYSTEMS ANALYSIS.)

PARAMETER—An entity in a model that is considered to be essential to the
model representation of the system under study and the value of which is
held constant during a particular use of the model. This is in contrast to
the variables of a model that assume different values so as to portray
the state of the system at each moment in time. Model parameters could
be, for example, the death rate or the rate of outward migration, if the
model is formulated so these values are fixed during a use of the model.
Of course, an entity may be a parameter at the level of model formulation
and a variable at a level of analysis that uses the model to study a specific
problem. (*See also* VARIABLE.)

QUEUING MODEL—A class of prototype mathematical models for determining
optimal policies for problems involving queues or waiting lines. The
application of queuing models contributes to the formulation of policies
that achieve an economic balance between the costs associated with providing service to arriving units and the costs associated with the units
waiting for the service. The application of queuing models provides information required for policy decisions by predicting various characteristics
of queues such as average waiting times and average service times for
problem situations. Queuing models generally represent the arrival of items
for service and the time required to service items in the form of probability
distributions. Queuing models differ in mathematical structure according
to whether they represent a single queue or multiple queues, and according
to the form of the probability distributions representing the arrivals for
service and the time required to service items.

RATE VARIABLE—A type of variable introduced in a model to assume values
that represent the rates of flow between the levels of a system at an in-

stant in time. The rate variables represent the activities in the system that produce the levels of the system. Some examples of rate variables are the migration of population, generation of orders for goods, and construction of housing. (*See also* LEVEL VARIABLE and VARIABLE.)

REGRESSION ANALYSIS—A statistical technique that determines from empirical data the extent to which a change in the value of one or more variables, regarded as independent variables for the purpose of the analysis, is accompanied by a change in a single variable, regarded as dependent on the independent variables. The technique takes different forms and is referred to by different names, depending on the number of independent variables involved in the analysis and the form of the functional relationship that relates the variables. If only one independent variable is involved, the technique is called a simple-regression analysis. If two or more independent variables are involved, it is called a multiple-regression analysis. If the functional relationship is a linear one, or a straight line, it is referred to as a linear regression. If the functional form is not linear, which indicates that the change in the dependent variable associated with a change in the independent variable does not occur at a constant rate over the range of the independent variable, the analysis is referred to as a curvilinear-regression analysis.

SENSITIVITY ANALYSIS—A mode of analysis that varies the values of the parameters of a model and runs the model to determine how significant parameter changes are to model results. Sensitivity analysis can be conducted to identify the most critical parameters in terms of influence on model results so that the values for the most critical parameters can be estimated very carefully. Sensitivity analysis also is useful when there is uncertainty with respect to the value of some parameters to determine the variations in model results for a range of values of those parameters. (*See also* PARAMETER.)

SIMULATION—A methodology for the study of systems by conducting experiments with mathematical and logical models that describe the behavior of the system over time. Simulation is the general methodological approach that includes both computer simulation and gaming simulation. (*See also* COMPUTER SIMULATION and GAMING SIMULATION.)

SIMULATION LANGUAGE—A type of computer software designed to assist in the preparation of computer programs to implement computer simulation and gaming simulation models. Simulation languages allow the researcher to specify his model in an algebraic-like language. They assist in conceptualizing simulations, reduce the effort required for the computer programming of simulation models, and assist in modifying computer programs as dictated by experimentation with the model. There are more than two dozen simulation languages in current use, with Simscript and General Purpose System Simulator (GPSS) the most widely used. Dynamo is a simulation language that was developed to implement industrial dynamics models. (*See also* DYNAMO.)

SYSTEMS ANALYSIS—The application of the scientific method to broad, long-range problems of managing organized systems and to provide guidance in the decision making related to achieving systems objectives. Systems analysis has much in common with operations research. Usually, however, systems analysis is said to apply to complex situations involving vague objectives and multiple criteria, whereas operations research deals with the simpler problems to which mathematical techniques more readily apply. There is considerable disagreement on the distinction between systems analysis and operations research, and many contend that there is no real distinction. (*See also* OPERATIONS RESEARCH.)

TECHNOLOGICAL FORECASTING—A group of methods and techniques for predicting trends in technological development. Technological forecasting may be undertaken to identify the sequences of technological developments, to support the achievement of a specified goal, or to identify the range of possible technological futures and the likelihood of each. Techniques include the use of expert opinion—perhaps through a survey of experts, or by an approach combining the opinion of a number of experts, such as the Delphi method. Trend analysis and projection techniques also are used, including crucial indicators to project technological trends and curve fitting and extrapolation techniques to make projections. Probability models also are used. These models represent the possible paths of development to achieve a goal, the interdependencies of the supporting technological developments, and the probabilities of achieving each supporting development. (*See also* DELPHI METHOD.)

VARIABLE—An entity introduced into a model to represent some aspect of the system being modeled by assuming different values to represent the aspect of the system at each moment in time. Examples of variables that might be represented in a model are population, birth rate, and average annual income. Variables are classified in a number of ways: in regression analysis and correlation analysis, they are either independent or dependent; in feedback-loop structures, they are either levels or rates. (*See also* CORRELATION ANALYSIS, FEEDBACK LOOPS, LEVEL VARIABLE, RATE VARIABLE, and REGRESSION ANALYSIS.)

Fortran Computer Program for Urban Dynamics Model

In his developmental work with the urban dynamics model, Forrester used a computer program written in the Dynamo computer language, which he and his associates devised and used at MIT.[1] Because the Dynamo language is not widely used, however, a Fortran-language version of the model was developed and used in this study; of the high-level computer languages, Fortran is the most widely used. Although not designed specifically for simulation modeling, there is no difficulty in representing such models in Fortran.

Other Fortran representations of the urban dynamics model have been developed, but these programs do not meet the needs of this study. One Fortran version uses a computer program that performs a Dynamo-to-Fortran translation, which produces a program that computes results identical to those of Forrester's Dynamo version of the model.[2] It is very difficult, however, to interpret the underlying concepts of the model when using this Fortran program, because the translation is a mechanical one that reorders the Dynamo language so it is computa-

---

[1] Alexander L. Pugh III. *DYNAMO User's Manual.* Cambridge, Mass., MIT Press, 1963; 2nd Edition, 1967; 3rd Edition, 1970.

[2] James N. Gray. "A FORTRAN Version of Forrester's Urban Dynamics Model." *In: Urban Dynamics: Extensions and Reflections.* Edited by Kan Chen. San Francisco, San Francisco Press, 1972, pp. 280–287.

219

tionally feasible, but almost entirely arbitrary, from the standpoint of the model's logic. Babcock's [3] Fortran version of the model is much better, because an attempt is made to keep the statements for each model sector contiguous. His program, however, includes a number of modifications to the original urban dynamics model that are needed to support his study, and contains few comments to interpret the Fortran statements in terms of the logic of the urban dynamics model.

The objective in developing the Fortran version discussed here is to obtain a computer program that can be easily modified to represent the sequential stages in the development of the model representation of Washington, D. C. The program contains sufficient comments to relate the Fortran statements to the logic of the urban dynamics model in a general way. Also, in the process of translating the Dynamo version to Fortran, a detailed understanding of the model is developed that is generally helpful and, in fact, essential in making modifications to the model.

The following discussion will provide insights into the type of problems that were encountered in translating the model into Fortran. First, a characterization of the Dynamo and Fortran computer languages is furnished. Then some of the specific problems are discussed, with an example illustrating the details of the translation process. Finally, a listing of the Fortran version of the model is presented, indicating its features. Although a general knowledge of Fortran is assumed, a knowledge of Dynamo is not essential because of the considerable carry-over from Fortran.

CHARACTERISTICS OF FORTRAN AND DYNAMO

Fortran is a widely used, algebraic-like, general-purpose computer programming language, designed to handle a broad class of problems rather than specific problems such as performing statistical computations or implementing simulation models. It is a procedural language: The language statements must indicate the ordered sequence of computational steps that must be performed to obtain the desired results. This procedural orientation contrasts with that of some other programming languages in which the computer automatically derives the sequence of computational steps from a problem-oriented description of the problem.

Dynamo is a special-purpose computer programming language, de-

---

[3] Daniel L. Babcock. "Analysis and Improvement of a Dynamic Urban Model." Doctoral Dissertation. Los Angeles, University of California, 1970, pp. 345–356.

signed for use in developing computer programs for simulation models. It also is algebraic-like and is not unlike Fortran in its basic notation. Dynamo, however, embodies several features, not available in Fortran, that ease the task of developing computer programs for the type of simulation models the language is designed to represent. Dynamo was designed to assist with the computer implementation of system dynamics models that incorporate multiple-loop, nonlinear, feedback structures. The basic variables in these models are continuous and have first derivatives with respect to time. Dynamo approximates continuous processes by a set of first-order difference equations that express the relationships among the variables of the model.[4] Its representation of model variables in continuous form sets it apart from the more widely used simulation languages, such as Simscript and General Purpose System Simulator (GPSS), which represent model variables in discrete form.

Two special features of Dynamo that assist in translating the concepts of a model into a computer program are the mechanism the language provides for representing time and the classification of language statements according to their functions. A general description of these features follows.

Dynamo provides seven types of language statements, each of which has a distinct function. Most important are the statements describing the computation of level variables and rate variables. These two types of statements relate directly to Forrester's concept of feedback loops as fundamental model-building blocks; of feedback loops composed of level variables representing accumulations at specific points in a system; and of rate variables controlling the flows in a system. The representation of time in level and rate variable statements, as well as in other types of statements, is achieved in Dynamo by referencing three points in time, denoted by J, K, and L: K is the current time, J is the point one time period earlier, and L is one time period later. The time intervals JK and KL are of unit length and denote the previous and next time intervals, respectively. The solution interval is denoted by DT and represents the number of unit-time intervals between evaluations of the model equations. The value of DT will vary according to the resolution of time needed to approximate the values of the continuous variables of the model by solving the set of first-order difference equations.[5]

The user of Dynamo describes the model relationships for time K, and the equations are used for each successive period for which com-

---

[4] Jean E. Sammet. *Programming Languages: History and Fundamentals.* Englewood Cliffs, N. J., Prentice-Hall, 1969, p. 651.

[5] Alexander L. Pugh III. *DYNAMO User's Manual*, 2nd Edition, pp. 4–7.

putations are made. Certain restrictions must be observed. For example, the value of a level variable at time K must depend only on the value of levels at time J, and on the value of rate variables for time JK. An example of a level variable equation is

$$\text{POP.K} = \text{POP.J} + \text{DT}(\text{BIRTHS.JK} - \text{DEATHS.JK}),$$

which indicates that the population at time K is calculated from the population at time J and the births and deaths during the previous time interval multiplied by the solution interval DT. Note that, in Dynamo, the subscripts associated with variables are set apart from the variable name by a period rather than parentheses, as in many languages. Also, the multiplication of births and deaths for a unit period by DT is indicated implicitly, rather than explicitly, as in most programming languages. Rate variables for an interval depend on levels at the preceding instant, and, in some cases, on the rates during the preceding time interval. An example of a rate equation is

$$\text{BIRTHS.JK} = (\text{POP.J})\,(\text{BRATE})$$

where BRATE is the basic birth rate expressed as the fraction of births per person per unit time period. In this equation, births during the period are computed as the product of the population at the beginning of the period and the birth rate.

Unlike Fortran, Dynamo is nonprocedural, so the user may express the model relationships without regard to the order in which the model variables must be computed. The Dynamo software automatically rearranges model equations into a feasible computational order, and the user need not be aware of this process. As indicated above, Dynamo provides other types of language statements in addition to the statements for specifying the computation of level variables and rate variables. Other types include statements for computing auxiliary variables, computing supplementary variables, setting initial values for variables, setting constants, and creating tables of values for use in tabular functions.[6]

PROBLEMS OF CONVERSION

The special features that assist Dynamo users in representing a model are primary problems in converting a computer program from Dynamo to Fortran. Three of the most common problems are:

---

[6] *Ibid.,* pp. 4–7, 44–47.

1. Organizing the Fortran program to represent the treatment of time so it is equivalent to that provided by Dynamo.

2. Reordering the model equations into computational order as required by Fortran.

3. Providing a means for dealing with the tabular functions provided in Dynamo.

The following discussion of these problems as they apply to the urban dynamics model will illustrate how the model's Fortran version handles them. A short section of the model equations will be used to illustrate the details of the conversion process.

Treatment of Time

Organization of the Fortran computer program to deal with the time dimension in a manner equivalent to that of the Dynamo version involves a number of considerations. The approach to this problem is patterned after the one Babcock [7] used in developing his Fortran program for the urban dynamics model. The basic idea is to provide a vector of storage for each model quantity that changes over time. If vectors containing a cell for each year for which computations were to be made could be provided, then the value of the model variables for successive time periods could be stored in successive cells of the vectors. Under such a storage arrangement, there would be access to the model values for times J, K, and L, or the last, present, and next time periods, while computations were performed for period K, thereby providing the same access to values for previous and past periods as provided by Dynamo. It is not desirable, however, to provide vectors with a cell for each year for which computations are to be made because of the large amount of storage this requires. For example, if model computations are carried out for a 250-year period, as Forrester did, 250 words of computer storage would be required for each of more than 150 model quantities, for a total of nearly 40,000 words. Although computations for 250-year periods are unnecessary in this study, Forrester's 250-year computation is reproduced to assure that the Fortran version of the model is equivalent to the published Dynamo version.

The vectors for storage of model quantities will be made shorter than one cell per year by adopting the computational convention of storing and retaining in the vectors the computed results for only those years for which results are to be printed. In this way, if com-

---

[7] Babcock. "Analysis and Improvement of a Dynamic Urban Model," pp. 345–356.

putations are performed for a 250-year period, and the model results are printed for every 10th year, then the computations can be carried out with vectors of 26 words each; this includes one word for model initialization or time zero, and 25 words for the results for each 10th year of the 250-year period. If computations are made for a 40-year period, and results are to be printed for every 5th year, then vectors of nine words will be needed. Under this approach, results are computed for each year, the same as in the Dynamo version of urban dynamics. As the results are computed for each year, they are stored back into the same vector cells where the results for the previous year were stored; however, after computing a year for which results are to be printed, the results for the next year are stored in the next cells of the model quantity vectors. This process continues until results have been computed for as many years as desired.

The costs of using this storage arrangement are small, from the standpoint of additional computer programming. A few additional computer programming statements are required to compute the LST and NXT indexes, which are the indexes used to indicate the location in the model quantity vectors of the results for the last year and next year, respectively, corresponding to J and L in Dynamo. These programming statements must take into consideration the aforementioned rationale for the storage of computed results in vectors. This requires that the LST and NXT indexes be advanced in concert with the specified interval of years for which model results are to be printed. The number of years to be computed and the frequency with which results are to be printed will be set by the model user.

Another consideration in the treatment of time is the observation of model variable dependencies on values computed in previous time periods. Dynamo takes care of this consideration automatically to a great extent. The convention adopted here is to compute the nine basic level variables one time period prior to computing rate and other variables. This is always possible, because level variables depend on the values of level variables and rate variables in the previous period. The basic variables are the three population groups: manager-professional (MP), labor (L), and underemployed (U); the three classes of housing: premium housing (PH), worker housing (WH), and under-employed housing (UH); and the three classes of business/industry: new enterprise (NE), mature business (MB), and declining industry (DI). The other 11 level variables in the model are secondary, in the sense that the 9 basic level variables are dependent indirectly on the values of the 11 secondary level variables in the previous period; therefore, the 11 variables need not be computed one time period ahead.

To implement this treatment of time in the computer program, the model equations in the Fortran version are controlled by two computational loops, which are Fortran DO loops. The primary loop controls the number of years for which printed model results are computed and retained in the aforementioned storage vectors. Each time the index for the primary loop is advanced, the computed results for a single year are printed. There is a secondary loop within the primary loop that controls the computation of results for each year. The secondary loop is satisfied each time results have been computed for enough years to create results that are to be printed for one year. Each time the loop is satisfied, control reverts to the primary loop that prints the results. In the listing of the computer program in Figure 3, the primary and secondary loops are set to replicate Forrester's 250-year computation. The primary loop is set to be executed 26 times, and the secondary loop is set to be executed 10 times for each time the primary loop is executed. These settings cause the program to compute results for 250 years and to print results for an initial or zero year and for each 10th year through the 250th year. The settings controlling the loops can be readily modified to compute the number of years and to print results as desired by the model user.

Ordering of Model Equations

The principal consideration in ordering the model relationships for the urban dynamics Fortran program is to observe dependencies among the model variables. In Fortran, the user is responsible for specifying that quantities are computed prior to being used. Because Dynamo does not require equations to be written in computational order and handles the reordering during the computational process, the order of the equations in the Fortran program will be different from the order in Forrester's Dynamo program. In ordering the equations, it is necessary to keep the model sectors intact as much as possible so the computer program will be coherent.

The model consists of 11 basic sectors plus an Urban Development Programs part, which also may be regarded as a sector. The sectors are kept in the same order in both the Fortran and Dynamo programs, with two exceptions. The major difference is that the Urban Development Programs Sector, Tax Sector, and Job Sector, which were located at the end of the Dynamo program, are placed first in the Fortran program. Another difference is that a Construction Goals and Multipliers section is included near the beginning of the Fortran program. This is not a sector, but it consists of a number of relationships that

```
C
C
C    THIS PROGRAM IS A FORTRAN VERSION OF FORRESTER'S URBAN DYNAMICS MODEL
C    WHICH WAS INITIALLY PROGRAMMED IN DYNAMO.   THE PROGRAM IS ORGANIZED
C    INTO THE FOLLOWING PRINCIPAL SECTIONS:
C        COMPUTER PROGRAM INITIALIZATION
C        URBAN DYNAMICS MODEL COMPUTATIONS
C            INITIALIZATION OF BASIC MODEL LEVEL VARIABLES
C            INITIALIZATION OF COMPUTATION CONTROL LOOPS
C            EQUATIONS FOR MODEL SECTORS
C            PRINTING OF MODEL RESULTS
C
C
C - - - - - - - - - - - - - - - - - - - - - - - - - - - - - - - - - - - -
C - - - COMPUTER PROGRAM INITIALIZATION - - - - - - - - - - - - - - - - -
C - - - - - - - - - - - - - - - - - - - - - - - - - - - - - - - - - - - -
C        THIS SECTION IS CONCERNED WITH STORAGE ALLOCATION AND
C        SPECIFYING CONVENTIONS TO BE USED FOR NAMING INTEGER AND REAL
C        VARIABLES.
C
C        THE RANGE OF FORTRAN REAL AND INTERGER VARIABLES IS SET SO
C        THAT THE URBAN DYANMICS MODEL VARIABLES WILL BE REAL--THERE
C        ARE NO MODEL VARIABLE NAMES WHICH BEGIN WITH THE LETTERS I, J,
C        AND K SO THESE WILL BE USED FOR OTHER PURPOSES.
     IMPLICIT REAL (A-H,L-Z), INTEGER (I-K)
C        THE FOLLOWING MUST BE INTEGERS
     INTEGER PRINT, FREQ, LST, NXT
C
C        THE FOLLOWING ARE STORAGE ALLOCATIONS FOR THE TABLES USED IN
C        TABULAR FUNCTIONS.   EACH TABLE IS ALLOCATED 15 WORDS, ALTHOUGH
C        THEY ALL USE LESS.
     DIMENSION
    1   BDMT(15) , DIEMT(15) ,DILMT(15),EDMT(15) , EGMT(15) , ELJMT(15),
    2   ELMT(15) , EMMT(15) , ETMT(15) , LAHMT(15) ,LAJMT(15) ,LATMT(15) ,
    3   LAUMT(15) ,LCRT(15) , LDMT(15) , LEMT(15) , LLFT(15) , LSMT(15) ,
    4   LUMT(15) , MAHMT(15) ,MAJMT(15) ,MAPMT(15) ,MATMT(15) ,MDMT(15) ,
    5   MLMT(15) , MSMT(15) , PEMT(15) , PHAMT(15) ,PHEMT(15) ,PHGMT(15) ,
    6   PHLMT(15) ,PHOMT(15) ,PHPMT(15) ,PHTMT(15) ,SHAMT(15) ,SHLMT(15) ,
    7   TCMT(15) , TRT(15) ,  UAMMT(15) ,UDMT(15) , UEMT(15) , UFWT(15) ,
    8   UHMT(15) , UHPMT(15) ,UJMT(15) , ULJRT(15) ,WHAMT(15) ,WHEMT(15) ,
    9   WHGMT(15) ,WHOMT(15) , WHUMT(15) ,WHTMT(15) ,WHLMT(15)
C
C        THE FOLLOWING ARE STORAGE ALLOCATIONS FOR THE MODEL VARIABLES
C        WHICH ARE COMPUTED EACH TIME PERIOD.   30 WORDS ARE ALLOCATED
C        FOR EACH VARIABLE.
     DIMENSION
    A   AMM(30) ,   AMMP(30) ,  AV(30) ,    BAV(30) ,   BDM(30) ,   DI(30) ,
    B   DID(30) ,   DIDM(30) ,  DIDP(30) ,  DIEM(30) ,  DILM(30) ,  EDM(30) ,
    C   EGM(30) ,   ELJM(30) ,  ELM(30) ,   EM(30) ,    EMM(30) ,   ETM(30) ,
    D   HAV(30) ,   HUT(30) ,   L(30) ,     LA(30) ,    LAHM(30) ,  LAJM(30) ,
    E   LAM(30) ,   LAMP(30) ,  LATM(30) ,  LAUM(30) ,  LB(30) ,    LCHCD(30) ,
    F   LCHP(30) ,  LCR(30) ,   LD(30) ,    LDC(30) ,   LDI(30) ,   LDM(30) ,
    G   LEM(30) ,   LFO(30) ,   LHR(30) ,   LJ(30) ,    LLF(30) ,   LMM(30) ,
    H   LMMP(30) ,  LR(30) ,    LRP(30) ,   LSM(30) ,   LTM(30) ,   LTPG(30) ,
    I   LTU(30) ,   LUM(30) ,   LUR(30) ,   MA(30) ,    MAHM(30) ,  MAJM(30) ,
```

FIGURE 3   Fortran program for urban dynamics model.

```
      J    MAM(30),    MAMP(30),   MAPM(30),   MATM(30),   MB(30),    MBD(30),
      K    MD(30),     MDM(30),    MHR(30),    MJ(30),     MLM(30),   MLR(30),
      L    MP(30),     MPB(30),    MPR(30),    MR(30),     MSM(30),   NE(30),
      M    NEA(30),    NEC(30),    NECL(30),   NECP(30),   NED(30),   NEGR(30),
      N    P(30),      PEM(30),    PH(30),     PHA(30),    PHAM(30),  PHC(30),
      O    PHCD(30)
         DIMENSION
      A    PHCP(30),   PHEM(30),   PHGM(30),   PHGR(30),   PHLM(30),  PHM(30),
      B    PHO(30),    PHOM(30),   PHPM(30),   PHTM(30),   PUT(30),   SHAM(30),
      C    SHD(30),    SHDM(30),   SHDP(30),   SHLM(30),   TAI(30),   TC(30),
      D    TCM(30),    TN(30),     TPCR(30),   TPCSP(30),  TR(30),    TRN(30),
      E    TRNP(30),   U(30),      UA(30),     UAMM(30),   UB(30),    UD(30),
      F    UDM(30),    UEM(30),    UFW(30),    UH(30),     UHM(30),   UHPM(30),
      G    UHPR(30),   UHR(30),    UJ(30),     UJM(30),    UJP(30),   ULJR(30),
      H    UM(30),     UMM(30),    UMMP(30),   UR(30),     UTL(30),   UTLN(30),
      I    UTLP(30),   UTP(30),    UW(30),     WH(30),     WHA(30),   WHAM(30),
      J    WHC(30),    WHCD(30),   WHCP(30),   WHEM(30),   WHGM(30),  WHGR(30),
      K    WHLM(30),   WHM(30),    WHO(30),    WHOM(30),   WHTM(30),  WHUM(30)
C
C - - - - - - - - - - - - - - - - - - - - - - - - - - - - - - - - - - - -
C - - - URBAN DYNAMICS MODEL COMPUTATIONS - - - - - - - - - - - - - - - - -
C - - - - - - - - - - - - - - - - - - - - - - - - - - - - - - - - - - - -
C
C     THE MODEL COMPUTATIONS ARE ORGANIZED INTO FOUR SECTIONS:
C      -INITIALIZATION OF BASIC MODEL LEVEL VARIABLES
C      -INITIALIZATION OF COMPUTATION CONTROL LOOPS
C      -EQUATIONS FOR MODEL SECTORS
C      -PRINTING OF MODEL RESULTS
C     THE THIRD SECTION IS ORGANIZED INTO A NUMBER OF SUBSECTIONS WHICH
C     DEAL WITH DIFFERENT ASPECTS OF THE MODEL.  THE NUMBERS AT THE
C     RIGHT-HAND SIDE OF STATEMENTS REFER TO THE STATEMENT NUMBERS
C     WHICH FORRESTER USED FOR THE ANALOGOUS STATEMENT IN HIS DYNAMO
C     LANGUAGE VERSION OF THE MODEL.  SINCE A NUMBER OF THE STATEMENTS
C     IN THE FORTRAN VERSION HAVE NO ANALOGUE IN THE DYNAMO VERSION,
C     MANY FORTRAN STATEMENTS WILL NOT CARRY A STATEMENT NUMBER AT
C     THEIR RIGHT-HAND END.
C
C - - - - - - - - - - - - - - - - - - - - - - - - - - - - - - - - - - - -
C - - - INITIALIZATION OF BASIC MODEL LEVEL VARIABLES - - - - - - - - - - -
C
C     POPULATION LEVELS: MANAGER-PROFESSIONAL (MP), LABOR (L), AND
C     UNDEREMPLOYED (U)
      MP(1) = 3900.                                                  52.1
      L(1)  = 14000.                                                 29.1
      U(1)  = 1200.                                                  16.1
C
C     HOUSING LEVELS: PREMIUM HOUSING (PH), WORKER HOUSING (WH),
C     AND UNDEREMPLOYED HOUSING (UH).
      PH(1) = 5000.                                                  78.1
      WH(1) = 21000.                                                 81.1
      UH(1) = 1100.                                                  95.1
C
C     BUSINESS-INDUSTRY LEVELS: NEW ENTERPRISE (NE), MATURE BUSINESS
C     (MB), AND DECLINING INDUSTRY (DI).
      NE(1) = 200.                                                  100.1
      MB(1) = 1000.                                                 113.1
```

FIGURE 3   (continued)

```
        DI(1) = 100.                                                    116.1
C
C - - - - - - - - - - - - - - - - - - - - - - - - - - - - - - - - - - - -
C - - - INITIALIZATION OF COMPUTATION CONTROL LOOPS - - - - - - - - - - - -
C - - - - - - - - - - - - - - - - - - - - - - - - - - - - - - - - - - - -
C
C        HERE PARAMETERS ARE SET AND THE PRIMARY AND SECONDARY DO LOOPS
C        WHICH CONTROL THE COMPUTATION ARE INITIALIZED.
C
C        PRINT IS SET TO INDICATE THE NUMBER OF MODEL YEARS FOR WHICH
C        RESULTS ARE TO BE PRINTED.  FREQ IS SET TO INDICATE THE
C        FREQUENCY WITH WHICH RESULTS ARE TO BE PRINTED (I.E. THE
C        NUMBER OF MODEL YEARS COMPUTED BETWEEN PRINTINGS).  THE NUMBER
C        OF MODEL YEARS ACTUALLY COMPUTED WILL BE FREQ*(PRINT - 1) PLUS
C        THE ZEROTH YEAR.
C
        PRINT = 26
        FREQ = 10
C        DT--THE SOLUTION INTERVAL
        DT = 1.                                                         151
C
C        THE PRIMARY AND SECONDARY LOOPS ARE INITIALIZED
        DO 2200 I = 1, PRINT
        DO 2000 J = 1, FREQ
C
C        THE VALUES K, LST, AND NXT MUST BE COMPUTED SO THEY MAY BE
C        USED THROUGHOUT THE MODEL COMPUTATIONS TO REFERENCE THE CELLS
C        IN THE STORAGE VECTORS WHICH CORRESPOND TO THE YEAR BEING
C        COMPUTED, THE YEAR LAST COMPUTED, AND THE YEAR TO BE COMPUTED
C        NEXT.
        K = I
        LST = K - 1
        IF((J.GT.1).OR.(I.EQ.1)) LST = K
        NXT = K
        IF((J.EQ.FREQ).OR.(I.EQ.1)) NXT = K + 1
C
C - - - - - - - - - - - - - - - - - - - - - - - - - - - - - - - - - - - -
C - - - EQUATIONS FOR MODEL SECTORS - - - - - - - - - - - - - - - - - - - -
C - - - - - - - - - - - - - - - - - - - - - - - - - - - - - - - - - - - -
C
C        THIS SECTION CONTAINS THE RELATIONSHIPS FOR THE MODEL SECTORS.
C        THE SECTION IS DIVIDED INTO THE FOLLOWING SUBSECTIONS:
C        -URBAN DEVELOPMENT PROGRAMS SECTOR
C        -TAX SECTOR
C        -CONSTRUCTION GOALS AND MULTIPLIERS
C        -JOB SECTOR
C        -UNDEREMPLOYMENT SECTOR
C        -LABOR SECTOR
C        -MANAGERIAL-PROFESSIONAL SECTOR
C        -PREMIUM HOUSING SECTOR
C        -WORKER HOUSING SECTOR
C        -UNDEREMPLOYED HOUSING SECTOR
C        -NEW ENTERPRISE SECTOR
C        -MATURE BUSINESS SECTOR
C        -DECLINING INDUSTRY SECTOR
C
```

FIGURE 3   (continued)

```
C
C
C - - - URBAN DEVELOPMENT PROGRAMS SECTOR - - - - - - - - - - - - - - - - -
C
C           THIS SECTION REPRESENTS A NUMBER OF URBAN DEVELOPMENT PROGRAMS
C           WHICH PROVIDE A MEANS OF TESTING THE INFLUENCE OF VARIOUS
C           EXTERNALLY SUPPORTED EFFORTS TO IMPROVE CONDITIONS.  THESE
C           PROGRAMS ARE NOT ACTIVATED HERE AND ARE ONLY INCLUDED FOR
C           COMPLETENESS.  PROGRAMS CAN BE ACTIVATED BY SETTING THE
C           APPROPRIATE PROGRAM PARAMETERS TO VALUES OTHER THAN ZERO.
C           THESE ARE THE URBAN PROGRAMS FORRESTER USED IN HIS ANALYSIS
C           OF THE IMPACT OF TRADITIONAL APPROACHES TO URBAN DEVELOPMENT.
C
C           INITIALIZATION OF PROGRAM PARAMETERS
      IF(K.GT.1) GO TO 50
      UTR = 0.                                                     140.1
      LTR =0.                                                      141.1
      PHCR = 0.                                                    142.1
      WHCR = 0.                                                    143.1
      SHDR = 0.                                                    144.1
      NECR = 0.                                                    145.1
      DIDR = 0.                                                    146.1
      TPCS = 0.                                                    147.1
      UJPC = 0.                                                    148.1
      LCHPC = 0.                                                   150.1
C
C           THE FOLLOWING ITEMS MUST BE COMPUTED PRIOR TO THE SECTOR
C           EQUATIONS, ALTHOUGH THE ITEMS LOGICALLY BELONG WITH OTHER
C           SECTORS.
C
   50 IF(K.GT.1) GO TO 55
      LPH = .1                                                     69.1
      LPP = .2                                                     69.2
      AREA = 100000.                                               69.3
   55 HUT(K) = PH(K) + WH(K) + UH(K)                               70
      PUT(K) = NE(K) + MB(K) + DI(K)                               71
      LFO(K) = (HUT(K)*LPH + PUT(K)*LPP) / AREA                    69
      PHLM(K) = TABLE(PHLMT,LFO(K),.0,1.,.1)                       68
      DATA PHLMT /.4,.9,1.3,1.6,1.8,1.9,1.8,1.4,.7,.2,.0/          68.1
      WHLM(K) = TABLE(WHLMT,LFO(K),.0,1.,.1)                       86
      DATA WHLMT /.4,.9,1.3,1.6,1.8,1.9,1.8,1.4,.7,.2,.0/          86.1
      ELM(K) = TABLE(ELMT,LFO(K),.0,1.,.1)                         105
      DATA ELMT /1.,1.15,1.3,1.4,1.45,1.4,1.3,1.,.7,.4,.0/         105.1
C
C           SECTOR EQUATIONS
C           (THE EQUATION FOR LOW-COST-HOUSING PROGRAM (LCHP) IS COMPUTED
C           IN THE JOB SECTOR SINCE IT DEPENDS ON VALUES COMPUTED THERE.)
C
C           UNDEREMPLOYED-TRAINING PROGRAM (UTP)
      UTP(K) = UTR*U(K)                                            140
C
C           LABOR-TRAINING PROGRAM (LTPG)
      LTPG(K) = LTR*L(K)                                           141
C
C           PREMIUM-HOUSING CONSTRUCTION PROGRAM (PHCP)
```

FIGURE 3   (continued)

```
      PHCP(K) = PHCB*PH(K)*PHLM(K)                              142
C
C        WORKER-HOUSING CONSTRUCTION PROGRAM (WHCP)
      WHCP(K) = WHCR*HUT(K)*WHLM(K)                             143
C
C        SLUM-HOUSING-DEMOLITION PROGRAM (SHDP)
      SHDP(K) = SHDB*UH(K)                                      144
C
C        NEW-ENTERPRISE-CONSTRUCTION PROGRAM (NECP)
      NECP(K) = NECR*PUT(K)*ELM(K)                              145
C
C        DECLINING-INDUSTRY-DEMOLITION PROGRAM (DIDP)
      DIDP(K) = DIDR*DI(K)                                      146
C
C        TAX/PER-CAPITA-SUBSIDY PROGRAM (TPCSP)
      TPCSP(K) = TPCS                                           147
C
C        UNDEREMPLOYED-JOB PROGRAM (UJP)
      UJP(K) = UJPC*U(K)                                        148
C
C        LOW-COST-HOUSING CONSTRUCTION DESIRED (LCHCD).   USED IN
C        COMPUTING LCHP IN JOB SECTOR.
      LCHCD(K) = LCHPC*U(K)*WHLM(K)                             150
C
C
C
C - - - TAX SECTOR - - - - - - - - - - - - - - - - - - - - - - - - - - - -
C
C        THE TAX COLLECTIONS (TC) ARE COMPUTED AS THE PRODUCT OF ASSESS-
C        ED VALUE (AV), WHICH INCLUDES BOTH BUSINESS ASSESSED VALUE
C        (BAV) AND HOUSING ASSESSED VALUE (HAV), BY THE TAX ASSESSMENT
C        NORMAL (TAN), BY THE TAX RATIO (TR).   THE TAX RATIO HAS
C        INFLUENCE AT A NUMBER OF POINTS IN THE MODEL ON MOBILITY AND
C        CONSTRUCTION.
C
C - - - - INITIALIZATION
C
  100 IF(K.GT.1) GO TO 110
      TAN = 50.                                                121.1
      TRNPT = 30.                                              123.2
      THP = 150.                                               126.1
      TLP = 200.                                               126.2
      TUP = 300.                                               126.3
      PHAV = 30.                                               129.1
      WHAV = 15.                                               129.2
      UHAV = 5.                                                129.3
      NEAV = 500.                                              130.1
      MBAV = 300.                                              130.2
      DIAV = 100.                                              130.3
      MPFS = 5.                                                9.1
      LFS = 6.                                                 9.2
      UFS = 8.                                                 9.3
  110 CONTINUE
C
C - - - - SECTOR EQUATIONS
```

FIGURE 3   (continued)

```
C
      BAV(K) = NEAV*NE(K)  +  MBAV*MB(K)  +  DIAV*DI(K)            130
      HAV(K) = PHAV*PH(K)  +  WHAV*WH(K)  +  UHAV*UH(K)            129
      AV(K)  = HAV(K)  +  BAV(K)                                  128
C        LABOR/UNDEREMPLOYED RATIO (LUR) IS COMPUTED AT THIS POINT
C        BECAUSE ITS NEEDED TO COMPUTE THE TAX COLLECTION MULTIPLIER
C        (TCM).
      LUR(K) = L(K)  / U(K)                                        26
      TCM(K) = TABLE(TCMT,LUR(K),0.,3.,.5)                        127
      DATA TCMT /2.,1.6,1.3,1.1,1.,.9,.8/                         127.1
      TN(K)  = (TMP*MPFS*MP(K) + TLP*LFS*L(K)  + TUP*UFS*U(K)) * TCM(K)   126
      TAI(K) = TN(K)/AV(K)                                        125
      TRN(K) = TAI(K)/TAN                                         124
      IF(K.GT.1) GO TO 120
      TRNP(K) = TRN(K)                                            123.1
      GO TO 130
  120 CONTINUE
      TRNP(K) = TRNP(LST)  + (DT/TRNPT)*(TRNX - TRNP(LST))
  130 TRNX = TRN(K)                                               123
      TR(K)  = TABLE(TRT,1.44*ALOG(TRNP(K)),-2.,4.,1.)
      DATA TRT /.3,.5,1.,1.8,2.8,3.6,4./                          122
      TC(K)  = AV(K)*TAN*TR(K)                                    122.1
C                                                                 121
C
C - - - CONSTRUCTION GOALS AND MULTIPLIERS  - - - - - - - - - - - - - - - - - - - -
C
C
C        THIS SECTION COMPUTES THE DESIRED LEVELS OF CONSTRUCTION
C        FOR PREMIUM HOUSING (PHCD), WORKER HOUSING (WHCD), AND NEW
C        ENTERPRISES (NECD).  IT IS NECESSARY TO COMPUTE THESE BEFORE
C        THE JOB SECTOR COMPUTATIONS.  AS A PRELIMINARY STEP TO
C        COMPUTING THESE CONSTRUCTION GOALS, MULTIPLIERS PHM, WHM, AND
C        EM ARE COMPUTED FOR PREMIUM HOUSING, WORKER HOUSING, AND
C        ENTERPRISES, RESPECTIVELY.  THESE MULTIPLIERS WILL BE USED
C        LATER IN THE PREMIUM HOUSING, WORKER HOUSING, AND NEW
C        ENTERPRISE SECTORS.  THE MULTIPLIERS ARE DETERMINED FROM A
C        NUMBER OF ATTRACTIVENESS TERMS AND EXPRESS THE MULTIPLE OF
C        THE NORMAL LEVEL OF CONSTRUCTION DESIRED FOR THE SECTOR.
C
C - - - - GROWTH RATES FOR HOUSING AND ENTERPRISES.
C        GROWTH RATES ARE COMPUTED FOR PREMIUM HOUSING (PHGR), WORKER
C        HOUSING (WHGR), AND NEW ENTERPRISES (NEGR).  THESE ARE ALL
C        COMPUTED BY THE SAME BASIC RELATIONSHIP, WHICH CONSISTS OF
C        SUBTRACTING AN EARLIER VALUE OF HOUSING OR ENTERPRISE LEVEL
C        (PHA, WHA, NEA) FROM THE PRESENT LEVEL (PH, WH, NE) AND
C        DIVIDING THIS DIFFERENCE BY A TIME DELAY (PHAT, WHAT, NEAT)
C        AND BY THE PRESENT LEVEL (PH, WH, NE) TO CONVERT IT TO A
C        FRACTIONAL GROWTH RATE.
C
C        FOR THE INITIAL YEAR CERTAIN VALUES MUST BE SET OR COMPUTED
      IF(K.GT.1) GO TO 210
      PHAT = 10.
      WHAT = 10.                                                  77.2
      NEAT = 10.                                                  92.2
      PHGRI = .03                                                 110.2
      WHGRI = .03                                                 77.3
                                                                  92.3
```

FIGURE 3   (continued)

```
      NEGRI = .03                                          110.3
      PHA(K) = PH(K) - PHGRI*PHAT*PH(K)                    77.1
      WHA(K) = WH(K) - WHGRI*WHAT*WH(K)                    92.1
      NEA(K) = NE(K) - NEGRI*NEAT*NE(K)                    110.1
      GO TO 215
C
C          THE AVERAGE LEVELS OF HOUSING AND NEW ENTERPRISE ARE
C          COMPUTED FOR ALL YEARS EXCEPT THE FIRST BY THE FOLLOWING
C          FORMULA. NOTE THAT THE PREVIOUS LEVELS OF PH, WH, AND NE
C          ARE STORED IN PHX, WHX, AND NEX, RESPECTIVELY, SO THEY WILL
C          BE AVAILABLE FOR USE IN COMPUTING THE NEXT YEAR.
C                                                          77
  210 PHA(K) = PHA(LST) + (DT/PHAT)*(PHX - PHA(LST))       92
      WHA(K) = WHA(LST) + (DT/WHAT)*(WHX - WHA(LST))       110
      NEA(K) = NEA(LST) + (DT/NEAT)*(NEX - NEA(LST))
C
  215 PHX = PH(K)
      WHX = WH(K)
      NEX = NE(K)
C                                                          76
      PHGR(K) = (PH(K) - PHA(K)) / (PH(K)*PHAT)            91
      WHGR(K) = (WH(K) - WHA(K)) / (WH(K)*WHAT)            109
      NEGR(K) = (NE(K) - NEA(K)) / (NE(K)*NEAT)
C
C          PREMIUM-HOUSING MULTIPLIER (PHM) IS COMPUTED AS THE PRODUCT
C          OF SIX TERMS-
C              PHAM - PREMIUM-HOUSING-ADEQUACY MULTIPLIER
C              PHLM - PREMIUM-HOUSING LAND MULTIPLIER
C              PHPM - PREMIUM-HOUSING POPULATION MULTIPLIER
C              PHTM - PREMIUM-HOUSING TAX MULTIPLIER
C              PHEM - PREMIUM-HOUSING ENTERPRISE MULTIPLIER
C              PHGM - PREMIUM-HOUSING-GROWTH MULTIPLIER
C          IN ADDITION A PREMIUM HOUSING FACTOR (PHF) IS INCLUDED IN
C          THE EQUATION AS A TECHNICAL PARAMETER WHICH PERMITS
C          SENSITIVITY EXPERIMENTATION WITH THE EFFECT OF THIS
C          EQUATION. THE SIX FACTORS WHICH CONTRIBUTE TO PHM ARE
C          COMPUTED BELOW, EXCEPT PHLM WHICH WAS COMPUTED EARLIER
C          BECAUSE IT IS USED IN THE URBAN DEVELOPMENT PROGRAMS SECTOR.
C
      IF(K.GT.1) GO TO 220                                 66.1
      PHF = 1.                                             61.1
      PHPD = 3.                                            61
  220 HHR(K) = (HP(K)*HPFS) / (PH(K)*PHPD)                 67
      PHAM(K) = TABLE(PHAMT,HHR(K),.0,2.,.25)              67.1
      DATA PHAMT /.0,.001,.01,.2,1.,.3-,.4.6,5.6,6./       58
      HPR(K) = HP(K) / (L(K) + U(K))                       72
      PHPM(K) = TABLE(PHPMT,HPR(K),.0,.1,.02)              72.1
      DATA PHPMT /.3,.7,1.,1.2,1.3,1.3/                    73
      PHTM(K) = TABLE(PHTMT,1.44*ALOG(TR(K)),-2.,.4.,.2.)  73.1
      DATA PHTMT /1.2,1.,.7,.3/                            74
      PHEM(K) = TABLE(PHEMT,NEGR(K),-1,.15,.05)            74.1
      DATA PHEMT/.2,.6,1.,1.4,1.8,2.2/                     75
      PHGM(K) = TABLE(PHGMT,PHGR(K),-1,.15,.05)            75.1
      DATA PHGMT /.2,.6,1.,1.4,1.8,2.2/                    66
      PHM(K) = PHAM(K)*PHLM(K)*PHPM(K)*PHTM(K)*PHEM(K)*PHGM(K)*PHF
C
```

FIGURE 3   (continued)

```
C          PREMIUM-HOUSING CONSTRUCTION DESIRED (PHCD) IS COMPUTED AS
C          THE PRODUCT OF PREMIUM-HOUSING CONSTRUCTION NORMAL (PHCN),
C          THE CURRENT LEVEL OF PREMIUM HOUSING (PH), AND THE PREMIUM
C          HOUSING MULTIPLIER (PHM), JUST COMPUTED.  IN ADDITION AN
C          EXTERNALLY IMPOSED PREMIUM-HOUSING CONSTRUCTION PROGRAM CAN
C          BE ADDED THROUGH THE TERM PHCP, FROM THE URBAN DEVELOPMENT
C          PROGRAMS SECTOR.
       IF(K.GT.1) GO TO 225
       PHCN = .03
   225 PHCD(K) = PHCN*PH(K)*PHM(K)  + PHCP(K)                         65.1
C                                                                     65
C
C          WORKER-HOUSING MULTIPLIER (WHM) IS COMPUTED IN THE SAME WAY
C          AS THE PREMIUM-HOUSING MULTIPLIER WAS ABOVE, AS THE PRODUCT
C          OF SIX TERMS -
C             WHAM - WORKER-HOUSING-ADEQUACY MULTIPLIER
C             WHLM - WORKER-HOUSING LAND MULTIPLIER
C             WHUM - WORKER-HOUSING UNDEREMPLOYED MULTIPLIER
C             WHTM - WORKER-HOUSING TAX MULTIPLIER
C             WHEM - WORKER-HOUSING ENTERPRISE MULTIPLIER
C             WHGM - WORKER-HOUSING GROWTH MULTIPLIER
C          IN ADDITION A WORKER HOUSING FACTOR (WHF) IS INCLUDED IN THE
C          EQUATION AS A TECHNICAL PARAMETER WHICH PERMITS SENSITIVITY
C          EXPERIMENTATION WITH THE EFFECTS OF THIS EQUATION.   THE SIX
C          FACTORS WHICH CONTRIBUTE TO WHM ARE COMPUTED BELOW, EXCEPT
C          WHLM WHICH WAS COMPUTED EARLIER BECAUSE IT WAS USED IN THE
C          URBAN DEVELOPMENT PROGRAMS SECTOR.
C
       IF(K.GT.1) GO TO 230
       WHF = 1.
       WHPD = 6.                                                      84.1
C                                                                     48.1
   230 LHR(K) = (L(K)*LFS) / (WH(K)*WHPD)
       WHAM(K) = TABLE(WHAMT,LHR(K),.0,2.,.25)                        48
       DATA WHAMT /.0,.05,.1,.3,1.,1.8,2.4,2.8,3./                    85
       WHUM(K) = TABLE(WHUMT,LUR(K),.0,5.,1.)                         85.1
       DATA WHUMT /.5,.8,1.,1.2,1.3,1.3/                              87
       WHTM(K) = TABLE(WHTMT,1.44*ALOG(TR(K)),-2.,4.,2.)             87.1
       DATA WHTMT /1.2,1.,.7,.3/                                      88
       WHEM(K) = TABLE(WHEMT,NEGR(K),-.2,.3,.1)                       88.1
       DATA WHEMT /.3,.7,1.,1.2,1.3,1.4/                              89
       WHGM(K) = TABLE(WHGMT,WHGR(K),-.1,.15,.05)                     89.1
       DATA WHGMT /.2,.6,1.,1.4,1.8,2.2/                              90
       WHM(K) = WHAM(K)*WHLM(K)*WHUM(K)*WHTM(K)*WHEM(K)*WHGM(K)*WHF   90.1
C                                                                     84
C          WORKER-HOUSING CONSTRUCTION DESIRED (WHCD) IS COMPUTED AS
C          THE PRODUCT OF WORKER HOUSING CONSTRUCTION NORMAL (WHCN),
C          THE CURRENT LEVEL OF WORKER HOUSING(WH), AND THE WORKER
C          HOUSING MULTIPLIER (WHM) JUST COMPUTED.  IN ADDITION AN
C          EXTERNALLY IMPOSED WORKER HOUSING CONSTRUCTION PROGRAM CAN BE
C          ADDED THROUGH THE TERM WHCP, FROM THE URBAN DEVELOPMENT
C          PROGRAMS SECTOR.
       IF(K.GT.1) GO TO 235
       WHCN = .03
   235 WHCD(K) = WHCN*WH(K)*WHM(K)  + WHCP(K)                         83.1
                                                                      83
```

FIGURE 3   (continued)

```
C
C         ENTERPRISE MULTIPLIER (EM) IS COMPUTED AS THE PRODUCT OF FIVE
C         TERMS -
C            EMM - ENTERPRISE MANAGER/JOB MULTIPLIER
C            ELM - ENTERPRISE LAND MULTIPLIER
C            ELJM - ENTERPRISE LABOR/JOB MULTIPLIER
C            ETM - ENTERPRISE TAX MULTIPLIER
C            EGM - ENTERPRISE-GROWTH MULTIPLIER
C         IN ADDITION AN ENTERPRISE FACTOR (EF) IS INCLUDED IN THE
C         EQUATION AS A TECHNICAL PARAMETER WHICH PERMITS SENSITIVITY
C         EXPERIMENTATION WITH THE EFFECTS OF THIS EQUATION.  THE FIVE
C         FACTORS WHICH CONTRIBUTE TO EM ARE COMPUTED BELOW EXCEPT
C         ELM WHICH WAS COMPUTED EARLIER FOR USE IN THE URBAN
C         DEVELOPMENT PROGRAMS SECTOR.
C
      IF(K.GT.1) GO TO 240                                              103.1
      EF = 1.                                                            37.1
      NEM = 4.                                                           37.2
      MBM = 2.                                                           37.3
      DIM = 1.                                                          139.2
      LRPT = 5.                                                          37
  240 MJ(K) = NE(K)*NEM + MB(K)*MBM + DI(K)*DIM                          36
      MR(K) = MP(K) / MJ(K)                                             104
      EMM(K) = TABLE(EMMT,MR(K),.0,2.,.25)                              104.1
      DATA EMMT /.1,.15,.3,.5,1.,1.4,1.7,1.9,2./                        139
      LRP(K) = LRP(LST) + (DT/LRPT)*(LR(LST) - LRP(LST))               139.1
      IF(K.EQ.1) LRP(K) = 1.                                           106
      ELJM(K) = TABLE(ELJMT,LRP(K),.0,2.,.25)                          106.1
      DATA ELJMT /.0,.05,.15,.4,1.,1.5,1.7,1.8,1.8/                    107
      ETM(K) = TABLE(ETMT,1.44*ALOG(TR(K)),-2.,4.,1.)                  107.1
      DATA ETMT /1.3,1.2,1.,.8,.5,.25,.1/                              108
      EGM(K) = TABLE(EGMT,NEGR(K),-1.,15,.05)                          108.1
      DATA EGMT /.2,.6,1.,1.4,1.8,2.2/                                 103
      EM(K) = EMM(K)*ELM(K)*ELJM(K)*ETM(K)*EGM(K)*EF
C
C         NEW ENTERPRISE CONSTRUCTION DESIRED (NECD) IS COMPUTED AS
C         THE PRODUCT OF NEW ENTERPRISE CONSTRUCTION NORMAL (NECN), A
C         WEIGHTED SUM OF THE THREE CURRENT LEVELS OF ENTERPRISES
C         (NE, MB, DI), AND THE ENTERPRISE MULTIPLIER (EM) JUST
C         COMPUTED.  IN ADDITION AN EXTERNALLY IMPOSED ENTERPRISE
C         CONSTRUCTION PROGRAM CAN BE ADDED THROUGH THE TERM NECP, FROM
C         THE URBAN DEVELOPMENT PROGRAMS SECTOR.
      IF(K.GT.1) GO TO 245                                             102.4
      NECN = .05                                                       102.1
      NECF = 1.                                                        102.2
      MBCF = .5                                                        102.3
      DICF = .3
  245 NECD(K) = NECN*(NECF*NE(K) + MBCF*MB(K) + DICF*DI(K))*EM(K)      102
     1 + NECP(K)
C
C - - - JOB SECTOR - - - - - - - - - - - - - - - - - - - - - - - - - -
C
C         IN THIS SECTOR EMPLOYMENT RATIOS FOR LABOR AND UNDEREMPLOYED
C         CATEGORIES ARE COMPUTED.  A LABOR CONSTRUCTION RATIO (LCR) IS
C         COMPUTED FOR LATER USE IN THE HOUSING SECTOR TO CONSTRAIN
```

FIGURE 3   (continued)

```
C             CONSTRUCTION TO THE LABOR SUPPLY.
C
C             INITIALIZATIONS
       IF(K.GT.1) GO TO 310
C             PREMIUM-HOUSING, WORKER-HOUSING, NEW ENTERPRISE, AND LOW-COST-
C             HOUSING CONSTRUCTION LABOR (PHCL, WHCL, NECL, LCHCL), EXPRESS-
C             ED IN MAN-YEARS/HOUSING UNIT.
       PHCL = 2.                                                  131.1
       WHCL = 1.                                                  131.2
       NECL = 20.                                                 131.3
       LCHCL = .6                                                 131.4
C             NEW-ENTERPRISE, MATURE-BUSINESS, AND DECLINING-INDUSTRY LABOR
C             (NEL, MBL, DIL), EXPRESSED IN MEN/PRODUCTIVE UNIT.
       NEL = 20.                                                  132.1
       MBL = 15.                                                  132.2
       DIL = 10.                                                  132.3
C
C             SECTOR EQUATIONS
C
C             TOTAL LABOR JOBS (LJ) ARE DETERMINED BY COMPUTING AND THEN
C             SUMMING THE LABOR DESIRED FOR CONSTRUCTION (LDC) AND LABOR
C             DESIRED FOR INDUSTRY (LDI).
   310 LDC(K) = PHCD(K)*PHCL + WHCD(K)*WHCL + NECD(K)*NECL
      1  + LCHCD(K)*LCHCL                                         131
       LDI(K) = NE(K)*NEL + MB(K)*MBL + DI(K)*DIL                 132
       LJ(K) = LDC(K) + LDI(K)                                    133
C
C             LABOR/JOB RATIO (LR)
       LR(K) = L(K) / LJ(K)                                      134
C
C             UNDEREMPLOYED JOBS (UJ) ARE COMPUTED AS A FUNCTION OF THE
C             LABOR/JOB RATIO JUST COMPUTED PLUS UNDEREMPLOYED-JOB PROGRAM
C             (UJP) JOBS.
       ULJR(K) = TABLE(ULJRT,LR(K),.0,2.,.5)                      135
       DATA ULJRT /1.15,.8,.5,.25,.1/                             135.1
       UJ(K) = LJ(K)*ULJR(K) + UJP(K)                            136
C
C             UNDEREMPLOYED/JOB RATIO (UR)
       UR(K) = U(K) / UJ(K)                                      137
C
C             LABOR CONSTRUCTION RATIO (LCR) EXPRESSES THE INFLUENCE OF
C             AVAILABLE LABOR ON HOUSING AND ENTERPRISE CONSTRUCTION.
       LCR(K) = TABLE(LCRT,LR(K),.0,2.,.5)                        138
       DATA LCRT /.0,.5,.9,1.1,1.15/                              138.1
C             LOW-COST-HOUSING PROGRAM (LCHP) WHICH BELONGS WITH THE
C             URBAN DEVELOPMENT PROGRAMS SECTOR CAN NOW BE COMPUTED.
       LCHP(K) = LCHCD(K)*LCR(K)                                  149
C
C             LABOR/JOB RATIO PERCEIVED (LRP) WHICH BELONGS WITH THIS SECTOR
C             WAS COMPUTED EARLIER FOR USE IN ABOVE SECTORS.
C
C
C
C - - - UNDEREMPLOYED SECTOR - - - - - - - - - - - - - - - - - - - - - -
```

FIGURE 3   (continued)

```
C         THE NUMBER OF UNDEREMPLOYED (U) FOR A PERIOD IS REPRESENTED AS
C         THE LEVEL OF UNDEREMPLOYED IN THE PREVIOUS PERIOD PLUS THE
C         CHANGE IN THE LEVEL OF UNDEREMPLOYED POPULATION DUE TO THE
C         FOLLOWING FIVE RATES OF FLOW DURING THE PREVIOUS PERIOD--
C             UA - UNDEREMPLOYED ARRIVALS
C             UB - UNDEREMPLOYED BIRTHS
C             LTU - LABOR TO UNDEREMPLOYED
C             UD - UNDEREMPLOYED DEPARTURES
C             UTL - UNDEREMPLOYED TO LABOR.
C         EACH OF THESE FLOWS IS COMPUTED IN TURN BELOW AND THEN THE
C         UNDEREMPLOYED LEVEL FOR THE NEXT PERIOD IS COMPUTED.
C
C         INITIALIZATIONS
      IF(K.GT.1) GO TO 410
C         PERCEPTION TIMES--FOR UNDEREMPLOYED TO LABOR (UTLPT),
C         ATTRACTIVENESS-FOR MIGRATION MULTIPLIER (AMMPT), UNDEREMPLOYED
C         MOBILITY MULTIPLIER(UMMPT).                                    20.2
      UTLPT = 10.                                                        2.2
      AMMPT = 20.                                                        22.2
      UMMPT = 10.
C         UNDEREMPLOYED NORMAL RATES--FOR ARRIVALS (UAN), DEPARTURES
C         (UDN), MOBILITY (UMN).                                         1.1
      UAN = .05                                                          13.1
      UDN = .02                                                          17.1
      UMN = .1
C         UNDEREMPLOYMENT-HOUSING POPULATION DENSITY (UHPD)              6.1
      UHPD = 12.
C         TAX PER CAPITA NORMAL                                          8.1
      TPCN = 250.
C         UNDEREMPLOYED BIRTH RATE                                       15.1
      UBR = .015
C         SENSITIVITY EXPERIMENTATION FACTORS--FOR ATTRACTIVENESS FOR
C         MIGRATION (AMF) AND UNDEREMPLOYED MOBILITY (UMF).              3.1
      AMF = 1.                                                           23.1
      UMF = 1.
  410 CONTINUE
C
C         SECTOR EQUATIONS
C
C         UNDEREMPLOYED ARRIVALS (UA)
C         THE ATTRACTIVENESS-FOR-MIGRATION MULTIPLIER (AMM) IS COMPUTED
C         FOR USE IN DETERMINING UNDEREMPLOYED ARRIVALS (UA) AND FOR
C         USE LATER IN DETERMINING UNDEREMPLOYED DEPARTURES (UD).   AMM
C         IS THE PRODUCT OF SIX FACTORS--UNDEREMPLOYED-ARRIVALS-
C         MOBILITY MULTIPLIER (UAMM), UNDEREMPLOYED/HOUSING MULTIPLIER
C         (UHM), PUBLIC-EXPENDITURE MULTIPLIER (PEM), UNDEREMPLOYED/
C         JOB MULTIPLIER (UJM), UNDEREMPLOYED-HOUSING-PROGRAM
C         MULTIPLIER (UHPM), AND ATTRACTIVENESS FOR MIGRATION FACTOR
C         (AMF), FOR SENSITIVITY EXPERIMENTATION.                        20
      UTLP(K) = UTLP(LST) + (DT/UTLPT)*(UTL(LST) - UTLP(LST))            20.1
      IF(K.EQ.1) UTLP(K) = 75.                                          21
      UM(K) = UTLP(K) / U(K)                                            4
      UAMM(K) = TABLE(UAMMT,UM(K),-0,-15,-025)                          4.1
      DATA UAMMT /-3,-7,1.,1-2,1-3,1-4,1-5/
```

FIGURE 3   (continued)

```
        UHR(K) = (U(K)*UPS) / (UH(K)*UHPD)                              6
        UHM(K) = TABLE(UHMT,UHR(K),.0,2.,.25)                           5
        DATA UHMT /2.5,2.4,2.2,1.7,1.,.4,.2,.1,.05/                     5.1
        P(K) = MP(K)*MPPS + L(K)*LPS + U(K)*UPS                         9
        TPCR(K) = ((TC(K)/P(K)) + TPCSP(K))/TPCN                        8
        PEM(K) = TABLE(PEMT,TPCR(K),.0,3.,.5)                           7
        DATA PEMT /.2,.6,1.,1.6,2.4,3.2,4./                             7.1
        UJM(K) = TABLE(UJMT,UR(K),.0,3.,.25)                            10
        DATA UJMT /2.,2.,1.9,1.6,1.,.6,.4,.3,.2,.15,.1,.05,.02/         10.1
        UHPR(K) = LCHP(K) / U(K)                                        12
        UHPM(K) = TABLE(UHPMT,UHPR(K),.0,.05,.01)                       11
        DATA UHPMT /1.,1.2,1.5,1.9,2.4,3./                              11.1
C       SAVE AMM(LST) FOR USE JUST BELOW IN COMPUTING AMMP(K).
        AMMLST = AMM(LST)
        AMM(K) = UAMM(K)*UHM(K)*PEM(K)*UJM(K)*UHPM(K)*AMF              3
C           ATTRACTIVENESS-FOR-MIGRATION MULTIPLIER PERCEIVED (AMMP) AND
C           THE UNDEREMPLOYED ARRIVALS (UA) CAN BE DETERMINED.
        AMMP(K) = AMMP(LST) + (DT/AMMPT)*(AMMLST - AMMP(LST))          2
        IF(K.EQ.1) AMMP(K) = 1.                                        2.1
        UA(K) = (U(K) + L(K))*UAN*AMMP(K)                             1
C
C
C       UNDEREMPLOYED BIRTHS (UB)
C           BIRTHS ARE COMPUTED BY APPLYING A NET BIRTH RATE TO THE
C           UNDEREMPLOYED POPULATION.
        UB(K) = U(K) * UBR                                             15
C
C
C       LABOR TO UNDEREMPLOYED
C           THE FLOW OF LABOR TO UNDEREMPLOYED (LTU) DEPENDS ON THE
C           LABOR-LAYOFF FRACTION (LLF) WHICH DEPENDS IN TURN ON THE
C           PREVIOUSLY COMPUTED LABOR/JOB RATIO (LR).
        LLF(K) = TABLE(LLFT,LR(K),.0,2.,.5)                            31
        DATA LLFT /.0,.01,.03,.1,.3/                                   31.1
        LTU(K) = L(K) * LLF(K)                                         30
C
C
C       UNDEREMPLOYED DEPARTURES (UD)
C           UD DEPENDS ON THE UNDEREMPLOYED (U) POPULATION, A RATE OF
C           UNDEREMPLOYED DEPARTURES NORMAL (UDN), AND AN UNDEREMPLOYED-
C           DEPARTURE MULTIPLIER (UDM). UDM DEPENDS ON THE PREVIOUSLY
C           COMPUTED ATTRACTIVENESS-FOR-MIGRATION MULTIPLIER (AMM).
        UDM(K) = TABLE(UDMT,1.44*ALOG(AMM(K)),-3.,3.,1.)              14
        DATA UDMT /8.,4.,2.,1.,.5,.25,.125/                            14.1
        UD(K) = UDN * U(K) * UDM(K)                                    13
C       UNDEREMPLOYED TO LABOR (UTL)
C           THE UNDEREMPLOYED-MOBILITY MULTIPLIER (UMM) IS FIRST
C           COMPUTED FOR USE IN DETERMINING UTL. UMM IS THE PRODUCT OF
C           FOUR FACTORS--LABOR-SUPPLY MULTIPLIER (LSM), LABOR/UNDER-
C           EMPLOYED MULTIPLIER (LUM), UNDEREMPLOYMENT EDUCATIONAL
C           MULTIPLIER (UEM), AND UNDEREMPLOYED-MOBILITY FACTOR (UMF),
C           FOR SENSITIVITY EXPERIMENTATION.
        LSM(K) = TABLE(LSMT,LR(K),.0,2.,.5)                            24
        DATA LSMT /2.4,2.,1.,.4,.2/                                    24.1
        LUM(K) = TABLE(LUMT,LUR(K),.0,5.,1.)                           25
        DATA LUMT /.2,.7,1.,1.2,1.3,1.4/                               25.1
        UEM(K) = TABLE(UEMT,TPCR(K),.0,3.,.5)                          27
        DATA UEMT /.2,.7,1.,1.3,1.5,1.6,1.7/                           27.1
```

FIGURE 3 (continued)

```
C           SAVE UMM (LST) FOR USE JUST BELOW IN COMPUTING UMMP(K)
       UMMLST = UMM (LST)                                                    23
       UMM(K) = LSM(K)*LUM(K)*UEM(K)*UMF
C           UNDEREMPLOYED-MOBILITY MULTIPLIER PERCEIVED (UMMP) CAN BE
C           DETERMINED.                                                      22
       UMMP(K) = UMMP(LST) + (DT/UMMPT)*(UMMLST - UMMP(LST))                 22.1
       IF(K.EQ.1) UMMP(K) = 1.
C           UNDEREMPLOYED TO LABOR (UTL) DEPENDS ON THE UNDEREMPLOYED
C           WORKING (UW), UNDEREMPLOYED MOBILITY NORMAL (UMN) RATE, AND
C           THE UNDEREMPLOYED- MOBILITY MULTIPLIER PERCEIVED (UMMP).   IN
C           ADDITION THE UNDEREMPLOYED-TRAINING PROGRAM (UTP) MAY PROVIDE
C           AN INCREMENT TO LABOR FROM THE UNDEREMPLOYED.
C                                                                           19
       UFW(K) = TABLE(UFWT,UR(K),-0,4.,1.)                                  19.1
       DATA UFWT /.9,.8,.5,.33,.25/                                         18
       UW(K) = U(K) * UFW(K)                                                17
       UTL(K) = UMN*UW(K)*UMMP(K) + UTP(K)

C
C           UNDEREMPLOYED (U) MAY NOW BE DETERMINED.                        16
       U(NXT) = U(K) + DT*(UA(K) + UB(K) + LTU(K) - UD(K) - UTL(K))
C
C           UNDEREMPLOYED TO LABOR NET (UTLN) MAY NOW BE COMPUTED--THIS
C           HAS NO FUNCTION EXCEPT OUTPUT                                   154
       UTLN(K) = UTL(K) - LTU(K)

C
C
C - - - LABOR SECTOR - - - - - - - - - - - - - - - - - - - - - - - - - - -
C
C           THE LABOR (L), OR SKILLED WORKERS, ARE REPRESENTED BY THE SAME
C           TYPE OF FUNCTIONAL FORM AS THE UNDEREMPLOYED WERE ABOVE.  THE
C           LABOR FOR A PERIOD IS EQUAL TO THE LABOR LEVEL OF THE PREVIOUS
C           PERIOD PLUS THE CHANGE IN LEVEL DUE TO THE FOLLOWING SIX RATES
C           OF FLOW DURING THE PREVIOUS PERIOD -
C               UTL - UNDEREMPLOYED TO LABOR
C               LB - LABOR BIRTHS
C               LTM - LABOR TO MANAGER
C               LA - LABOR ARRIVALS
C               LD - LABOR DEPARTURES
C               LTU - LABOR TO UNDEREMPLOYED
C           TWO OF THESE RATES, UTL AND LTU, WERE COMPUTED IN THE UNDER-
C           EMPLOYED SECTOR.  THE OTHER FOUR ARE COMPUTED HERE.
C
C           INITIALIZATIONS
       IF(K.GT.1) GO TO 510
C           PERCEPTION TIMES--FOR LABOR-MOBILITY-MULTIPLIER PERCEPTION
C           TIME (LMMPT) AND LABOR-ARRIVAL-MULTIPLIER PERCEPTION TIME
C           (LAMP).                                                         33.2
       LMMPT = 15.                                                          42.2
       LAMPT = 15.
C           LABOR NORMAL RATES--FOR ARRIVALS (LAN), DEPARTURES (LDN),
C           AND MOBILITY (LMN).                                             41.1
       LAN = .03                                                            49.1
       LDN = .02                                                            32.1
       LMN = .02
C           UNDEREMPLOYED BIRTH RATE                                        28.1
       LBR = .01
```

FIGURE 3   (continued)

```
C           SENSITIVITY EXPERIMENTATION FACTORS--FOR LABOR MOBILITY (LMF)
C           AND LABOR ARRIVALS (LAF).
        LMF = 1.                                                            34.1
        LAF = 1.                                                            43.1
  510 CONTINUE
C
C           LABOR BIRTHS (LB)
C           BIRTHS ARE COMPUTED BY APPLYING A NET BIRTH RATE TO THE
C           LABOR POPULATION.
        LB(K) = L(K) * LBR                                                  28
C
C           LABOR TO MANAGER (LTM)
C           THE LABOR-MOBILITY MULTIPLIER (LMM) IS FIRST COMPUTED FOR
C           USE IN COMPUTING LTM.  LMM IS THE PRODUCT OF FOUR FACTORS--
C           MANAGER-SUPPLY MULTIPLIER (MSM), MANAGER/LABOR MULTIPLIER
C           (MLM), LABOR EDUCATIONAL MULTIPLIER (LEM), AND LABOR-
C           MOBILITY FACTOR (LMF), FOR SENSITIVITY EXPERIMENTATION.
        MSM(K) = TABLE(MSMT,MR(K),.0,2.,.25)                                35
        DATA MSMT /2.3,2.2,2.,1.6,1.,.5,.2,.1,.05/                          35.1
        MLR(K) = MP(K) / L(K)                                              39
        MLM(K) = TABLE(MLMT,MLR(K),.0,.2,.05)                              38
        DATA MLMT /.2,.7,1.,1.2,1.3/                                       38.1
        LEM(K) = TABLE(LEMT,TPCR(K),.0,3.,.5)                              40
        DATA LEMT /.2,.7,1.,1.3,1.5,1.6,1.7/                               40.1
C           SAVE LMM(LST) FOR USE JUST BELOW IN COMPUTING LMMP(K).
        LMMLST = LMM(LST)
        LMM(K) = MSM(K)*MLM(K)*LEM(K)*LMF                                   34
C           LABOR-MOBILITY MULTIPLIER PERCEIVED (LMMP) CAN NOW BE
C           DETERMINED.
        LMMP(K) = LMMP(LST) + (DT/LMMPT)*(LMMLST - LMMP(LST))               33
        IF(K.EQ.1) LMMP(K) = 1.                                            33.1
C           LABOR TO MANAGER (LTM) DEPENDS ON THE LABOR (L) LEVEL,
C           LABOR MOBILITY NORMAL (LMN) RATE, AND THE LABOR-MOBILITY
C           MULTIPLIER PERCEIVED (LMMP).  IN ADDITION THE LABOR-TRAINING
C           PROGRAM (LTPG) MAY CONTRIBUTE.
        LTM(K) = LMN*L(K)*LMMP(K) + LTPG(K)                                32
C
C           LABOR ARRIVALS (LA)
C           THE LABOR-ARRIVAL MULTIPLIER (LAM) IS COMPUTED FOR USE IN
C           DETERMINING LABOR ARRIVALS (LA) AND FOR LATER USE IN
C           COMPUTING LABOR DEPARTURES (LD).  LAM IS THE PRODUCT OF FIVE
C           FACTORS--LABOR-ARRIVAL JOB MULTIPLIER (LAJM), LABOR-ARRIVAL
C           UNDEREMPLOYED MULTIPLIER (LAUM), LABOR-ARRIVAL TAX
C           MULTIPLIER (LATM), LABOR-ARRIVAL HOUSING MULTIPLIER (LAHM),
C           AND LABOR-ARRIVAL FACTOR (LAF), FOR SENSITIVITY TESTING.
C
        LAJM(K) = TABLE(LAJMT,LR(K),.0,2.,.25)                              44
        DATA LAJMT /2.6,2.6,2.4,1.8,1.,.4,.2,.1,.05/                        44.1
        LAUM(K) = TABLE(LAUMT,LUR(K),.0,5.,.1.)                            45
        DATA LAUMT /.4,.8,1.,1.2,1.3,1.3/                                  45.1
        LATM(K) = TABLE(LATMT,1.44*ALOG(TR(K)),-2.,.4.,.2.)                46
        DATA LATMT /1.2,1.,.7,.3/                                          46.1
        LAHM(K) = TABLE(LAHMT,LHR(K),.0,3.,.5)                             47
        DATA LAHMT /1.3,1.2,1.,.5,.2,.1,.05/                               47.1
C           SAVE LAM(LST) FOR USE JUST BELOW IN COMPUTING LAMP(K).
```

FIGURE 3   (continued)

```
      LAMLST = LAM(LST)
      LAM(K) = LAJM(K) * LAUM(K) * LATM(K) * LAHM(K) * LAF          43
C
C         LABOR-ARRIVAL MULTIPLIER PERCEIVED (LAMP) AND THE LABOR
C         ARRIVALS (LA) CAN NOW BE COMPUTED.
      LAMP(K) = LAMP(LST) + (DT/LAMPT)*(LAMLST - LAMP(LST))          42
      IF(K.EQ.1) LAMP(K) = 1.                                       42.1
      LA(K) = LAN * L(K) * LAMP(K)                                  41
C
C         LABOR DEPARTURES (LD)
C         LD DEPENDS ON THE LABOR (L) LEVEL, THE RATE OF LABOR
C         DEPARTURES NORMAL (LDN), AND A LABOR DEPARTURE MULTIPLIER
C         (LDM). LDM DEPENDS ON THE LABOR-ARRIVAL MULTIPLIER WHICH
C         WAS PREVIOUSLY COMPUTED.
      LDM(K) = TABLE(LDMT,1.44*ALOG(LAM(K)),-3.,3.,1.)               50
      DATA LDMT /8.,4.,2.,1.,.5,.25,.125/                           50.1
      LD(K) = LDN * L(K) * LDM(K)                                    49
C
C         LABOR (L) MAY NOW BE COMPUTED
      L(NXT) = L(K) + DT*(UTL(K)+LB(K)-LTM(K)+LA(K)-LD(K)-LTU(K))     29
C
C - - - MANAGER-PROFESSIONAL SECTOR - - - - - - - - - - - - - - - - - - -
C
C         THE MANAGERIAL-PROFESSIONAL (MP) POPULATION IS REPRESENTED IN
C         TERMS OF THE MANAGERIAL-PROFESSIONAL LEVEL IN THE PREVIOUS
C         PERIOD PLUS THE CHANGE IN LEVEL DUE TO THE FOLLOWING FOUR RATES
C         OF FLOW DURING THE PREVIOUS PERIOD--
C         LTM - LABOR TO MANAGER
C         MPB - MANAGER-PROFESSIONAL BIRTHS
C         MA - MANAGER ARRIVALS
C         MD - MANAGER DEPARTURES
C         LTM WAS COMPUTED ABOVE IN THE LABOR SECTOR.  THE OTHER THREE
C         RATES ARE COMPUTED BELOW.
C
C         INITIALIZATIONS
      IF(K.GT.1) GO TO 610
C         MANAGER-PROFESSIONAL BIRTH RATE
      MPBR = .0075                                                   51.1
C         MANAGER-ARRIVAL MULTIPLIER PERCEPTION TIME.
      MAMPT = 10.                                                    54.2
C         MANAGER NORMAL RATES--FOR ARRIVALS (MAN) AND FOR DEPARTURES
C         (MDN).
      MAN = .03                                                      53.1
      MDN = .02                                                      62.1
C         MANAGER-ARRIVAL FACTOR (MAF) FOR SENSITIVITY TESTING.
      MAF = 1.                                                       55.1
  610 CONTINUE
C
C         MANAGERIAL-PROFESSIONAL BIRTHS
C         BIRTHS ARE COMPUTED BY APPLYING A NET BIRTH RATE (MPB) TO
C         THE MANAGERIAL-PROFESSIONAL POPULATION LEVEL (MP).
      MPB(K) = MP(K) * MPBR                                          51
C
C         MANAGER ARRIVALS
C         THE MANAGER-ARRIVAL MULTIPLIER (MAM) IS COMPUTED FOR USE IN
```

FIGURE 3   (continued)

```
C           DETERMINING MANAGER ARRIVALS (MA).  MAM IS THE PRODUCT OF
C           FIVE FACTORS--MANAGER-ARRIVAL JOB MULTIPLIER (MAJM),
C           MANAGER-ARRIVAL POPULATION MULTIPLIER (MAPM), MANAGER-ARRIVAL
C           TAX MULTIPLIER (MATM), MANAGER-ARRIVAL HOUSING MULTIPLIER
C           (MAHM), AND MANAGER-ARRIVAL FACTOR (MAF), FOR USE IN
C           SENSITIVITY TESTING.
      MAJM(K) = TABLE(MAJMT,MR(K),.0,2.,.25)                            56
      DATA MAJMT /2.7,2.6,2.4,2.,1.,.4,.2,.1,.05/                       56.1
      MAPM(K) = TABLE(MAPMT,MPR(K),.0,.1,.02)                           57
      DATA MAPMT /.3,.7,1.,1.2,1.3,1.3/                                 57.1
      MATM(K) = TABLE(MATMT,1.44*ALOG(TR(K)),-2.,4.,2.)                 59
      DATA MATMT /1.4,1.,.7,.3/                                         59.1
      MAHM(K) = TABLE(MAHMT,MHR(K),.0,3.,.5)                            60
      DATA MAHMT /1.3,1.2,1.,.5,.2,.1,.05/                              60.1
C           SAVE MAM(LST) FOR USE JUST BELOW IN COMPUTING MAMP(K).
      MAMLST = MAM(LST)
      MAM(K) = MAJM(K)*MAPM(K)*MATM(K)*MAHM(K)*MAF                      55
C           MANAGER-ARRIVAL MULTIPLIER PERCEIVED (MAMP) AND THE MANAGER
C           ARRIVALS (MA) CAN NOW BE COMPUTED.
      MAMP(K) = MAMP(LST) + (DT/MAMPT)*(MAMLST - MAMP(LST))             54
      IF(K.EQ.1) MAMP(K) = 1.                                          54.1
      MA(K) = MAN*MP(K)* MAMP(K)                                        53
C
C           MANAGER DEPARTURES
C           MANAGER DEPARTURES (MD) DEPEND ON THE MANAGER-PROFESSIONAL
C           (MP) LEVEL, A RATE OF MANAGER DEPARTURES NORMAL (MDN), AND A
C           MANAGER DEPARTURE MULTIPLIER (MDM).  MDM IS A FUNCTION OF THE
C           PREVIOUSLY COMPUTED MANAGER-ARRIVAL MULTIPLIER (MAM).
      MDM(K) = TABLE(MDMT,1.44*ALOG(MAM(K)),-3.,3.,1.)                  63
      DATA MDMT /8.,4.,2.,1.,.5,.25,.125/                              63.1
      MD(K) = MDN*MP(K)*MDM(K)                                          62
C
C           MANAGER-PROFESSIONAL (MP) LEVEL MAY NOW BE DETERMINED.
      MP(NXT) = MP(K) + DT*(LTM(K) + MPB(K) + MA(K) - MD(K))            52
C
C - - - PREMIUM HOUSING SECTOR  - - - - - - - - - - - - - - - - - - - -
C
C           PREMIUM HOUSING (PH) LEVEL FOR A PERIOD IS A FUNCTION OF THE
C           LEVEL IN THE PREVIOUS PERIOD, PLUS THE INCREASE FOR PREMIUM-
C           HOUSING CONSTRUCTION (PHC) LESS THE DECREASE FOR PREMIUM-HOUSING
C           OBSOLESCENCE (PHO).  (THE PREMIUM-HOUSING MULTIPLIER (PHM) AND
C           PREMIUM-HOUSING CONSTRUCTION DESIRED (PHCD) WERE COMPUTED IN
C           THE ABOVE SECTION ON CONSTRUCTION GOALS AND MULTIPLIERS.)
C           INITIALIZATIONS
      IF(K.GT.1) GO TO 710
C           PREMIUM-HOUSING OBSOLESCENCE NORMAL
      PHON = .03                                                       79.1
  710 CONTINUE
C           SECTOR EQUATIONS
      PHOM(K) = TABLE(PHOMT,1.44*ALOG(PHM(K)),-3.,3.,1.)                80
      DATA PHOMT /2.8,2.6,2.,1.,.5,.3,.2/                              80.1
      PHO(K) = PHON * PH(K) * PHOM(K)                                   79
      PHC(K) = PHCD(K) * LCR(K)                                         64
      PH(NXT) = PH(K) + DT*(PHC(K) - PHO(K))                           78
C
```

FIGURE 3   (continued)

```
C - - - WORKER HOUSING SECTOR - - - - - - - - - - - - - - - - - - - -
C
C          WORKER HOUSING (WH) LEVEL IS EXPRESSED AS A FUNCTION OF WH IN
C          THE PREVIOUS PERIOD, PLUS THE FILTER DOWN OF PREMIUM-HOUSING
C          OBSOLESCENCE (PHO) COMPUTED ABOVE, PLUS THE INCREASE DUE TO
C          WORKER-HOUSING CONSTRUCTION (WHC), LESS THE DECREASE DUE TO
C          WORKER-HOUSING OBSOLESCENCE (WHO).  (THE WORKER-HOUSING
C          MULTIPLIER (WHM) AND WORKER-HOUSING CONSTRUCTION DESIRED (WHCD)
C          WERE COMPUTED IN THE ABOVE SECTION ON CONSTRUCTION GOALS AND
C          MULTIPLIERS.)
C          INITIALIZATIONS
       IF (K.GT.1) GO TO 810
C          WORKER-HOUSING OBSOLESCENCE NORMAL                           93.1
       WHON = .02
   810 CONTINUE
C          SECTOR EQUATIONS                                             94
       WHOM(K) = TABLE(WHOMT,1.44*ALCG(WHM(K)),-3.,3.,1.)               94.1
       DATA WHOMT /2.2,2.,1.6,1.,.7,.5,.4,/                             93
       WHO(K) = WHON * WH(K) * WHCM(K)                                  82
       WHC(K) = WHCD(K) * LCR(K)                                        81
       WH(NXT) = WH(K) + DT*(PHO(K) + WHC(K) - WHO(K))
C
C
C - - - UNDEREMPLOYED HOUSING SECTOR - - - - - - - - - - - - - - - - - -
C
C          UNDEREMPLOYED HOUSING (UH) LEVEL IS EXPRESSED AS THE LEVEL IN
C          THE PREVIOUS PERIOD, PLUS THE FILTER DOWN OF WORKER-HOUSING
C          OBSOLESCENCE (WHO), LESS THE SLUM-HOUSING DEMOLITION (SHD),
C          PLUS THE LOW-COST-HOUSING PROGRAM (LCHP) LEVEL.  WHO AND LCHP
C          WERE COMPUTED EARLIER.  SHD IS COMPUTED BY FIRST COMPUTING A
C          SLUM-HOUSING-DEMOLITION MULTIPLIER (SHDM) WHICH IS APPLIED TO
C          THE UH LEVEL.  IN ADDITION THE SLUM-HOUSING-DEMOLITION PROGRAM
C          (SHDP) MAY CONTRIBUTE TO THE SHD LEVEL.
C          INITIALIZATIONS
       IF(K.GT.1) GO TO 910
C          SLUM-HOUSING-DEMOLITION NORMAL                               96.1
       SHDN = .02
C          SLUM-HOUSING-DEMOLITION FACTOR--FOR SENSITIVITY TESTING      97.1
       SHDF = 1.
   910 CONTINUE
C          SECTOR EQUATIONS                                             99
       SHLM(K) = TABLE(SHLMT,LFO(K),.8,1.,.05)                          99.1
       DATA SHLMT /1.,1.2,1.6,2.2,6./                                   98
       SHAM(K) = TABLE(SHAMT,UHR(K),.0,2.,.5)                           98.1
       DATA SHAMT /3.6,2.,1.,.6,.4/                                     97
       SHDM(K) = SHAM(K) * SHLM(K) * SHDF                               96
       SHD(K) = SHDN * UH(K) * SHLM(K) + SHDP(K)                        95
       UH(NXT) = UH(K) + DT*(WHO(K) - SHD(K) + LCHP(K))
C
C
C - - - NEW ENTERPRISE SECTOR - - - - - - - - - - - - - - - - - - - - -
C
C          NEW ENTERPRISE (NE) LEVEL FOR A PERIOD IS A FUNCTION OF THE
C          LEVEL IN THE PREVIOUS PERIOD, PLUS THE INCREASE FOR NEW-
C          ENTERPRISE CONSTRUCTION (NEC) LESS THE DECREASE FOR NEW-
```

FIGURE 3   (continued)

```
C         ENTERPRISE DECLINE (NED).  (THE ENTERPRISE MULTIPLIER (EM) AND
C         NEW-ENTERPRISE CONSTRUCTION DESIRED (NECD) WERE COMPUTED IN THE
C         ABOVE SECTION ON CONSTRUCTION GOALS AND MULTIPLIERS.)
C
C         INITIALIZATIONS
      IF(K.GT.1) GO TO 1010
C         NEW-ENTERPRISE DECLINE NORMAL
      NEDN = .08
 1010 CONTINUE                                                      111.1
C
C         SECTOR EQUATIONS
      EDM(K) = TABLE(EDMT,1.44*ALOG(EM(K)),-3.,3.,1.)                 112
      DATA EDMT /2.,1.8,1.5,1.,.7,.5,.5/                            112.1
      NED(K) = NEDN * NE(K) * EDM(K)                                  111
      NEC(K) = NECD(K) * LCR(K)                                       101
      NE(NXT) = NE(K) + DT*(NEC(K) - NED(K))                          100
C
C
C - - - MATURE BUSINESS SECTOR - - - - - - - - - - - - - - - - - - - - -
C
C         MATURE BUSINESS (MB) LEVEL FOR A PERIOD IS A FUNCTION OF THE
C         LEVEL IN THE PREVIOUS PERIOD, PLUS THE NEW-ENTERPRISE DECLINE
C         (NED) AND LESS THE MATURE-BUSINESS DECLINE (MBD) DURING THE
C         PREVIOUS PERIOD.  (THE ENTERPRISE MULTIPLIER (EM) WAS COMPUTED
C         ABOVE IN THE SECTION ON CONSTRUCTION GOALS AND MULTIPLIERS.)
C
C         INITIALIZATIONS
      IF(K.GT.1) GO TO 1110
C         MATURE-BUSINESS DECLINE NORMAL
      MBDN = .05
 1110 CONTINUE                                                      114.1
C
C         SECTOR EQUATIONS
      BDM(K) = TABLE(BDMT,1.44*ALOG(EM(K)),-3.,3.,1.)                 115
      DATA BDMT /2.,1.8,1.5,1.,.7,.5,.4/                            115.1
      MBD(K) = MBDN * MB(K) * BDM(K)                                  114
      MB(NXT) = MB(K) + DT*(NED(K) - MBD(K))                          113
C
C
C - - - DECLINING INDUSTRY SECTOR - - - - - - - - - - - - - - - - - - -
C
C         DECLINING INDUSTRY (DI) LEVEL FOR A PERIOD IS EQUAL TO THE
C         LEVEL IN THE PREVIOUS PERIOD, PLUS THE MATURE-BUSINESS DECLINE
C         (MBD) COMPUTED ABOVE AND LESS THE DECLINING-INDUSTRY DEMOLITION
C         (DID).  (THE ENTERPRISE MULTIPLIER (EM) WAS COMPUTED ABOVE IN
C         THE SECTION ON CONSTRUCTION GOALS AND MULTIPLIERS.)
C
C         INITIALIZATIONS
      IF(K.GT.1) GO TO 1210
C         DECLINING-INDUSTRY DEMOLITION NORMAL
      DIDN = .03                                                     117.1
C         DECLINING-INDUSTRY-DEMOLITION FACTOR--FOR SENSITIVITY TESTING
      DIDF = 1.                                                      118.1
 1210 CONTINUE
C
C         SECTOR EQUATIONS
```

FIGURE 3   (continued)

```
      DIEM(K) = TABLE(DIEMT,1.44*ALCG(EM(K)),-3.,3.,1.)         119
      DATA DIEMT /.4,.5,.7,1.,1.6,2.4,4./                       119.1
      DILM(K) = TABLE(DILMT,BFO(K),.8,1.,.05)                   120
      DATA DILMT /1.,1.2,1.6,2.2,6./                            120.1
      DIDM(K) = DIEM(K) * DILM(K) * DIDF                        118
      DID(K) = DIDN * DI(K) * DIDM(K) + DIDP(K)                 117
      DI(NXT) = DI(K) + DT*(MBD(K) - DID(K))                    116
C
      IF(I.EQ.1) GO TO 2100
 2000 CONTINUE
C
C
C - - - - - - - - - - - - - - - - - - - - - - - - - - - - - - - - - - - -
C - - - PRINTING OF MODEL RESULTS - - - - - - - - - - - - - - - - - - - - -
C
C
C         THIS SECTION PRINTS THE RESULTS FOR THE LAST YEAR COMPUTED
C         WHEN IT IS ENTERED.  RESULTS ARE PRINTED FOR 124 MODEL
C         VALUES IN THE SAME FORMAT AS IN 'URBAN DYNAMICS' BOOK PAGES
C         42-43.
C
 2100 PRINT 9991
      PRINT 9991
 9990 FORMAT (1H ,-3P3F14.3,0P6F14.3)
      PRINT 9990,
     1    AV  (K),    MB  (K),    U   (K),    AMM (K),    LAJM(K),    LSM (K),
     2    MSM (K),    SHLM(K),    UMM (K),    DI  (K),    MBD (K),    UA  (K),
     3    AMMP(K),    LAM (K),    LUM (K),    NEGR(K),    TCM (K),    UMMP(K),
     4    DID (K),    MD  (K),    UD  (K),    BDM (K),    LAMP(K),    LUR (K),
     5    PEM (K),    TPCR(K),    UR  (K),    DIDP(K),    MP  (K),    UH  (K),
     6    DIDM(K),    LATM(K),    MAHM(K),    PHAM(K),    TR  (K),    WHAM(K),
     7    L   (K),    NE  (K),    UJ  (K),    DIEM(K),    LAUM(K),    MAJM(K),
     8    PHEM(K),    TEN (K),    WHEM(K),    LA  (K),    NEC (K),    UJP (K),
     9    DILM(K),    LCR (K),    MAM (K),    PHGM(K),    UAMM(K),    WHGM(K),
     A    LCHP(K),    NECP(K),    UTL (K),    EDM (K),    LDM (K),    MAMP(K),
     B    PHGR(K),    UDM (K),    WHGR(K)
      PRINT 9991
 9991 FORMAT (1H0)
      PRINT 9990,
     1    LD  (K),    P   (K),    UTLN(K),    EGM (K),    UEM (K),    MAPM(K),
     2    PHLM(K),    UEM (K),    WHLM(K),    LDC (K),    PH  (K),    UTP (K),
     3    ELJM(K),    LFO (K),    MATM(K),    PHM (K),    UFW (K),    WHM (K),
     4    LDI (K),    PHC (K),    UW  (K),    ELM (K),    LHR (K),    MDM (K),
     5    PHOM(K),    UHM (K),    WHOM(K),    LJ  (K),    PHCP(K),    WH  (K),
     6    EM  (K),    LLF (K),    MHR (K),    PHPM(K),    UHPR(K),    WHTM(K),
     7    LTM (K),    PHO (K),    WHC (K),    EMM (K),    LMM (K),    MLM (K),
     8    PHTM(K),    UHR (K),    WHUM(K),    LTU (K),    SHD (K),    WHCP(K),
     9    ETM (K),    LMMP(K),    MLR (K),    SHAM(K),    UJM (K),    UTP (K),
     A    MA  (K),    SHDP(K),    WHO (K),    LAHM(K),    LR  (K),    MR  (K),
     B    SHDM(K),    UM  (K)
C
C
C     END OF LOOP FOR COMPUTING AND PRINTING RESULTS FOR A YEAR
 2200 CONTINUE
      STOP
      END
```

FIGURE 3   (continued)

```
      FUNCTION TABLE(TBL,VAR,VLO,VHI,STEP)
C
C     THIS FUNCTION PERFORMS THE SAME OPERATION AS THE TABLE OPERATION
C     IN THE DYNAMO LANGUAGE.  A LINEAR INTERPOLATION IS PERFORMED IN
C     TABLE OF VALUES TBL TO OBTAIN A VALUE WHICH CORRESPONDS TO THE
C     ARGUMENT VALUE VAR.  VLO, VHI, AND STEP SPECIFY THE HIGH VALUE, LOW
C     VALUE, AND STEP SIZE, RESPECTIVELY, FOR THE INDEPENDENT VARIABLE
C     SO THAT A CORRESPONDENCE IS SET UP BETWEEN THE INDEPENDENT VARIABLE
C     VALUES AND THE TABLE OF VALUES SPECIFIED IN THE TBL BY THE CALLING
C     PROGRAM.  IF THE SPECIFIED VALUE OF VAR IS OUTSIDE THE RANGE
C     VLO-VHI, THEN VAR IS ASSIGNED THE FIRST VALUE IN TBL IF VAR IS LESS
C     VLO AND VAR IS ASSIGNED THE LAST VALUE IN TBL IF VAR IS GREATER
C     THAN VHI.
      DIMENSION TBL(15)
      IF(VAR.LT.VLO) GO TO 100
      IF(VAR.GT.VHI) GO TO 200
      STEPS = (VAR - VLO)/STEP + 1.
      N = INT(STEPS)
      TABLE = TBL(N) + (STEPS - FLOAT(N)) * (TBL(N+1) - TBL(N))
      RETURN
  100 TABLE = TBL(1)
      RETURN
  200 K = INT((VHI - VLO)/STEP) + 1
      TABLE = TBL(K)
      RETURN
      END
```

FIGURE 3   (continued)

appear in the housing and business/industry sectors in the Dynamo program. These relationships are collected and placed near the beginning of the Fortran program because of their pervasive influence in other sectors. This is the major exception in which relationships are not kept together by model sector, as they are in the Dynamo version. There are other minor violations in trying to keep relationships for each sector together as a unit, and these are noted in the comments included in the Fortran program.

Within the model sectors, the order of the relationships in the Fortran and Dynamo programs also will differ. This kind of reordering will be illustrated in the example discussed later in this appendix.

Tabular Functions

Dynamo provides tabular functions to conveniently express functional relationships, and such tabular functions are used frequently in the urban dynamics computer program. The basic idea in a tabular function is to express the relationship between two model quantities through a table of values; that is, the programmer provides a table that specifies values of a dependent variable for equal-distance values in an independent variable range. Then, for a specified value of the independent variable, Dynamo will perform a table look-up and linear interpolation to provide a value of the dependent variable corresponding to the specified value of the independent variable.

An example of a tabular function will clarify how they are used and operate. In urban dynamics, a tabular function is used to compute an underemployed arrivals mobility multiplier (UAMM) from underemployed mobility (UM). In the Dynamo language, this is accomplished by the following statements:

UAMM.K = TABLE(UAMMT,UM.K,0,.15,.025)
UAMMT = .3/.7/1/1.2/1.3/1.4/1.5.[8]

The first line indicates that UAMM at time K is to be computed by a tabular function with a table called UAMMT, and the value of UM at time K is the independent variable in this table look-up. The numbers 0,.15,.025 indicate that the range of the independent variable is from 0 to .15 in steps of .025. This means that the seven independent variable values of 0, .025, .05, . . ., .15 correspond, respectively, to the seven values carried in the example's second line, which specifies the table. If an independent variable value is less than 0, the dependent

---

[8] Jay W. Forrester. *Urban Dynamics.* Cambridge, Mass., MIT Press, 1969, p. 26.

variable is assigned a value of .3. If an independent variable is greater than the high range of .15, the dependent variable is given a value of 1.5. If the value of the independent variable is in the 0–.15 range, then a table look-up and interpolation is performed to obtain the value of the dependent variable. For example, for an independent variable value of .0625, a dependent variable value of 1.1 will be computed.

The capability to handle tabular functions in the Fortran version of urban dynamics is provided by developing and using a Fortran function subprogram. The subprogram, TABLE, and its parameters are in the same order as in the Dynamo TABLE operation, which makes statements appear as similar as possible in the two languages. In Fortran, the DATA statement is used to set up the table of values. With this approach, the example given in the preceding paragraph will appear as follows in the Fortran version of the model:

UAMM(K) = TABLE(UAMMT,UM(K),0,.15,.025)
DATA UAMMT / .3,.7,1,1.2,1.3,1.4,1.5/,

which is very similar to its appearance in the Dynamo version.

An Illustrative Example

To provide a more concrete idea of the Dynamo to Fortran translation process, a short sector of the urban dynamics model will be examined in both languages. Figure 4 presents the model relationships for the Underemployed Housing Sector in Dynamo language, and Figure 5 presents the Fortran version of the same relationships.

The format of the Dynamo statements consists of a statement number on the left, followed by a symbol indicating the type of statement, followed by the algebraic-like statement of the model relationship.

94.5	NOTE	**********UNDEREMPLOYED HOUSING SECTOR
95	L	UH.K=UH.J+(DT)(WHO.JK-SHD.JK+LCHP.JK)
95.1	N	UH=1100
96	R	SHD.KL=(SHDN)(UH.K)(SHDM.K)+SHDP.K
96.1	C	SHDN=.02
97	A	SHDM.K=(SHAM.K)(SHLM.K)(SHDF)
97.1	C	SHDF=1
98	A	SHAM.K=TABLE(SHAMT,UHR.K,0,2,.5)
98.1	T	SHAMT=3.6/2/1/.6/.4
99	A	SHLM.K=TABHL(SHLMT,LFO.K,.8,1,.05)
99.1	T	SHLMT=1/1.2/1.6/2.2/6

FIGURE 4 Underemployed housing sector of urban dynamics expressed in Dynamo computer language.

```
C - - - UNDEREMPLOYED HOUSING SECTOR - - - - - - - - - - - - - -
C
C        UNDEREMPLOYED HOUSING (UH) LEVEL IS EXPRESSED AS THE LEVEL IN
C        THE PREVIOUS PERIOD, PLUS THE FILTER DOWN OF WORKER-HOUSING
C        OBSOLESCENCE (WHO), LESS THE SLUM-HOUSING DEMOLITION (SHD),
C        PLUS THE LOW-COST-HOUSING PROGRAM (LCHP) LEVEL.  WHO AND LCHP
C        WERE COMPUTED EARLIER.  SHD IS COMPUTED BY FIRST COMPUTING A
C        SLUM-HOUSING-DEMOLITION MULTIPLIER (SHDM) WHICH IS APPLIED TO
C        THE UH LEVEL.  IN ADDITION THE SLUM-HOUSING-DEMOLITION PROGRAM
C        (SHDP) MAY CONTRIBUTE TO THE SHD LEVEL.
C        INITIALIZATIONS
         IF(K.GT.1) GO TO 910
C .      SLUM-HOUSING-DEMOLITION NORMAL
         SHDN = .02                                              96.1
C        SLUM-HOUSING-DEMOLITION FACTOR--FOR SENSITIVITY TESTING
         SHDF = 1.                                               97.1
     910 CONTINUE
C        SECTOR EQUATIONS
         SHLM(K) = TABLE(SHLMT,LFO(K),.8,1.,.05)                 99
         DATA SHLMT /1.,1.2,1.6,2.2.6./                          99.1
         SHAM(K) = TABLE(SHAMT,UHR(K),.0,2.,.5)                  98
         DATA SHAMT /3.6,2.,1.,.6,.4/                            98.1
         SHDM(K) = SHAM(K) * SHLM(K) * SHDF                      97
         SHD(K) = SHDN *UH(K) * SHDM(K) + SHDP(K)                96
         UH(NXT) = UH(K) + DT*(WHO(K) - SHD(K) + LCHP(K))        95
```

FIGURE 5   Underemployed housing sector of urban dynamics expressed in Fortran computer language.

There are seven types of statements, including c, which sets a constant; a, which computes an auxiliary variable; l, which computes a level variable; r, which computes a rate variable; n, which sets an initial value; t, which creates a table; and s, which computes a supplementary variable.[9] All seven types are represented in Figure 4, except for type s, which is used infrequently.

The Fortran version of the Underemployed Housing Sector begins with a set of comments that indicate the general logic of the sector, but these comments have no other function in the computer program. Note that the two Dynamo type c statements that set constants are placed first in the Fortran version and are controlled by an IF statement, so the constants are set only the first time the sector computations are performed. The initial value setting for UH is not shown in Figure 5, because all initial values for the model are set in a preliminary section of the Fortran program. In the sector equations, the ordering of the statements is changed from the Dynamo version to put them into a feasible computational order for Fortran. All quantities are computed for time K except the basic level variable UH, which is

[9] *Ibid.*, p. 267.

computed for time NXT, as previously discussed. Rate variables, such as SHD, represent change over an interval; in the Fortran version, time K denotes the interval KL when associated with rate variables. The Fortran statements carry the Dynamo statement numbers at the righthand side of the statements when the statements have a Dynamo counterpart. The only function of these numbers is to provide a mapping between the two versions of the model. Also, it may be noted in Figure 4 that Dynamo allows tabular functions to be indicated by either the name TABLE or TABHL.

FORTRAN VERSION OF URBAN DYNAMICS

Figure 3 provides a listing of the Fortran program for the urban dynamics model developed for use in this study. This program serves as a starting point for developing the model representation of the District of Columbia. The program is successively modified in developing an urban dynamics representation of Washington, and the successive changes will reflect the four stages of model development.

In terms of overall structure, the computer program is organized into the following principal sections:

Computer Program Initialization
Urban Dynamics Model Computations

    Initialization of Basic Model Level Variables
    Initialization of Computation Control Loops
    Equations for Model Sectors
    Printing of Model Results.

The computer program initialization section is concerned with the allocation of computer storage and with specifying conventions regarding which variable names will be integer and which will be real numbers. This section contains programming technicalities. The model computations section contains model-related parts of the program and is divided into four principal subsections. The general function of these subsections has already been mentioned, and more specific information is provided by the comments carried in the computer program. The subsection containing the equations for model sectors is further subdivided into model sector components, as previously discussed. The Fortran subprogram for handling tabular functions appears in Figure 3 following the main program.

As mentioned earlier, if Fortran statements have a counterpart in the Dynamo version of urban dynamics, then the Fortran statements carry the Dynamo statement numbers at the right end of the statements. This provides a means of readily locating the Dynamo statements corresponding to Fortran program statements. A listing of the Dynamo version of urban dynamics is provided in Appendix E of *Urban Dynamics.*[10] These Dynamo statement numbers also furnish easy reference to Appendix A of *Urban Dynamics,*[11] which explains each statement in the Dynamo version of the model, in order, by statement number.

The Fortran program in Figure 3 reproduces the results that Forrester obtained with his Dynamo program. This involves running the program to simulate a 250-year period with the initial values and model parameters that Forrester used for his hypothetical city. The Fortran program reproduces and prints the 124 model values published by Forrester.[12]

---

[10] *Ibid.,* pp. 274–280.
[11] *Ibid.,* pp. 133–217.
[12] *Ibid.,* pp. 42–43.

APPENDIX C

Estimation of Parameter Values
for Washington, D.C. Model

This appendix presents the approach taken in estimating initial values and parameters to initialize the urban dynamics model representation of the District of Columbia at the beginning of 1960. More than 80 initial values and parameters will be examined, and area-specific values will be estimated for them, to the extent that relevant data are found. The examination includes the parameters and initial values for which area-specific values are introduced in the first two stages of development. It does not cover the tabular functions used in the model, although area-specific values are incorporated for a number of tabular functions in the final stage, as discussed in Chapter 5.

A listing of the set of initial values and parameters that are examined is provided in Table 9, which is organized into five sections corresponding to the organization of this discussion: population, housing, business/industry, land utilization, and taxes. Four items of information for each of the model quantities are presented in Table 9. The first column gives the symbol for the model quantity used by Forrester and in the Fortran computer programs presented in Appendixes B and D; the next column gives the name of the model quantity and the dimensions in which it is expressed in the model; the third column indicates whether the quantity is an initial value

251

TABLE 9 Initial Values and Parameters for Urban Dynamics Washington Model

	Symbol	Name and Dimension	Type	Value
Population				
	*MP	Manager-professional, men	Initial	81,335
	*L	Labor, men	Initial	252,814
	*U	Underemployed, men	Initial	34,541
	*MAMP	Manager arrival multiplier perceived, dimensionless	Initial	1
	*LAMP	Labor arrival multiplier perceived, dimensionless	Initial	1
	*AMMP	Attractiveness for migration multiplier perceived, dimensionless	Initial	1
	*LMMP	Labor mobility multiplier perceived, dimensionless	Initial	1
	*UMMP	Underemployed mobility multiplier perceived, dimensionless	Initial	1
	*LRP	Labor/job ratio perceived, dimensionless	Initial	1
	MPBR	Manager-professional birth rate, fraction/year	Parameter	.011
	LBR	Labor birth rate, fraction/year	Parameter	.013
	UBR	Underemployed birth rate, fraction/year	Parameter	.016
	*MPFS	Manager-professional family size, people/man	Parameter	1.79
	*LFS	Labor family size, people/man	Parameter	2.10
	*UFS	Underemployed family size, people/man	Parameter	2.52
	MAMPT	Manager arrival multiplier perception time, years	Parameter	10
	LAMPT	Labor arrival multiplier perception time, years	Parameter	15
	AMMPT	Attractiveness for migration multiplier perception time, years	Parameter	20
	LMMPT	Labor mobility multiplier perception time, years	Parameter	15
	UMMPT	Underemployed mobility multiplier perception time, years	Parameter	10
	UTLPT	Underemployed to labor perception time, years	Parameter	10
	LRPT	Labor/job ratio perception time, years	Parameter	5
	MAN	Manager arrivals normal, fraction/year	Parameter	.036

TABLE 9 (continued)

MDN	Manager departures normal, fraction/year	Parameter	.064
LAN	Labor arrivals normal, fraction/year	Parameter	.026
LDN	Labor departures normal, fraction/year	Parameter	.044
UAN	Underemployed arrivals normal, fraction/year	Parameter	.039
UDN	Underemployed departures normal, fraction/year	Parameter	.067
LMN	Labor mobility normal, fraction/year	Parameter	.02
UMN	Underemployed mobility normal, fraction/year	Parameter	.1
*UTLP	Underemployed to labor perceived, dimensionless	Initial	1,727

Housing

*PH	Premium housing, housing units	Initial	49,122
*WH	Worker housing, housing units	Initial	181,155
*UH	Underemployed housing, housing units	Initial	32,364
*PHPD	Premium housing population density, people/housing unit	Parameter	3.05
*WHPD	Worker housing population density, people/housing unit	Parameter	3.03
*UHPD	Underemployed housing population density, people/housing unit	Parameter	3.03
PHA	Premium housing average, housing units	Initial	Computed
WHA	Worker housing average, housing units	Initial	Computed
PHAT	Premium housing averaging time, years	Parameter	10
WHAT	Worker housing averaging time, years	Parameter	10
PHGRI	Premium housing growth rate initial, fraction/year	Parameter	.017
WHGRI	Worker housing growth rate initial, fraction/year	Parameter	.017
PHCN	Premium housing construction normal, fraction/year	Parameter	.017
WHCN	Worker housing construction normal, fraction/year	Parameter	.017

TABLE 9 (continued)

*PHAV	Premium housing assessed value, thousand dollars/ housing unit	Parameter	14.05
*WHAV	Worker housing assessed value, thousand dollars/housing unit	Parameter	4.70
*UHAV	Underemployed housing assessed value, thousand dollars/ housing unit	Parameter	2.00
PHCL	Premium housing construction labor, man-years/housing unit	Parameter	1.7
WHCL	Worker housing construction labor, man-years/housing unit	Parameter	.6
PHON	Premium housing obsolescence normal, fraction/year	Parameter	.010
WHON	Worker housing obsolescence normal, fraction/year	Parameter	.014
SHDN	Slum housing demolition normal, fraction/year	Parameter	.080

Business/ Industry

*NE	New enterprise, productive units	Initial	13,824
*MB	Mature business, productive units	Initial	17,280
*DI	Declining industry, productive units	Initial	12,096
NEDN	New enterprise decline normal, fraction/year	Parameter	.125
MBDN	Mature business decline normal, fraction/year	Parameter	.083
DIDN	Declining industry demolition normal, fraction/year	Parameter	.047
NEA	New enterprise average, productive units	Initial	Computed
NEAT	New enterprise averaging time, years	Parameter	10
NECF	New enterprise construction factor, dimensionless	Parameter	1
MBCF	Mature business construction factor, dimensionless	Parameter	.5
DICF	Declining industry construction factor, dimensionless	Parameter	.3
NECN	New enterprise construction normal, fraction/year	Parameter	.063

TABLE 9 (continued)

NEGRI	New enterprise growth rate initial, fraction/year	Parameter	.119
*NEAV	New enterprise assessed value, thousand dollars/productive unit	Parameter	30.40
*MBAV	Mature business assessed value, thousand dollars/productive unit	Parameter	22.60
*DIAV	Declining industry assessed value, thousand dollars/ productive unit	Parameter	9.10
NECL	New enterprise construction labor, man-years/productive unit	Parameter	3.4
*NEM	New enterprise management, men/productive unit	Parameter	3.1
*NEL	New enterprise labor, men/ productive unit	Parameter	6.2
*MBM	Mature business management, men/productive unit	Parameter	1.8
*MBL	Mature business labor, men/ productive unit	Parameter	5.5
*DIM	Declining industry management, men/productive unit	Parameter	.6
*DIL	Declining industry labor, men/ productive unit	Parameter	2.5

Land Utilization

*AREA	Land area, acres	Parameter	40,154
*LPH	Land per house, acres/housing unit	Parameter	.09
*LPP	Land per productive unit, acres/productive unit	Parameter	.37

Taxes

TRNP	Tax ratio needed perceived, dimensionless	Initial	Computed
*TAN	Tax assessment normal, dollars/ year/thousand dollars	Parameter	110
*TMP	Tax per management person, dollars/person/year	Parameter	475
*TLP	Tax per labor person, dollars/ person/year	Parameter	275
*TUP	Tax per underemployed person, dollars/person/year	Parameter	400

TABLE 9 (continued)

TPCN	Tax per capita normal, dollars/ year/person	Parameter	330
TRNPT	Tax ratio needed perception time, years	Parameter	30

or a parameter; and the last column shows the value of the adopted quantity used in developing the urban dynamics model of Washington.

The initial values and parameters, which are regarded as basic model quantities, are indicated in the table by an asterisk to the left of the symbol for the quantity. The 25 parameters and 16 initial values constitute the set of values incorporated into Forrester's model during the first stage of developing the Washington urban dynamics model. These 41 quantities are the set that Forrester[1] suggests should be estimated empirically to develop an urban dynamics model of a particular urban area. The second stage in the development of the Washington model incorporates the full set of model values shown in Table 9.

Various problems associated with estimating values for model quantities arise, because urban dynamics was developed with very little attention to the availability of supporting data. For most of the model quantities, relevant data are available; however, in many cases, it is necessary to make a number of assumptions to relate these data to the concepts of the model. In some instances, the particular assumption adopted to relate data and model is only one of a number of assumptions that could have been adopted; in this sense, the approach taken at many points is only one of a number of possible approaches. For some model quantities, no data are found to provide a basis for establishing values. Perception-time parameters, which are related primarily to population migration and mobility behavior, are an example of such quantities. These parameters specify the number of years of delay by population groups in perceiving the actual value of a model quantity that influences the group behavior. These perception-time delays, as Babcock noted, are very difficult to quantify; Forrester's values and his general reasoning for the values adopted are accepted.

Of the 86 model quantities included in Table 9, the values adopted for 66 are estimated empirically. In addition, four initial values are computed by model equations from other model quantities and are

---

[1] Jay W. Forrester. *Urban Dynamics.* Cambridge, Mass., MIT Press, 1969, pp. 36–37.

included in the table only for completeness. This leaves 16 quantities for which data were not found: 8 perception-time parameters, 2 interclass-mobility parameters, 3 averaging-time parameters, and 3 construction-averaging factors. These 16 and the other model quantities are discussed in the context of the estimates for each model sector.

POPULATION

The structure of the model's population subsystem consists of three categories: manager-professional, labor, and underemployed, each with its characteristic birth rate and family size. Each category has a normal rate of in-migration and out-migration, and the normal rates are influenced by a number of factors to determine the effective migration rates at a particular point in time. In addition, mobility from the underemployed to labor, labor to manager-professional, and labor to underemployed classifications is represented. The subsystem formulation includes 31 initial values and parameters, discussed in terms of seven groups.

Labor-force Levels:
MP, L, U

Forrester's criteria for dividing the labor force into manager-professional, MP, labor, L, and underemployed, U, components appear to be based mainly on the nature of occupations. The manager-professional group includes the entrepreneurial and managerial elements of the labor force. "The labor is skilled labor fully participating in the urban economy. Underemployed workers include, in addition to the unemployed and unemployable, people in unskilled jobs, those in marginal economic activity, and those not seeking employment who might work in a period of intense economic activity." [2] From these characterizations, the nine occupational groups used in the 1960 Census may be mapped into three labor-force components of the model. The unemployed reported in the census are included in the underemployed component. This correspondence between the labor-force components of the model and the occupations, as shown in the listing that follows, is used to estimate the initial values for the labor-force components from 1960 Census data.

[2] *Ibid.,* p. 19.

Labor-Force Components	*Census Occupations*
Manager-professional (MP)	Professional, technical, and kindred workers
	Managers, officials, and proprietors
Labor (L)	Clerical and kindred workers
	Sales workers
	Craftsmen, foremen, and kindred workers
	Operatives and kindred workers
	Private household workers
	Service workers, except private household
Underemployed (U)	Laborers, except mine [3]

With this definition of labor-force group occupations, the 305,671 persons in the census who reported their occupations are classified as 69,671 manager-professional, 218,860 labor, and 17,140 underemployed. This leaves the 35,891 not reporting their occupations, 15,238 unemployed, and 11,889 military [4] to be dealt with. Those not reporting their occupations are divided among the three labor-force groups in the same proportions as those reporting their occupations. The unemployed are included in the underemployed category. The military are allocated to the manager-professional and labor categories in the same proportions as the male labor-force reporting occupation is distributed between these two groups. Carrying out these distributions provides estimates of the three labor-force components as follows:

MP = 81,335 men
L = 252,814 men
U = 34,541 men,

which are assumed to represent the District of Columbia at the beginning of 1960, although the census was conducted on April 1. In view of the slow rate of population change in the District during 1950–1970, this three-month period would result in a very small population change.

---

[3] U. S. Bureau of the Census. *Census of Population and Housing: 1960, Census Tracts.* Final Report PHC(1)-166, Washington, D. C.-Md.-Va. SMSA. Washington, D. C., U. S. Government Printing Office, 1962, p. 106.
[4] *Ibid.*

Perceived Multipliers:
MAMP, LAMP, AMMP, LMMP, UMMP, LRP

Each of these perceived multipliers represents the time-lagged value of a multiplier computed within the model. The perceived-multiplier values govern the behavior of population groups. The manager arrival multiplier perceived, MAMP, labor arrival multiplier perceived, LAMP, and attractiveness-for-migration multiplier perceived, AMMP, are lagged values of the manager arrival multiplier, MAM, labor arrival multiplier, LAM, and attractiveness-for-migration multiplier, AMM, respectively; and these perceived multiplier values govern the migration behavior of the manager-professional, labor, and underemployed population groups. The labor mobility multiplier perceived, LMMP, and underemployed mobility multiplier perceived, UMMP, are lagged values of the labor mobility multiplier, LMM, and underemployed mobility multiplier, UMM, respectively, which govern the interclass mobility of population groups. The labor/job ratio perceived, LRP, is a lagged value of the labor/job ratio, LR, and influences the amount of new construction undertaken.[5] Technically, these perceived multipliers are level variables, so initial values must be set for them, although in many respects they operate as if they were rate variables.

The six perceived multipliers are initialized at a value of unity, the same as they were initialized by Forrester, for two related reasons. First, the basic assumption is made in estimating values for model quantities that 1960, or the year for which the model is initialized, is a normal year. Forrester makes the same assumption, that the year for which the model is initialized is a normal year in that it is a base year. Many model quantities for years subsequent to the initial or base year are computed on the basis of change relative to the initial or normal year. The second reason for setting the perceived multipliers at unity, which is closely related to the first, is that it is consistent with the manner in which empirical estimates of other model quantities are developed. How the manager arrival multiplier perceived, MAMP, is put to use in the model illustrates this. The number of manager arrivals, MA, during year K is computed as

$$MA(K) = MAN * MP(K) * MAMP(K),$$

where MAN is the manager arrivals normal rate expressed in fractional increase per year, and MP is the level of the manager-professional

---

[5] Forrester. *Urban Dynamics*, pp. 136–137, 150, 156, 159, 166, 210.

labor-force group at time K in terms of men.[6] The manager arrivals normal rate, MAN, is based on historical data for the five years preceding 1960; these data and, hence, MAN include the influence of any distortion existing between the manager-professional group's perception of what is happening and what is actually happening. Therefore, by setting MAMP = 1, the computation for the initial year for which computations are made determines the manager arrivals, MA, as the product of the manager arrivals rate, MAN, and the manager-professional level, MP. This is consistent with the empirical estimate for MAN. In the computations for subsequent years, the value of MAMP is determined by model equations as a lagged value of the manager arrival multiplier, MAM. These same considerations apply to all of the perceived multipliers related to population behavior.

Birth Rates: MPBR, LBR, UBR

In urban dynamics, the birth rate parameters for each population group are the manager-professional birth rate, MPBR, labor birth rate, LBR, and underemployed birth rate, UBR, and are expressed as net births per labor-force member per year. In model computations, the birth rate for each labor-force component is multiplied by the level of the labor-force component to obtain the yearly increase in that component. The current level of a labor-force component, multiplied by the family-size parameter for the labor component, gives the population of that labor group, and the sum of the three population groups is the total population of the urban area.[7]

Vital statistics, such as birth and death rates, are not readily available for the labor-force components of the model, because most vital statistics of this type are collected and published only in terms of attributes such as area of residence, age, race, and sex. To estimate the net birth rates for the model, data from the 1960 Census are combined with vital statistics for the District. First, the census data are used to compute relative birth rates for the labor-force components. Then the relative birth rates are used with birth and death data to estimate the net birth rates for the three labor-force components.

The relative birth rates are estimated from census data that give the number of children born in the District of Columbia through April 1, 1960 to women residents between the ages of 35 and 44, by occupations

---

[6] *Ibid.*, p. 166.
[7] *Ibid.*, pp. 142, 145, 153, 164.

of their husbands. The census occupational groups are combined into model labor-force groups according to the mapping developed previously in estimating population levels. These tabulations show 7,193 women and 13,564 children for the manager-professional group, 17,492 women and 38,788 children for the labor group, and 2,971 women and 7,900 children for the underemployed group.[8] Computing a relative birth rate for each group, then normalizing relative to the manager-professional rate, which is set to unity, gives birth rates of 1.00, 1.17, and 1.41 for the manager-professional, labor, and underemployed groups, respectively. These rates represent the relative fertility of the three labor-force components, which rests on the general assumption that the occupation of the husband in 1960 indicates the labor-force component with which the children should be associated.

In the District of Columbia in 1960, there were 9,745 more births than deaths.[9] Because the model represents net births as the fractional increase in labor-force participants, only that proportion of births is of interest. Of the 1960 total population of 763,956,[10] 368,690 are included in the foregoing labor-force estimates. Therefore, an increase in the number of labor-force participants, equivalent to 48.26 percent of the net births or 4,703 more participants, is expected to result from the 1960 net births. The model's assumption is that this number of new labor-force participants percolates upward through the population system, and not that the newly born immediately become labor-force participants.

Using the relative birth rates and net births with the previously estimated 1960 manager-professional, labor, and underemployed labor-force levels of 81,335, 252,814, and 34,541, respectively, the following relationship must hold:

$$(81,335)(\text{MPBR}) + (252,814)(1.17)(\text{MPBR}) + (34,541)(1.41)(\text{MPBR}) = 4,703,$$

and, from this,

MPBR $= .011$ fraction/year
LBR $\ \ = .013$ fraction/year
UBR $\ \ = .016$ fraction/year.

---

[8] U. S. Bureau of the Census. *Census of Population: 1960, Subject Reports. Women by Number of Children Ever Born.* Final Report PC(2)–3A. Washington, D. C., U. S. Government Printing Office, 1964, p. 272.

[9] U. S. Bureau of the Census. *Statistical Abstract of the United States: 1962.* 83rd Edition. Washington, D. C., U. S. Government Printing Office, 1962, pp. 55, 64.

[10] U. S. Bureau of the Census. *Census of Population and Housing: 1960, Census Tracts*, p. 15.

Family Sizes: MPFS, LFS, UFS

Forrester considers a family as having a single working member,[11] which is an unrealistic representation of labor-force participation in today's urban areas; however, an interpretation of the model parameters is made to allow the number of workers per family to be other than one. To do this, the parameters MPFS, LFS, and UFS are estimated to represent population per worker for the three labor-force groups. This fragments families, but later, in estimating the housing density parameters for each labor-force group, the density parameters are set to ensure that the proper number of persons is included in each type of housing unit and, hence, that family fragments are combined.

In estimating family sizes, it is assumed that the population per labor-force member for the three labor-force groups is proportional to the relative birth rates previously developed. This assumption is generally reasonable. Its impact on model computations is limited, however, because the family-size parameters are used only in population accounting and in computing the population-to-housing capacity ratios for each labor-force group. Using this assumption and the previously estimated 1960 labor-force estimates of 81,335 manager-professionals, 252,814 laborers, and 34,541 underemployeds, the following relationship holds:

$$(81,335)(\text{MPFS}) + (252,814)(1.17)(\text{MPFS}) + (34,541)(1.41)(\text{MPFS}) = 763,956,$$

where 763,956 is the estimated 1960 population of the city.[12] Solving this for MPFS and setting LFS and UFS in proportion to MPFS according to the relative birth rates, results in

MPFS $= 1.79$ people/man
LFS $ = 2.10$ people/man
UFS $ = 2.52$ people/man.

As noted, Forrester's dimension of people per man for these parameters is interpreted as people per labor-force member.

Perception Times: MAMPT, LAMPT, AMMPT, LMMPT, UMMPT, UTLPT, LRPT

Seven parameters represent the perception-time lags between the actual value of model quantities and their perceived values. These lags are

---

[11] Forrester. *Urban Dynamics*, pp. 141–142.

[12] U. S. Bureau of the Census. *Census of Population and Housing: 1960, Census Tracts*, p. 15.

represented in the model as first-order exponential delays, so that in each time period the perceived value shows improvement in moving toward the actual value. As indicated earlier, Forrester's perception-time values are used in the Washington model, mainly because they are difficult to estimate from available data. In addition, Forrester found that the perception times had "no influence on the equilibrium conditions of the system and rather minor influence on transient behavior."[13]

The first three parameters are the perception times associated with the manager-professional, labor, and underemployed groups perceiving the attractiveness of the city for in-migration. Forrester assigned values of 10, 15, and 20 years, respectively, to the manager-professional, MAMPT, the labor, LAMPT, and underemployed, AMMPT, attractiveness for migration perception times. He based his values on the general premise that the more productive groups have greater awareness and more rapid perception of reality.[14] The second three parameters are perception times related to interclass mobility. LMMPT and UMMPT represent the "training time and time necessary for social influences to become effective" [15] for the labor and underemployed groups to achieve upward mobility to the next higher labor class. Forrester assigns LMMPT and UMMPT values of 15 and 10 years, respectively. In addition, the underemployed are subject to a delay in perceiving the opportunity for upward mobility expressed by the parameter UTLPT, which is assigned a value of 10 years. The last of the parameters, LRPT, expresses the perception delay between the availability of labor for use in construction and the undertaking of construction, and the parameter is assigned a value of five years.[16]

Normal Migration Rates:
MAN, MDN, LAN, LDN, UAN, UDN

As previously indicated, each of the three labor-force groups in the model has its own normal in-migration and out-migration rate. These rates are expressed as the fraction of the labor-force group migrating inward or outward per year. The manager arrivals normal, MAN, and manager departures normal, MDN, are the rates for the manager-professional group; the labor arrivals normal, LAN, and labor departures normal, LDN, are the rates for the labor groups; and the underemployed arrivals normal, UAN, and underemployed departures normal, UDN, are

[13] Forrester. *Urban Dynamics*, p. 150.
[14] *Ibid.*, p. 166.
[15] *Ibid.*, p. 150.
[16] *Ibid.*, pp. 150, 156, 210.

the underemployed rates. Values for these rates are arrived at by first estimating relative migration rates for the three labor-force groups represented in the model. These relative migration rates are used with census estimates of migration to and from the District of Columbia during the 1955–1960 period to estimate area-specific in-migration and out-migration rates for each of the three labor-force groups.

The relative migration rates for the three labor-force groups are based on data from the 1960 Census, which provides estimates of U. S. movers and nonmovers by occupational category. Here, a mover is regarded as a labor-force member who moved from one county to another, or from one country to another, during the 1955–1960 period covered by the census data. Nonmovers are all others, although nonmovers actually may have moved within a county. Tabulating these data into the three model labor-force components by using the previously established mapping of census occupations and urban dynamics labor-force groups results in the following statistics:

Labor-Force Component	Movers	Nonmovers
Manager-professional (MP)	3,158,954	9,411,318
Labor (L)	6,821,498	34,759,330
Underemployed (U)	1,415,448	6,513,722 [17]

From this tabulation, 28 percent of the labor-force movers are manager-professionals, 60 percent are in the labor classification, and 12 percent are underemployed. These percentages may be assumed to represent the relative propensity of the three labor-force groups to move over county or country boundaries, and, by regarding the District of Columbia as a county, these rates may be assumed to be the relative propensity of the groups to move into and out of the District.

Since estimates of migration into and out of the District for the 1955–1960 period are available only for the total population, it is necessary to convert the relative migration rates for labor-force groups to relative migration rates for population groups. This is done by weighting the labor-force rates by the previously estimated family sizes of 1.79, 2.10, and 2.52, respectively, per manager-professional, labor, and underemployed labor-force member, resulting in relative migration rates of 24 percent, 61 percent, and 15 percent for the manager-professional, labor, and underemployed groups, respectively. The total migration to the District during the 1955–1960 period was

[17] U. S. Bureau of the Census. *Census of Population: 1960, Subject Reports. Mobility for States and State Economic Areas.* Final Report PC(2)–2B. Washington, D. C., U. S. Government Printing Office, 1963, pp. 23–27.

111,170, and the out-migration for the same period was 193,343.[18] Assuming that these relative migration rates for the three population groups hold for the District, the migrations for the 1955–1960 period are distributed as follows:

Population Group	In-Migrants	Out-Migrants
Manager-professional (MP)	26,625	46,306
Labor (L)	67,736	117,804
Underemployed (U)	16,809	29,233
Total	111,170	193,343

Now, converting these migrations back into a labor-force member basis by using the previously estimated family-size parameters and then expressing migrations as an annual fraction of the previously estimated 1960 labor force provides an estimate of the required parameters. The estimation of MAN illustrates the procedure.

$$\text{MAN} = ((26,625)/(1.79)(5))/81,335$$
$$\text{MAN} = .036 \text{ fraction/year.}$$

Similarly, the estimates for the other parameters are

$$\text{MDN} = .064 \text{ fraction/year}$$
$$\text{LAN} = .026 \text{ fraction/year}$$
$$\text{LDN} = .044 \text{ fraction/year}$$
$$\text{UAN} = .039 \text{ fraction/year}$$
$$\text{UDN} = .067 \text{ fraction/year.}$$

Mobility Rates: *LMN, UMN, UTLP*

The parameters LMN and UMN express the normal mobility rates for the labor and underemployed groups, respectively, as the fraction of the group moving upward to the next higher economic group each year. Forrester's values of .02 for the labor mobility normal, LMN, and .1 for the underemployed mobility normal, UMN,[19] are used in the Washington model because of a lack of data for estimating values. It should be noted, however, that in the last stage of the Washington model development, discussed in Chapter 5, it is necessary to adjust some of the parameters controlling interclass flows.

The underemployed to labor perceived, UTLP, is a level variable that

[18] *Ibid.*, p. 177.
[19] Forrester. *Urban Dynamics*, pp. 147, 154.

represents the underemployed group's perceived flow per year to labor-group status.[20] It is assumed that the underemployed-to-labor flow is occurring at the normal rate in the initial year, 1960, and that only one-half the flow is perceived by the underemployed group. Using this and the previously estimated underemployed level of 34,541, the initial setting for UTLP is (.5)(LMN)(U) or (.5)(.1)(34,541) or 1,727 men/year.

HOUSING

The basic structure of the housing subsystem is that there are three types of housing—premium, worker, and underemployed—corresponding to the three population groups, and that each group occupies its category of housing according to the group's density parameter. Only premium- and worker-level housing is constructed, and only underemployed housing is lost through demolition. Premium units filter downward to become worker units, and worker units become underemployed units. Each of the three types of units has an assessed value for tax purposes. The housing subsystem is formulated in terms of 22 initial values and parameters, and values for most of them can be estimated from statistical data sources. The discussion of the approach taken in estimating values is divided into six sections.

Housing Levels and Population Densities:
PH, WH, UH, PHPD, WHPD, UHPD

The 1960 levels and population densities or average household sizes for each of the three types of housing are estimated as follows: First, an estimate is made of the number of households in each of the three population groups so that the total number of households agrees with the total number of occupied housing units in 1960. This provides a basis for computing values of the three household population density parameters and also gives a distribution of the occupied housing units among the three classes of housing. Second, the unoccupied housing units are distributed among the three classes of housing and added to the distribution of occupied units to estimate the 1960 level of housing for each class.

In 1960, there were 252,066 occupied housing units in the District of Columbia. The assumption here is that the entire population was distributed among these 252,066 households, although, actually, ap-

[20] *Ibid.,* p. 150.

proximately 5 percent of the 1960 population was in group quarters not regarded as households.[21] The assumption relied on in distributing households among the three population groups is that the number of households in each group is proportional to the number of adults in the group. The results of estimating the distribution of households are:

Population Group	Population	Children	Adults	Households
Manager-professional (MP)	145,400	44,621	100,779	47,640
Labor (L)	531,492	160,219	371,273	175,690
Underemployed (U)	87,064	26,356	60,708	28,736
Total	763,956	231,196	532,760	252,066

The first column shows the population for each of the three population groups, which is the product of the previously estimated labor-force component and its corresponding estimated family size or people per labor-force member parameter. The second column gives an estimate of the distribution of the 231,196 children in the city.[22] The number of children is distributed among the three population groups in proportion to the products of the labor-force levels and the labor-force birth rates previously estimated. The third column provides the adult population, by reducing the population by the estimated number of children. The fourth column shows the distribution of the 252,066 households in proportion to the entries in the third column.

These results provide estimates for the premium housing population density, PHPD, the worker housing population density, WHPD, and the underemployed housing population density, UHPD, parameters. Each is expressed in terms of people per housing unit.

PHPD $= 145,400/47,640 = 3.05$ people/housing unit
WHPD $= 531,492/175,690 = 3.03$ people/housing unit
UHPD $= 87,064/28,736 = 3.03$ people/housing unit

The foregoing results provide the distribution of occupied housing units among the premium, worker, and underemployed housing categories as 47,640, 175,690, and 28,736, respectively. In addition to the occupied units, in 1960, there were 10,575 unoccupied housing units in the city, of which 7,841 were judged available for occupancy and 2,734, not available.[23] The available units are assumed to be distributed pro-

---

[21] U. S. Bureau of the Census. *Census of Population and Housing: 1960, Census Tracts*, pp. 15, 180.

[22] *Ibid.*, p. 46.

[23] *Ibid.*, p. 149.

portionally among the three categories of housing, and other units are assumed unsuitable for occupancy and in the underemployed category. Under these assumptions, the levels of housing are estimated as

PH = 49,122 housing units
WH = 181,155 housing units
UH = 32,364 housing units.

Average Housing Levels and Averaging Times:
PHA, WHA, PHAT, WHAT

In urban dynamics, the growth rates of premium and worker housing for the current year are computed as average growth rates over a number of years prior to the current year. This is accomplished by computing estimated housing levels for a previous year, referred to as the premium housing average, PHA, and worker housing average, WHA, levels, which are used with the levels for the current year to compute average growth rates for each type of housing over the past period. These average growth rates are subsequently modified by other factors to determine the actual rate of growth for each type of housing during the current year.[24]

There is no need to estimate initial values for the average levels, PHA and WHA, because they are computed in the model from other initial values and parameters. The parameters for the premium housing averaging time, PHAT, and worker housing averaging time, WHAT, must be specified. Forrester used averaging times of 10 years for both premium and worker housing,[25] and these averaging times are used in the Washington model. This is appropriate, because the most important consideration in setting averaging times is that they be long enough to represent a growth trend. In estimating housing construction rate parameters, it is important to use a period of the same length for the sake of consistency.

Housing Construction Rates:
PHGRI, WHGRI, PHCN, WHCN

These parameters are the initial and normal rates of construction for premium- and worker-level housing. The only use of the premium housing growth rate initial, PHGRI, and worker housing growth rate initial, WHGRI, parameters is in computing the average housing levels

---

[24] Forrester. *Urban Dynamics,* pp. 177–178, 185.
[25] *Ibid.,* pp. 178, 185.

previously discussed, and, as indicated, these parameters are estimated for the 10-year period preceding 1960, corresponding to the 10-year averaging time adopted. The other two parameters, premium housing construction normal, PHCN, and worker housing construction normal, WHCN, are regarded as the normal construction rates. Because 1960 is taken as the normal year, these parameters are set equal to the corresponding initial rates for premium and worker housing. It is not possible to separate the premium- and worker-housing construction in the data used in the estimates; therefore, it is assumed that the premium- and worker-level units are constructed at the same rate. These two assumptions together mean that the four parameters are set to the same value, consistent with the way Forrester set these four parameters in his computations.

Housing construction in the District during the 1950–1959 period is taken as equal to the following authorized construction levels:

Year	Housing Units
1950	4,857
1951	4,494
1952	4,751
1953	5,384
1954	2,984
1955	2,796
1956	2,176
1957	3,082
1958	4,975
1959	1,624
Total	37,123 [26]

From these data, the average rate of increase during the period is computed as the ratio of the average yearly construction to the average housing level. From the previous estimates, the 1960 housing level was 262,641 units, and approximately 88 percent of these were premium- and worker-level units. Assuming that the same proportion of the 229,738 units in the city in 1950 [27] were premium and worker units, the average level of premium and worker units combined for the 1950–1959 period is (.88)(262,641+229,738)/2, or approximately 216,600 units. The rate of increase for the period, then, is 37,123/216,600, or

[26] U. S. Bureau of the Census. *Housing Construction Statistics: 1889–1964*. Washington, D. C., U. S. Government Printing Office, 1966, p. 203.

[27] U. S. Bureau of the Census. *Statistical Abstract of the United States: 1956*. 77th Edition. Washington, D. C., U. S. Government Printing Office, 1956, p. 780.

1.7 percent per year. Because the parameters are expressed as fractions per year, the four rate parameters are set to a .017 value.

Housing Assessed Values: PHAV, WHAV, UHAV

Although Forrester is not explicit as to whether his assessed housing values represent taxable or market values, the taxable assessed value is adopted for use in the Washington model. The important point is that the assessed values for housing be consistent with the assessed values for business/industry units estimated later, because, in the model, a single tax rate is applied to all real property.

There are three steps in estimating the premium housing assessed value, PHAV, worker housing assessed value, WHAV, and underemployed housing assessed value, UHAV, parameters. First, the distribution of assessed taxable values of single-family housing units in the District at the beginning of 1960 is estimated. Second, the distribution of the assessed taxable values of multifamily housing units is estimated for the same point in time. Third, both distributions are combined to obtain a composite distribution of assessed taxable values for all housing. The composite distribution is divided into premium, worker, and underemployed units, and the average assessed value for each type of housing unit is estimated. This particular approach is motivated primarily by the available data related to the problem.

The estimated distribution of the assessed values of single-family units is based on data from the 1960 census of housing, which provide the following figures on the market value of the city's owner-occupied, single-family units:

Market Value	Number of Units
Less than $5,000	356
$5,000 to $7,499	1,634
$7,500 to $9,999	4,258
$10,000 to $12,499	10,587
$12,500 to $14,999	16,648
$15,000 to $17,499	12,913
$17,500 to $19,999	6,443
$20,000 to $24,999	7,269
$25,000 to $34,999	5,797
$35,000 or more	5,401
Total	71,306 [28]

[28] U. S. Bureau of the Census. *Census of Housing: 1960. Vol. I. States and Small Areas—District of Columbia.* Final Report HC(1)–10. Washington, D. C., U. S. Government Printing Office, 1962, p. 8.

Some shortcomings exist in these data, in that only approximately 75 percent of the city's owner-occupied, single-family units are included, and the market values are based on the owner's estimate. The fact that only 75 percent of the units are included may introduce some bias, because the single-family units that are owner-occupied may tend to be valued at lower rates.

For 1960, the total number of single-family units in the city is estimated as 99,639, with a total assessed value of $886,429,000, obtained by reducing the estimates for 1961 for 100,000 units with a taxable assessed value of $891,000,000 [29] by the 1960 construction of 361 units with an assessed taxable value of $4,571,000.[30] This total number of units and assessed taxable values are distributed according to the distribution of assessed market values previously given, which results in the following distribution for single-family assessed taxable values:

Assessed Value	Number of Units
$1,227	498
3,044	2,292
4,272	5,978
5,499	14,746
6,727	23,316
7,954	18,035
9,182	8,968
11,023	10,163
14,705	8,071
20,867	7,572
Total	99,639

This distribution is computed by replacing each interval of the previously presented market value distribution by the interval's mean value. To do this, a lower bound of zero and an upper bound of $50,000 were adopted for the first and last interval, respectively, of the market value distribution. The distribution of numbers of units was adjusted proportionally to raise the total to the 99,639 units for 1960. Market values were adjusted proportionally so the sum of the products of unit numbers by their assessed value equals the $886,429,000 estimated assessed taxable value of single-family housing.

Much the same procedure is followed in estimating an assessed taxable value distribution for multifamily housing. In this case, the

[29] U. S. Bureau of the Census. *Census of Governments: 1962. Vol. II. Taxable Property Values.* Washington, D. C., U. S. Government Printing Office, 1963, pp. 32, 36.

[30] U. S. Bureau of the Census. *Housing Construction Statistics, 1889–1964,* p. 57.

distribution is based on the gross monthly rents of units as reported in the 1960 Census:

Monthly Rent	Number of Units
Less than $20	212
$20 to $29	1,141
$30 to $39	3,747
$40 to $49	8,406
$50 to $59	11,891
$60 to $69	22,907
$70 to $79	34,182
$80 to $99	50,185
$100 to $119	16,804
$120 to $149	12,962
$150 to $199	6,869
$200 or more	3,831
Total	173,137 [31]

Using this distribution to represent all multifamily units ignores the fact that the figures include some single-family units that are rented and fail to include some multifamily units that are owned. It is assumed that these two factors do not create an unacceptable bias in the resulting distribution. It is further assumed that reported unit rents are proportional to the assessed taxable value of the units.

For 1960, the number of multifamily units in the city is estimated as 163,002, with a total assessed value of $516,839,000. The number of units is estimated by reducing the previously estimated total of 262,641 housing units by the 99,639 single-family units estimated in the foregoing. The assessed value is estimated by reducing the assessed value of $536,000,000 for the city's 1961 multifamily units [32] by the assessed value of the 1960 multifamily construction. [33] Proportionally adjusting the distribution of monthly rents to conform to these estimates of numbers of units and assessed values results in the distribution of assessed taxable values of multifamily units, as shown in the listing that follows. The same adjustments are made as in estimating the distribution for single-family units. First, mean values are adopted for the rent intervals; then the numbers of units are adjusted proportionally to meet the estimated total number of multifamily units; and rent

[31] U. S. Bureau of the Census. *Census of Housing, 1960. Vol. I. States and Small Areas—District of Columbia*, p. 8.

[32] U. S. Bureau of the Census. *Census of Governments: 1962*, p. 32.

[33] U. S. Bureau of the Census. *Housing Construction Statistics: 1889–1964*, p. 57.

Assessed Value	Number of Units
$357	163
875	1,141
1,231	3,586
1,589	7,824
1,946	11,247
2,303	21,516
2,660	32,112
3,016	47,271
3,909	15,811
4,801	12,225
6,229	6,520
10,709	3,586
Total	163,002

amounts are adjusted proportionally to obtain the estimated assessed values so that the sum of the assessed values meets the estimated total.

The distribution of assessed taxable values of single- and multifamily housing may be merged, divided into three parts corresponding to the three types of housing, and the average assessed value for each type of housing computed. The 49,122 housing units with the lowest assessed value are assumed to be underemployed units. From the two distributions, the lowest valued 49,122 units have an assessed value of $98,323,344 and an average assessed value of $2,002. The highest valued 32,364 units are premium units, which have a total value of $454,407,106 and an average assessed value of $14,040. The middle group, which corresponds to the 181,155 worker-level units, has an assessed value of $849,682,252 and an average assessed value of $4,690. These estimates are rounded out to the nearest $50 to obtain parameter values of

PHAV $= 14.05$ thousand dollars/housing unit
WHAV $= 4.70$ thousand dollars/housing unit
UHAV $= 2.00$ thousand dollars/housing unit.

Housing Construction Labor: PHCL, WHCL

These parameters indicate the labor requirements for construction of premium and worker housing units in terms of man-years per housing unit. Values for these parameters are developed by estimating the average market value of premium and worker units for 1960, estimating the proportion of the value of the units required for wages and salaries, and converting the wage and salary requirements to man-years for both types of housing.

In 1960, there were 2,778 housing units authorized for construction in the District, with an assessed taxable value of $22,393,000.[34] The market value of housing units is approximately 2.1 times the assessed taxable value, according to sales in the District over a six-month period in 1961.[35] This ratio of market to taxable values is assumed to hold for the 1960 construction. It is further assumed that the 2,778 units constructed in 1960 are divided between premium and worker units in the same proportion as premium and worker units are represented in the 1960 housing inventory, and that the average market value of the new premium and worker units is proportional to the previously estimated average assessed taxable values for those units. On the basis of these assumptions, the 1960 construction consists of 592 premium units and 2,186 worker units, and the market value of worker units, wv, is .334 times the value of premium units, PV. Because the sum of the market value of all units must equal the total market value, the following relationships hold:

$$592\text{PV} - 2186\text{wv} = (2.1)(\$22,393,000)$$
$$592\text{PV} - (2186)(.334)\text{PV} = \$47,025,300$$
$$\text{PV} = \$35,570$$
$$\text{wv} = \$11,880.$$

In 1960, the average market values are $35,570 and $11,880 for premium and worker units, respectively.

From national aggregate data, it is estimated that, for 1960, approximately 27 percent of the market value of new construction represents expenditures of wages and salaries for labor. This estimate is based on 1958 data—the year closest to 1960 for which data were found, but there would be practically no change in this technological relationship during a two-year period. For 1958, the total value of new construction produced was $52,416,000,[36] and the total payments of wages and salaries for the new construction industry was $14,025,000.[37] From this, the labor costs of new construction are estimated to be 27 percent of the

[34] *Ibid.*

[35] U. S. Bureau of the Census. *Census of Governments: 1962*, p. 143.

[36] National Planning Association. *Input-Output Analysis: Two Reports on Its Scope and Application.* Report No. 65-A. Washington, D. C., September 1965, p. 34.

[37] U. S. Office of Business Economics. *The National Income and Product Accounts of the United States, 1929–1965.* Statistical Tables. Washington, D. C., U. S. Government Printing Office, 1966, p. 97.

value produced. Using this factor, the labor costs of premium and worker units are $9,600 and $3,200, respectively. These costs may be converted to man-years by using the 1960 average weekly wages of $113.04 for contract construction workers [38] and assuming a 50-week work year, providing parameter values of

PHCL $= 1.7$ man-years/housing unit
WHCL $= .6$ man-years/housing unit.

Housing Obsolescence and Demolition Rates:
PHON, WHON, SHDN

These parameters govern the filtering and demolition of housing units. Only the underemployed level units are lost through demolition, and the basic rate of loss is indicated by the slum housing demolition normal, SHDN, parameter. This parameter is estimated first, and then the normal obsolescence parameters, PHON and WHON, which control the basic rates of filtering of premium and worker units, are estimated. The three parameters are normal or basic rates; they are modified as they are applied in the model for each year to reflect the influence of other factors.

Time series data on housing demolitions in the District are not available, but two housing studies conducted in the 1960s for the metropolitan Washington area used a yearly demolition rate of 1 percent of the housing stock. This rate was based on analyses of data on demolitions from the 1960 Census and other studies and has been assumed to hold for each of the jurisdictions, including the District of Columbia.[39] The 1 percent rate is adopted for use in the Washington model; and the entire 1 percent loss must be made from the underemployed housing stock. Using the previous estimates for 1960, of 262,641 for total housing and 32,364 for underemployed housing, the parameter is estimated as

SHDN $= (.01)(262,641)/32,364$
SHDN $= .080$ fraction/year.

In estimating filter rates for premium and worker housing, the assumption is made that, under normal conditions, the distribution

[38] U. S. Bureau of Labor Statistics. *Employment and Earnings Statistics for the United States, 1909–1967.* Bulletin No. 1312–5. Washington, D. C., U. S. Government Printing Office, 1967, p. xxxvi.

[39] Metropolitan Washington Council of Governments. *Housing Gap Quantification: A Methodology.* Washington, D. C., 1968, p. 38.

of the three types of housing is fixed. Normal conditions means that the previously estimated normal growth rates for premium and worker housing and the normal demolition rate for underemployed housing are not modified by the influence of other factors. Under this assumption, if the previously estimated normal construction rates, PHCN and WHCN, and the slum housing demolition normal, SHDN, rate are applied for one year, the resulting housing will be distributed in the same proportions as in the previous year. Consider the previously estimated levels for 1960, for which the total housing is 262,641, consisting of 49,122 premium, 181,155 worker, and 32,364 underemployed units. Applying the previously estimated construction and demolition rates results in total housing of 263,967, consisting of 49,957 premium, 184,235 worker, and 29,775 underemployed units. In order for the same distribution of housing to be preserved, these 263,967 units must be distributed as 49,450 premium, 182,070 worker, and 32,447 underemployed. This implies a filtering of 507 units from premium to worker status and the filtering of 2,672 units from worker to underemployed status. Thus, the values for the filtering parameters become

PHON $= 507/49,122 = .010$ fraction/year
WHON $= 2,672/181,155 = .014$ fraction/year.

BUSINESS/INDUSTRY

The business/industry subsystem of the model is organized around a life-cycle concept, wherein units of business/industry begin as new enterprises, age to become units of mature business, and age further to become units of declining industry. Only new enterprise units are constructed, and only declining industry units are lost through demolition. Just as in housing, each of the three classes of business/industry units has an assessed value for tax purposes. The business/industry subsystem is formulated in terms of 23 initial values and parameters. The discussion of the procedures used in estimating values for these initial values and parameters is organized into five sections.

Industry Initial Levels and Decline Rates:
NE, MB, DI, NEDN, MBDN, DIDN

The three initial values NE, MB, and DI specify the 1960 levels of new enterprise, mature business, and declining industry, respectively. The parameters NEDN, MBDN, and DIDN specify the normal rates of decline for each class of business/industry in terms of the fraction of units per year that decline to the next lower level or, in the case of declining-industry units, that are demolished. The reciprocals of these normal rate-of-decline parameters for the three classes of industry indicate the normal life span expected for each of the three phases of the life cycle.[40] The six values embody the heart of Forrester's life-cycle concept of the business/industry subsystem.

There are two principal steps in the estimation of these values. First, the length of the three phases of the business/industry life cycle and the distribution of the District's 1960 business enterprises among these three phases is estimated. Second, the total number of business/industry units in the city in 1960 is estimated. The estimation of the six model values follows immediately after these two problems are dealt with.

A body of data developed by the National Planning Association is useful in estimating the lengths of the business/industry life-cycle phases and the 1960 distribution of business/industry units among these phases. These data provide estimates of the age distribution of productive units for approximately 80 economic sectors for a number of regions in the United States, and were developed with a life-cycle concept somewhat like Forrester's concept, which treats business/industry enterprises as consisting of a combination of plant and equipment that deteriorates over time. Under National Planning's concept, a mean service life or expected capital stock lifetime is estimated for each economic sector by taking a weighted average of the typical lives of 16 different types of plant and equipment assets used in the sector. The weights used in the averaging are the proportions of total investment expended for each type of asset in the typical annual investment for the sector. A sector's capital stock lifetime is broken into two periods, referred to as the fixed-life period and the declining-life period. The fixed-life period is the number of years for which the sector's capital stock is regarded as certain to last. The declining-life period is the average number of years for which the capital stock of the sector will be serviceable beyond the fixed-life period.[41] For example, in the household furniture manufacturing sector, the average life of capital stock is 27.5 years, consisting of a fixed-life period of 16.0 years and a declining-life period of 11.5 years.[42]

[40] Forrester. *Urban Dynamics,* pp. 195–198.

[41] Graham Cecil Scott. "Industrial Production and Investment in a Dynamic, Multiregional, Interindustry Model of the United States." Doctoral Dissertation. Durham, N. C., Duke University, 1972, pp. 41–43.

[42] National Planning Association. "Capital Stock by Industry and Region 1947–1963." Washington, D. C., 1969. Computer listing, unnumbered.

These data on capital stock lifetimes and age distributions of capital stock are available for approximately 80 economic sectors by regions of the United States. In order to be consistent with urban dynamics, it is necessary to combine the sectors into a single business/industry sector and to estimate capital stock data for the District of Columbia from data for the South Atlantic region, of which the District is a part. A summary of the steps taken in combining the sectors follows: First, data for the 80 sectors are consolidated into the 13-sector industry classification used by the Bureau of the Census in the 1960 Census. This provides the information for the 13 economic sectors of the South Atlantic region. Four items of information are known for each sector: the length of the sector's fixed-life period, the length of the sector's declining-life period, the dollar value of the sector's capital stock in the fixed-life phase, and the dollar value of the sector's capital stock in the declining-life phase. These dollar values of capital stock are for 1960; all values are in 1963 dollars. Because the capital stock values are in constant dollars, the distribution of capital stock between the fixed-life and declining-life phases provides an approximate age distribution of the capital stock for a sector.

The next step in this process is estimating the capital stock data for these 13 sectors of the District of Columbia. For each sector, the proportion of the sector's regional capital stock is allocated to the District, according to the ratio of the District's 1960 employment in the sector to the region's 1960 employment in the sector. The employment ratios are computed from census data.[43] (It is assumed that the fixed-life and declining-life phases are the same length for economic sectors in the District and in the region.) Then the 13 economic sectors for the District are combined into a single sector. Thus, the fixed-life and declining-life phase lengths for the composite sector are computed as a weighted average of the phase lengths of the 13 sectors, with the employment levels of the sectors taken as weights; and the capital stock values are computed as the sum of the 13 sectors. This estimated composite, District of Columbia economic sector has a fixed-life phase of 17 years and a declining-life phase of 24 years. The 1960 distribution of capital stock is $1,641,618,000 in the fixed-life phase and $767,227,000 in the declining-life phase.

The life-cycle concepts used by the National Planning Association and by Forrester are generally compatible. The urban dynamics

[43] U. S. Bureau of the Census. *Census of Population: 1960, General Social and Economic Characteristics, United States Summary.* Final Report PC(1)–1c. Washington, D. C., U. S. Government Printing Office, 1962, p. 280.

business/industry lifetime, however, is divided into three phases, whereas the National Planning lifetime is divided into two phases. To reconcile this difference and to make use of the estimates previously developed, the 41-year lifetime of the District's business/industry is divided somewhat arbitrarily into three phases of 8, 12, and 21 years each. This division makes the total agree with the preceding empirically based estimate and divides the business/industry lifetime into three phases proportional to the 12-, 20-, and 33-year phases used by Forrester.[44] The normal decline rates of business/industry units must be consistent with the lengths of the three phases adopted. This implies that the normal or equilibrium rates of decline are the reciprocals of the phase lengths and results in the following normal decline rates for new enterprise, mature business, and declining industry:

$$\text{NEDN} = 1/8 = .125 \text{ fraction/year}$$
$$\text{MBDN} = 1/12 = .083 \text{ fraction/year}$$
$$\text{DIDN} = 1/21 = .047 \text{ fraction/year}.$$

With this adopted division of the business/industry lifetime, the preceding estimated dollar value of the capital stock in the fixed-life and declining-life phases can be apportioned to the three phases by allocating 8/17 of the fixed-life capital to the new enterprise category; the remainder of the fixed-life capital and 3/24 of the declining-life capital to the mature-business category; and the remainder of the declining-life capital to the declining-industry category. This results in values of $772,545,000, $964,976,000, and $671,324,000, respectively, for the capital stock in the new enterprise, mature business, and declining-industry phases. Because the dollar values of the capital stock are in constant dollars, the preceding distribution of capital stock investment may be taken to represent the distribution of units among the three industry phases. This distribution is 32 percent new enterprise, 40 percent mature business, and 28 percent declining industry units. Assumed to be the 1960 distribution of types of units for the District, this distribution is applied after estimating the total number of business/industry units.

The last step in estimating initial industry levels is to estimate the total number of business/industry units for the District of Columbia for 1960. In estimating the number of units, a relationship is used to

[44] Forrester. *Urban Dynamics*, pp. 195–198.

estimate the total number of business firms as a function of total personal income. The number of government units is then estimated and added to the business firms to obtain a total number of business/industry units.

The relationship used in estimating the number of business firms is an empirically developed one that has been used to estimate the total number of business firms for the states and the District of Columbia as a function of total personal income. The form of the relationship adopted for use is

$$\log y = -1.967 + 1.015 \log x$$

where y is the number of firms represented in thousands and x is the personal income represented in millions of dollars. This relationship was tested with data for a number of years through 1954 and was found to be quite stable.[45] Using this relationship with the 1960 estimated total personal income for the District of $2.311 billion [46] gives an estimate of 28,100 business firms.

It is assumed that governmental organizations are divided into the same size units as business firms. For 1960, the estimated total employment in the District is 483,228;[47] of these, 168,991 are federal employees, including employees of the District government.[48] On the preceding assumption, and assuming also that 483,228 minus 168,991, or 314,237, are employees of business firms, there are 43,200 business/industry units, which include both business firms and governmental organizations. Distributing these 43,200 business/industry units according to the previously estimated distribution of 32, 40, and 28 percent of new enterprise, mature business, and declining industry units, respectively, gives the following 1960 estimates of business/industry levels:

NE = 13,824 productive units
MB = 17,280 productive units
DI = 12,096 productive units.

---

[45] Betty C. Churchill. "State Distribution of Business Concerns." *Survey of Current Business, 34*:16–22, November 1954.

[46] Regional Economic Division Staff. "State Personal Income, 1948–65." *Survey of Current Business, 46*:12, August 1966.

[47] U. S. Bureau of the Census. *Census of Population and Housing: 1960, Census Tracts,* p. 106.

[48] Metropolitan Washington Council of Governments. *Statistics—Washington Metropolitan Area.* Washington, D. C., January 1968, p. 66.

New Enterprise Average Level and Averaging Time:
NEA, NEAT

The new enterprise average level, NEA, and the new enterprise averaging time parameter, NEAT, are analogous to the average levels and averaging times used in the housing subsystem, except that, in the business/industry subsystem, only one type of business/industry unit is constructed. NEA represents the level of new enterprise units for a previous year, and NEAT, which is referred to as the averaging time, is the number of years the level represented by NEA is at prior to the current year. There is no necessity to estimate the initial value for NEA, because it is computed in the model from other model quantities. As in the housing subsystem, Forrester used an averaging time of 10 years. This value is used in the Washington model, because it appears long enough to represent the growth trend for new enterprise units.

New Enterprise Construction Factors and Growth Rates:
NECF, MBCF, DICF, NECN, NEGRI

There are two growth rate parameters for the business/industry subsystem: the new enterprise growth rate initial, NEGRI, and the new enterprise construction normal, NECN. Both parameters represent the fractional annual increment of new business/industry units, but the increment is represented relative to a different base in the two parameters. NEGRI represents the fractional annual increment relative to the number of new enterprise units. NECN represents the fractional annual increment in business/industry units relative to a weighted average of the three types of business/industry units. The weights used in the averaging process are the new enterprise construction factor, NECF, mature business construction factor, MBCF, and declining industry construction factor, DICF. Forrester assigned values of 1, .5, and .3, respectively, to the construction factor parameters, NECF, MBCF, and DICF, on the premise that new business units are associated more strongly with the formation of additional business/industry units.[49] Here, the same weights as Forrester's are used, because the weights are not estimated readily from available data.

The approach in estimating values for the growth rates is to estimate the number of business/industry units constructed during each year of the 1955–1959 period and then to compute parameter values based on the average rates over this five-year period. Following is a summary

[49] Forrester. *Urban Dynamics*, p. 195.

of the steps taken in estimating the number of business/industry units constructed.

Year	Business/ Industry Units (thousands)	Net New Units (thousands)	Replacement Units (thousands)	Total New Units (thousands)
1955	38.2	1.1	.5	1.6
1956	39.3	.4	.5	.9
1957	39.7	.8	.5	1.3
1958	40.5	1.5	.5	2.0
1959	42.0	1.2	.6	1.8
1960	43.2			

This number is arrived at in the same way the number of units was estimated previously for 1960, which involves the use of the previously discussed relationship to estimate the number of operating business firms from personal income for the District, which is estimated as $1.949, $2.019, $2.061, $2.133, $2.228, and $2.311 billion for the successive years of the 1955–1960 period.[50] The number of business firms for each year is then adjusted upward to reflect the federal employment in the District, estimated as 163,316, 165,818, 164,664, 162,672, 166,265, and 168,991 for the same years,[51] resulting in the estimates of the business/industry units shown in the first column. The second column represents estimated net increases in business/industry units and is obtained by subtracting the number of units in each year from the number in the next year. The third column represents the new business/industry units that must be constructed to replace units lost through demolition. These estimates are made by applying the previously estimated decline rate for declining industry units, DIDN, to the number of declining-industry units, which, for each year, is assumed to be the 1960 proportion, or 28 percent, of the total number of business/industry units for the year. The final column sums the net increase in units and the units needed for replacement of lost units to provide the total number of new units constructed each year.

The two growth-rate parameters are estimated from the preceding time series of new enterprise construction for 1955–1959. The growth rates for each year follow:

---

[50] Regional Economic Division Staff. "State Personal Income, 1948–65," p. 12.

[51] Metropolitan Washington Council of Governments. *Statistics—Washington Metropolitan Area*, p. 66.

Year	Weighted Fraction Increase	New Enterprise Fraction Increase
1955	.069	.131
1956	.038	.071
1957	.054	.102
1958	.082	.154
1959	.071	.134

Both rates are based on the assumption that the total business/industry units for each year are distributed the same way as they were in 1960; namely, that 32 percent of the units are new-enterprise, 40 percent are mature-business, and 28 percent are declining-industry units. The rates in the first column express the total new units for the year as a fraction of the weighted sum of the three types of business/industry units, using the weights previously discussed. Rates in the second column express the total new units as a fraction of the new-enterprise level for the year. The weighted fractional increase corresponds to the NECN parameter, and its value is taken as the average rate over the 1955–1959 period, which is

NECN = .063 fraction/year.

Similarly, the new enterprise growth rate initial parameter, NEGRI, which expresses the construction of new units relative to the new-enterprise level, is taken as the average of the growth rates in the second column, or

NEGRI = .119 fraction/year.

Business/Industry Assessed Values and Construction Labor: NEAV, MBAV, DIAV, NECL

The three parameters NEAV, MBAV, and DIAV specify the assessed values of new-enterprise, mature-business, and declining-industry units, respectively. The new enterprise construction labor parameter, NECL, specifies the labor requirements for the construction of new-enterprise units. These parameters are analogous to model parameters in the housing subsystem.

In estimating assessed values for the categories of business/industry units, it is assumed that the assessed value of units decreases at a constant rate over the 41-year average unit life. Using this rate, the average assessed value of each type of unit is taken as the value at the midpoint of its life in that phase. From earlier calculations, the phase lengths for new-enterprise, mature-business, and declining-industry units are 8, 12, and 21 years, respectively, and the relative assessed values of new-enterprise, mature-business, and declining-industry units are 90, 66, and 26. Because the 1960 distribution of business/industry units is estimated as 32 percent new enterprise, 40 percent mature business, and 28 percent declining industry, the total assessed value of business enterprises is distributed at (90)(32):(66)(40):(26)(28) or .46:.42:.12 among the new-enterprise, mature-business, and declining-industry categories.

In 1960, the estimated total assessed value of real property in the District is $2.32 billion.[52] Subtracting from this the previously estimated $1.40 billion assessed value of 1960 housing, gives a total assessed value of business/industry units of $0.92 billion. Allocating the total among the three categories according to the distribution previously estimated gives assessed values of $0.42 billion, $0.39 billion, and $0.11 billion for the new-enterprise, mature-business, and declining-industry categories, respectively. Division of the total assessed value of each category by the previously estimated number of units in the category results in estimated values of $30,400, $22,600, and $9,100 for the three types of units. Parameter values are taken as

$\text{NEAV} = 30.4$ thousand dollars/productive unit
$\text{MBAV} = 22.6$ thousand dollars/productive unit
$\text{DIAV} = 9.1$ thousand dollars/productive unit.

With the assessed value of new-enterprise units and some of the relationships developed for the housing subsystem, the parameter, NECL, which expresses the man-years of labor required to construct a new-enterprise unit, is estimated. From the housing subsystem estimates, it was estimated that the market value of new construction for 1960 is 2.1 times its assessed value; that 27 percent of the market value of new construction is an expenditure for labor; and that the 1960 cost of labor is $5,652 per man-year. From these estimations, the average assessed value of new-enterprise units is $30,400. Because this represents 90 percent of a new unit's assessed value, the assessed value of a new unit is $33,800, and the estimated market value of a new unit is (2.1)($33,800), or $70,980. If 27 percent of the market value is labor cost at $5,652 per man-year, then

$\text{NECL} = 3.4$ man-years/productive unit.

[52] U. S. Bureau of the Census. *Census of Governments: 1962*, p. 142.

Business/Industry Labor Utilization Rates:
NEM, NEL, MBM, MBL, DIM, DIL

These six parameters specify the number of manager-professional and labor persons employed in each of the three types of business/industry units. In adopting values for these parameters, Forrester's basic idea is followed; namely, that the personnel mix of business/industry units changes as new enterprise units age into the mature-business and declining-industry categories. This idea assumes that the proportion of management personnel declines as business/industry declines. Neither data nor support for this idea is found to provide a basis for setting values of the business/industry employment ratios. The approach taken in setting values for these parameters is to assume ratios of manager-professional and labor employment that reflect the composition of the District's 1960 labor force, and then to adjust the ratios to reflect the size of the labor-force components estimated earlier. It should be noted that these parameters do not include the underemployed group, because jobs for the underemployed are represented in the model as a fraction of the number of labor jobs, with the fraction varying according to the ratio of labor workers to labor jobs.[53]

The ratios of manager-professional to labor employment are assumed to be 1:2 for new-enterprise units, 1:3 for mature-business units, and 1:4 for declining-industry units. Although these ratios include proportionally more manager-professionals than Forrester's ratios of 1:5, 1:7.5, and 1:10 for the three categories of business/industry,[54] the ratios adopted reflect the District of Columbia's 1960 ratio of manager-professional and labor components of approximately 1:3. In addition, it is assumed that each category of business/industry units uses a combined number of manager-professional and labor persons, approximately proportional to its assessed value, which was estimated previously. Taking this and the size of the manager-professional labor force, previously estimated at 81,335, into consideration gives the following parameter values for the manager-professional component:

NEM $= 3.1$ men/productive unit.
MBM $= 1.8$ men/productive unit
DIM $= 0.6$ men/productive unit.

These values, multiplied by the corresponding numbers of business/industry units, account for the District's manager-professional employment. Next, by applying the previously adopted ratios of manager-

[53] Forrester. *Urban Dynamics*, pp. 19–20.
[54] *Ibid.*

professional to labor persons for each industry type gives the following parameter values for the labor level component:

NEL $=6.2$ men/productive unit
MBL $=5.5$ men/productive unit
DIL $=2.5$ men/productive unit.

These six parameter values related the city's manager-professional and labor groups to the previously estimated numbers of business/industry units within the assumed pattern of labor utilization.

LAND UTILIZATION

The basic concept of land utilization in urban dynamics is that all usable land in the city is occupied either by housing or business/industry units, or is vacant. This leaves the way land is used for overhead purposes, such as parks, streets, sidewalks, and utility rights-of-way, open to interpretation. The approach here is to allocate proportionally the land used for overhead purposes to housing and business/industry uses. By so doing, all the land in the city is included in the model's land accounting.

There are three model parameters related to land utilization: the city's total land area, AREA, expressed in acres; the land per house, LPH, expressed in acres per unit; and the land per productive unit, LPP, expressed in acres per business/industry unit. To estimate values for these parameters for 1960, to initialize the model for Washington, data from the Metropolitan Washington Council of Governments'[55] empiric model data file are used, which provides the following information on land utilization for the city as of the beginning of 1960:

Land-Use Category	Acres
Residential	14,169
Industrial	1,775
Commercial	2,771
Institutional	5,346
Parks	7,085
Vacant	779
Residual	8,229
Total	40,154

[55] Metropolitan Washington Council of Governments. "Empiric Model Calibration Data File: 1960 and 1968." Washington, D. C., June 1973. Computer listing, unnumbered.

These data are based on an analysis of the land assessor's records, supplemented by data from aerial photographs. The residual category includes streets, sidewalks, and utility rights-of-way. It is assumed that these industrial, commercial, and institutional categories correspond to the land used for business/industry units in urban dynamics. Using this assumption and proportionally allocating the parks and residual acreage according to the land used for housing and business results in:

Land-Use Category	Acres
Housing	23,204
Business/industry	16,171
Vacant	779
Total	40,154

From earlier computations, the total number of housing units for the city at the beginning of 1960 was 262,641, and the number of business/industry units was 43,200. The three parameters for land utilization are then estimated to have the following values:

AREA $= 40,154$ acres
LPH $= 23,204/262,641 = 0.09$ acres/house
LPP $= 16,171/ 43,200 = 0.37$ acres/unit.

TAXES

The tax sector in urban dynamics is very summary, in that the only revenue source represented is real property, and expenditures are represented in terms of per capita expenditures for each of the model's three population groups. The tax sector has one initial value and six parameters. There is no need to estimate the initial value, which is the tax ratio needed perceived, TRNP, because it is computed by the model equations as a time-delayed value of the ratio of the tax assessment rate currently needed and the normal tax assessment rate. Forrester's value of 30 years for the tax ratio needed perception time, TRNPT, is used in the Washington model. The five parameter values estimated are the tax per capita normal, TPCN, the tax assessment normal, TAN, and the tax expenditure per capita rates for the three population groups.

In estimating the parameters for the tax sector, it is assumed that all of the District's general tax revenue can be subsumed under the property tax represented in the model. Although this produces some distortions, because some taxes—such as sales tax—are not proportional to the assessed value of property owned, it does have the advantage of accounting for all general tax revenue within the model structure. Also, the general assumption previously relied on is made, that parameter values estimated for the initial year of model computations are normal parameter values.

The tax per capita normal, TPCN, represents per capita tax expenditures and is expressed in terms of dollars per year per person. An estimate of this parameter for the beginning of 1960 is provided by the District's 1959 per capita expenditure of \$329.40.[56] From this amount, the value of the parameter is taken as

TPCN $=330$ dollars/year/person.

The tax assessment normal, TAN, parameter governs the tax revenue obtained from real property tax and is expressed in dollars per year per \$1,000 of assessed value. The parameter is estimated as the ratio of the revenue needed by the city and the assessed value of real property. The tax needed is estimated by allowing the \$330 per person annual expenditure previously estimated for the city's 1960 population of 763,956, which indicates a needed tax of \$252,110,000. The total assessed value of the real property in the District in 1960 was \$2.32 billion.[57] This provides an estimate of

TAN $=252.11/2.32=108.5$ dollars/year/thousand.

The estimated value is rounded off to provide a parameter value of

TAN $=110$ dollars/year/thousand.

As mentioned earlier, this estimate subsumes all tax revenue under the real property tax.

The other three parameters for the tax sector express the per capita tax expenditures for each of the model's three population classes. Because data directly related to these parameters were not found, estimates are made in the following way. The per capita expenditures by broad category for the District in 1969 were

Education	\$65.71
Highways	35.48
Public Welfare	21.31

[56] U. S. Bureau of the Census. *Statistical Abstract of the United States: 1961.* 82nd Edition. Washington, D. C., U. S. Government Printing Office, 1961, p. 411.

[57] U. S. Bureau of the Census. *Census of Governments: 1962*, p. 142.

Health and Hospitals	46.55
Other	160.35 [58]

These 1959 expenditures are apportioned to the three population classes according to three assumptions and are used to initialize the model for 1960. First, it is assumed that education expenditures are distributed over the entire population on a per capita basis. Second, it is assumed that public welfare expenditures are made entirely to the underemployed population group. Third, it is assumed that the other three categories of expenditures are distributed among the three population groups in proportion to the assessed value of residential property for the groups. Applying these assumptions by using the population and assessed value of housing developed earlier provides the following estimates of per capita expenditures:

	Manager-professional	Labor	Underemployed
Education	$ 65.71	$ 65.71	$ 65.71
Public Welfare	—	—	187.03
All Other	412.05	211.36	148.99
Total	$477.76	$277.07	$401.73

Rounding out these estimates results in the following values for taxes per management person, TMP, taxes per labor person, TLP, and taxes per underemployed person, TUP:

TMP = 475 dollars/person/year
TLP = 275 dollars/person/year
TUP = 400 dollars/person/year.

[58] U. S. Bureau of the Census. *Statistical Abstract of the United States: 1961*, p. 411.

Fortran Computer Program for Washington, D.C. Urban Dynamics Model

Appendix D provides a listing of the computer program for the urban dynamics model representation of Washington, D. C. developed in this study. The program was developed by beginning with the Fortran-language version of Forrester's urban dynamics model, which appears in Appendix B, and incorporating the four stages of model modifications that were made in developing the representation of Washington. The modifications introduced in each of the four stages are discussed in Chapter 5, and the estimation of model initial values and parameters introduced in the modifications is discussed in Appendix C.

Figure 6 is a listing of the computer program that represents the stage 4 version of the Washington model discussed in Chapter 5. The program entries that were modified or introduced in each of the four stages of model development are coded in the listing to indicate the stage in which they were modified or introduced. These codes, carried in the two character positions at the extreme right of the entries, indicate the last of the four stages in which the entry was changed and make it possible to reconstruct the computer program for the previous stages. The codes used are A, B, C, and D to represent stages 1, 2, 3, and 4, respectively. Letter codes are distinguished easily from Forrester's statement numbers, which also are carried near the right end of the program entries. All of the initial values and parameters examined in Appendix c are coded with an A for stage 1 and a B for stage 2, although Forrester's values are used in a number of instances, as the discussion in Appendix c indicates. In a few cases, stage 4 changes override changes made in stages 1 and 2. In such cases, the entries are coded *D in the two extreme character positions at the right, and an explanatory note appears below such entries to indicate the modifications used in the previous stage. Starting with the listing from Appendix B and using the information provided by the codes and explanatory notes in the listing in Figure 6, a computer program representation for stages 1, 2, or 3 of the Washington model can be constructed.

```
C
C
C    THIS PROGRAM IS A FORTRAN VERSION OF FORRESTER'S URBAN DYNAMICS MODEL
C    WHICH WAS INITIALLY PROGRAMMED IN DYNAMO.  THE PROGRAM IS ORGANIZED
C    INTO THE FOLLOWING PRINCIPAL SECTIONS:
C        COMPUTER PROGRAM INITIALIZATION
C        URBAN DYNAMICS MODEL COMPUTATIONS
C            INITIALIZATION OF BASIC MODEL LEVEL VARIABLES
C            INITIALIZATION OF COMPUTATION CONTROL LOOPS
C            EQUATIONS FOR MODEL SECTORS
C            PRINTING OF MODEL RESULTS
C
C
C - - - - - - - - - - - - - - - - - - - - - - - - - - - - - - - - - - - -
C - - - COMPUTER PROGRAM INITIALIZATION - - - - - - - - - - - - - - - - -
C - - - - - - - - - - - - - - - - - - - - - - - - - - - - - - - - - - - -
C        THIS SECTION IS CONCERNED WITH STORAGE ALLOCATION AND
C        SPECIFYING CONVENTIONS TO BE USED FOR NAMING INTEGER AND REAL
C        VARIABLES.
C
C        THE RANGE OF FORTRAN REAL AND INTERGER VARIABLES IS SET SO
C        THAT THE URBAN DYANMICS MODEL VARIABLES WILL BE REAL--THERE
C        ARE NO MODEL VARIABLE NAMES WHICH BEGIN WITH THE LETTERS I, J,
C        AND K SO THESE WILL BE USED FOR OTHER PURPOSES.
      IMPLICIT REAL (A-H,L-Z), INTEGER (I-K)
C        THE FOLLOWING MUST BE INTEGERS
      INTEGER PRINT,FREQ,LST,NXT,YEAR
C
C        THE FOLLOWING ARE STORAGE ALLOCATIONS FOR THE TABLES USED IN
C        TABULAR FUNCTIONS.  EACH TABLE IS ALLOCATED 15 WORDS, ALTHOUGH
C        THEY ALL USE LESS.
      DIMENSION
     1   BDMT(15), DIEMT(15), DILMT(15),EDMT(15), EGMT(15), ELJMT(15),
     2   ELMT(15), EMMT(15), ETMT(15), LAHMT(15),LAJMT(15),LATMT(15),
     3   LAUMT(15), LCRT(15), LDMT(15), LEMT(15), LLFT(15), LSMT(15),
     4   LUMT(15), MAHMT(15),MAJMT(15),MAPMT(15),MATMT(15),MDMT(15),
     5   MLMT(15), MSMT(15), PEMT(15), PHAMT(15),PHEMT(15),PHGMT(15),
     6   PHLMT(15), PHOMT(15),PHPMT(15),PHTMT(15),SHAMT(15),SHLMT(15),
     7   TCMT(15), TRT(15),  UAMMT(15),UDMT(15), UEMT(15), UFWT(15),
     8   UHMT(15), UHPMT(15),UJMT(15), ULJRT(15),WHAMT(15),WHEMT(15),
     9   WHGMT(15),WHOMT(15),WHUMT(15),WHTMT(15),WHLMT(15)
C
C        THE FOLLOWING ARE STORAGE ALLOCATIONS FOR THE MODEL VARIABLES
C        WHICH ARE COMPUTED EACH TIME PERIOD.  30 WORDS ARE ALLOCATED
C        FOR EACH VARIABLE.
      DIMENSION
     A   AMM(30),  AMMP(30), AV(30),   BAV(30),  BDM(30),  DI(30),
     B   DID(30),  DIDM(30), DIDP(30), DIEM(30), DILM(30), EDM(30),
     C   EGM(30),  ELJM(30), ELM(30),  EM(30),   EMM(30),  ETM(30),
     D   HAV(30),  HUT(30),  L(30),    LA(30),   LAHM(30), LAJM(30),
     E   LAM(30),  LAMP(30), LATM(30), LAUM(30), LB(30),   LCHCD(30),
     F   LCHP(30), LCR(30),  LD(30),   LDC(30),  LDI(30),  LDM(30),
     G   LEM(30),  LFO(30),  LHR(30),  LJ(30),   LLF(30),  LMM(30),
     H   LMMP(30), LR(30),   LRP(30),  LSM(30),  LTM(30),  LTPG(30),
     I   LTU(30),  LUM(30),  LUR(30),  MA(30),   MAHM(30), MAJM(30),
```

```
J     MAM(30),    MAMP(30),   MAPM(30),   MATM(30),   MB(30),     MBD(30),
K     MD(30),     MDM(30),    MHR(30),    MJ(30),     MLM(30),    MLR(30),
L     MP(30),     MPB(30),    MPR(30),    MR(30),     MSM(30),    NE(30),
M     NEA(30),    NEC(30),    NECD(30),   NECP(30),   NED(30),    NEGR(30),
N     P(30),      PEM(30),    PH(30),     PHA(30),    PHAM(30),   PHC(30),
O     PHCD(30)
      DIMENSION
A     PHCP(30),   PHEM(30),   PHGM(30),   PHGR(30),   PHLM(30),   PHM(30),
B     PHO(30),    PHOM(30),   PHPM(30),   PHTM(30),   PUT(30),    SHAM(30),
C     SHD(30),    SHDM(30),   SHDP(30),   SHLM(30),   TAI(30),    TC(30),
D     TCM(30),    TN(30),     TPCR(30),   TPCSP(30),  TR(30),     TRN(30),
E     TRNP(30),   U(30),      UA(30),     UAMM(30),   UB(30),     UD(30),
F     UDM(30),    UEM(30),    UFW(30),    UH(30),     UIHM(30),   UHPM(30),
G     UHPR(30),   UHR(30),    UJ(30),     UJM(30),    UJP(30),    ULJR(30),
H     UM(30),     UMM(30),    UMMP(30),   UR(30),     UTL(30),    UTLN(30),
I     UTLP(30),   UTP(30),    UW(30),     WH(30),     WHA(30),    WHAM(30),
J     WHC(30),    WHCD(30),   WHCP(30),   WHEM(30),   WHGM(30),   WHGR(30),
K     WHLM(30),   WHM(30),    WHO(30),    WHOM(30),   WHTM(30),   WHUM(30)
C
C
C         THE FOLLOWING VECTORS ALLOCATE STORAGE FOR THE THREE
C         SURROUNDING LABOR FORCE GROUPS.  EACH VECTOR WILL CARRY THE
C         SURROUNDING LABOR FORCE LEVEL BY YEAR.
      DIMENSION MPSY(50), LSY(50), USY(50)
C         SET VECTORS
      MPSY(1) = 181304.
      LSY(1) = 300612.
      USY(1) = 21128.
      DO 3 I=2,50
      MPSY(I) = 1.022*MPSY(I-1)
      LSY(I) = 1.022*LSY(I-1)
    3 USY(I) = 1.022*USY(I-1)
C
C - - - - - - - - - - - - - - - - - - - - - - - - - - - - - - - -
C - - - URBAN DYNAMICS MODEL COMPUTATIONS - - - - - - - - - - - - - - -
C - - - - - - - - - - - - - - - - - - - - - - - - - - - - - - - -
C
C         THE MODEL COMPUTATIONS ARE ORGANIZED INTO FOUR SECTIONS:
C          -INITIALIZATION OF BASIC MODEL LEVEL VARIABLES
C          -INITIALIZATION OF COMPUTATION CONTROL LOOPS
C          -EQUATIONS FOR MODEL SECTORS
C          -PRINTING OF MODEL RESULTS
C         THE THIRD SECTION IS ORGANIZED INTO A NUMBER OF SUBSECTIONS WHICH
C         DEAL WITH DIFFERENT ASPECTS OF THE MODEL.  THE NUMBERS AT THE
C         RIGHT-HAND SIDE OF STATEMENTS REFER TO THE STATEMENT NUMBERS
C         WHICH FORRESTER USED FOR THE ANALOGOUS STATEMENT IN HIS DYNAMO
C         LANGUAGE VERSION OF THE MODEL.  SINCE A NUMBER OF THE STATEMENTS
C         IN THE FORTRAN VERSION HAVE NO ANALOGUE IN THE DYNAMO VERSION,
C         MANY FORTRAN STATEMENTS WILL NOT CARRY A STATEMENT NUMBER AT
C         THEIR RIGHT-HAND END.
C
C - - - - - - - - - - - - - - - - - - - - - - - - - - - - - - - -
C - - - INITIALIZATION OF BASIC MODEL LEVEL VARIABLES - - - - - - - - - - - -
C
C         POPULATION LEVELS: MANAGER-PROFESSIONAL (MP), LABOR (L), AND
C         UNDEREMPLOYED (U)
      MP(1) = 81335.                                            52.1 A
```

FIGURE 6   (continued)

```
                                                                    29.1 A
      L(1)  = 252814.                                               16.1 A
      U(1)  = 34541.
C
C          HOUSING LEVELS: PREMIUM HOUSING (PH), WORKER HOUSING (WH),
C          AND UNDEREMPLOYED HOUSING (UH).                          78.1 A
      PH(1) = 49122.                                                81.1 A
      WH(1) = 181155.                                               95.1 A
      UH(1) = 32364.
C
C          BUSINESS-INDUSTRY LEVELS: NEW ENTERPRISE (NE), MATURE BUSINESS
C          (MB), AND DECLINING INDUSTRY (DI).                       100.1 A
      NE(1) = 13824.                                                113.1 A
      MB(1) = 17280.                                                116.1 A
      DI(1) = 12096.
C
C - - - - - - - - - - - - - - - - - - - - - - - - - - - - - - - - - - - -
C - - - INITIALIZATION OF COMPUTATION CONTROL LOOPS - - - - - - - - - - -
C - - - - - - - - - - - - - - - - - - - - - - - - - - - - - - - - - - - -
C          HERE PARAMETERS ARE SET AND THE PRIMARY AND SECONDARY DO LOOPS
C          WHICH CONTROL THE COMPUTATION ARE INITIALIZED.
C
C          PRINT IS SET TO INDICATE THE NUMBER OF MODEL YEARS FOR WHICH
C          RESULTS ARE TO BE PRINTED.  FREQ IS SET TO INDICATE THE
C          FREQUENCY WITH WHICH RESULTS ARE TO BE PRINTED (I.E. THE
C          NUMBER OF MODEL YEARS COMPUTED BETWEEN PRINTINGS).  THE NUMBER
C          OF MODEL YEARS ACTUALLY COMPUTED WILL BE FREQ*(PRINT - 1) PLUS
C          THE ZEROTH YEAR.
C
      PRINT = 26
      FREQ = 1
      YEAR =0
C          DT--THE SOLUTION INTERVAL                                151
      DT = 1.
C
C          THE PRIMARY AND SECONDARY LOOPS ARE INITIALIZED
      DO 2200 I = 1, PRINT
      DO 2000 J = 1, FREQ
C
C          THE VALUES K, LST, AND NXT MUST BE COMPUTED SO THEY MAY BE
C          USED THROUGHOUT THE MODEL COMPUTATIONS TO REFERENCE THE CELLS
C          IN THE STORAGE VECTORS WHICH CORRESPOND TO THE YEAR BEING
C          COMPUTED, THE YEAR LAST COMPUTED, AND THE YEAR TO BE COMPUTED
C          NEXT.
      K = I
      LST = K - 1
      IF((J.GT.1).OR.(I.EQ.1)) LST = K
      NXT = K
      IF((J.EQ.FREQ).OR.(I.EQ.1)) NXT = K + 1
C                                                                      C
C          MPS LS, AND US ARE SET TO REPRESENT THE SURROUNDING         C
C          POPULATION FOR THE YEAR BEING COMPUTED.                     C
      YEAR = YEAR + 1                                                  C
      MPS = MPSY(YEAR)                                                 C
      LS = LSY(YEAR)                                                   C
      US = USY(YEAR)
```

FIGURE 6   (continued)

```
C
C - - - - - - - - - - - - - - - - - - - - - - - - - - - - - - - - - - - -
C - - - EQUATIONS FOR MODEL SECTORS - - - - - - - - - - - - - - - - - - - - -
C - - - - - - - - - - - - - - - - - - - - - - - - - - - - - - - - - - - -
C
C         THIS SECTION CONTAINS THE RELATIONSHIPS FOR THE MODEL SECTORS.
C         THE SECTION IS DIVIDED INTO THE FOLLOWING SUBSECTIONS:
C         -URBAN DEVELOPMENT PROGRAMS SECTOR
C         -TAX SECTOR
C         -CONSTRUCTION GOALS AND MULTIPLIERS
C         -JOB SECTOR
C         -UNDEREMPLOYMENT SECTOR
C         -LABOR SECTOR
C         -MANAGERIAL-PROFESSIONAL SECTOR
C         -PREMIUM HOUSING SECTOR
C         -WORKER HOUSING SECTOR
C         -UNDEREMPLOYED HOUSING SECTOR
C         -NEW ENTERPRISE SECTOR
C         -MATURE BUSINESS SECTOR
C         -DECLINING INDUSTRY SECTOR
C
C
C
C - - - URBAN DEVELOPMENT PROGRAMS SECTOR - - - - - - - - - - - - - - - - - -
C
C         THIS SECTION REPRESENTS A NUMBER OF URBAN DEVELOPMENT PROGRAMS
C         WHICH PROVIDE A MEANS OF TESTING THE INFLUENCE OF VARIOUS
C         EXTERNALLY SUPPORTED EFFORTS TO IMPROVE CONDITIONS.  THESE
C         PROGRAMS ARE NOT ACTIVATED HERE AND ARE ONLY INCLUDED FOR
C         COMPLETENESS.  PROGRAMS CAN BE ACTIVATED BY SETTING THE
C         APPROPRIATE PROGRAM PARAMETERS TO VALUES OTHER THAN ZERO.
C         THESE ARE THE URBAN PROGRAMS FORRESTER USED IN HIS ANALYSIS
C         OF THE IMPACT OF TRADITIONAL APPROACHES TO URBAN DEVELOPMENT.
C
C         INITIALIZATION OF PROGRAM PARAMETERS
      IF(K.GT.1) GO TO 50
      UTR = 0.                                                    140.1
      LTR =0.                                                     141.1
      PHCR = 0.                                                   142.1
      WHCR = 0.                                                   143.1
      SHDR = 0.                                                   144.1
      NECR = 0.                                                   145.1
      DIDR = 0.                                                   146.1
      TPCS = 0.                                                   147.1
      UJPC = 0.                                                   148.1
      LCHPC = 0.                                                  150.1
C
C         THE FOLLOWING ITEMS MUST BE COMPUTED PRIOR TO THE SECTOR
C         EQUATIONS, ALTHOUGH THE ITEMS LOGICALLY BELONG WITH OTHER
C         SECTORS.
C
   50 LPH = .088 - FLOAT(YEAR) * .000625                            *D
      IF (YEAR.GT.16) LPH=.078                                      *D
      LPP = .37 - FLOAT(YEAR) *  .0075                              *D
      IF(YEAR.GT.11) LPP=.287                                       *D
```

FIGURE 6   (continued)

```
C       (THE ABOVE FOUR LINES CORRESPOND TO FORRESTER EQUATIONS 69.1
C       AND 69.2.  IN STAGE 1 LPH=.09 AND LPP=.37 WERE USED, AND
C       IN STAGE 4 THESE PARAMETERS WERE MADE TO VARY WITH TIME.)          69.3 A
        AREA = 40154.                                                      70
   55 HUT(K) = PH(K) + WH(K) + UH(K)                                       71
        PUT(K) = NE(K) + MB(K) + DI(K)                                     69
        LFO(K) = (HUT(K)*LPH + PUT(K)*LPP) / AREA                          68
        PHLM(K) = TABLE(PHLMT,LFO(K),.0,1.,.1)                             68.1
        DATA PHLMT /.4,.9,1.3,1.6,1.8,1.9,1.8,1.4,.7,.2,.0/                86
        WHLM(K) = TABLE(WHLMT,LFO(K),.0,1.,.1)                             86.1
        DATA WHLMT /.4,.9,1.3,1.6,1.8,1.9,1.8,1.4,.7,.2,.0/                105
        ELM(K) = TABLE(ELMT,LFO(K),.0,1.,.1)                               105.1
        DATA ELMT /1.,1.15,1.3,1.4,1.45,1.4,1.3,1.,.7,.4,.0/
C
C           SECTOR EQUATIONS
C           (THE EQUATION FOR LOW-COST-HOUSING PROGRAM (LCHP) IS COMPUTED
C           IN THE JOB SECTOR SINCE IT DEPENDS ON VALUES COMPUTED THERE.)
C
C               UNDEREMPLOYED-TRAINING PROGRAM (UTP)                       140
C
        UTP(K) = UTR*U(K)
C
C               LABOR-TRAINING PROGRAM (LTPG)                             141
C
        LTPG(K) = LTR*L(K)
C
C               PREMIUM-HOUSING CONSTRUCTION PROGRAM (PHCP)               142
C
        PHCP(K) = PHCR*PH(K)*PHLM(K)
C
C               WORKER-HOUSING CONSTRUCTION PROGRAM (WHCP)                143
C
        WHCP(K) = WHCR*HUT(K)*WHLM(K)
C
C               SLUM-HOUSING-DEMOLITION PROGRAM (SHDP)                    144
C
        SHDP(K) = SHDR*UH(K)
C
C               NEW-ENTERPRISE-CONSTRUCTION PROGRAM (NECP)                145
C
        NECP(K) = NECR*PUT(K)*ELM(K)
C
C               DECLINING-INDUSTRY-DEMOLITION PROGRAM (DIDP)              146
C
        DIDP(K) = DIDR*DI(K)
C
C               TAX/PER-CAPITA-SUBSIDY PROGRAM (TPCSP)
C
        TPCSP(K) = TPCS
C
C               UNDEREMPLOYED-JOB PROGRAM (UJP)                           148
C
        UJP(K) = UJPC*U(K)
C
C           LOW-COST-HOUSING CONSTRUCTION DESIRED (LCHCD).  USED IN
C           COMPUTING LCHP IN JOB SECTOR.
C
        LCHCD(K) = LCHPC*U(K)*WHLM(K)
C
C
C
C - - - TAX SECTOR - - - - - - - - - - - - - - - - - - - - - - - - - - -
C
C           THE TAX COLLECTIONS (TC) ARE COMPUTED AS THE PRODUCT OF ASSESS-
C           ED VALUE (AV), WHICH INCLUDES BOTH BUSINESS ASSESSED VALUE
C
```

FIGURE 6 (continued)

```
C            (BAV) AND HOUSING ASSESSED VALUE (HAV), BY THE TAX ASSESSMENT
C            NORMAL (TAN), BY THE TAX RATIO (TR).  THE TAX RATIO HAS
C            INFLUENCE AT A NUMBER OF POINTS IN THE MODEL ON MOBILITY AND
C            CONSTRUCTION.
C
C - - - - INITIALIZATION
C
   100 IF(K.GT.1) GO TO 110
            TAN = 110.
            TRNPT = 30.                                                 121.1 A
            TMP = 475.                                                  123.2 B
            TLP = 275.                                                  126.1 A
            TUP = 400.                                                  126.2 A
            PHAV = 14.050                                               126.3 A
            WHAV = 4.700                                                129.1 A
            UHAV = 2.000                                                129.2 A
            NEAV = 30.4                                                 129.3 A
            MBAV = 22.6                                                 130.1 A
            DIAV = 9.1                                                  130.2 A
            MPFS = 1.79                                                 130.3 A
            LFS = 2.10                                                    9.1 A
            UFS = 2.52                                                    9.2 A
   110 CONTINUE                                                           9.3 A
C
C - - - - SECTOR EQUATIONS
C
            BAV(K) = NEAV*NE(K) + MBAV*MB(K) + DIAV*DI(K)               130
            HAV(K) = PHAV*PH(K) + WHAV*WH(K) + UHAV*UH(K)              129
            AV(K) = HAV(K) + BAV(K)                                    128
C            LABOR/UNDEREMPLOYED RATIO (LUR) IS COMPUTED AT THIS POINT
C            BECAUSE ITS NEEDED TO COMPUTE THE TAX COLLECTION MULTIPLIER
C            (TCM).
            LUR(K) = L(K) / U(K)                                       26
            TCM(K) = TABLE(TCMT,LUR(K),0.,3.,.5)                       127
            DATA TCMT /2.,1.6,1.3,1.1,1.,.9,.8/                        127.1
            TN(K) = (TMP*MPFS*MP(K) + TLP*LFS*L(K) + TUP*UFS*U(K)) * TCM(K)  126
            TAI(K) = TN(K)/AV(K)                                       125
            TRN(K) = TAI(K)/TAN                                        124
            IF(K.GT.1) GO TO 120
            TRNP(K) = TRN(K)
            GO TO 130                                                  123.1
   120 CONTINUE
            TRNP(K) = TRNP(LST) + (DT/TRNPT)*(TRNX - TRNP(LST))
   130 TRNX = TRN(K)                                                   123
            TR(K) = TABLE(TRT,1.44*ALOG(TRNP(K)),-2.,4.,1.)
            DATA TRT /.3,.5,1.,1.8,2.8,3.6,4./                         122
            TC(K) = AV(K)*TAN*TR(K)                                    122.1
C                                                                      121
C
C - - - CONSTRUCTION GOALS AND MULTIPLIERS  - - - - - - - - - - - - - - - -
C
C            THIS SECTION COMPUTES THE DESIRED LEVELS OF CONSTRUCTION
C            FOR PREMIUM HOUSING (PHCD), WORKER HOUSING (WHCD), AND NEW
C            ENTERPRISES (NECD).  IT IS NECESSARY TO COMPUTE THESE BEFORE
C            THE JOB SECTOR COMPUTATIONS.  AS A PRELIMINARY STEP TO
```

FIGURE 6   (continued)

```
C        COMPUTING THESE CONSTRUCTION GOALS, MULTIPLIERS PHM, WHM, AND
C        EM ARE COMPUTED FOR PREMIUM HOUSING, WORKER HOUSING, AND
C        ENTERPRISES, RESPECTIVELY.  THESE MULTIPLIERS WILL BE USED
C        LATER IN THE PREMIUM HOUSING, WORKER HOUSING, AND NEW
C        ENTERPRISE SECTORS.  THE MULTIPLIERS ARE DETERMINED FROM A
C        NUMBER OF ATTRACTIVENESS TERMS AND EXPRESS THE MULTIPLE OF
C        THE NORMAL LEVEL OF CONSTRUCTION DESIRED FOR THE SECTOR.
C
C - - - GROWTH RATES FOR HOUSING AND ENTERPRISES.
C        GROWTH RATES ARE COMPUTED FOR PREMIUM HOUSING (PHGR), WORKER
C        HOUSING (WHGR), AND NEW ENTERPRISES (NEGR).  THESE ARE ALL
C        COMPUTED BY THE SAME BASIC RELATIONSHIP, WHICH CONSISTS OF
C        SUBTRACTING AN EARLIER VALUE OF HOUSING OR ENTERPRISE LEVEL
C        (PHA, WHA, NEA) FROM THE PRESENT LEVEL (PH, WH, NE) AND
C        DIVIDING THIS DIFFERENCE BY A TIME DELAY (PHAT, WHAT, NEAT)
C        AND BY THE PRESENT LEVEL (PH, WH, NE) TO CONVERT IT TO A
C        FRACTIONAL GROWTH RATE.

C        FOR THE INITIAL YEAR CERTAIN VALUES MUST BE SET OR COMPUTED
         IF(K.GT.1) GO TO 210                                              77.2 B
         PHAT = 10.                                                        92.2 B
         WHAT = 10.                                                       110.2 B
         NEAT = 10.                                                        77.3 B
         PHGRI = .017                                                      92.3 B
         WHGRI = .017                                                     110.3 B
         NEGRI = .119                                                      77.1
         PHA(K) = PH(K) - PHGRI*PHAT*PH(K)                                 92.1
         WHA(K) = WH(K) - WHGRI*WHAT*WH(K)                                110.1
         NEA(K) = NE(K) - NEGRI*NEAT*NE(K)
         GO TO 215
C
C        THE AVERAGE LEVELS OF HOUSING AND NEW ENTERPRISE ARE
C        COMPUTED FOR ALL YEARS EXCEPT THE FIRST BY THE FOLLOWING
C        FORMULA.  NOTE THAT THE PREVIOUS LEVELS OF PH, WH, AND NE
C        ARE STORED IN PHX, WHX, AND NEX, RESPECTIVELY, SO THEY WILL
C        BE AVAILABLE FOR USE IN COMPUTING THE NEXT YEAR.
  210 PHA(K) = PHA(LST) + (DT/PHAT)*(PHX - PHA(LST))                       77
      WHA(K) = WHA(LST) + (DT/WHAT)*(WHX - WHA(LST))                       92
      NEA(K) = NEA(LST) + (DT/NEAT)*(NEX - NEA(LST))                      110
C
  215 PHX = PH(K)
      WHX = WH(K)
      NEX = NE(K)
C
      PHGR(K) = (PH(K) - PHA(K)) / (PH(K)*PHAT)                            76
      WHGR(K) = (WH(K) - WHA(K)) / (WH(K)*WHAT)                            91
      NEGR(K) = (NE(K) - NEA(K)) / (NE(K)*NEAT)                           109
C
C        PREMIUM-HOUSING MULTIPLIER (PHM) IS COMPUTED AS THE PRODUCT
C        OF SIX TERMS-
C            PHAM - PREMIUM-HOUSING-ADEQUACY MULTIPLIER
C            PHLM - PREMIUM-HOUSING LAND MULTIPLIER
C            PHPM - PREMIUM-HOUSING POPULATION MULTIPLIER
C            PHTM - PREMIUM-HOUSING TAX MULTIPLIER
C            PHEM - PREMIUM-HOUSING ENTERPRISE MULTIPLIER
```

FIGURE 6   (continued)

```
C              PHGM - PREMIUM-HOUSING-GROWTH MULTIPLIER
C          IN ADDITION A PREMIUM HOUSING FACTOR (PHF) IS INCLUDED IN
C          THE EQUATION AS A TECHNICAL PARAMETER WHICH PERMITS
C          SENSITIVITY EXPERIMENTATION WITH THE EFFECT OF THIS
C          EQUATION.  THE SIX FACTORS WHICH CONTRIBUTE TO PHM ARE
C          COMPUTED BELOW, EXCEPT PHLM WHICH WAS COMPUTED EARLIER
C          BECAUSE IT IS USED IN THE URBAN DEVELOPMENT PROGRAMS SECTOR.
C
      PHF = 1.                                                      66.1
      PHPD = 3.05 - (FLOAT(YEAR) - 1.) * .02                          *D
      IF(YEAR.GT.21) PHPD=2.65                                        *D
C     (THE ABOVE TWO LINES CORRESPOND TO FORRESTER EQUATION 61.1.
C       IN STAGE 1 PHPD=3.05 WAS USED, IN STAGE 4 THIS PARAMETER WAS
C       MADE TO VARY OVER TIME.)
  220 MHR(K) = (MP(K)*MPFS) / (PH(K)*PHPD)                          61
      PHAM(K) = TABLE(PHAMT,MHR(K),.0,2.,.25)                       67
      DATA PHAMT /.0,.001,.01,.2,1.,3.,4.6,5.6,6./                  67.1
      MPR(K) = MP(K) / (L(K) + U(K))                                58
      PHPM(K) = TABLE(PHPMT,MPR(K),.0,.1,.02)                       72
      DATA PHPMT /.3,.7,1.,1.2,1.3,1.3/                             72.1
      PHTM(K) = TABLE(PHTMT,1.44*ALOG(TR(K)),-2.,4.,2.)             73
      DATA PHTMT /1.2,1.,,.7,.3/                                    73.1
      PHEM(K) = TABLE(PHEMT,NEGR(K),-.1,.15,.05)                    74
      DATA PHEMT/.2,.6,1.,1.4,1.8,2.2/                              74.1
      PHGM(K) = TABLE(PHGMT,PHGR(K),-.1,.15,.05)                    75
      DATA PHGMT /.2,.6,1.,1.4,1.8,2.2/                             75.1
      PHM(K) = PHAM(K) * PHPM(K) * PHEM(K) * PHGM(K) * PHF          66   D
C
C          PREMIUM-HOUSING CONSTRUCTION DESIRED (PHCD) IS COMPUTED AS
C          THE PRODUCT OF PREMIUM-HOUSING CONSTRUCTION NORMAL (PHCN),
C          THE CURRENT LEVEL OF PREMIUM HOUSING (PH), AND THE PREMIUM
C          HOUSING MULTIPLIER (PHM), JUST COMPUTED.  IN ADDITION AN
C          EXTERNALLY IMPOSED PREMIUM-HOUSING CONSTRUCTION PROGRAM CAN
C          BE ADDED THROUGH THE TERM PHCP, FROM THE URBAN DEVELOPMENT
C          PROGRAMS SECTOR.
      IF(K.GT.1) GO TO 225
      PHCN = .017                                                   65.1 B
  225 PHCD(K) = PHCN*PH(K)*PHM(K) + PHCP(K)                         65
C
C
C          WORKER-HOUSING MULTIPLIER (WHM) IS COMPUTED IN THE SAME WAY
C          AS THE PREMIUM-HOUSING MULTIPLIER WAS ABOVE, AS THE PRODUCT
C          OF SIX TERMS -
C              WHAM - WORKER-HOUSING-ADEQUACY MULTIPLIER
C              WHLM - WORKER-HOUSING LAND MULTIPLIER
C              WHUM - WORKER-HOUSING UNDEREMPLOYED MULTIPLIER
C              WHTM - WORKER-HOUSING TAX MULTIPLIER
C              WHEM - WORKER-HOUSING ENTERPRISE MULTIPLIER
C              WHGM - WORKER-HOUSING GROWTH MULTIPLIER
C          IN ADDITION A WORKER HOUSING FACTOR (WHF) IS INCLUDED IN THE
C          EQUATION AS A TECHNICAL PARAMETER WHICH PERMITS SENSITIVITY
C          EXPERIMENTATION WITH THE EFFECTS OF THIS EQUATION.  THE SIX
C          FACTORS WHICH CONTRIBUTE TO WHM ARE COMPUTED BELOW, EXCEPT
C          WHLM WHICH WAS COMPUTED EARLIER BECAUSE IT WAS USED IN THE
C          URBAN DEVELOPMENT PROGRAMS SECTOR.
```

FIGURE 6   (continued)

```
C                                                                        84.1
      WHF = 1.
      WHPD = 3.03 - (FLOAT(YEAR) - 1.) * .02                              *D
      IF(YEAR.GT.21) WHPD=2.63                                           *D
C     (THE ABOVE TWO LINES CORRESPOND TO FORRESTER EQUATION 48.1.
C      IN STAGE 1 WHPD=3.03 WAS USED, IN STAGE 4 THIS PARAMETER WAS
C      MADE TO VARY OVER TIME.)
C
  230 LHR(K) = (L(K)*LFS) / (WH(K)*WHPD)                                  48
      WHAM(K) = TABLE(WHAMT,LHR(K),.0,2.,.25)                             85
      DATA WHAMT /.0,.05,.1,.3,1.,1.8,2.4,2.8,3./                        85.1
      WHUM(K) = TABLE(WHUMT,LUR(K),5.,10.,1.)                            87    D
      DATA WHUMT /.5,.8,1.,1.2,1.3,1.3/                                  87.1
      WHTM(K) = TABLE(WHTMT,1.44*ALOG(TR(K)),-2.,4.,2.)                  88
      DATA WHTMT /1.2,1.,.7,.3/                                          88.1
      WHEM(K) = TABLE(WHEMT,NEGR(K),-.2,.3,.1)                           89
      DATA WHEMT /.3,.7,1.,1.2,1.3,1.4/                                  89.1
      WHGM(K) = TABLE(WHGMT,WHGR(K),-.1,.15,.05)                         90
      DATA WHGMT /.2,.6,1.,1.4,1.8,2.2/                                  90.1
      WHM(K) = WHAM(K) * WHUM(K) * WHEM(K) * WHGM(K) * WHF               84    D
C
C             WORKER-HOUSING CONSTRUCTION DESIRED (WHCD) IS COMPUTED AS
C             THE PRODUCT OF WORKER HOUSING CONSTRUCTION NORMAL (WHCN),
C             THE CURRENT LEVEL OF WORJER HOUSING (WH), AND THE WORKER
C             HOUSING MULTIPLIER (WHM) JUST COMPUTED.  IN ADDITION AN
C             EXTERNALLY IMPOSED WORKER HOUSING CONSTRUCTION PROGRAM CAN BE
C             ADDED THROUGH THE TERM WHCP, FROM THE URBAN DEVELOPMENT
C             PROGRAMS SECTOR.
      IF(K.GT.1) GO TO 235
      WHCN = .017                                                        83.1  B
  235 WHCD(K) = WHCN*WH(K)*WHIM(K) + WHCP(K)                             83
C
C             ENTERPRISE MULTIPLIER (EM) IS COMPUTED AS THE PRODUCT OF FIVE
C             TERMS -
C                 EMM - ENTERPRISE MANAGER/JOB MULTIPLIER
C                 ELM - ENTERPRISE LAND MULTIPLIER
C                 ELJM - ENTERPRISE LABOR/JOB MULTIPLIER
C                 ETM - EMTERPRISE TAX MULTIPLIER
C                 EGM - ENTERPRISE-GROWTH MULTIPLIER
C             IN ADDITION AN ENTERPRISE FACTOR (EF) IS INCLUDED IN THE
C             EQUATION AS A TECHNICAL PARAMETER WHICH PERMITS SENSITIVITY
C             EXPERIMENTATION WITH THE EFFECTS OF THIS EQUATION.  THE FIVE
C             FACTORS WHICH CONTRIBUTE TO EM ARE COMPUTED BELOW EXCEPT
C             ELM WHICH WAS COMPUTED EARLIER FOR USE IN THE URBAN
C             DEVELOPMENT PROGRAMS SECTOR.
C
      IF(K.GT.1) GO TO 240                                               103.1
      EF = 1.                                                            37.1  A
      NEM = 3.1                                                          37.2  A
      MBM = 1.8                                                          37.3  A
      DIM = .6                                                           139.2 B
      LRPT = 5.                                                          37
  240 MJ(K) = NE(K)*NEM + MB(K)*MBM + DI(K)*DIM                          36    C
      MR(K) = (MPS + MP(K)) / (MPS + MJ(K))                             104
      EMM(K) = TABLE(EMMT,MR(K),.0,2.,.25)
```

FIGURE 6   (continued)

```
      DATA EMMT /.1,.15,.3,.5,1.,1.4,1.7,1.9,2./              104.1
      LRP(K) = LRP(LST) + (DT/LRPT)*(LR(LST) - LRP(LST))      139
      IF(K.EQ.1) LRP(K) = 1.                                  139.1 A
      ELJM(K) = TABLE(ELJMT,LRP(K),.0,2.,.25)                 106
      DATA ELJMT /.0,.05,.15,.4,1.,1.5,1.7,1.8,1.8/           106.1
      ETM(K) = TABLE(ETMT,1.44*ALOG(TR(K)),-2.,4.,1.)         107
      DATA ETMT /1.3,1.2,1.,.8,.5,.25,.1/                     107.1
      EGM(K) = TABLE(EGMT,NEGR(K),-.1,.15,.05)                108
      DATA EGMT /.2,.6,1.0,1.10,1.12,1.18/                    108.1 D
      EM(K) = EMM(K) * ELJM(K) * EGM(K) * EF                  103   D
C
C
C           NEW ENTERPRISE CONSTRUCTION DESIRED (NECD) IS COMPUTED AS
C           THE PRODUCT OF NEW ENTERPRISE CONSTRUCTION NORMAL (NECN), A
C           WEIGHTED SUM OF THE THREE CURRENT LEVELS OF ENTERPRISES
C           (NE, MB, DI), AND THE ENTERPRISE MULTIPLIER (EM) JUST
C           COMPUTED.  IN ADDITION AN EXTERNALLY IMPOSED ENTERPRISE
C           CONSTRUCTION PROGRAM CAN BE ADDED THROUGH THE TERM NECP, FROM
C           THE URBAN DEVELOPMENT PROGRAMS SECTOR.
      IF(K.GT.1) GO TO 245
      NECN = .063                                             102.4 B
      NECF = 1.                                               102.1 B
      MBCF = .5                                               102.2 B
      DICF = .3                                               102.3 B
  245 NECD(K) = NECN*(NECF*NE(K) + MBCF*MB(K) + DICF*DI(K))*EM(K)
     1  + NECP(K)                                             102
C
C - - - JOB SECTOR - - - - - - - - - - - - - - - - - - - - - - - - - - - - - -
C
C           IN THIS SECTOR EMPLOYMENT RATIOS FOR LABOR AND UNDEREMPLOYED
C           CATEGORIES ARE COMPUTED.  A LABOR CONSTRUCTION RATIO (LCR) IS
C           COMPUTED FOR LATER USE IN THE HOUSING SECTOR TO CONSTRAIN
C           CONSTRUCTION TO THE LABOR SUPPLY.
C
C           INITIALIZATIONS
      IF(K.GT.1) GO TO 310
C           PREMIUM-HOUSING, WORKER-HOUSING, NEW ENTERPRISE, AND LOW-COST-
C           HOUSING CONSTRUCTION LABOR (PHCL, WHCL, NECL, LCHCL), EXPRESS-
C           ED IN MAN-YEARS/HOUSING UNIT.
      PHCL = 1.7                                              131.1 B
      WHCL = .6                                               131.2 B
      NECL = 3.4                                              131.3 B
      LCHCL = .6                                              131.4
C           NEW-ENTERPRISE, MATURE-BUSINESS, AND DECLINING-INDUSTRY LABOR
C           (NEL, MBL, DIL), EXPRESSED IN MEN/PRODUCTIVE UNIT.
      NEL = 6.2                                               132.1 A
      MBL = 5.5                                               132.2 A
      DIL = 2.5                                               132.3 A
C
C           SECTOR EQUATIONS
C
C           TOTAL LABOR JOBS (LJ) ARE DETERMINED BY COMPUTING AND THEN
C           SUMMING THE LABOR DESIRED FOR CONSTRUCTION (LDC) AND LABOR
C           DESIRED FOR INDUSTRY (LDI).
  310 LDC(K) = PHCD(K)*PHCL + WHCD(K)*WHCL + NECD(K)*NECL
```

FIGURE 6   (continued)

```
     1   + LCHCD(K)*LCHCL                                              131
         LDI(K) = NE(K)*NEL + MB(K)*MBL + DI(K)*DIL                    132
         LJ(K) = LDC(K) + LDI(K)                                       133
C
C           LABOR/JOB RATIO (LR)
         LR(K) = (LS + L(K)) / (LS + LJ(K))                            134   C
C
C           UNDEREMPLOYED JOBS (UJ) ARE COMPUTED AS A FUNCTION OF THE
C           LABOR/JOB RATIO JUST COMPUTED PLUS UNDEREMPLOYED-JOB PROGRAM
C           (UJP) JOBS.
         ULJR(K) = TABLE(ULJRT,LR(K),.0,2.,.5)                         135
         DATA ULJRT /1.,.5,.09,.05,.02/                                135.1 D
         UJ(K) = LJ(K)*ULJR(K) + UJP(K)                                136
C
C           UNDEREMPLOYED/JOB RATIO (UR)
         UR(K) = (US + U(K)) / (US + UJ(K))                            137   C
C
C           LABOR CONSTRUCTION RATIO (LCR) EXPRESSES THE INFLUENCE OF
C           AVAILABLE LABOR ON HOUSING AND ENTERPRISE CONSTRUCTION.
         LCR(K) = TABLE(LCRT,LR(K),.0,2.,.5)                           138
         DATA LCRT /.0,.5,.9,1.1,1.15/                                 138.1
C           LOW-COST-HOUSING PROGRAM (LCHP) WHICH BELONGS WITH THE
C           URBAN DEVELOPMENT PROGRAMS SECTOR CAN NOW BE COMPUTED.
         LCHP(K) = LCHCD(K)*LCR(K)                                     149
C
C           LABOR/JOB RATIO PERCEIVED (LRP) WHICH BELONGS WITH THIS SECTOR
C           WAS COMPUTED EARLIER FOR USE IN ABOVE SECTORS.
C
C
C
C
C
C - - - UNDEREMPLOYED SECTOR - - - - - - - - - - - - - - - - - - - - - - - -
C
C           THE NUMBER OF UNDEREMPLOYED (U) FOR A PERIOD IS REPRESENTED AS
C           THE LEVEL OF UNDEREMPLOYED IN THE PREVIOUS PERIOD PLUS THE
C           CHANGE IN THE LEVEL OF UNDEREMPLOYED POPULATION DUE TO THE
C           FOLLOWING FIVE RATES OF FLOW DURING THE PREVIOUS PERIOD--
C             UA - UNDEREMPLOYED ARRIVALS
C             UB - UNDEREMPLOYED BIRTHS
C             LTU - LABOR TO UNDEREMPLOYED
C             UD - UNDEREMPLOYED DEPARTURES
C             UTL - UNDEREMPLOYED TO LABOR.
C           EACH OF THESE FLOWS IS COMPUTED IN TURN BELOW AND THEN THE
C           UNDEREMPLOYED LEVEL FOR THE NEXT PERIOD IS COMPUTED.
C
C           INITIALIZATIONS
         IF(K.GT.1) GO TO 410
C           PERCEPTION TIMES--FOR UNDEREMPLOYED TO LABOR (UTLPT),
C           ATTRACTIVENESS-FOR MIGRATION MULTIPLIER (AMMPT), UNDEREMPLOYED
C           MOBILITY MULTIPLIER(UMMPT).
         UTLPT = 10.                                                   20.2 B
         AMMPT = 20.                                                   2.2 B
         UMMPT = 10.                                                   22.2 B
C           UNDEREMPLOYED NORMAL RATES--FOR ARRIVALS (UAN), DEPARTURES
```

FIGURE 6 (continued)

```
C          (UDN), MOBILITY (UMN).
       UAN = .039                                                        1.1 B
       UDN = .067                                                        13.1 B
       UMN = .1                                                          17.1 B
C          TAX PER CAPITA NORMAL
       TPCN = 330.                                                       8.1  B
C          UNDEREMPLOYED BIRTH RATE
       UBR = .016                                                        15.1 B
C          SENSITIVITY EXPERIMENTATION FACTORS--FOR ATTRACTIVENESS FOR
C          MIGRATION (AMF) AND UNDEREMPLOYED MOBILITY (UMF).
       AMF = 1.                                                          3.1
       UMF = 1.                                                          23.1
  410 CONTINUE
C          UNDEREMPLOYMENT-HOUSING POPULATION DENSITY (UHPD)
       UHPD = 3.03 - (FLOAT(YEAR) - 1.) * .02                            *D
       IF(YEAR.GT.21) UHPD=2.63                                          *D
C     (THE ABOVE TWO LINES CORRESPOND TO FORRESTER EQUATION 6.1.
C     IN STAGE 1 UHPD=3.03 WAS USED, IN STAGE 4 THIS PARAMETER WAS
C     MADE TO VARY OVER TIME.)
C
C
C          SECTOR EQUATIONS
C
C          UNDEREMPLOYED ARRIVALS (UA)
C          THE ATTRACTIVENESS-FOR-MIGRATION MULTIPLIER (AMM) IS COMPUTED
C          FOR USE IN DETERMINING UNDEREMPLOYED ARRIVALS (UA) AND FOR
C          USE LATER IN DETERMINING UNDEREMPLOYED DEPARTURES (UD).  AMM
C          IS THE PRODUCT OF SIX FACTORS--UNDEREMPLOYED-ARRIVALS-
C          MOBILITY MULTIPLIER (UAMM), UNDEREMPLOYED/HOUSING MULTIPLIER
C          (UHM), PUBLIC-EXPENDITURE MULTIPLIER (PEM), UNDEREMPLOYED/
C          JOB MULTIPLIER (UJM), UNDEREMPLOYED-HOUSING-PROGRAM
C          MULTIPLIER (UHPM), AND ATTRACTIVENESS FOR MIGRATION FACTOR
C          (AMF), FOR SENSITIVITY EXPERIMENTATION.
       UTLP(K) = UTLP(LST) + (DT/UTLPT)*(UTL(LST) - UTLP(LST))           20
       IF(K.EQ.1) UTLP(K) = 1727.                                       20.1 A
       UM(K) = UTLP(K) / U(K)                                           21
       UAMM(K) = TABLE(UAMMT,UM(K),.0,.15,.025)                         4
       DATA UAMMT /.3,.7,1.,1.2,1.3,1.4,1.5/                            4.1
       UHR(K) = (U(K)*UFS) / (UH(K)*UHPD)                               6
       UHM(K) = TABLE(UHMT,UHR(K),.0,2.,.25)                            5
       DATA UHMT /2.5,2.4,2.2,1.7,1.,.4,.2,.1,.05/                      5.1
       P(K) = MP(K)*MPFS + L(K)*LFS + U(K)*UFS                          9
       TPCR(K) = ((TC(K)/P(K)) + TPCSP(K))/TPCN                         8
       PEM(K) = TABLE(PEMT,TPCR(K),.0,3.,.5)                            7
       DATA PEMT /.2,.6,1.,1.6,2.4,3.2,4./                              7.1
       UJM(K) = TABLE(UJMT,UR(K),.0,3.,.25)                             10
       DATA UJMT /2.,2.,1.9,1.6,1.,.6,.4,.3,.2,.15,.1,.05,.02/          10.1
       UHPR(K) = LCHP(K) / U(K)                                         12
       UHPM(K) = TABLE(UHPMT,UHPR(K),.0,.05,.01)                        11
       DATA UHPMT /1.,1.2,1.5,1.9,2.4,3./                               11.1
C          SAVE AMM(LST) FOR USE JUST BELOW IN COMPUTING AMMP(K).
       AMMLST = AMM(LST)
       AMM(K) = UAMM(K)*UHM(K)*PEM(K)*UJM(K)*UHPM(K)*AMF                3
C          ATTRACTIVENESS-FOR-MIGRATION MULTIPLIER PERCEIVED (AMMP) AND
C          THE UNDEREMPLOYED ARRIVALS (UA) CAN BE DETERMINED.
       AMMP(K) = AMMP(LST) + (DT/AMMPT)*(AMMLST - AMMP(LST))            2
```

FIGURE 6   (continued)

```
      IF(K.EQ.1) AMMP(K) = 1.                                           2.1 A
      UA(K) = U(K) * UAN * AMMP(K)                                      1   D
C
C        UNDEREMPLOYED BIRTHS (UB)
C           BIRTHS ARE COMPUTED BY APPLYING A NET BIRTH RATE TO THE
C           UNDEREMPLOYED POPULATION.
      UB(K) = U(K) * UBR                                                15
C
C        LABOR TO UNDEREMPLOYED
C           THE FLOW OF LABOR TO UNDEREMPLOYED (LTU) DEPENDS ON THE
C           LABOR-LAYOFF FRACTION (LLF) WHICH DEPENDS IN TURN ON THE
C           PREVIOUSLY COMPUTED LABOR/JOB RATIO (LR).
      LLF(K) = TABLE(LLFT,LR(K),.0,2.,.5)                               31
      DATA LLFT /.0,.005,.015,.05,.15/                                  31.1 D
      LTU(K) = L(K) * LLF(K)                                            30
C
C        UNDEREMPLOYED DEPARTURES (UD)
C           UD DEPENDS ON THE UNDEREMPLOYED (U) POPULATION, A RATE OF
C           UNDEREMPLOYED DEPARTURES NORMAL (UDN), AND AN UNDEREMPLOYED-
C           DEPARTURE MULTIPLIER (UDM).  UDM DEPENDS ON THE PREVIOUSLY
C           COMPUTED ATTRACTIVENESS-FOR-MIGRATION MULTIPLIER (AMM).
      UDM(K) = TABLE(UDMT,1.44*ALOG(AMM(K)),-3.,3.,1.)                  14
      DATA UDMT /8.,4.,2.,1.,.5,.25,.125/                               14.1
      UD(K) = UDN * U(K) * UDM(K)                                       13
C        UNDEREMPLOYED TO LABOR (UTL)
C           THE UNDEREMPLOYED-MOBILITY MULTIPLIER (UMM) IS FIRST
C           COMPUTED FOR USE IN DETERMINING UTL.  UMM IS THE PRODUCT OF
C           FOUR FACTORS--LABOR-SUPPLY MULTIPLIER (LSM), LABOR/UNDER-
C           EMPLOYED MULTIPLIER (LUM), UNDEREMPLOYMENT EDUCATIONAL
C           MULTIPLIER (UEM), AND UNDEREMPLOYED-MOBILITY FACTOR (UMF),
C           FOR SENSITIVITY EXPERIMENTATION.
      LSM(K) = TABLE(LSMT,LR(K),.0,2.,.5)                               24
      DATA LSMT /2.4,2.,1.,.4,.2/                                       24.1
      LUM(K) = TABLE(LUMT,LUR(K),.0,5.,1.)                              25
      DATA LUMT /.2,.7,1.,1.2,1.3,1.4/                                  25.1
      UEM(K) = TABLE(UEMT,TPCR(K),.0,3.,.5)                             27
      DATA UEMT /.2,.7,1.,1.3,1.5,1.6,1.7/                              27.1
C           SAVE UMM(LST) FOR USE JUST BELOW IN COMPUTING UMMP(K)
      UMMLST = UMM(LST)
      UMM(K) = LSM(K)*LUM(K)*UEM(K)*UMF                                 23
C           UNDEREMPLOYED-MOBILITY MULTIPLIER PERCEIVED (UMMP) CAN BE
C           DETERMINED.
      UMMP(K) = UMMP(LST) + (DT/UMMPT)*(UMMLST - UMMP(LST))             22
      IF(K.EQ.1) UMMP(K) = 1.                                          22.1 A
C           UNDEREMPLOYED TO LABOR (UTL) DEPENDS ON THE UNDEREMPLOYED
C           WORKING (UW), UNDEREMPLOYED MOBILITY NORMAL (UMN) RATE, AND
C           THE UNDEREMPLOYED- MOBILITY MULTIPLIER PERCEIVED (UMMP).  IN
C           ADDITION THE UNDEREMPLOYED-TRAINING PROGRAM (UTP) MAY PROVIDE
C           AN INCREMENT TO LABOR FROM THE UNDEREMPLOYED.
      UFW(K) = TABLE(UFWT,UR(K),.0,4.,1.)                               19
      DATA UFWT /.9,.8,.5,.33,.25/                                      19.1
      UW(K) = U(K) * UFW(K)                                            18
      UTL(K) = UMN*UW(K)*UMMP(K) + UTP(K)                              17
C
C        UNDEREMPLOYED (U) MAY NOW BE DETERMINED.
```

FIGURE 6   (continued)

```
        U(NXT) = U(K) + DT*(UA(K) + UB(K) + LTU(K) - UD(K) - UTL(K))        16
C
C               UNDEREMPLOYED TO LABOR NET (UTLN) MAY NOW BE COMPUTED--THIS
C               HAS NO FUNCTION EXCEPT OUTPUT
        UTLN(K) = UTL(K) - LTU(K)                                           154
C
C
C - - - LABOR SECTOR  - - - - - - - - - - - - - - - - - - - - - - - - - - - - - -
C
C               THE LABOR (L), OR SKILLED WORKERS, ARE REPRESENTED BY THE SAME
C               TYPE OF FUNCTIONAL FORM AS THE UNDEREMPLOYED WERE ABOVE.  THE
C               LABOR FOR A PERIOD IS EQUAL TO THE LABOR LEVEL OF THE PREVIOUS
C               PERIOD PLUS THE CHANGE IN LEVEL DUE TO THE FOLLOWING SIX RATES
C               OF FLOW DURING THE PREVIOUS PERIOD -
C                  UTL - UNDEREMPLOYED TO LABOR
C                  LB - LABOR BIRTHS
C                  LTM - LABOR TO MANAGER
C                  LA - LABOR ARRIVALS
C                  LD - LABOR DEPARTURES
C                  LTU - LABOR TO UNDEREMPLOYED
C               TWO OF THESE RATES, UTL AND LTU, WERE COMPUTED IN THE UNDER-
C               EMPLOYED SECTOR.  THE OTHER FOUR ARE COMPUTED HERE.
C
C                  INITIALIZATIONS
        IF(K.GT.1) GO TO 510
C                  PERCEPTION TIMES--FOR LABOR-MOBILITY-MULTIPLIER PERCEPTION
C                  TIME (LMMPT) AND LABOR-ARRIVAL-MULTIPLIER PERCEPTION TIME
C                  (LAMP).
        LMMPT = 15.                                                        33.2 B
        LAMPT = 15.                                                        42.2 B
C                  LABOR NORMAL RATES--FOR ARRIVALS (LAN), DEPARTURES (LDN),
C                  AND MOBILITY (LMN).
        LAN = .026                                                         41.1 B
        LDN = .044                                                         49.1 B
        LMN = .01                                                          32.1*D
C       (IN STAGE 1 LMN=.02 WAS USED WHICH IS FORRESTER VALUE)
C                  UNDEREMPLOYED BIRTH RATE
        LBR = .013                                                         28.1 B
C                  SENSITIVITY EXPERIMENTATION FACTORS--FOR LABOR MOBILITY (LMF)
C                  AND LABOR ARRIVALS (LAF).
        LMF = 1.                                                           34.1
        LAF = 1.                                                           43.1
    510 CONTINUE
C
C                  LABOR BIRTHS (LB)
C                  BIRTHS ARE COMPUTED BY APPLYING A NET BIRTH RATE TO THE
C                  LABOR POPULATION.
        LB(K) = L(K) * LBR                                                  28
C
C                  LABOR TO MANAGER (LTM)
C                  THE LABOR-MOBILITY MULTIPLIER (LMM) IS FIRST COMPUTED FOR
C                  USE IN COMPUTING LTM.  LMM IS THE PRODUCT OF FOUR FACTORS--
C                  MANAGER-SUPPLY MULTIPLIER (MSM), MANAGER/LABOR MULTIPLIER
C                  (MLM), LABOR EDUCATIONAL MULTIPLIER (LEM), AND LABOR-
```

FIGURE 6   (continued)

```
C            MOBILITY FACTOR (LMF), FOR SENSITIVITY EXPERIMENTATION.
      MSM(K) = TABLE(MSMT,MR(K),.0,2,.25)                              35
      DATA MSMT /2.3,2.2,2.,1.6,1.,.5,.2,.1,.05/                       35.1
      MLR(K) = MP(K) / L(K)                                           39
      MLM(K) = TABLE(MLMT,MLR(K),.0,.2,.05)                           38
      DATA MLMT /.2,.7,1.,1.2,1.3/                                    38.1
      LEM(K) = TABLE(LEMT,TPCR(K),.0,3.,.5)                           40
      DATA LEMT /.2,.7,1.,1.3,1.5,1.6,1.7/                            40.1
C            SAVE LMM(LST) FOR USE JUST BELOW IN COMPUTING LMMP(K).
      LMMLST = LMM(LST)
      LMM(K) = MSM(K)*MLM(K)*LEM(K)*LMF                               34
C            LABOR-MOBILITY MULTIPLIER PERCEIVED (LMMP) CAN NOW BE
C            DETERMINED.
      LMMP(K) = LMMP(LST) + (DT/LMMPT)*(LMMLST - LMMP(LST))           33
      IF(K.EQ.1) LMMP(K) = 1.                                         33.1 A
C            LABOR TO MANAGER (LTM) DEPENDS ON THE LABOR (L) LEVEL,
C            LABOR MOBILITY NORMAL (LMN) RATE, AND THE LABOR-MOBILITY
C            MULTIPLIER PERCEIVED (LMMP).  IN ADDITION THE LABOR-TRAINING
C            PROGRAM (LTPG) MAY CONTRIBUTE.
      LTM(K) = LMN*L(K)*LMMP(K) + LTPG(K)                             32
C
C         LABOR ARRIVALS (LA)
C            THE LABOR-ARRIVAL MULTIPLIER (LAM) IS COMPUTED FOR USE IN
C            DETERMINING LABOR ARRIVALS (LA) AND FOR LATER USE IN
C            COMPUTING LABOR DEPARTURES (LD).  LAM IS THE PRODUCT OF FIVE
C            FACTORS--LABOR-ARRIVAL JOB MULTIPLIER (LAJM), LABOR-ARRIVAL
C            UNDEREMPLOYED MULTIPLIER (LAUM), LABOR-ARRIVAL TAX
C            MULTIPLIER (LATM), LABOR-ARRIVAL HOUSING MULTIPLIER (LAHM),
C            AND LABOR-ARRIVAL FACTOR (LAF), FOR SENSITIVITY TESTING.
C
      LAJM(K) = TABLE(LAJMT,LR(K),.0,2.,.25)                          44
      DATA LAJMT /2.6,2.6,2.4,1.8,1.,.4,.2,.1,.05/                    44.1
      LAUM(K) = TABLE(LAUMT,LUR(K),4.,9.,1.)                          45    D
      DATA LAUMT /.4,.8,1.,1.2,1.3,1.3/                               45.1
      LATM(K) = TABLE(LATMT,1.44*ALOG(TR(K)),-2.,4.,2.)              46
      DATA LATMT /1.2,1.,.7,.3/                                       46.1
      LAHM(K) = TABLE(LAHMT,LHR(K),.0,3.,.5)                          47
      DATA LAHMT /1.3,1.2,1.,.5,.2,.1,.05/                            47.1
C            SAVE LAM(LST) FOR USE JUST BELOW IN COMPUTING LAMP(K).
      LAMLST = LAM(LST)
      LAM(K) = LAJM(K) * LAUM(K) * LATM(K) * LAHM(K) * LAF            43
C
C            LABOR-ARRIVAL MULTIPLIER PERCEIVED (LAMP) AND THE LABOR
C            ARRIVALS (LA) CAN NOW BE COMPUTED.
      LAMP(K) = LAMP(LST) + (DT/LAMPT)*(LAMLST - LAMP(LST))           42
      IF(K.EQ.1) LAMP(K) = 1.                                         42.1 A
      LA(K) = LAN * L(K) * LAMP(K)                                    41
C
C         LABOR DEPARTURES (LD)
C            LD DEPENDS ON THE LABOR (L) LEVEL, THE RATE OF LABOR
C            DEPARTURES NORMAL (LDN), AND A LABOR DEPARTURE MULTIPLIER
C            (LDM).  LDM DEPENDS ON THE LABOR-ARRIVAL MULTIPLIER WHICH
C            WAS PREVIOUSLY COMPUTED.
      LDM(K) = TABLE(LDMT,1.44*ALOG(LAM(K)),-3.,3.,1.)               50
      DATA LDMT /8.,4.,2.,1.,.5,.25,.125/                            50.1
```

FIGURE 6   (continued)

```
        LD(K) = LDN * L(K) * LDM(K)                                        49
C
C          LABOR (L) MAY NOW BE COMPUTED
        L(NXT) = L(K) + DT*(UTL(K)+LB(K)-LTM(K)+LA(K)-LD(K)-LTU(K))        29
C
C - - - MANAGER-PROFESSIONAL SECTOR - - - - - - - - - - - - - - - - - - - - - -
C
C          THE MANAGERIAL-PROFESSIONAL (MP) POPULATION IS REPRESENTED IN
C          TERMS OF THE MANAGERIAL-PROFESSIONAL LEVEL IN THE PREVIOUS
C          PERIOD PLUS THE CHANGE IN LEVEL DUE TO THE FOLLOWING FOUR RATES
C          OF FLOW DURING THE PREVIOUS PERIOD--
C          LTM - LABOR TO MANAGER
C          MPB - MANAGER-PROFESSIONAL BIRTHS
C          MA - MANAGER ARRIVALS
C          MD - MANAGER DEPARTURES
C          LTM WAS COMPUTED ABOVE IN THE LABOR SECTOR.  THE OTHER THREE
C          RATES ARE COMPUTED BELOW.
C
C          INITIALIZATIONS
        IF(K.GT.1) GO TO 610
C          MANAGER-PROFESSIONAL BIRTH RATE
        MPBR = .011                                                        51.1 B
C          MANAGER-ARRIVAL MULTIPLIER PERCEPTION TIME.
        MAMPT = 10.                                                        54.2 B
C          MANAGER NORMAL RATES--FOR ARRIVALS (MAN) AND FOR DEPARTURES
C          (MDN).
        MAN = .036                                                         53.1 B
        MDN = .064                                                         62.1 B
C          MANAGER-ARRIVAL FACTOR (MAF) FOR SENSITIVITY TESTING.
        MAF = 1.                                                           55.1
    610 CONTINUE
C
C          MANAGERIAL-PROFESSIONAL BIRTHS
C            BIRTHS ARE COMPUTED BY APPLYING A NET BIRTH RATE (MPB) TO
C
C            THE MANAGERIAL-PROFESSIONAL POPULATION LEVEL (MP).
        MPB(K) = MP(K) * MPBR                                              51
C          MANAGER ARRIVALS
C            THE MANAGER-ARRIVAL MULTIPLIER (MAM) IS COMPUTED FOR USE IN
C            DETERMINING MANAGER ARRIVALS (MA).  MAM IS THE PRODUCT OF
C            FIVE FACTORS--MANAGER-ARRIVAL JOB MULTIPLIER (MAJM),
C            MANAGER-ARRIVAL POPULATION MULTIPLIER (MAPM), MANAGER-ARRIVAL
C            TAX MULTIPLIER (MATM), MANAGER-ARRIVAL HOUSING MULTIPLIER
C            (MAHM), AND MANAGER-ARRIVAL FACTOR (MAF), FOR USE IN
C            SENSITIVITY TESTING.
        MAJM(K) = TABLE(MAJMT,MR(K),.0,2.,.25)                             56
        DATA MAJMT /2.7,2.6,2.4,2.,1.,.4,.2,.1,.05/                        56.1
        MAPM(K) = TABLE(MAPMT,MPR(K),.1,.6,.1)                             57    D
        DATA MAPMT /.3,.7,1.0,1.2,1.3,1.3/                                 57.1
        MATM(K) = TABLE(MATMT,1.44*ALOG(TR(K)),-2.,4.,2.)                  59
        DATA MATMT /1.4,1.,.7,.3/                                          59.1
        MAHM(K) = TABLE(MAHMT,MHR(K),.0,3.,.5)                             60
        DATA MAHMT /1.3,1.2,1.,.5,.2,.1,.05/                              60.1
C          SAVE MAM(LST) FOR USE JUST BELOW IN COMPUTING MAMP(K).
```

FIGURE 6   (continued)

```
      MAMLST = MAM(LST)
      MAM(K) = MAJM(K)*MAPM(K)*MATM(K)*MAHM(K)*MAF              55
C           MANAGER-ARRIVAL MULTIPLIER PERCEIVED (MAMP) AND THE MANAGER
C           ARRIVALS (MA) CAN NOW BE COMPUTED.
      MAMP(K) = MAMP(LST) + (DT/MAMPT)*(MAMLST - MAMP(LST))    54
      IF(K.EQ.1) MAMP(K) = 1.                                 54.1 A
      MA(K) = MAN*MP(K)* MAMP(K)                               53
C
C          MANAGER DEPARTURES
C          MANAGER DEPARTURES (MD) DEPEND ON THE MANAGER-PROFESSIONAL
C          (MP) LEVEL, A RATE OF MANAGER DEPARTURES NORMAL (MDN), AND A
C          MANAGER DEPARTURE MULTIPLIER (MDM).  MDM IS A FUNCTION OF THE
C          PREVIOUSLY COMPUTED MANAGER-ARRIVAL MULTIPLIER (MAM).
      MDM(K) = TABLE(MDMT,1.44*ALOG(MAM(K)),-3.,3.,1.)         63
      DATA MDMT /8.,4.,2.,1.,.5,.25,.125/                      63.1
      MD(K) = MDN*MP(K)*MDM(K)                                 62
C
C          MANAGER-PROFESSIONAL (MP) LEVEL MAY NOW BE DETERMINED.
      MP(NXT) = MP(K) + DT*(LTM(K) + MPB(K) + MA(K) - MD(K))   52
C
C - - - PREMIUM HOUSING SECTOR CTOR - - - - - - - - - - - - - - - - - - - -
C
C          PREMIUM HOUSING (PH) LEVEL FOR A PERIOD IS A FUNCTION OF THE
C          LEVEL IN THE PREVIOUS PERIOD, PLUS THE INCREASE FOR PREMIUM-
C          HOUSING CONSTRUCTION (PHC) LESS THE DECREASE FOR PREMIUM-HOUSING
C          OBSOLESCENCE (PHO).  (THE PREMIUM-HOUSING MULTIPLIER (PHM) AND
C          PREMIUM-HOUSING CONSTRUCTION DESIRED (PHCD) WERE COMPUTED IN
C          THE ABOVE SECTION ON CONSTRUCTION GOALS AND MULTIPLIERS.)
C          INITIALIZATIONS
      IF(K.GT.1) GO TO 710
C          PREMIUM-HOUSING OBSOLESCENCE NORMAL
      PHON = .010                                              79.1 B
  710 CONTINUE
C          SECTOR EQUATIONS
      PHOM(K) = TABLE(PHOMT,1.44*ALOG(PHM(K)),-3.,3.,1.)       80
      DATA PHOMT /2.8,2.6,2.,1.,.5,.3,.2/                      80.1
      PHO(K) = PHON * PH(K) * PHOM(K)                          79
      PHC(K) = PHCD(K) * LCR(K)                                64
      PH(NXT) = PH(K) + DT*(PHC(K) - PHO(K))                   78
C
C - - - WORKER HOUSING SECTOR - - - - - - - - - - - - - - - - - - - - - - -
C
C          WORKER HOUSING (WH) LEVEL IS EXPRESSED AS A FUNCTION OF WH IN
C          THE PREVIOUS PERIOD, PLUS THE FILTER DOWN OF PREMIUM-HOUSING
C          OBSOLESCENCE (PHO) COMPUTED ABOVE, PLUS THE INCREASE DUE TO
C          WORKER-HOUSING CONSTRUCTION (WHC), LESS THE DECREASE DUE TO
C          WORKER-HOUSING OBSOLESCENCE (WHO).  (THE WORKER-HOUSING
C          MULTIPLIER (WHM) AND WORKER-HOUSING CONSTRUCTION DESIRED (WHCD)
C          WERE COMPUTED IN THE ABOVE SECTION ON CONSTRUCTION GOALS AND
C          MULTIPLIERS.)
C          INITIALIZATIONS
      IF (K.GT.1) GO TO 810
C          WORKER-HOUSING OBSOLESCENCE NORMAL
      WHON = .014                                              93.1 B
  810 CONTINUE
```

FIGURE 6 (continued)

```
C          SECTOR EQUATIONS
           WHOM(K) = TABLE(WHOMT,1.44*ALOG(WHM(K)),-3.,3.,1.)              94
           DATA WHOMT /2.2,2.,1.6,1.,.7,.5,.4,/                            94.1
           WHO(K) = WHON * WH(K) * WHOM(K)                                 93
           WHC(K) = WHCD(K) * LCR(K)                                       82
           WH(NXT) = WH(K) + DT*(PHO(K) + WHC(K) - WHO(K))                 81
C
C
C - - - UNDEREMPLOYED HOUSING SECTOR - - - - - - - - - - - - - - - - - - -
C
C          UNDEREMPLOYED HOUSING (UH) LEVEL IS EXPRESSED AS THE LEVEL IN
C          THE PREVIOUS PERIOD, PLUS THE FILTER DOWN OF WORKER-HOUSING
C          OBSOLESCENCE (WHO), LESS THE SLUM-HOUSING DEMOLITION (SHD),
C          PLUS THE LOW-COST-HOUSING PROGRAM (LCHP) LEVEL. WHO AND LCHP
C          WERE COMPUTED EARLIER. SHD IS COMPUTED BY FIRST COMPUTING A
C          SLUM-HOUSING-DEMOLITION MULTIPLIER (SHDM) WHICH IS APPLIED TO
C          THE UH LEVEL. IN ADDITION THE SLUM-HOUSING-DEMOLITION PROGRAM
C          (SHDP) MAY CONTRIBUTE TO THE SHD LEVEL.
C             INITIALIZATIONS
           IF(K.GT.1) GO TO 910
C             SLUM-HOUSING-DEMOLITION NORMAL
           SHDN = .080                                                     96.1 B
C             SLUM-HOUSING-DEMOLITION FACTOR--FOR SENSITIVITY TESTING
           SHDF = 1.                                                       97.1
    910 CONTINUE
C          SECTOR EQUATIONS
           SHLM(K) = TABLE(SHLMT,LFO(K),.8,1.,.05)                         99
           DATA SHLMT /.8,.9,1.0,1.0,1.2/                                  99.1 D
           SHAM(K) = TABLE(SHAMT,UHR(K),.0,2.,.5)                          98
           DATA SHAMT /3.6,2.,1.,.6,.4/                                    98.1
           SHDM(K) = SHAM(K) * SHLM(K) * SHDF                              97
           SHD(K) = SHDN * UH(K) * SHDM(K) + SHDP(K)                       96
           UH(NXT) = UH(K) + DT*(WHO(K) - SHD(K) + LCHP(K))                95
C
C
C - - - NEW ENTERPRISE SECTOR - - - - - - - - - - - - - - - - - - - - - -
C
C          NEW ENTERPRISE (NE) LEVEL FOR A PERIOD IS A FUNCTION OF THE
C          LEVEL IN THE PREVIOUS PERIOD, PLUS THE INCREASE FOR NEW-
C          ENTERPRISE CONSTRUCTION (NEC) LESS THE DECREASE FOR NEW-
C          ENTERPRISE DECLINE (NED). (THE ENTERPRISE MULTIPLIER (EM) AND
C          NEW-ENTERPRISE CONSTRUCTION DESIRED (NECD) WERE COMPUTED IN THE
C          ABOVE SECTION ON CONSTRUCTION GOALS AND MULTIPLIERS.)
C
C             INITIALIZATIONS
           IF(K.GT.1) GO TO 1010
C             NEW-ENTERPRISE DECLINE NORMAL
           NEDN = .125                                                     111.1 B
   1010 CONTINUE
C
C          SECTOR EQUATIONS
           EDM(K) = TABLE(EDMT,1.44*ALOG(EM(K)),-3.,3.,1.)                 112
           DATA EDMT /2.,1.8,1.5,1.,.7,.5,.5/                              112.1
           NED(K) = NEDN * NE(K) * EDM(K)                                  111
           NEC(K) = NECD(K) * LCR(K)                                       101
```

FIGURE 6   (continued)

```
          NE(NXT) = NE(K) + DT*(NEC(K) - NED(K))                          100
C
C
C - - - MATURE BUSINESS SECTOR - - - - - - - - - - - - - - - - - - - -
C          MATURE BUSINESS (MB) LEVEL FOR A PERIOD IS A FUNCTION OF THE
C          LEVEL IN THE PREVIOUS PERIOD, PLUS THE NEW-ENTERPRISE DECLINE
C          (NED) AND LESS THE MATURE-BUSINESS DECLINE (MBD) DURING THE
C          PREVIOUS PERIOD.  (THE ENTERPRISE MULTIPLIER (EM) WAS COMPUTED
C          ABOVE IN THE SECTION ON CONSTRUCTION GOALS AND MULTIPLIERS.)
C
C          INITIALIZATIONS
       IF(K.GT.1) GO TO 1110
C          MATURE-BUSINESS DECLINE NORMAL
          MBDN = .083                                                    114.1 B
  1110 CONTINUE
C
C          SECTOR EQUATIONS
          BDM(K) = TABLE(BDMT,1.44*ALOG(EM(K)),-3.,3.,1.)                115
          DATA BDMT /2.,1.8,1.5,1.,.7,.5,.4/                             115.1
          MBD(K) = MBDN * MB(K) * BDM(K)                                 114
          MB(NXT) = MB(K) + DT*(NED(K) - MBD(K))                         113
C
C
C - - - DECLINING INDUSTRY SECTOR - - - - - - - - - - - - - - - - - - - -
C
C          DECLINING INDUSTRY (DI) LEVEL FOR A PERIOD IS EQUAL TO THE
C          LEVEL IN THE PREVIOUS PERIOD, PLUS THE MATURE-BUSINESS DECLINE
C          (MBD) COMPUTED ABOVE AND LESS THE DECLINING-INDUSTRY DEMOLITION
C          (DID).  (THE ENTERPRISE MULTIPLIER (EM) WAS COMPUTED ABOVE IN
C          THE SECTION ON CONSTRUCTION GOALS AND MULTIPLIERS.)
C          INITIALIZATIONS
       IF(K.GT.1) GO TO 1210
C          DECLINING-INDUSTRY DEMOLITION NORMAL
          DIDN = .047                                                    117.1 B
C          DECLINING-INDUSTRY-DEMOLITION FACTOR--FOR SENSITIVITY TESTING
          DIDF = 1.                                                      118.1
  1210 CONTINUE
C
C          SECTOR EQUATIONS
          DIEM(K) = TABLE(DIEMT,1.44*ALOG(EM(K)),-3.,3.,1.)              119
          DATA DIEMT /.4,.5,.7,1.,1.6,2.4,4./                            119.1
          DILM(K) = TABLE(DILMT,LFO(K),.8,1.,.05)                        120
          DATA DILMT /1.,1.2,1.6,2.2,6./                                 120.1
          DIDM(K) = DIEM(K) * DILM(K) * DIDF                             118
          DID(K) = DIDN * DI(K) * DIDM(K) + DIDP(K)                      117
          DI(NXT) = DI(K) + DT*(MBD(K) - DID(K))                         116
C
       IF(I.EQ.1) GO TO 2100
  2000 CONTINUE
C
C
C - - - - - - - - - - - - - - - - - - - - - - - - - - - - - - - - - - - -
C - - - PRINTING OF MODEL RESULTS - - - - - - - - - - - - - - - - - - - -
C
C          THIS SECTION PRINTS THE RESULTS FOR THE LAST YEAR COMPUTED
```

FIGURE 6 (continued)

```
C           WHEN IT IS ENTERED.  RESULTS ARE PRINTED FOR 124 MODEL
C           VALUES IN THE SAME FORMAT AS IN 'URBAN DYNAMICS' BOOK PAGES
C           42-43.
C
 2100 PRINT 9991
      PRINT 9991
 9990 FORMAT (1H ,-3P3F14.3,0P6F14.3)
      PRINT 9990,
     1    AV  (K),  MB  (K),  U   (K),  AMM (K),  LAJM(K),  LSM (K),
     2    MSM (K),  SHLM(K),  UMM (K),  DI  (K),  MBD (K),  UA  (K),
     3    AMMP(K),  LAM (K),  LUM (K),  NEGR(K),  TCM (K),  UMMP(K),
     4    DID (K),  MD  (K),  UD  (K),  BDM (K),  LAMP(K),  LUR (K),
     5    PEM (K),  TPCR(K),  UR  (K),  DIDP(K),  MP  (K),  UH  (K),
     6    DIDM(K),  LATM(K),  MAIM(K),  PHAM(K),  TR  (K),  WHAM(K),
     7    L   (K),  NE  (K),  UJ  (K),  DIEM(K),  LAUM(K),  MAJM(K),
     8    PHEM(K),  TRN (K),  WHEM(K),  LA  (K),  NEC (K),  UJP (K),
     9    DILM(K),  LCR (K),  MNM (K),  PHGM(K),  UAMM(K),  WHGM(K),
     A    LCHP(K),  NECP(K),  UTL (K),  EDM (K),  LDM (K),  MAMP(K),
     B    PHGR(K),  UDM (K),  WHGR(K)
      PRINT 9991
 9991 FORMAT (1H0)
      PRINT 9990,
     1    LD  (K),  P   (K),  UTLN(K),  EGM (K),  UEM (K),  MAPM(K),
     2    PHLM(K),  UEM (K),  WHLM(K),  LDC (K),  PH  (K),  UTP (K),
     3    ELJM(K),  LFO (K),  MATM(K),  PHM (K),  UFW (K),  WHM (K),
     4    LDI (K),  PHC (K),  UW  (K),  ELM (K),  LHR (K),  MDM (K),
     5    PHOM(K),  UHM (K),  WHOM(K),  LJ  (K),  PHCP(K),  WH  (K),
     6    EM  (K),  LLF (K),  MHR (K),  PHPM(K),  UHPR(K),  WHTM(K),
     7    LTM (K),  PHO (K),  WHC (K),  EMM (K),  LMM (K),  MLM (K),
     8    PHTM(K),  UHR (K),  WHUM(K),  LTU (K),  SHD (K),  WHCP(K),
     9    ETM (K),  LMMP(K),  MLR (K),  SHAM(K),  UJM (K),  UTP (K),
     A    MA  (K),  SHDP(K),  WHO (K),  LAHM(K),  LR  (K),  MR  (K),
     B    SHDM(K),  UM  (K)
C
C
C      END OF LOOP FOR COMPUTING AND PRINTING RESULTS FOR A YEAR
 2200 CONTINUE
C
      STOP
      END
```

FIGURE 6   (continued)

```
      FUNCTION TABLE(TBL,VAR,VLO,VHI,STEP)
C
C    THIS FUNCTION PERFORMS THE SAME OPERATION AS THE TABLE OPERATION
C     IN THE DYNAMO LANGUAGE.  A LINEAR INTERPOLATION IS PERFORMED IN
C     TABLE OF VALUES TBL TO OBTAIN A VALUE WHICH CORRESPONDS TO THE
C     ARGUMENT VALUE VAR.  VLO, VHI, AND STEP SPECIFY THE HIGH VALUE, LOW
C     VALUE, AND STEP SIZE, RESPECTIVELY, FOR THE INDEPENDENT VARIABLE
C     SO THAT A CORRESPONDENCE IS SET UP BETWEEN THE INDEPENDENT VARIABLE
C     VALUES AND THE TABLE OF VALUES SPECIFIED IN THE TBL BY THE CALLING
C     PROGRAM.  IF THE SPECIFIED VALUE OF VAR IS OUTSIDE THE RANGE
C     VLO-VHI, THEN VAR IS ASSIGNED THE FIRST VALUE IN TBL IF VAR IS LESS
C     VLO AND VAR IS ASSIGNED THE LAST VALUE IN TBL IF VAR IS GREATER
C     THAN VHI.
      DIMENSION TBL(15)
      IF(VAR.LT.VLO) GO TO 100
      IF(VAR.GT.VHI) GO TO 200
      STEPS = (VAR - VLO)/STEP + 1.
      N = INT(STEPS)
      TABLE = TBL(N) + (STEPS - FLOAT(N)) * (TBL(N+1) - TBL(N))
      RETURN
  100 TABLE = TBL(1)
      RETURN
  200 K = INT((VHI - VLO)/STEP) + 1
      TABLE = TBL(K)
      RETURN
      END
```

FIGURE 6   (continued)

Index

Aaron, Henry J., 149, 150
Abt Associates, Inc., 31
Ackoff, Russell L., 33
Adelman, Irma, 32
Alfeld, L., 13, 14
Allen, Jodie T., 45
American Association for the Advancement of Science (AAAs), 13
Analysis of variance, 24, 25, 210
Analytical mathematical models, 24, 26, 210
Ansoff, H. Igor, 11, 87
Anthony, Robert N., 79
Averch, Harvey A., 88, 104

Babcock, Daniel L., 13, 50, 93, 104–109, 117, 123, 132, 133, 135, 220, 223, 256
Bacon, Laura W., 49
Baltimore retail market potential model, 51, 55–56
Banks, James G., 147, 152
Barber, Thomas A., 11
Barringer, Robert L., 58
Bartos, Otomar J., 109, 110, 112, 113, 120
Batty, Michael, 66
Belkin, Jacob, 105
Berger, Edward, 95
Berman, Barbara R., 59, 98
Bernd, Joseph L., 7
Blalock, Hubert M., Jr., 37
Blumberg, Donald F., 65
Boston Regional Planning Project, 60
Boulay, Harvey, 95
Braybrooke, David, 21
Brewer, Garry D., 3, 4, 11
The Brookings Institution, 32
Brown, H. James, 56, 60

Buffalo regional growth model, 51, 58
Business/industry subsystem, *see* Urban dynamics model, business/industry subsystem; Urban dynamics Washington model, business/industry subsystem

Campbell, Donald T., 42–43
Catanese, Anthony J., 11, 78, 88, 92
Census, *see* U. S. Census
Charlesworth, James C., 11
Chen, Kan, 13, 90, 123, 219
Chicago area transportation model, 51, 54–55, 58, 62
Chinitz, Benjamin, 59, 98
Christakis, Alexander N., 11
Churchill, Betty C., 280
Closed-system boundary, 68, 86, 92–93, 210
Club of Rome, 14, 184
Cluster analysis, 24, 25, 211
Cole, H. S. D., 186
Collins, John F., 9, 67, 91
Complex system, 67, 86–87, 211
Computer language, *see* Computer simulation models, computer languages for; Dynamo; Fortran; GPSS; Simscript
Computer simulation
  areas of application, 32
  definitions, 28–30, 211
  and gaming simulation, 26
  growth in social sciences, 31–33
  policymaking uses of, 24, 32–33
  potential of, 2–3, 26–27, 30
  spectrum of policy uses of, 40
Computer simulation models
  and broad-aim policy problems, 40–46

313